TALKING ABOUT RACE

STUDIES IN COMMUNICATION, MEDIA, AND PUBLIC OPINION

A series edited by Susan Herbst and Benjamin I. Page

Talking about Race

Community Dialogues and the Politics of Difference

KATHERINE CRAMER WALSH

WITHDRAWN

THE UNIVERSITY OF CHICAGO PRESS

Chicago and London

KATHERINE CRAMER WALSH is associate professor of political science at the University of Wisconsin–Madison and the author of *Talking about Politics: Informal Groups and Social Identity in American Life*, also published by the University of Chicago Press.

The University of Chicago Press, Chicago 60637
The University of Chicago Press, Ltd., London
© 2007 by The University of Chicago
All rights reserved. Published 2007
Printed in the United States of America

16 15 14 13 12 11 10 09 08 07   1 2 3 4 5

ISBN-13: 978-0-226-86906-3   (cloth)
ISBN-13: 978-0-226-86907-0   (paper)
ISBN-10: 0-226-86906-7   (cloth)
ISBN-10: 0-226-86907-5   (paper)

Library of Congress Cataloging-in-Publication Data

Walsh, Katherine Cramer.
    Talking about race : community dialogues and the politics of difference / Katherine Cramer Walsh.
        p.   cm.
    Includes bibliographical references and index.
    ISBN-13: 978-0-226-86906-3 (cloth : alk. paper)
    ISBN-13: 978-0-226-86907-0 (pbk. : alk. paper)
    ISBN-10: 0-226-86906-7 (cloth : alk. paper)
    ISBN-10: 0-226-86907-5 (pbk. : alk. paper)   1. United States—
Race relations.   2. Intergroup relations—United States.
3. Discussion.   I. Title.
    E184.A1.W217   2007
    305.800973—dc22
                                            2006039089

♾ The paper used in this publication meets the minimum requirements of the American National Standard for Information Sciences—Permanence of Paper for Printed Library Materials, ANSI Z39.48-1992.

CONTENTS

In the fall of 2000, I woke up to an announcement on the radio asking for volunteers for the City of Madison Study Circles on Race. The brief ad said that participants would talk in small, racially diverse groups about race once a week for several months. The point was to improve race relations through better understanding.

It caught my attention.

I was in the midst of finishing up a study in which I had observed several groups of people for several years, trying to understand how they interpreted public affairs through their conversations. One of the things I learned was that through their talk, the people I spent time with clarified their own racial identities and used these as tools to make sense of politics. This on its own is not troubling, but what is troubling is that much of this talk perpetuated racial stereotypes and exclusionary identities. Also, in the neighborhood corner store that was the site of my main case, a group of retired white men met just ten steps away from a separate group of people who were primarily African Americans. They avoided each other, albeit cordially, every morning.

This lack of interracial interaction and the exclusionary identities that went along with it were not unique to the corner store. Nevertheless, watching it happen day after day left me convinced that if our society was ever to nurture social identities—which play a central role in individuals' attempts to understand public affairs—that were not racially exclusionary, we had to do so proactively, through fostering interaction across racial boundaries.

I was certainly not the first to come to this conclusion. Within academia alone, intergroup contact scholars had been saying similar things for about fifty years. These insights had in part fueled drives to desegregate public schools. More recently, social capital scholars had been making related calls for bridging social capital and intercommunal ties in order to strengthen democracy and minimize interethnic violence within particular cities.

But, when I heard the radio announcement about the race dialogues in my city, I knew we had much to learn from the way people were heeding the calls for more interracial interaction. I quickly contacted the local Urban League, the nonprofit entity that had contracted with the city of Madison to administer the program, and my university's human subjects committee. My goal was to study the identity development that occurred among participants. I expected that this interracial talk would help people develop overarching identities with one another that would minimize conflict and set the stage for future collective action.

I was wrong.

Over the course of the next few years, I administered pre/post surveys to participants in the Madison program as well as to participants in a similar program in Aurora, Illinois. Eventually, the program administrators agreed to allow me to give surveys to a quasi-control group of people on the waiting list. I used standard measures of social identity—closeness measures—among other things. I found that instead of feeling closer to people of other racial backgrounds and to members of the community as a whole, it seemed that if anything people were finding out just how *not* close they were to others through the course of the dialogues.

As part of this initial study, I observed a ten-week session in Madison, looking for the tools people used to connect with one another. I expected people to grope for shared values, experiences, identities, memberships— something on which they could find common ground and use to develop subsequent action. I found instead that people were not striving to figure out how underneath it all we really are alike. Our sessions were busy with the recognition and understanding of difference.

This book is about the way people around the country are actively creating a politics of their own from their deep aspiration for unity and their desire to proactively deal with the presence of difference in their own communities. The book seizes on programs like the Madison Study Circles— what I will call more generally civic intergroup dialogue programs—as opportunities to examine why, under what conditions, and how people are using face-to-face conversations to listen to, scrutinize, and make sense of racial difference. The practice of dialogue poses significant challenges to prevailing conceptions of good deliberation, ideal intergroup contact, and healthy democracy, and the aim of the book is to help us better understand each of these three areas of civic concern by learning from such programs.

I have benefited enormously from the wisdom of many people in writing this book. First, I would like to thank the many people who completed questionnaires, agreed to be interviewed, and allowed me to sit in on their dialogues for this study. I am deeply respectful of their efforts and grateful for their generosity. Special thanks also to Martha McCoy and the Study Circles Resource Center, the National League of Cities, and the National Coalition for Dialogue and Deliberation for feedback and access to invaluable information. Thank you to Mona Adams Winston, Hedi Rudd, and Gladis Benevides for granting me access to the City of Madison Study Circles on Race and for sharing their passion with me. Thank you also to Mary Jane Hollis of the Aurora Community Study Circles for providing insight on and access to that program and for her endless energy. My sincere thank you also to the many research assistants at the University of Wisconsin-Madison who lightened and enlivened this project by processing questionnaire data and gathering information on city and program characteristics: Kristine Berg, Tim Bagshaw, Melissa Brown, Adam Busch, Bryan Gadow, Patrick Guarasci, Rob Hunter, Patty LeBaron, Kerri Meulemans, Zach Mesenbourg, Hillary Schulman, and Kristin Wieben. My gratitude also to the UW Department of Political Science and the University of Wisconsin-Madison graduate school for financial support.

I had the good fortune to share this project with many seminar participants in the vibrant workgroups at the University of Wisconsin-Madison and at other universities. At Wisconsin-Madison, I am grateful for feedback from Joel Rivlin and David Canon and other members of the Political Behavior Research Group, Elspeth Wilson and other members of the Political Philosophy Colloquium, the Communication Science Colloquium, and the Mass Communication Research Seminar. Thank you also to participants in the Journey to Democracy Dialogues at Lewis and Clark University, the National Election Studies Fellows Workshop at the University of Michigan, the Department of Government at Cornell University, the Departments of Political Science and Psychology at the University of Minnesota, the Civic Engagement in the 21st Century Conference at the University of Southern California, the Conference on Framing at Texas A&M University, and the Princeton Conference on Deliberative Democracy.

I owe a very large debt to the wisdom a number of generous colleagues have shared with me through their feedback on this project. I am sincerely grateful for invaluable feedback from John Gastil and three other reviewers for Temple University Press and the University of Chicago Press. Jason Wittenberg, William Scheuerman, David Ryfe, Jamie Druckman, Paula Pickering, and Susan Herbst provided good sense and inspiration on early portions of this project. Kim Gross read over drafts of the first chapters and embraced me with enthusiasm for this project at a crucial time. Cara Wong read over the entire manuscript and provided incisive and extensive feedback. Dick Merelman shared numerous lunches and lively conversations about this project. Eric MacGilvray engaged me in stimulating and illuminating feedback on several chapters, particularly chapter 2. Jane Mansbridge, Nancy Burns, and several anonymous reviewers provided excellent feedback that greatly improved chapter 4. An earlier version of chapter 4 appeared as Katherine Cramer Walsh, "Communities, Race, and Talk: An Analysis of the Occurrence of Civic Dialogue Programs," *Journal of Politics* 68 [1]: 22–33.) Matt Leighninger read early papers as well as an entire draft of the manuscript and provided the keen eye of a dialogue practitioner. Amaal Tokars shared her compassionate, astute perceptions and suggestions for revisions on a full draft. John Tryneski, my editor at the University of Chicago Press, was, as always, a joy to work with. I also greatly appreciate the careful and insightful copy editing performed by Richard Allen, and the fine-tuning that Erik Carlson provided on the final version. Joe Soss nourished this project in many ways, with his stimulating questions, encouragement, and amazing generosity. I am forever grateful for the extensive feedback he provided on early papers as well as on two entire drafts of this manuscript. Those conversations enriched this project greatly and made writing this book a pleasure. I am seriously and sincerely grateful to all of these people for their help on this project and their support.

Finally, I owe a special thank you to my family, Pat, Kip, Joan, Scott, Ben, and Matt, and all the Cramers, Geissmans, and Walshes. In particular, I am eternally grateful to Bailey for kindness and understanding that continues to humble me on a daily basis. This book would not have been possible without you.

CHAPTER ONE

Race, Dialogue, and the Practice of Community Life

It is a sunny spring day in a midsized Midwestern city, and the parking lot of the police station is beginning to fill. Inside, in a stately conference room, a Latina woman is busy placing handouts and pamphlets at fifteen or so places around the table. She has already put out bottles of water, sugar cookies on paper napkins, and individually wrapped wintergreen LifeSavers on the table in front of each chair.

Gradually people filter in. An African-American man and woman enter and greet the woman warmly. Several white men in suits walk in and do the same. A white woman in a cozy sweater arrives, just in front of an African-American man. Then two East Asian men enter. Some people greet each other with smiles, handshakes, or jokes; others introduce themselves across the table. After several more white men and women (some in suits) and an African-American mother and daughter enter, the table is full. We begin.

"Good afternoon everyone. Welcome to this Diversity Circle. I am Maria[1] and I will be your facilitator." She says a bit more and then holds up a pamphlet.

> This is the book that you will be bringing back with you [for the other three sessions.] We are here to do dialogue. This describes what that is, the role of the participant, listening carefully to others, etcetera. We need to make sure—this is extremely important, everyone—that we keep the discussion on track. The important part of my job is to keep things moving along, important that you speak freely, but don't monopolize. Address remarks to the group rather than to me. Important that all of us value your own experiences and opinion, ok? And that you engage in friendly disagreement. Remember it is dialogue, and not debate.

What is going on here? What I've just described is the actual start of a dialogue group that met in a central Wisconsin city. They were meeting to talk about race.[2] This city, like many others, had chosen to use interracial face-to-face conversations about race as a way of improving race relations and the life of their community. The people wearing suits were public officials—elected officials and city government department heads.

This is striking behavior for a variety of reasons. First, these folks were about to voluntarily take part in an interracial discussion, not a typical behavior for most Americans.[3] Second, they were not just engaging in interracial discussion; they were doing so *about race*. Bringing up the topic of race in interracial settings is generally treated as a potential for disaster by politicians and ordinary citizens alike.[4] Third, it is a rare thing in public life to see a group of residents of a community sitting down around the same table with their public officials. Typically, when residents and officials engage in talk in a group, the format is a hearing or a meeting in which officials sit empowered at the front and residents sit passively in the audience.

Finally, this talk is also somewhat odd because these people were not about to engage in decision-making. Instead, as the facilitator said, what they were aiming for is *dialogue*—discussion intended to focus on personal experiences, emotions, and storytelling. As therapeutic and recreational as that may sound, the city manager, city council members, and other city employees were doing this on taxpayer time.

What these folks were doing is known generally as intergroup dialogue. Although it involves some behaviors that are rare in everyday American life, this type of program is not unique to this particular city. Since the early 1990s, more than 400 cities across the United States,[5] and many cities throughout the world,[6] have implemented programs like this in which diverse groups of volunteers are recruited to come together over repeated sessions to talk about race.

The actions of the people in this particular Midwestern city, as well as in cities around the country, are worth some attention because of all of the ways in which they are surprising, noted above. But they are particularly worthy of study by a political scientist because they constitute deliberative democracy in action. This is actual public talk, or interpersonal talk organized to address public issues. It is an attempt by real people in actual communities to confront the difficult public issue of race, and an attempt to enhance civic life in a context of cultural heterogeneity.

We have much to learn from what these people are doing. First, social psychologists have long suggested that interaction between people of different racial backgrounds is precisely what is needed to reduce prejudice. But much of what we know about intergroup contact is based on contact that has been manufactured by researchers. When, in contrast, do communities choose to foster interracial interaction—specifically about race? And what goes on when they do so?

Previous work on public talk suggests that it quickly becomes intractable when conducted across cultural divides or conflicting interests.[7] Does that happen in these groups? Or given that people volunteer themselves for the programs, perhaps the participants are already in agreement that they ought to focus on racial identity when they first sit down together. Maybe the conversations merely "preach to the choir." Perhaps these programs are the domain of left-leaning "multiculturalists," focusing on racial group identities rather than things that unite the American people.[8] If these intergroup programs intentionally draw attention to race, why do public officials volunteer for this seemingly divisive talk?

We also have much to learn about deliberative democracy from these groups. Democratic theory has taken a deliberative turn in the past several decades.[9] Scholarship in political psychology,[10] political communication,[11] and public policy has followed suit.[12] We now have not only multiple theories of what ideal deliberation ought to look like and what it can produce, but we also have a growing number of empirical studies that test, question, and expand these claims.

Thanks to recent studies, we now know more about who participates in various forms of deliberative participation, and even a bit about how this has changed over time.[13] But we know very little about why community leaders choose to provide opportunities for public talk or why they turn to such a strategy to address pressing public problems such as race. Taking the time to notice how communities around the country are using dialogues on race can provide valuable insights into how deliberative democracy comes into being.

Why Study This Aspect of the Deliberative System?

I take deliberative democracy to mean the range of acts of structured interpersonal discussion intended to address community problems. As the facilitator quoted at the start of this chapter asserts, the talk in these programs is "dialogue, not debate." It is a form of public talk in which the emphasis is on listening to and understanding others, not on reaching a decision. Thus it is not deliberation. However, it is one form of talk in the overall *deliberative system*—the range of acts from informal conversation to formal debate that collectively comprise deliberative democracy.[14]

Such civic dialogue provides an opportunity to understand why communities choose to confront public problems with organized, interpersonal, face-to-face talk. The insight we gain can not be generalized to all forms of public talk, but it can bring us closer to knowing the place that such communication plays in contemporary civic life.

This is all to say that these programs enable us to examine two pressing questions: How does public talk come into being? And what goes on within it?[15] We expect deliberation to achieve many things—better informed opinions, tolerance, efficacy, well-rounded decisions[16]—but before public talk can actually bring about these outcomes, people have to choose to pursue it. Because civic dialogue programs constitute a particularly difficult form of public talk within the deliberative system, understanding how this case comes into being can reveal more generally how deliberative democracy arises.[17]

Why are communities choosing dialogue as a means to address the issue of race relations? A skeptic might say that people cannot seriously expect this endeavor to improve race relations or to achieve any kind of social justice, because deliberative democracy is slow and likely to favor the status quo.[18] Even if the talk provides opportunities to question powerholders, doesn't it devolve into chaos? If it doesn't, isn't it too superficial or civil for anything productive to occur?[19] And in interracial forums, aren't the voices of marginalized racial groups ignored or silenced?[20] And doesn't the lack of interracial understanding simply cause the talk to collapse into disarray?[21] A skeptic might also question why public officials are involved. Aren't they just paying lip service to a deep problem that requires a much more proactive approach?[22] Finally, if this is really *dialogue* in which people actually listen to one another, rather than debate or make decisions, isn't it closer to a self-indulgent act of individual development rather than to political action?[23]

There are many reasons to be skeptical of this form of public talk. And yet the fact remains that many people in many communities around the country are turning to it. Examining what they are actually doing with these dialogues on race brings us closer to understanding the nature of deliberative democracy. And it also sheds light on yet another pressing topic in contemporary civic life: how to create bonds across social divides. In recent years, this has been called the problem of creating bridging social capital. Social capital, the capacity of a social network to collectively address public problems,[24] is particularly valued when it is created by relationships that bridge divisions across social groups. Although this "bridging" social capital is notoriously difficult to create, many claim that it is crucial for heterogeneous democracies.[25] It is the kind of social capital that scholars expect will lead to generalized trust in other people.[26] Without connections between members of different social groups, cities are vulnerable to intergroup violence,[27] and the lack of reciprocity and cooperation across social groups threatens to undermine the stability of democracy.[28]

These civic dialogue groups enable us to better understand how people go about building social capital across a particularly daunting social divide—race. We might expect that people would choose to build bridging social capital by focusing on what they have in common, or by working together on a common project, in a cooperative, not combative fashion.[29] Why do they choose instead to engage in dialogue that could focus on racial differences and interracial conflict? And what do they do with the opportunity when they choose to do so?

Because these programs are about race, they also allow us to study how people are dealing with this fundamental issue confronting American civic life. Although race is not a new issue in American cities, Hispanic and Latino immigration in the 1990s[30] and the terrorist attacks of September 11, 2001 have forced the issue of cultural diversity to the forefront in many smaller and medium-sized cities around the country. How are people of various racial backgrounds reconciling their identities as people of a particular race with their desire to bring the community as a whole together? How are people attempting to reconcile the desire to respect diversity with the desire to nevertheless come together as a community?

The Nature of Intergroup Dialogue Programs on Race

Intergroup dialogue programs on race relations are volunteer programs that organize interracial conversations about race over repeated sessions. The programs arise organically within particular communities, and then program administrators typically advertise through local media for volunteers. These volunteers are sorted into racially diverse groups of about ten to fifteen people who then meet once a week for about five weeks. At their meetings one or two facilitators lead them in two-hour-long discussions. They follow guidebooks that encourage people to talk openly about their personal experiences with race, their perceptions of race relations in their community, and their ideas about how they might individually and collectively improve race relations. When the program ends, participants are encouraged to pursue some of these actions, but they are not obligated to do so.

In some cities, the programs are sponsored by city or county governments. In others, they are sponsored by an existing nonprofit organization such as the YWCA or the National Conference for Community and Justice (NCCJ, formerly the National Conference on Christians and Jews), or an organization that has been created specifically to administer the program.

The programs have proliferated across the country since the 1990s, particularly around national events that highlighted existing racial tension such as the Rodney King and O. J. Simpson trials and the September 11 terrorist attacks.[31] Several national organizations have promoted the use of race dialogues, including the Study Circles Resource Center, the Hope in the Cities program, the YWCA, the NCCJ, the National League of Cities, the National Civic League, and President William Jefferson Clinton's Initiative on Race.[32]

Although the talk is not about policy decision-making per se, in most cases, public officials—elected and nonelected policymakers, and street-level bureaucrats[33]—participate in the programs alongside local residents. They participate as "equals" in the conversation—sitting in the same circle, following the same ground rules and taking turns like the other participants.

Although much of the emergence of intergroup dialogue programs can be attributed to national umbrella organizations, it is not the case that these organizations seek out communities that are fertile ground for a dialogue program and then try to sell them the program. Instead, people within particular cities hear about intergroup dialogue programs through acquaintances, mass media, or professional organizations and contact the national dialogue organizations for help. Also, national offices of organizations such as the YWCA, the League of Women Voters, the NCCJ and the National League of Cities encourage their affiliates or member cities to use intergroup dialogue as one of many of their strategies to enhance civic life. In some cities, administrators have transformed the dialogue program into its own organization.

Thus the emergence of civic dialogue programs has an organic nature. People involved mention similar problems when explaining why they chose to pursue it—intractable race relations, a desire to know their neighbors better, a desire to invigorate participation in civic life—and yet they explain the need as specific to their community. At this point in the history of race relations in the United States, people around the country are finding it necessary to dialogue in order to improve their civic life.

What Do We Hear?

What do these dialogues on race reveal? Listening closely, we hear talk that is neither tuned to unity nor fixed on cultural differences. Despite the self-selection that brings people to these programs, we see participants we might not expect—police officers, firefighters, self-labeled conservatives. The participants are ordinary people, not leftist intellectuals. They are not uniformly wedded to the idea of placing racial identity before community or national identity. They approach the dialogues from a variety of perspectives and often convey that they prefer a politics of unity rather than a politics of difference. However, the format of the dialogues fosters listening and the telling of stories that insert attention to difference into the conversations. As people tell their stories and use these appeals to authenticity to exert power over the conversation, the groups struggle with a balance between unity and difference.

Rather than perpetuate a politics of unity or promote a politics of difference, these dialogues do something else: they engage in a practical politics. I call this a practical politics because it is conducted by people who are steeped in the idea that in order to deal with difference we have to focus on unity; and yet they are reminded in the course of the dialogues that race matters in their everyday lives, particularly in the lives of people of color in their communities. These reminders are not taken from the pages of multiculturalist theorists, however. They come from the real lives of neighbors, who are themselves wanting to see "people as people."

This is a practical politics also because people use it to achieve something they perceive as necessary in their increasingly heterogeneous towns: improved communication and understanding across racial lines. In aggregate analyses of objective indicators and individual-level investigations of perspectives of this talk, we see evidence that this is not about individual self-fulfillment, but about concrete community change. Examining the characteristics of the cities in which these programs arise and listening to the explanations that program practitioners give for them, we learn that people use the dialogues as a step toward social justice. This kind of public talk shows up in poor communities as well as in wealthy ones. And it is most closely associated with conditions related to attempts to address racial inequality, rather than with a context in which the goal is primarily self-actualization. Also, governments pursue the programs under the same conditions as do nongovernmental organizations, which are often explicitly focused on social justice, suggesting that public officials are involved for more than symbolic reasons.

Yet other evidence that this is not "just talk" comes from listening to the way people who have implemented these programs explain their choice. They do not describe dialogue as a luxury or as a means of self-fulfillment. They tend to talk about it as a necessity, a complement to other forms of action, and a step toward significant change. They do not talk about the decision to promote dialogue as a choice. Instead, they treat it as an obvious, essential component of a healthy civic life in a racially diverse city. They tend to be people who have pursued interracial dialogue throughout much of their lives.

Another reason why I say that these dialogues constitute a practical politics is that they are far from ideal. They are messy. In them, people attempt to be civil but find it necessary at times to disobey the mantra of "dialogue, not debate." Some aspects of difference, such as language differences, are treated as too threatening to the fabric of civic life to tolerate. Although the practice of listening lends authority to marginalized racial groups, some groups are perceived as more legitimate than others. As we listen to what goes on, we see people in real communities struggle to craft something positive from the racial tension that brought them to the group.

While these conversations are not devoid of domination and some of the downsides of deliberative democracy that critics lament, the practice of this form of public talk teaches us that people around the country are finding a way to engage in the struggle of balancing unity and difference. They do so in ways that opens the eyes of community members and public officials alike. When they confront race head-on, the discussions neither explode nor shift permanently to safer ground. Instead the participants compel each other to face the reality of different realities. As they listen to and scrutinize each other, they hear that everyday life in their city can vary starkly by race. Through this talk, residents and public officials build a practical politics informed by the struggles of their own particular community.

Listening as a Methodological Approach

Listening is an integral part of these race dialogue programs. It is also at the heart of the methods I employ. Intergroup dialogues are new to political scientists' purview. While scholars in other fields have investigated such programs as instances of interpersonal and group communication, and also of intergroup contact, I sought to understand them as instances of civic engagement and policy choice. While previous studies of intergroup dialogues have investigated these programs in controlled or manufactured settings, I wanted to know how they work in settings chosen and structured by community members themselves. Also, while political scientists have observed civic deliberation directly, this is one of the first studies to examine intergroup dialogue programs initiated by community members.[34] Therefore, I sought methods that would enable me to learn from and structure the direction of my study around the behavior of people implementing and participating in this form of public talk.

The result is that I use strategies that enabled me to listen directly to the content of dialogues and to attend to the perspectives of people engaging in them, as well as strategies that enabled me to step back from their first-hand accounts. At the earliest stages of this study, I conducted a pilot study of participant observation of one round of a city-sponsored dialogue program in Madison, Wisconsin. My purpose was to understand how people were using this type of civic program. At the same time, I worked with the local Urban League, which was administering the program on behalf of the city, to conduct an evaluation study via paper-and-pencil questionnaires. I continued to administer pre-test and post-test questionnaires to participants in Madison, as well as to adults and high school students in a similar program in Aurora, Illinois, over several years. These questionnaires provided insight into the attitudes and demographics associated with participants. They also provided insight into a large number of participants' perceptions about the nature of the communication within the dialogues and their aspirations for this talk. To expand my understanding of the perceptions held by people conducting dialogue beyond Madison and Aurora, I interviewed people throughout the broader Midwest, primarily through face-to-face interviews, and supplemented this with archival research and observation at local political events.

Much of this early work was inductive—I asked people to tell me why these programs were important, what went on within them, and what they hoped they would achieve. I drew conclusions about the types of communities that were pursuing such programs, and attempted to understand in particular when local governments sought to sponsor them.

Drawing on these insights as well as urban politics literature, I conducted a deductive study of the conditions under which communities pursue these programs. I collected data on the characteristics of cities with and without programs that various theories suggest we ought to observe coinciding with the choice to pursue these programs. These data allowed me to test, using objective indicators, different explanations for the existence of civic intergroup dialogue.

The analyses of city characteristics are suggestive and have the benefit of avoiding the biases of self-reports. But I am also a firm believer in the revelatory powers of narrative—that is, in the many things that people reveal when they explain themselves to you.[35] A large portion of the community-level data was drawn from the Census, but I and an energetic group of undergraduate research assistants obtained a good deal of it through calling city clerks, local activists, and newspaper editors. While doing this detective work, I talked and listened to the people I encountered. I used these in-depth interviews to understand the choice to pursue dialogue. Asking these people to explain their choices revealed things that I, as the learner, would not otherwise have thought to ask about. It properly turned the tables on who had expertise in the research situation. And it revealed important things about how the people I talked to see themselves as well as their communities.

Obviously, there are problems with self-reports. Were people accurately recalling the past?[36] When accurate data about the past is what I needed, I was sure to collect corroborating evidence. But the particularities of how different people explained their choice to pursue dialogue were partly what I was after. Did public officials view dialogue differently than people administrating dialogue through nonprofit organizations? Mindful that the responses I received could very well be influenced by the nature of the interview context, especially because we were talking about race relations,[37] I sought to learn from patterns across interviews. I proceeded on the premise that the way people perceive their alternatives and explain their motives constrains their behavior.[38] The ways people explained themselves to me served as indicators of their *perspectives* or *interpretations* of the choice. Capturing those perspectives was my goal.

Listening was a key method in this study in yet another way: I used participant observation. To understand what goes on in the process of civic intergroup dialogue programs, I needed to observe these discussions directly. I observed a variety of one-day dialogues on race in Madison, Wisconsin, including two YWCA lunchtime brown bag discussions and six screenings of PBS documentaries on race paired with community discussions afterward. More importantly, I conducted participant observation of six different intergroup dialogue groups in four different cities in Illinois and Wisconsin. Each of these groups met once a week for a month or more.

One of my goals was to characterize the content of these deliberations, but I wanted to do more than count how much each participant spoke and whether or not they disagreed with one another. In order to understand the role of intergroup dialogue in civic life, I needed to confront claims that public talk silences certain *perspectives*. Thus I needed to know not only who spoke, but the frame in which they said it, and how, collectively, the group understood the issues it confronted. In the interviews, I wanted to know how people understood this experience—how they perceived it, how they understood the role of dialogue in their attempts to make sense of civic life in contexts of difference, and how collectively, they made sense of good citizenship together. In other words, I analyzed my observation and interview data largely using what researchers call an interpretivist approach. I tried to understand the frameworks and perspectives through which people were understanding and conducting dialogue.[39]

I observed these dialogues as a participant, interacting with the other participants, attending other events with them, and spending time in their communities.[40] Participating as a member of the groups, albeit a relatively quiet one, enabled me to pay attention to aspects of the rooms and buildings in which they met, seating arrangements, body language and facial expressions, and the tone in which people contributed to the conversation. It also allowed me to interact with the participants—to probe, pose questions, and in turn, answer theirs. In this way, my method and my project were one and the same. The individuals I was studying were trying to use dialogue to understand "others." This dialogue involved listening and exchange. I followed their lead. I listened and I also opened myself to their questions and the relationships that they, and I, expected would further understanding.

I am not the first to listen in on actual civic deliberation or civic dialogue for the purposes of analyzing its content.[41] But this study is unique in its intensive attention to intergroup dialogues on race in particular, in the questions it asks, and in its combination of large-N aggregate level analyses with intensive methodologies. My purpose in relying on an original multi-city data set as well as the intensive methods of interviews and observation was to combine the strengths of deductive and inductive approaches. In addition, I wanted to make use of the knowledge that political scientists, communications scholars, and social psychologists had already accumulated but also wanted to enable myself to learn from the expertise gathered by the people actually doing dialogue around the country. Using a multi-method approach that incorporated listening allowed me to do so.

One final note for the moment on my approach: I focus primarily on medium-sized cities across the United States, in other words cities with populations between 50,000 and 250,000. I chose to do so in order to limit the scope of the study, to control for the different nature of political processes that may occur in cities of different size, and because the struggle with intergroup conflict is relatively new in cities of this size. Most of these places have been home to people of a variety of racial and ethnic backgrounds for nearly a century or more. But recent immigration has brought these conflicts to the fore. As these communities choose to innovate (or not) to address this public issue, they represent an important laboratory for the rest of the nation. Even though the observations and multi-city study are conducted on medium-sized cities, I interviewed people conducting dialogue in larger cities as well, in order to estimate how my conclusions extrapolate to these places.

Outline of This Book

In the following chapter, I visit the ways in which democratic theorists argue that the existence of public talk constitutes healthy democracy. Within that general argument, however, there are two main ways of characterizing what we hope this talk sounds like. In short, one focuses on unity, the other on difference. I examine these arguments in detail, drawing on scholarship on democratic theory, political behavior, and intergroup conflict. I use these arguments to set up expectations about the conditions under which these programs come into being, how people explain these programs, and what takes place within them.

In chapter 3, I compare the contours of civic intergroup dialogue programs to the more general class of civic deliberative programs. Using interviews with national organizations that promote these programs and analyses of program literature, I show that civic dialogue programs on race are promoted as difference-focused communication that nevertheless focuses on the common good. I discuss how this form of communication resembles "dialogue" as described by communications scholars, and yet emphasize that it remains an empirical question whether dialogue (i.e., difference-focused communication) actually occurs in these programs.

Chapter 4 investigates when these programs arise, using aggregate-level analyses of a nationally representative sample of medium-sized cities. Using the original data set of community characteristics and the incidence of dialogue programs on race, I test various explanations for these programs derived from urban politics literature. In particular, I examine whether the programs are consistent with an emphasis on postmaterialist concerns, in other words arise in contexts oriented toward lifestyle and consumption concerns, or whether they arise in conditions that suggest they are used to pursue social justice. I find weak support for the postmaterialist model but strong support for the social justice model. I also find that the conditions that give rise to government-sponsored versus merely government-endorsed programs are nearly identical. Taken together, these results suggest that communities are using dialogue about race not as a leisure-time activity, but as an earnest step toward improved race relations.

In chapter 5, I move away from this objective data to the explanations of dialogue practitioners themselves. Using semi-structured interviews, I listen to the explanations people in cities around the country give for implementing dialogue programs and probe what their reasons suggest about the functions and uses of such groups. Despite the many reasons that could lead us not to expect social justice activists to use interracial dialogue, people who do tend to explain it as a necessity. They do not talk about it as a fallback or compromise strategy, but as an integral part of striving for social justice.

Chapter 6 begins the examination of what takes place within these dialogue programs. I demonstrate that listening to difference does indeed go on. But this is only part of the story. I show that these dialogues consist of a constant struggle with the desire to find common ground and yet respect difference. It is through the acts of members of marginalized racial groups pulling the whites in their groups back from unity that this negotiation of unity and difference takes place. The results suggest that the deliberative system can and does include listening to difference. At the same time, the manner in which this difference-focused talk is intertwined with attention to unity suggests that it may not be the threat to unity that theorists and social psychologists assume that a recognition of difference poses. The results help us rethink what people are using public talk for. They demonstrate that organized community forums can function to address public problems and also serve as sites in which people struggle to define citizenship and community identity.

Chapter 7 builds on these analyses to probe the types of communication that are at work in these dialogues. Storytelling plays a central role in the conversations, and yet its function differs from what previous studies lead us to expect. When people engage in storytelling, the result is not necessarily greater unity but instead greater attention to difference. Also, we see a challenge to expectations that listening, as opposed to debate or combative speech, helps reconcile inequalities that plague many forms of civic deliberation. It is participants' use of debate as well as dialogue, despite facilitators' injunctions, that allows them to demonstrate greater respect for each other.

Chapter 8 uses the observations of civic dialogue to address how people negotiate power in these groups. I focus on discussions on four issues, reparations, affirmative action, immigration, and language policy, and probe how people negotiate consensus and disagreement on them. I demonstrate how people make appeals to racial identity to confer legitimacy on their comments and to assert authority over the conversation. I show that even in these forums that are fertile ground for listening, people avoid the most controversial issues and do not pay attention to all differences equally. However, people do bring difficult issues to the fore, despite resistance, partly through the use of personal stories related to the issue. An analysis of who speaks, and of who asks for and is asked for justification, shows that alternative perspectives and experiences are represented and that people of color as well as whites exert power in these conversations.

Chapter 9 examines the nature of the interaction between residents and public officials in these dialogues. I find that the nature of the conversations involving public officials is much akin to the nature of dialogues when officials are not present. Instead of deference to public officials, officials treat residents' stories as expertise. The analyses question our notions of expertise in the deliberative system, and the assumption that citizens will either defer to or lash out at officials when presented with the opportunity to confront them directly. They also suggest that government–resident communication that involves listening, on the part of both residents as well as officials, can ease the job of local government actors.

In the final chapter, I revisit these results and argue that they call into question common assumptions about public talk, the best way to build bridging social capital, characterizations of the public's stance toward multiculturalism, and the role of the government in the public sphere. We see that in contrast to calls for appealing to overarching identities as the way to build a stronger civic life, many communities—low- and high-income, university and blue-collar—are intentionally taking a different route. At the heart of their strategy is an emphasis on listening rooted in the practical need to learn to communicate across lines of difference. We see government actors creating the opportunity for people of different perspectives to come together, enabling this aspect of the public sphere to arise. I conclude that people implementing and participating in civic dialogues around the country are pursuing a practical politics that balances unity and diversity, listening and scrutiny, and dialogue and debate. The results suggest a rethinking of the place of conflict in deliberative democracy and an acknowledgement that it is the ongoing struggle with difference that provides unity in contemporary civic life.

CHAPTER TWO

Unity and Difference in Civic Life

Deliberation among citizens holds a central place in democratic theory for the ends it brings about, but also for the character of life it enables. Many democratic thinkers, from ancient to contemporary times, argue that deliberation brings about improved opinion and more capable citizens.[1] But a broad array of theorists likewise value the *existence* of deliberative democracy as a form of civic life. They regard it as a process by which the public constitutes itself and gives itself meaning.

Jürgen Habermas, for one, has vigorously defended the idea that democracies ought to have ongoing critical discussion about public problems by members of the public. His work argues that such communication is essential for forming public opinion and keeping a check on government.[2] Part of the value of this communication is its collective, ongoing nature, according to Habermas. He argues that democracies achieve reason through communication among people, not through individuals independently identifying the truth. Rather than reasoning on the basis of fixed moral principles, Habermas argues, people discover, through discourse with one another, principles for judging public policy that are appropriate to their historical and political context.[3] In other words, deliberation with others forms the basis of reason itself.[4] Its *existence* is a democratic good.

John Dewey also argued that collective discussion of public affairs is integral to democracy. In fact, in his work, democracy seems to actually reside in the act of public-focused communication among citizens. Democracy is "a social idea" that "remains barren and empty save as it is incarnated in human relationships."[5] Dewey did not value mere associating together. He wanted *intentional* public talk that consciously appreciated the consequences of that interaction.[6] He conceptualized the democratic project as engaged progressive action that people generated through analysis of public concerns.[7] Such engaged deliberation was important for societies to reach their full potential, according to Dewey, but it also enabled individual fulfillment. He argued that it allowed for equality, in the sense of widespread sharing in the fruits of associating with others (as opposed to equality in the sense of sameness);[8] enabled liberty, in the sense of freely exercising one's talents in the course of engaging with others (as opposed to isolation and thus the absence of opportunity to have this freedom);[9] and enabled people to learn to be truly human, or to have "an effective sense of being an individually distinctive member of a community; one who understands and appreciates its beliefs, desires and methods, and who contributes to a further conversion of organic powers into human resources and values."[10]

Hannah Arendt also valued deliberative democracy as both a democratic good and a route to self-actualization. Interaction among members of the public, in her work, is the practice by which people create "the public."[11] We can think about her conceptualization in the following way. Imagine for the moment an object. People, being the unique individuals that we are, each have a particular perspective of this object. To Arendt, individuals' unique perspectives function like lights to collectively illuminate the objects of our attention. If the object we are focusing on is a sphere, for example, in private our individual lights allow us to see *part* of this sphere. But in a public realm, something transformative happens: multiple people, all shining their individual lights on this object, reveal a depth and richness to it that is not visible to an individual viewing it alone. It is through interaction that an object—whether a sphere or a public issue—becomes illuminated. Together, in interaction, we make the object public and in doing so define what public life is.

Because human interaction gives meaning to public life, Arendt highly valued the freedom to engage in it. She contrasted the existence of a public realm against mob behavior and fascism. In terms of the globe and light metaphor, under fascism multiple people may consider the same object, but all of their lights are constrained to shine at the same point on the globe. This is not a truly public life. Also, according to Arendt, people can occupy a space, but if they fail to engage with one another, public life does not exist. It is communication, particularly among people who hold a variety of perspectives, that constitutes a public realm in Arendt's work.

Arendt built this idea of the public realm around classical Greek theory, and, like those conceptions, viewed the existence of the public realm as important for self-actualization. She held up participation in public life as "intrinsically rewarding" and regarded it as the realm in which people could attain excellence and distinguish themselves.[12] She saw the public realm as so important for this purpose that she wished to exclude some topics, and people, from access to it. In particular, she expected the topic of poverty to threaten the public realm, because it would invite the rage of the poor and laborers and therefore disrupt impartiality. Such disruption would prevent people from using the public realm to record a spot for themselves in history,[13] and would threaten to degrade the public realm into a forum for merely utilitarian pursuits, not the broader project of self-development.[14]

But if Arendt's citizens "begin to resemble posturing little boys clamoring for attention ('Look at me! I'm the greatest!' 'No, look at *me!*'),"[15] this is only a partial understanding of what Arendt intended with the public realm. She sought to ensure that the public realm is a site of collective self-determination as well as for individual development and achievement. Hannah Pitkin comments on and clarifies these arguments:

> Political life is not some leisure-time sport for aristocrats, in which they may cultivate their honor and display their prowess. It is the activity through which relatively large and permanent groups of people determine what they will collectively do, settle how they will live together, and decide their future, to whatever extent that is within human power.[16]

Human beings are not only products of our society but also "creators of culture."[17] Because we create our cultures, Pitkin explains, we need to not just let culture happen to us. We need to intentionally engage in the act of creating who we are. Public life is important because it is the realm in which we do this, *together.*[18] "What distinguishes public life, then, is not that it has important substantive consequences for many people; for that could be true of large-scale private power, or economic activity, or child-rearing practices."[19] It is where we collectively discover our connections to others and learn to care about those connections.[20]

In the work of Arendt, as in that of Dewey and Habermas, public talk is important for its very existence as well as for the decisions and actions that flow from it. Even though these theorists are working from different philosophical traditions, they all value the *existence* of public talk, aside from its effects on policy outcomes.[21]

If the public realm is where we collectively create who we are, we face the dilemma over how to deal with different perspectives of who we are. While including a diversity of perspectives in the public realm might be valuable for illuminating public issues, it threatens to undermine the stability or cohesion of the public. How, in the course of public life, should people deal with the tension between unity and diversity?

TABLE 2.1: Comparing the politics of unity and the politics of difference

	Politics of unity	*Politics of difference*
Outlines in democratic theory	Deliberation can foster democracy in contexts of cultural difference because it can help identify or forge similarity; Just societies are achieved by abiding by universal principles; National identity is preferred over subgroup identity	Deliberation perpetuates marginalization by privileging the language and perspectives of dominant groups; Social group identities are empowering; Difference should be dealt with through recognition, not overlooked; Deliberative system ought to include alternative modes of communication
	Echoes in empirical work	
Intergroup contact research	Reduce prejudice by focusing on overarching identities (recategorization), or draw attention away from subgroup identity (decategorization)	Alternative models suggest prejudice best reduced by paying attention to subgroup and overarching categories simultaneously
Political communication	Diversity of frames inhibits political understanding	. . .
Public planning	Focus on similarities to overcome diversity of cultural narratives	. . .
Public talk	Contexts of intergroup conflict require focus on unity	Deliberation does tend toward consensus, marginalizes racial minorities; needs to incorporate challenges to mainstream conceptions
Collective action	Frame alignment necessary for action	. . .
Public opinion	General disdain for hard multiculturalism	. . .
Questions for the study of civic dialogue	Do people use civic dialogue to identify or forge similarities, shared identities? Discussions with public officials converge on status quo? Is conflict treated as an obstacle? Focus on difference shunned as elitist?	Do people use civic dialogue to pay attention to cultural difference? Do activists avoid dialogue because of its tendency to support the status quo? Do public officials avoid multiculturalist dialogue? Does storytelling insert the perspectives of marginalized groups? Do people treat conflict as productive?

This question lies at the heart of a longstanding debate within democratic theory and American political culture. The remainder of this chapter examines the debate over privileging unity versus privileging cultural difference,[22] and uses this debate to illuminate the tensions we ought to expect in the practice of civic dialogue. Table 2.1 provides an overview of the major arguments.

Unity

How does a public constitute itself as a whole when it is characterized by ethnic, racial, and cultural differences? For many theorists, the answer is deliberation. They argue that deliberation can hold heterogeneous democracies together by legitimating decisions,[23] conferring tolerance and mutual respect,[24] and "encourage[ing] public-spirited perspectives on public issues."[25] Others expect deliberation to do yet even more: *unify* diverse publics. They claim that beyond holding different groups together, deliberation can *forge* unity in the shape of consensus on problem areas,[26] policy ends,[27] or means. Some say it can create unity by helping people identify common ground such as a shared membership in a "new" or "expanded" social category[28] or collective identity,[29] or uncover shared values or principles.[30] And some assert that deliberation can forge these things through the process itself.[31] In short, various theorists assert that deliberation can solve the problem of cultural heterogeneity by providing unity in the form of consensus, shared membership, or shared values.

The desire to address diversity by focusing on unity runs strong in American political culture. The principle of unity is imbedded in the ideology of classical liberalism, which has pervaded American political institutions and political theory since the founding of the United States. Classical liberalism regards the individual as the essence of civic life, and it revolves around the principle that all individual citizens should be treated equally and given the same rights.[32]

This central principle leads to a politics of unity in the following way. When confronting how to sustain a democracy that encompasses many cultures, classical liberalism answers that a polity must be driven by universal principles and a consistent standard of reason. The result is a belief that the proper way to deal with diversity or cultural pluralism is to allow individuals to do what they will, as long as they buy into certain fundamental beliefs, premises, and norms.[33] Defenders of such a view argue that if we do otherwise—if we implement policies that enable members of subgroups to abide by principles and practices particular to their own culture—we threaten the central principle of the protection of rights and liberties. These arguments are apparent, for example, in U.S. immigration policy, which has been structured around the idea that a nation of immigrants will only endure if newcomers adopt the cultural practices, language, and principles of the dominant culture.[34]

Since the social movements of the 1960s, many have questioned whether protecting individual rights and liberties is enough to ensure equality, and have questioned whether consensus on basic moral questions is possible. Such dissenters call for an alternative to the politics of unity. They seek a politics of difference that recognizes that the perspectives and practices of some cultural groups diverge from the mainstream, and that therefore enables minorities to freely express and be recognized for their unique cultural practices.

But proponents of classical liberalism point out the dangers of this politics of difference. They argue that if we emphasize groups rather than individual rights and the good of the whole, we actually enable members of dominant groups to privilege their own groups at the expense of minorities, thus trampling individual liberty.

One of the most comprehensive arguments in favor of a politics of unity as opposed to a politics of difference is put forth by Brian Barry.[35] He notes that arguing for more attention to the perspectives of particular cultural groups falls dangerously close to assuming that all members of a given social group have identical preferences.[36] Also, contrary to claims that democracies should not only tolerate and respect social groups but publicly recognize them as well,[37] Barry argues that some cultures should not be recognized because they do not sufficiently value the protection of individual liberty. And perhaps most centrally, Barry and other classical liberals assert that relaxing the principle of unity is inherently divisive.[38]

Some classical liberals do profess a respect for cultural difference.[39] However, they hold that identification with the nation as a whole is far more important for democratic stability than identification with individual subgroups.[40] Also, Barry argues that there are certain values that all people within a nation can agree upon,[41] and adds that all citizens have to be willing "to make sacrifices for the common good" and be "capable of recognizing a common good."[42] In addition, Barry argues that privileging unity does not require people to give up who they are. He points to the ability of people to learn multiple languages as evidence that subgroup and national identities can actually coexist.[43]

Arguments from Empirical Studies

The unity versus difference debate among theorists centers on whether consensus on basic moral questions is possible in principle. Empirical scholars take up this question by focusing on whether a politics of unity is the best way to improve the fabric of community. They ask: Does focusing on unity reduce prejudice, promote communication, and foster collective action? As in political theory, scholarship on this topic does tend to conclude that focusing on unity is preferable to a politics of difference.

Take, for example, scholarship among social psychologists on how to reduce racial prejudice. Since the 1940s, scholars have prescribed direct, face-to-face contact as a remedy for animosity between people of different racial and ethnic backgrounds.[44] In 1954, Gordon Allport reviewed existing research and historical examples and argued that if members of a dominant social group are hostile toward members of a racial outgroup, this is driven largely by uncertainty stemming from a lack of interaction. His solution for reducing intergroup conflict therefore was to prescribe intergroup contact.[45]

But Allport specified that a particular kind of contact is necessary to reduce prejudice, because contact can just as easily exacerbate conflict as minimize it.[46] Specifically, Allport argued the contact ought to be cooperative and oriented toward a common goal,[47] have the sanction of the community,[48] and take place among people of equal status.[49] Over fifty years later, these remain the main tenets of the "contact hypothesis."[50]

As research on the contact hypothesis progressed, scholars began conceptualizing the problem of intergroup conflict as one of categorization. To make sense of the world, people categorize objects, including themselves and other people, and form identities with ingroups and outgroups accordingly.[51] And even though we might expect that globalization and advanced mass communication would foster identities that cut across subgroup boundaries, identities with specific ingroups continue to persist in modern society.[52] Moreover, social categorization is ubiquitous because it serves a positive function: identification with social groups contributes to self-esteem.[53] Even among people who think of themselves as tolerant or unprejudiced, there is a pervasive tendency to notice social group categories and for these categories to affect information processing.[54]

As scholars have recognized the ubiquity of social categorization, they have conceptualized intergroup conflict as a problem of carving up the world into "us" and "them."[55] Thus conceived, a prevailing prescription for reducing prejudice has been to get people to stop thinking in terms of these categories. Leading explanations for the reasons that Allport's optimal conditions of contact reduce prejudice assert that the conditions work because they draw attention to a common identity or because they draw attention away from subgroup identities. Specifically, *decategorization* theory holds that contact reduces prejudice by encouraging people to think of others as individuals, not as members of outgroups.[56] *Recategorization* theory asserts that contact reduces prejudice if it encourages people to think of others as co-members of an overarching social category.[57] In other words, many social psychologists expect that working on a common task fosters solidarity by focusing attention on unity rather than the differences that divide people.

Scholars working in the field of political communication likewise tend to suggest that unity is better for civic life than is difference. They tend to be wary of the existence of divergent perspectives among members of the public. Some scholars expect that the competition of frames, or "central organizing idea[s]," in news coverage hinders the ability of the public to collectively make sense of public affairs.[58] They worry about the capacity of ordinary citizens to make sense of the complexity of political life and their ability to engage in "public discussion" if political rhetoric does not provide a unified frame for understanding an issue.[59]

Literature on public planning is yet another vein of scholarship that alerts us to the complications that different perspectives pose for civic life. In the racial and ethnic diversity of U.S. cities, planners often confront the challenge of relating to community residents who communicate about public problems through narratives, cultural scripts and codes with which they are unfamiliar.[60] The common form of dealing with such obstacles in the course of planning is to focus on similarities—to privilege unity over difference—because directly addressing conflict and divergences among interpretations is much more difficult to do.[61]

Scholarship on public talk likewise tends to suggest that deliberative democracy is best practiced by privileging unity over diversity. For example, in a recent study of a public forum called Americans Discuss Social Security in Mesa, Arizona, published in the leading political science journal, Jason Barabas defines deliberation as "an enlightened and open-minded search for consensus amid diverse participants."[62] And in a study of deliberation in town hall meetings in New Jersey on school desegregation, Tali Mendelberg and John Oleske conclude that public talk is *not* the answer when it comes to issues infused with intergroup conflict. They state that the only way it might serve to improve desegregation is if it focuses on unity, not difference.[63]

There is yet more scholarship related to community and public life that upholds the benefits of focusing on unity over difference. Scholarship on social movements asserts that collective action is not only assisted when actors share a common frame, but that frame alignment is *necessary* for action to occur.[64] Also, those who wish to foster bridging social capital argue that the way to achieve it is to focus on shared social identities or shared values.[65] Finally, others praise unity in the form of widespread identification with the nation as a whole because such attachment tends to coincide with high levels of political engagement and compliance with laws.[66]

All of these different lines of theorizing and research suggest that the best way to foster democracy in contexts of difference is to strive for unity. Proponents of this view often label arguments to the contrary—which I examine in depth below—as elitist and the product of intellectuals who are out of touch with mainstream public opinion.[67] Existing studies of public opinion support these claims. Opinion poll results show little support for multicultural orientations toward public policy among members of the American public. Sears, Citrin, Cheleden, and van Laar define "multiculturalism" as an alternative vision to the "traditional ideal of American integration."[68] They distinguish two versions of multiculturalism: "soft" versions that are "pluralistic" and "emphasize the need for mutual recognition, respect and tolerance among diverse ethnic groups, as in the 'melting pot' or 'salad bowl' metaphors, and no longer evoke much controversy";[69] and a "hard" version which is "particularistic" and

> asserts the viability and merit of multiple cultures within a society and advocates government action to maintain these equally worthy cultures. As an ideal image of society, [this] multiculturalism rejects the assimilationist ethos of the melting pot in favor of the mosaic, which typically consists of differently colored tiles isolated from each other by impenetrable grout. It construes racial or ethnic identity as the preferred choice of self-definition.[70]

The evidence these authors offer up to assert that multiculturalism is not supported by most Americans comes from a national sample of 1,496 adults through the 1994 General Social Survey.[71] Their analysis of these data shows that majorities of whites, blacks, and Hispanics favor multiculturalism to some extent—they favored bilingual education and election ballots printed in languages other than English (64, 76, and 86 percent, respectively).[72] However, Sears et al. found little support for national identity that stresses subgroups over the nation as a whole. When asked whether it is better for the country's different ethnic groups to "blend into the larger society" or to "maintain their distinct cultures," only 32 percent gave the group-oriented response.[73] And even members of marginalized racial groups were just as or more likely to identify with a national identity rather than a subgroup identity, although to a lesser extent than were whites.[74]

When asked specifically about "hard" multiculturalism—whether members of ethnic or racial groups should "maintain distinct cultures" or "blend in, as in a melting pot"—fewer than a third of whites and Hispanics supported this vision, and less than a majority of blacks did so.[75]

Even among younger generations, a large majority stated that they think of themselves "mainly as just an American" on "all or most issues," as opposed to the hard mutliculturalist position of thinking of oneself "as a member of your ethnic, racial, or nationality group,"[76] although support for hard multiculturalism was slightly stronger among younger generations.[77]

Deborah Schildkraut's work on national identity and language policy also corroborates the view that few people support hard multiculturalism.[78] She used public opinion polls and focus groups to examine the presence of the three primary traditions of national identity that Rogers Smith identifies: liberalism, civic republicanism, and ethnoculturalism (or nativism, the support for extreme unity in the belief that only one type of people should be considered true Americans).[79] She found little support for either ethnoculturalism or "hard" multiculturalism, but instead found that the typical conception of national identity consists of a balance between these two extremes. She calls this tradition "incorporationism" and defines it as a vision of the United States as a nation of immigrants that includes *both* melting pot assimilation and multiculturalism. Just as many theorists and empirical scholars privilege unity over difference in contexts of cultural heterogeneity, the American public as a whole disdains attention to subgroup categories and identities without a simultaneous striving for unity.

Implications for the Study of Civic Dialogue

Unity-focused conceptions of how democracies ought to deal with difference raise various questions about civic intergroup dialogue programs on race, and suggest what we might expect to see in these discussions. First of all, when considering the question of how race dialogues come into being, the unity perspective would lead us to ask whether these programs are implemented in ways and under conditions that are consistent with a concern with unity. Do communities turn to intergroup dialogue as a way to get beyond racial difference and instead forge a common identity? Do the individuals implementing this talk conceptualize it as a way to recognize unity in the form of shared values, beliefs, and experiences? Do they expect it to forge unity in the form of shared identity, or agreement on which problems to pursue and how to pursue them? Do they expect it to overcome divides and celebrate the things that people have in common as a step toward a renewed civic life and opportunities for collective interaction?

A unity-focused perspective also leads to questions regarding how people actually use this form of public talk. Do they shun hard multiculturalism in favor of constituting themselves as a unified public that shares perspectives, identities, and goals? Do they strive to discover similarities and try to settle on agreed ways of interpreting public problems? In dialogues between residents and public officials, do public officials exert authority over the discussion, use the opportunity to justify existing public policy, and therefore bring about convergence around the status quo? Also, among people who claim that they want to use the dialogues productively, do they treat conflict—either in terms of sudden awareness of cultural difference, or disagreement over preferences—as something to be gotten past, not as something they wish to stimulate? In these various ways, the politics of unity could show through in the existence and practice of these programs.

We can also formulate a set of assumptions about race dialogues that do not follow a logic of unity. From a unity perspective we would expect that communication that pays attention to social group difference divides people and exacerbates conflict. And because a focus on cultural difference as opposed to overarching identities runs against the grain of mainstream public opinion, we would also expect that such talk would be elitist, or pursued by people who are out of touch with ordinary citizens and who hold radical leftist political ideologies.

Difference

In all of the research traditions we have visited—democratic theory, intergroup contact research, public opinion research—there is an alternative point of view that privileges difference rather than unity in the quest for a healthy civic life. In all of these realms, it is a minority point of view. I use the term "minority" intentionally to convey that this is both a dissenting point of view as well as a view that is typically associated with concerns about adequate representation of people of color, women, and other minority social groups.[80]

Within democratic theory, this politics of difference argues that assuming that consensus on basic moral questions is possible inevitably leads to the oppression of minority groups.[81] "Difference democrats" argue that deliberation is particularly guilty of perpetuating oppression, because they perceive it to be a procedure that is oriented toward identifying or creating consensus.[82] Even though many proponents of deliberation deny that it is inherently focused on unity, others assert that the focus on consensus is actually the characteristic of deliberative democracy that makes it distinct from other forms of democratic governance.[83]

One of the clearest demonstrations of how deliberation can perpetuate marginalization comes from Lynn Sanders's review of studies of jury deliberation. She argues that juries—quintessential democratic deliberative bodies—often do not proceed on the basis of the best possible argument, as proponents of deliberation would hope. Rather than take advantage of the breadth of experience among all the members assembled, juries' decisions are often clouded by perceptions of status. They tend to defer to those with social group characteristics that people widely associate with expertise. For example, juries often choose those who are dominant in the discussions to lead the deliberation, and these people tend to be high-status individuals, namely, highly educated white males with prior experience seemingly relevant to jury deliberation. Related studies show that the dominance of high-status individuals in group discussions is not correlated with superior decision-making ability.[84]

Critics also assert that deliberation tends toward domination because being successful in deliberation requires winning the support of a majority of the group. And this requires using language, words, expressions, frames, and arguments that will be understood by the widest array of people.[85] If not cast in these terms, members of dominant groups may not listen to minority voices, even if people are present to speak them.[86] In addition, people who do not speak in ways that dominant groups consider articulate will not receive as much respect during deliberation and their arguments will therefore carry less weight.[87]

Notice that these worries about deliberation are therefore much deeper than who speaks and how much.[88] The concern is that certain *perspectives* will not be aired or listened to. Even if there are no patterns of inequality in who participates in deliberation, what gets said and heard is expected to be biased toward the status quo and dominant frames of understanding.

Proponents of deliberation have argued that the reasons people offer up during deliberation do not have to be agreed upon by all participants. Instead, deliberation merely requires that reasons be "acceptable" to all— reasons that people in the public can understand even if they oppose.[89] One example that Amy Gutmann and Dennis Thompson provide is, "Deliberative arguments for universal health care, for example, would appeal to a mutually recognized principle of basic opportunity for all citizens or to another such principle that serves a moral purpose."[90]

But the requirement of publicly acceptable reasons may also be too restrictive, according to difference democrats. They say that it may exclude some arguments or modes of argumentation that are more familiar and advantageous to nondominant groups, such as "pictures, song, poetic imagery, and expressions of mockery and longing performed in rowdy and even playful ways aimed not at commanding assent, but disturbing complacency."[91] Moreover, difference democrats say that even if the requirement is merely that contributions be reasonable, definitions of "reasonableness" are likely to exclude legitimate challenges to the status quo.[92] Part of this worry is a concern that the expression of emotion is often viewed as the opposite of reason and antithetical to the goals of deliberation.[93] Based on claims that displaying emotion is an effective way to challenge dominant positions, some argue that disdaining such expressions is yet another way that deliberation silences alternative views.[94]

Much of what difference democrats are reacting to is the tendency toward unity in classical liberalism, but they criticize the other dominant model of civic life—civic republicanism—for this tendency as well. Civic republicanism centers on the community as the important unit of democracy, in contrast to the individual-centered vision of classical liberalism. Young argues that many civic republicans, such as Benjamin Barber and Habermas, seem to strive to pay attention to difference or at least avoid group-based oppression.[95] However, she argues, their priority is the common good, and they privilege the community over the particularities of groups.[96] In her view, although civic republicans want to respect difference, they tend to see it not as a value but as an obstacle.[97] By presuming that public life can be constituted around a universal conception of the common good, difference is not incorporated but instead excluded.[98]

Difference democrats expect that the lines of exclusion often coincide with social group categories.[99] A politics of difference differs from a politics of unity in its claim that although social group categories can be vehicles of oppression in social, economic, and political life, they also can be liberating as sources of positive identity.[100]

In the United States, the dimension of group difference that is often at the center of debates over the need for attention to difference is race. As Danielle Allen eloquently notes, fifty years after the school desegregation case of *Brown v. Board of Education,* we remain a nation of strangers.[101] *Brown* declared that the United States would no longer tolerate separate civic lives for people of different racial backgrounds. And yet, the passage of time has not produced unity. Citizens of different racial groups still do not know how to interact and treat each other as citizens.

Allen suggests that democracy in a context of difference requires that people have the capacity to interact with strangers and foster "political friendship." Such friendship is not intimacy but is instead a willingness to encounter difference, sincerely consider the interests of others, and learn from these experiences. Allen's conception of democracy is a participatory one in which the central project of democracy is neither voting nor the identification of the proper institutions for reconciling differences. Instead, Allen suggests that the central project of democracy ought to be the development of practices that enable us to define how we are going to live with one another.

Consistent with the politics of difference, Allen does not argue that the importance of interpersonal communication is to find out how we are all alike. Instead, she argues that people should actively try to forge relationships by acknowledging difference. She draws on Aristotle to explain how political friendship might work:

> Friendship begins in the recognition that friends have a *shared* life—not a "common" nor an identical life—only one with common events, climates, built-environments, fixations of the imagination, and social structures. Each friend will view all these phenomena differently, but they are not the less shared for that. The same is true of democracy. The inhabitants of a polity have a shared life in which each citizen and noncitizen has an individual perspective on a set of phenomena relevant to all. Some live behind one veil, and others behind another, but the air that we all breathe carries the same gases and pollens through those veils. More important, our shared elements . . . are made out of the combination of all our interactions with each other.[102]

Instead of the rhetoric of unity or "oneness" as she calls it, she urges a focus on "wholeness." She demonstrates wholeness with a photograph: a picture of a group of people standing around a piano, singing together.[103] In this metaphor of her ideal civic life, people are not "one"—they do not have the same voice. Instead, they create "wholeness" or harmony through the act of singing together.

Allen's call for wholeness resembles difference democrats' call for recognition of group difference: neither portrays the recognition of subgroup identities as a necessary evil. Instead, they view recognizing differences as empowering. They treat subgroup identity as something to celebrate and something that individuals themselves define, rather than a label that is imposed by others.[104] Recognizing difference is expected to encourage self-reflection among members of dominant groups, increasing the chance that group memberships will seem less remarkable, thereby defusing their potency as sources of dominance.[105] Recognizing difference may also empower people by replacing individualism with group solidarity,[106] and may foster collective action along group lines.[107]

Calling for Alternative Modes

Theorists who criticize the ability of deliberation to incorporate minority viewpoints into democratic life do not rule out *all* forms of communication.

Instead, they call for *alternative* forms of communication.[108] They call for an opening up of the deliberative system to include talk that challenges the discourses of mainstream society,[109] "to make us wonder about what we are doing, to rupture a stream of thought, rather than to weave an argument."[110] In their accounts, democracies ought to expand their deliberative systems to include forms of communication that focus on difference as opposed to unity.[111]

They call for public life to include an *ongoing process* of contestation to ensure that any understanding reached through public talk does not repress marginalized perspectives.[112] The idea is not that consensus or shared identity must be avoided at all costs. Instead, difference democrats argue for a civic life in which notions of consensus and shared categories are continually called into question.[113]

Specifically, difference democrats call for communication that forces people in power to listen to voices of marginalized groups. Sanders has called for testimony, a form of communication that she argues would reveal the perspectives of those normally ignored during public discussion.[114] Young has called for greeting, storytelling, and rhetoric, three forms of communication that involve listening to, and acknowledging, others.[115] Greeting, because it requires recognition of others, is a means toward establishing a bond of "trust necessary to sustain a discussion about issues that face us together."[116] Rhetoric requires people to pose arguments in terms the audience can understand, again forcing attention to difference. Young's call for storytelling—much akin to Sanders's "testimony"—has a particular focus on marginalized perspectives. The expectation is that the act of telling stories about one's own experience and listening to others' stories helps people understand others' experiences and worldviews and reveals the "source of values, priorities, or cultural meanings."[117]

Arguments from Empirical Studies

Empirical work on deliberative democracy suggests that, in practice, deliberation does tend toward unity. And in fact, such research questions whether the deliberative system can even function without a source of unity such as shared identity or shared interests. Jane Mansbridge, in her intensive study of a town meeting in Vermont and a small democratic workplace, argues that in situations in which deliberators do not have established friendships that consist of a sense of equality and shared respect, and thus do not recognize shared interests, it is difficult if not impossible to make decisions through public talk.[118] Dryzek and Braithwaite, using an analysis of subjects' orientations to contemporary political debates in

Australia, similarly conclude that in contexts of divergent value orientations, people will have little success reaching agreement through talk.[119]

Thus in the contemporary United States, the use of deliberation to address issues related to race seems particularly problematic. Race may be the single most divisive feature of American life, and, if unity is what deliberation needs, then deliberation about race just might be impossible. Discrimination, misunderstanding, and uncertainty prevent interracial talk from occurring. And in a context of racial diversity, the unity on which public talk is expected to rely seems to evaporate. Interracial deliberative forums are often devoid of the shared respect and equality that deliberation requires.[120] The fact that on many issues "whites and blacks see different worlds" also calls into question the possibility of interracial deliberation.[121]

Even if deliberation does occur within racially diverse groups, work on civic deliberation and small group discussion confirms difference democrats' fears that this public talk tends toward consensus and subjugates minority viewpoints. Karpowitz and Mansbridge assert simply that "*because deliberative norms tend toward consensus*, participants must try to alert themselves to possible enduring conflicts in interest and deeply held opinion" (emphasis added).[122] Similarly, Button and Mattson observed a tendency toward consensus in an observation and survey study of seven different deliberative forums.[123] They note that in these examples of deliberation in actual civic life,

> all participants' desire for education, information-sharing, and the pursuit of consensus and unity tended to push aside conflict. This meant not only the relative displacement of one or more different orientations to deliberation, but the more significant loss of the voices of those who, at least initially, approached political discussion in these alternative modes.[124]

The avoidance of alternative views shows up in many other studies of actual deliberation, from Mansbridge's study of the Vermont town meeting to Coote and Lenaghan's study of citizens' juries in the United Kingdom (structured four-day discussions among small, representative groups of people combined with plenary sessions with experts intended to produce policy solutions).[125] Finally, laboratory analyses of small group dynamics add fuel to this argument against the utility of deliberation in contexts of racial difference by revealing how difficult it is to induce dominant groups to listen to members of minority groups.[126]

The result of these observations is that within empirical studies of deliberation, as in political theory, we see a dissenting view that calls for attention to difference rather than a focus on unity. Karpowitz and Mansbridge argue that organizers of deliberation need to structure attention to conflict directly into public talk, in order to avoid the otherwise inevitable reversion to consensus and subsequent backlash from those whose concerns have been ignored, and also to avoid damaging "the good name and reputation of deliberation itself."[127] They call for *dynamic updating* in which participants in deliberation probe conflicts and "update their understandings of common and conflicting interests as the process evolves."[128]

Dissents in favor of a politics of difference show up in another area of empirical research as well—intergroup conflict. In contrast to theories of decategorization or recategorization, some research in the contact hypothesis tradition suggests that deemphasizing subgroup categories may not always be advantageous. Positive interaction with members of outgroups is most likely to generalize to outgroup members beyond the contact situation if the contact involves some attention to subgroup identities.[129] Also, contact seems to most effectively reduce prejudice when it involves emphasis of both subgroup *and* superordinate identities.[130]

Thus research on intergroup conflict has produced two dissenting models: the mutual intergroup differentiation model[131] and the dual identity approach.[132] These models advocate attention to both similarities and differences, and attention to both subgroup and overarching identities, respectively. These alternative theories discourage looking beyond or deemphasizing subgroup identities, based on evidence that such attachments have positive effects on self-esteem.[133] For example, among students in a university curriculum designed to draw attention to group differences, those who were members of dominant social groups showed an increase in the belief that such interaction has positive democratic consequences. Subordinate group members reported more positive interactions with members of outgroups compared to a control group that was not exposed to the curriculum.[134] Also, students who engaged in intergroup dialogues in the program learned about group differences, and this in turn seemed both to spur beliefs that such interaction is important and to nourish confidence in pursuing such contact.[135]

Although these studies on difference-focused intergroup contact challenge the unity-focused decategorization and recategorization models, proponents of the latter at times acknowledge that focusing on subgroup identities can be valuable. For example, Marilynn Brewer, a proponent of decategorization, points to her own work on individuals' dual needs for assimilation and differentiation in maintaining positive self-esteem[136] to recognize the utility of paying attention to subgroup identities.[137] Also, she and Samuel Gaertner, and also Thomas Pettigrew, propose that decategorization, recategorization, and the alternative models that prescribe a focus on subgroups are complementary processes that are best fostered at different stages and conditions of intergroup contact.[138] Thus it is not the case that scholars who point to the positive effects of an overarching identity do not acknowledge that such a focus can have oppressive consequences.

However, the field of intergroup contact has nevertheless maintained its focus on unity-centered intergroup contact.[139] For example, as recently as 1999, a volume that reviewed the state of the literature included an article by Gurin and colleagues on the value of difference-focused intergroup contact in a university setting,[140] but also included a chapter by Gaertner and colleagues on recategorization (attention to overarching identities) that won the 1998 Gordon Allport Intergroup Relations Prize awarded by the Society for the Psychological Study of Social Issues and the Gordon W. Allport Memorial Fund.[141]

Implications for the Study of Intergroup Dialogue

In democratic theory and empirical studies of civic life, the debate between unity and difference continues. Viewed from the perspective of theorists and empirical scholars who argue that paying attention to difference is valuable, the tension provides an alternative set of expectations surrounding the practice of civic intergroup dialogue programs. When asking how programs that involve repeated discussions about race come into being, we can ask: Do these programs arise in conditions that are associated with a concern with racial difference? Do the people implementing the dialogues talk about their choice as one stemming from a desire to pay attention to the demands, interests, and perspectives of marginalized racial groups? Do they intend for these forums to be agonistic forums in which people scrutinize and challenge white, mainstream conceptions of national identity and perspectives of public problems? We would expect that activists would not choose to pursue public talk, particularly talk with public officials, given the potential for such forums to silence dissent and contestation of the status quo. Finally, we would not expect public officials to pursue or support public talk that involves listening to the views of racial minorities, especially if these views directly challenge conventional wisdom or mainstream modes of conceptualizing public problems.

Furthermore, when considering what actually happens during these dialogues, we would ask whether the participants spend their time focusing on racial subgroup identities and different perspectives and experiences across members of the community. Do they talk about race? Or do they talk about wanting to get beyond race? Do they call into question assumptions of similarity, such as shared identity, experience, values, and perspectives? Do participants use the opportunity to challenge dominant conceptions of public policy related to race? When programs do foster alternative forms of communication, like storytelling or testimony, is their value in interjecting the perspectives and experiences of members of marginalized groups? Do racial minorities resist the tendency toward unity? Do participants treat conflict as productive rather than inherently divisive? In dialogues that take place between residents and public officials, do officials use the talk to better understand the perspectives of people of various cultural backgrounds?[142] Do people create a context in which norms of civility are relaxed enough that residents can directly challenge officials' interpretations of public problems?

The examination of various conceptions of democratic theory and of empirical studies of political communication and political behavior in this chapter reveals a pervasive divide between unity- and difference-focused approaches to dealing with diversity in civic life. Political theorists and empirical researchers disagree about what approaches ought to be pursued and are even feasible. But it remains to be seen why ordinary citizens, in the course of civic life, choose to foster communication that addresses racial difference in public life, what they intend for it to achieve, and the type of focus they imbue it with when they do so. The remainder of this book focuses on these questions.

CHAPTER THREE

Public Talk That Aims
to Listen to Difference

Civic intergroup dialogue programs on the surface appear to have the difference-focused quality that difference democrats hope to inject into the deliberative system. But do they? This chapter describes these programs in relation to deliberation, or decision-making public talk, to set the stage for the subsequent analyses of how these programs come into being and what actually takes place within them. Using interviews with race dialogue practitioners and program promotional materials, I identify the traits that should lead us to expect that civic dialogue listens to difference more than other forms of civic deliberation, and yet identify why civic dialogue may nevertheless focus on unity.

The basic distinction between civic deliberation and civic dialogue is that deliberation is focused on weighing options to produce a decision, while dialogue is about increasing understanding among people. Because dialogue is not generated for the purposes of decision-making, we should expect it to have a qualitatively different character.[1]

John Gastil defines *public* (or what I call "civic") deliberation as

> discussion that involves judicious argument, critical listening, and earnest decision making. Following the writings of John Dewey, full deliberation includes a careful examination of a problem or issue, the identification of possible solutions, the establishment or reaffirmation of evaluative criteria, and the use of these criteria in identifying an optimal solution. Within a specific policy debate or in the context of an election, deliberation sometimes starts with a given set of solutions, but it always involves problem analysis, criteria specification, and evaluation.[2]

Dialogue, on the other hand, is "an orientation to conflict that is open to changing not just what one believes but also how one talks and even thinks about an issue."[3] It is often conceptualized as a precursor to deliberation, a way to increase mutual understanding before engaging in argumentation. This shows up in theory as well as in practice.[4] Some public talk practitioners advocate this intertwining, calling the combination "deliberative dialogue."[5] They argue that deliberation needs dialogue to bridge gaps in understanding in diverse communities, and dialogue also needs deliberation to move talk into action.

Nevertheless, these programs clearly aim for communication that is "dialogue and not debate." For example, guidelines for discussions organized through the NCCJ read: "Dialogue is not a debate, in which one can expect to id a 'winner' or a 'loser.' In dialogue, the goal is not for one party to impose ideas on the other; rather, to see afresh issues or positions that seemed non-negotiable."[6] Unlike deliberation, dialogue programs are not about reaching a decision or a policy choice. "Exploration, not agreement, is the objective" reads a pamphlet describing the Kenosha/Racine Diversity Circles. The SCRC facilitator guide includes an entire page outlining the distinction between debate and dialogue.[7] Contributions to the discussions are intended to take the form of testimony or personal stories, not statements on behalf of a particular stance on an issue, especially in the first meetings of the group.[8]

The Varieties of Public Talk

Civic intergroup dialogue programs have emerged alongside other types of public talk, as activists and organizations around the country have turned to organized interpersonal talk to solve public problems.[9] Many of the people involved in implementing these forums have roots in social movement organizing of the 1960s, and their efforts are often intertwined with a desire to revitalize the notion of citizens as active producers of civic life rather than as passive consumers of it.[10]

These initiatives include forums geared toward dialogue as well as forums for deliberation, and thus I refer to them generally as "public talk," and reserve the term "civic deliberation" for programs that are specifically intended to produce decisions. There are many examples of public talk programs, but some of the more widely known include Deliberative Polls, Citizen Juries, National Issues Forums, 21st Century Town Hall Meetings, and Study Circles.[11]

The National Issues Forums are typically one-day forums on public issues involving discussion among citizens from one geographic community and often from within one organization. The idea was developed by David Matthews with the help of Daniel Yankelovich through the Kettering

Foundation.[12] The forums are sponsored by a variety of organizations from colleges to correction facilities. The Kettering Foundation and the Public Agenda Foundation publish policy books each year that address several public issues, provide alternative solutions to the policy problems, and describe the consequences of these alternatives. Participants in the forums use the books to deliberate about the suggested options. The Forums were developed in the early 1980s, and by 1986 over 100,000 people were participating per year. By 1999, twenty-two regional Public Policy Institutes had been established to train conveners and facilitators.[13]

Another prominent example of civic deliberation is the America*Speaks* program, headquartered in Washington, D.C. America*Speaks* uses technology to engage large numbers of people in one-day forums in which people discuss and reach judgments on public policy issues. Participants are clustered into small groups and then engage in facilitator-led discussion. The facilitator summarizes the groups' ideas and communicates them to a "lead team" via a computer at the table. This team aggregates the thoughts of all of the groups and broadcasts these results back to the forum as a whole. America*Speaks* has trademarked this model and calls it the "21st Century Town Meeting." The most prominent example of such a meeting to date was the convening of over 4,300 people in 2002 in New York City's Jacob Javits Center to deliberate about the fate of Ground Zero.[14]

The NIF and America*Speaks* are just two examples of the many types of public talk arising around the United States. Some of this growth has been spurred by governments, as federal agencies and local governments have sought to increase communication between governments and residents and increase resident input in the governing process through face-to-face discussion, as well as through the use of the Internet.[15] Changes in journalism have also spurred more public talk. A civic or public journalism movement spread throughout the media industry in the 1990s and sought to engage the public in addressing issues of concern and to establish greater trust among residents, local media, and public officials. Many of these efforts involve forums sponsored by local media that provide an opportunity for citizens to learn about and discuss public issues, and enable journalists to hear and report on these concerns.[16]

One sign of the growth of the practice of focused discussion about public problems by ordinary people—not just legislators—is the start of several international professional organizations for practitioners of public talk. The National Coalition for Dialogue and Deliberation held its first annual conference in October 2002 in Arlington, Virginia, during which 240 scholars and practitioners engaged in several days of workshops and discussions. The organization's website states that the membership had grown "eight-fold" in the two years following the conference. In addition, the Deliberative Democracy Consortium is an organization of practitioners and academics who are attempting to improve the practice of public talk through collaboration and research.[17]

Civic dialogue programs constitute a subset of these many public talk initiatives. The name of the national organization for public talk practitioners—the National Coalition of Dialogue and Deliberation—signifies that people involved in public talk often distinguish dialogue from deliberation. And although political theorists often use the terms "dialogue" and "deliberation" interchangeably, work by communications scholars provides precedents for differentiating the two.[18] Drawing on theorists including Habermas, Bakhtin, Gadamer, Buber, and Bohm, scholars in the field of communication describe dialogue as the act of sharing information about perspectives, rather than debate.[19] They often regard dialogue as an essential precursor to deliberation in situations in which participants tend to approach a problem from disparate cultural perspectives.[20] The expectation is that if participants keep an open mind and allow themselves enough time, they can develop shared understandings, or a new "language" jointly understood by all parties. At a less advanced stage, dialogue can produce active listening, or empathy.[21]

The use of dialogue in civic life stems from a variety of traditions, including intergroup contact research, conflict resolution work, and social justice organizing.[22] University and college administrators are increasingly implementing intergroup dialogue on campuses to try to deal with cultural diversity. David Schoem, Sylvia Hurtado, Patricia Gurin, and others have implemented intergroup dialogue at the University of Michigan,[23] and Gurin's involvement in particular was instrumental in defending that university's affirmative action policies in the 2003 U.S. Supreme Court Case, *Grutter v. Bollinger*.[24] Other universities that have implemented intergroup dialogue programs include Princeton University, the University of Massachusetts, the School of Social Work at the University of Washington, Arizona State University, the University of Maryland at College Park, and the University of New Hampshire.[25] The diffusion of dialogue on campuses continues as numerous scholars and professional organizations, such as the Center for Values in Higher Education, promote the idea of dialogue as an integral component of education in a diverse democracy.[26]

Intergroup dialogue has become a facet of deliberative democracy off of college campuses as well.[27] Much of the awareness of civic dialogue is due in large part to promotional efforts by national organizations such as the Study Circles Resource Center. The SCRC was started by Paul Aicher, who had made a fortune in the metals industry and chose later in his career to target some of it toward improving civic life. In 1982 he sold his business, Technical Materials Inc., and started the Topsfield Foundation (renamed the Paul J. Aicher Foundation after his death in 2002). During the 1980s, he focused the foundation on international peace efforts and affordable housing in Connecticut, where the foundation is located. During this work, he noticed a need for dialogue and came across the work of Leonard Oliver, an associate of the Kettering Foundation. Oliver had written a book on the century-old idea of study circles, or small discussion groups popularized in New York in the 1870s through the Chautauqua adult education movement.[28] Inspired by Oliver's work, Aicher formed the SCRC in 1989.[29] As the foundation developed guidelines for dialogue, initially around race and racism, it moved from advocating one-time events to advocating a series of meetings, so that participants could develop understanding as well as engage in deliberation about the future actions they wished to pursue.[30]

While Aicher was turning toward dialogue and founding the SCRC, a variety of religious and political leaders were trying to establish interracial communication in Richmond, Virginia. In 1990, they started Hope in the Cities, an interfaith, interracial dialogue program aimed at racial healing. Several years later, they started using the organization to help cities across the nation engage in similar programs.[31] In addition, the National Conference for Communities and Justice had been using intercultural dialogue to bridge tensions in communities and foster a "spirit of understanding" since the 1920s.[32]

These and other uses of dialogue to address race relations attracted the attention of national leaders in the late 1990s. Bob Knight, the mayor of Wichita, used his platform as president and first vice president of the National League of Cities in the late 1990s and 2000 to promote greater attention to reducing racism in cities across the country. Through speaking engagements, the annual NLC conference, and publications distributed by the NLC, Knight promoted the use of interracial dialogue programs.[33]

Even more prominently, President Bill Clinton's Initiative on Race promoted talk about race through its town hall meetings on the topic, and promoted civic dialogue programs specifically. His administration identified and publicized race dialogue programs as some of the "best practices" for improving race relations.[34] Another prominent national politician, Bill Bradley, while a U.S. senator from New Jersey, also gave visible support to intergroup dialogue programs when he attended a SCRC-assisted Days of Dialogue program in Los Angeles following the O. J. Simpson trial verdict in 1995.

Civic intergroup dialogue has also spread outside of the United States. Scholars and practitioners have turned to dialogue to reconcile some of the most violent intergroup conflicts around the world, including the 1994 genocide in Rwanda.[35] Indeed, Barbara Nelson, Linda Kaboolian, and Kathryn Carver have found that organizations in the United States, Northern Ireland, South Africa, and Israel that seek to bring people together across longstanding divides commonly use the strategy of dialogue.[36] Such organizations, which they call "concord organizations,"[37] include the Center for Conflict Resolutions in South Africa, the Community Relations Council in Northern Ireland, the Network for Life and Choice in many cities in the United States, and the Parents' Circle-Families Forum and Bereaved Families Supporting Reconciliation, Tolerance, and Peace in Israel and Palestine.

Sketching the Distinctiveness of Civic Intergroup Dialogue

Civic dialogue programs are a recognized component of the deliberative system, but should we expect them to produce communication that is qualitatively different from civic deliberation? In particular, should we expect them to pay attention to difference more than other forms of public talk? To investigate, I compare descriptions of this form of communication provided by representatives of national dialogue organizations and also promotional materials and facilitator guides against criteria of ideal deliberation.[38] I say "ideal deliberation" intentionally to note that this characterization may not match the actual practice of any one example of deliberation, but that it serves as an ideal type, or a standard of comparison. For these characteristics, I rely on work by Jane Mansbridge,[39] and Tali Mendelberg and John Oleske,[40] which synthesizes a broad range of political theory on deliberation. Mansbridge offers up seven common requirements of good deliberation: equality of access, publicity, reciprocity, reasonableness, freedom from power, accountability, and a focus on consensus or common ground. She derives publicity, accountability, and reciprocity from Gutmann and Thompson's *Deliberative Democracy*. The remaining criteria are adapted primarily from Joshua Cohen's work.[41] These criteria closely match those that Mendelberg and Oleske "distill" from a variety of theorists.[42] In the following, I sketch the outlines of civic dialogue with respect to these seven criteria. Table 3.1 summarizes this comparison.

Equality of Access

When deliberative theorists talk about equality of access in the discussion, they are referring to the physical presence of people representing a wide

TABLE 3.1: Comparing criteria of good deliberation against descriptions of civic dialogue

	Deliberation	Dialogue
Overall purpose	Decision making; selection of solutions; agreement	Improved understanding; attention to varieties of perspectives; exploration
Equality of access	Presence of people representing a wide range of views	Attempts to attract a range of participants by connecting the dialogue to policy making; treats inclusivity as a topic of discussion
Publicity and reciprocity	Participants offer publicly acceptable reasons; open-mindedness	Programs relax the constraint of publicity, make discussions confidential; create "safe" space in order to enable challenging of dominant perspectives
Considered debate	Reasonable, not necessarily dispassionate discussion	Welcomes expression of emotion as route to challenge dominant perspectives
Freedom from power	Prevent social inequalities from influencing content of deliberation	Treats inequalities of power as a focus of discussion
Accountability	Participants exhibit accountability to constituents	Urges attentiveness to the common good; mindfulness of concerns of other community members
Focus on consensus or common good	Focus on a goal of unity	Cautious encouragement to focus on unity and the common good

range of views. Program literature and people who promote civic dialogue convey a good deal of concern with this criterion. In addition to caring about equality in principle, they perceive that recruiting participants is much easier if the steering committee and previous participants represent a broad cross-section of the community.[43]

Achieving equality in dialogue programs is difficult. Many practitioners interviewed for this study reported that their programs have a difficult time recruiting people of color.[44] For example, Dean Lovelace, a Dayton, Ohio, city commissioner who started a dialogue program in that city, stated that as an African-American city official in a city in which 43 percent of the population in 2000 identified as black, and a majority of the elected city officials are African American, his recruitment concerns are dominated by the dilemma of attracting blacks who are particularly upset with the state of race relations. He said, "My concern is, 'How do you get angry brothers and sisters involved?'"

One way in which practitioners have tried to enhance equality is by inviting public officials or by attempting to connect the discussion to formal channels of policy decision-making. Some say that without the potential to impact policy, why, indeed, would angry brothers and sisters choose to be involved?[45]

Dialogue programs may not meet the criterion on equality in another respect: they are often criticized for "preaching to the choir," in other words, only attracting people who already perceive that racism in their community is a problem and are willing to do something about it.

Despite the difficulties with racial and ethnic inclusivity, dialogue programs do appear to improve the equality of the deliberative system with respect to gender. Women may speak less during the dialogues, a possibility suggested by previous research on jury and legislative deliberation,[46] small group discussions,[47] New England town meetings,[48] the public forum of talk radio,[49] and in everyday political discourse.[50] However, the volunteers for dialogue programs tend to be female,[51] a result that is consistent with other recent studies of deliberative democracy.[52]

Civic dialogue programs may struggle with equality, but this does not distinguish them from civic deliberation. Some civic deliberation programs go to such lengths to achieve inclusivity that they recruit participants through random sampling, such as Deliberative Polls[53] and Citizen Juries.[54] What distinguishes dialogue programs is that equality is often a topic of the discussion itself. For example, the SCRC curriculum guide encourages participants to talk about institutional racism, and about the ways in which laws and entrenched practices limit access and voice for people of marginalized racial groups, starting in the second session.[55] Thus with respect to this criterion, we have reason to expect a focus on difference in the form of direct attention to inequality in participation.

Publicity and Reciprocity

Turning to other criteria of good deliberation reveals that dialogue programs tend to have built-in mechanisms for fostering openness and the revelation of perspectives and experiences, again suggesting a focus on difference. "Publicity" is the term democratic theorists use to describe deliberation that is open to public scrutiny. The hope, expressed by Bohman for example, is that the legitimacy of outcome decisions is enhanced if the participants offer up *publicly acceptable* reasons, or reasons that all citizens can at least understand, if not agree with.[56] However, what constitutes an acceptable reason is a subjective question. When faced with speaking in public, participants may be more likely to contribute reasons that appeal to the majority, thereby perpetuating intercultural conflict.

Dialogue programs relax the constraint of publicity by requiring that the communication is private and *removed* from public scrutiny.[57] Participants commonly agree on their ground rules collectively at the start of the first session, and these often include an agreement to keep the conversations confidential.[58] Respecting confidentiality is typically emphasized in facilitator and participant guides.[59]

Analyzing publicity requires a consideration of reciprocity as well. Reciprocity is a willingness to listen to and potentially agree with others' reasons. It is the criterion of open-mindedness, mutual respect, and civility.[60] Program guides ask participants to be civil in the sense of listening to all reasons, stories, and viewpoints—especially if people do not find them acceptable at first. The guides ask participants to keep their minds open and to try to understand others' views, especially when the views conflict with their own. The following series of "Tips for study circle participants," published in the SCRC guide given to participants and facilitators, illustrates this point:

1. Make a good effort to attend all meetings. The comfort level and depth of conversation depend upon familiarity with other participants.
2. Think together about what you want to get out of your conversation.
3. Help keep the discussion on track. Make sure your remarks are relevant.
4. Speak your mind freely, but don't monopolize the conversation.
5. Really try to understand what others are saying and respond to their ideas, especially when their thinking is different from yours. (In other words, seek first to understand, then to be understood.)
6. Be open to changing your mind. This will help you really listen to others' views.
7. When disagreement occurs, don't personalize it. Try to identify the ideas that are in conflict. Search for the common concerns beneath the surface.
8. Don't waste time arguing about points of fact. For the time being, you

may need to agree to disagree and then move on. You might decide to
check out the facts together before your next meeting.

9. Value one another's experiences. Think about how your own
   experiences have contributed to your thinking.
10. Help to develop one another's ideas. Listen carefully, and ask clarify-
    ing questions.[61]

Instructions to "Really try to understand what others are saying" (tip
number 5), and "Be open to changing your mind" (number 6) illustrate the
ways dialogue programs encourage participants to keep an open mind.

Other programs provide similar guidelines. The guide for the Hope in
the Cities program urges facilitators to "make it clear [to participants] that
there are no right or wrong responses for the purposes of these dialogues,"
to convey respect for each member of the group,[62] and suggests that one
of the ground rules include "listen[ing] carefully and respectfully to each
other."[63] For the NCCJ, a handout on dialogue states: "Primary requirements are a willingness to act civilly, both in listening to the other and in
expressing one's convictions. It also involves a willingness to learn from
others, to clarify, even change perceptions without forfeiting individual
values and identity."[64] The St. Louis Bridges program similarly uses the
terms "open mind" and "respect" to describe the form that comments
should take during discussion.[65]

Although examination of this criterion suggests that dialogue programs
foster attention to subgroup identities and divisions, the many injunctions
to practice civility might actually interfere with something else that difference democrats call for: the direct challenging of dominant perspectives
on public issues. An atmosphere of open-mindedness may make people
more comfortable and perhaps more likely to contribute, but it does not
necessarily make the talk more beneficial when the goal is social justice.
Calls for civility have at times been used to alienate some members of the
public from participation.[66] As Young suggests, to give due consideration
to marginalized voices, democracy needs a space in which these voices
can "rupture a stream of thought."[67] Civil contexts are not synonymous
with attention to minority perspectives. "[S]ubordinates sometimes need
the battering ram of rage."[68] And, "Democracy may sometimes require
that your interlocutor does not wait politely for you to finish but shakes
you by the collar and cries, 'Listen! For God's sake!'"[69]

It may be, however, that the relaxed criterion of publicity enables
enough incivility that people can indeed engage in the agonistic communication difference democrats prescribe for the deliberative system. Dialogue
practitioners say that the key to creating a space in which people are both

willing to participate and yet willing to say publicly unpalatable things is "safety." The participant guidelines cited above suggest that the goal is to provide a forum in which people can say whatever is on their mind (tip number 4), but not be hurt by the comments of others (number 7). On the one hand, this is civility. On the other, it is an attempt to not restrict what gets said. It remains to be seen, however, what actually occurs in practice.

Considered Debate

The criterion of "considered debate" pertains to whether or not good deliberation involves the expression of emotion. The role that emotions ought to play is, ironically, hotly contested. Some stipulate that deliberation ought to consist of the careful consideration of opinions,[70] or the cool voice of reason.[71] Yet outlawing emotion ignores evidence that citizens use emotion as a source of information when trying to make sense of public issues.[72] Moreover, as noted in chapter 2, some theorists argue that emotions such as compassion and solidarity are important contributions to public debate, and suggest that we ought to strive for "considered" rather than "reasoned" deliberation.[73]

Civic intergroup dialogue practitioners seem to try to encourage participants to expect and value the expression of emotion. For example, the SCRC guide starts with a "note to readers" that acknowledges: "It is hard to talk about race. Conversations are likely to touch on power and privilege, fear and anger, hope and disappointment."[74] The guide to Hope in the Cities Honest Conversations describes the expression of emotions as a sign of attaining a goal of the program:

HOW TO KNOW . . . WHEN YOU ARE HAVING AN HONEST CONVERSATION

When you say the things you <u>need</u> to say
When you say things to <u>reveal</u> your feelings
When you say things to <u>disclose</u> your own reality
When you say things that you <u>really</u> believe
When you say things in such a way that indicates an openness to <u>growth</u>
   and the <u>future</u>

INSTEAD OF

When you say things you <u>want</u> to say
When you say things to <u>accuse</u> others
When you say things to <u>control</u> another person's reality
When you say what's <u>expected</u> or <u>stereotypical</u>
When you speak only to the <u>past</u>[75]

This program focuses on "racial reconciliation," in particular, acknowledging history. Program administrators strive for this by taking "walks through history," or guided tours of a city during which the participants consider significant events in the history of race relations in their community. The program guide privileges the expression of emotion in this process: "Facts are important, but historical memory may be more powerful. Facts have emotional components which are attached to our hearts and spirits. We need to look within the 'package of pain' where historical facts are packed. It is not the facts that challenge us racially; it is the pain that we choose to not get beyond."[76]

This and other programs treat the discussions as a kind of *haven* for emotions. For example, Roseann Mason, who runs the Kenosha/Racine Diversity Circles, has held discussions among prison inmates. She notes that the discussions are perhaps the one place in prison life where the expression of emotions is acceptable, and are a valuable resource for participants in that respect.

Because these programs welcome the expression of passionate views that may challenge dominant perspectives, we have yet more reason to expect that civic dialogue will consist of difference-focused talk.

Freedom from Power

The prescription that good deliberation be "free from power" is an instruction to prevent inequalities in society from influencing the process of deliberation. There is, of course, reason to wonder whether any form of communication can be free from power.[77] A difference democrat might ask, how can public talk—whether deliberation or dialogue—ever be free from power, because it is highly unlikely that those with and those without power are equally familiar and comfortable using the same language and set of symbols to convey meaning?[78]

The way in which civic dialogues on race measure up to this criterion again suggests that the talk in these programs may focus on difference as much as strive for unity. Rather than chase the elusive condition of freedom from power, dialogue programs focus on imbalances of power directly. For example, the curriculum guide for the second session of Study Circles on race suggests that groups discuss "What is the nature of the problem?" It gives participants six different viewpoints, and then asks them to discuss which comes closest to their own view. These viewpoints include (1) "History is at the root of the problem"; (2) "The real problem is institutional racism"; (3) "The problem is that many people of color lack economic opportunity"; (4) "The problem is that too many people of color are not taking advantage of the opportunities available to them"; (5) "Separation and prejudice are still our major problems"; and (6) "The problem is our lack of strong leadership."[79]

The goal of focusing on imbalances in power puts a premium on encouraging people to listen to the stories of those who have experienced such disparities. In practice, this results in attempts to ensure equality in participation during the conversations. Tips for Study Circles facilitators include instructions such as "It is important to hear from everyone" and "Don't let anyone dominate; try to involve everyone."[80] Other programs set similar goals such as "We will insure the participation of all[81] and instructions to arrange chairs in a circle and not around a table such that that there is no back row.[82] The SCRC and the St. Louis Bridges program both advise discussion groups to have a racially diverse team of co-facilitators to make it as comfortable as possible for people of a variety of racial backgrounds to talk. In these ways, the programs exude a self-conscious attempt to address inequality.

Accountability

Ideal deliberation requires that the participants are accountable to their constituents.[83] This might seem irrelevant with respect to civic dialogue programs, because the participants are not elected or representatives of a constituency in any formal sense. In addition, program guides urge facilitators to not treat individual participants as representatives of any given social group.[84] However, part of what interpersonal talk accomplishes is the clarification of "to whom am I responsible?"[85] Neither interviews with program promoters nor dialogue program literature revealed the use of the terms "accountability," "responsibility to others," or "obligation to others." But occasionally, these interviewees or guidebooks would emphasize common good and "unity," suggesting that proponents of these programs expect that the dialogues lead participants to understand their preferences in ways that are attentive to the common good as opposed to only a sensitivity to a particular racial group.

Focus on Consensus or the Common Good

The focus on unity in the form of consensus or the common good is the final criterion that Mansbridge and Mendelberg and Oleske identify, and it is the one that perhaps sits at the heart of the question of whether civic dialogue programs exhibit the tendency toward unity for which difference democrats criticize deliberation. Program literature presents a mixed view. The names of programs themselves often convey a simultaneous desire for a unified community and respect for cultural difference. For example, a program in Kansas City, Missouri, is called "Harmony," and another in Miami, Florida, was called "Many Voices, One Community."

But Sirianni and Friedland claim that in civic renewal efforts, metaphors of common ground *dominate* rather than co-exist with calls for respecting difference.[86] And although SCRC promotional materials encourage participants to avoid striving for consensus, they clearly encourage people to seek unity in the sense of seeking common concerns. For example, instructions to Study Circles facilitators read: "Help participants identify 'common ground,' but don't force consensus"[87] and "While our differences may separate us on some matters, we have enough in common as human beings to allow us to talk together in a constructive way."[88] However, some dispute resolution organizations that use dialogue do advocate consensus and even include the word in their organizations' titles (e.g., Consensus Council, Inc.)[89] Postings on the listserve for the National Coalition for Dialogue and Deliberation also reveal that not all practitioners (in the United States or elsewhere) agree whether consensus should be a goal. Their exchanges exhibit a good deal of disagreement about the proper balance between a focus on difference and a focus on unity.

Another example of a desire for unity in dialogue programs comes from dialogues sponsored by The National Endowment for the Humanities in 1995 and 1996. The initiative, called the National Conversation on American Pluralism and Identity, consisted of single-event as well as repeated-session discussions in a study circle format. The NEH promoted them as a way to focus on shared values and a unified American identity—a type of unity.[90]

Listening to Difference?

This comparison of civic intergroup dialogue programs on race and ideal deliberation suggests that these programs do involve listening to difference, and they challenge the idea that public talk by definition tends toward unity. The focus on listening and understanding, the provisions for confidentiality, the welcoming of emotion, and the scrutiny of power structures and patterns of accountability hold open the possibility that the deliberative system can give attention to marginalized views.

However, there are reasons to wonder just how far this attention to difference extends. The focus on civility hints at the possibility that civic dialogue might not involve the agonistic communication that difference democrats call for. It may be the case that in practice the desire for civility overrides the desire to allow emotional outbursts and unpopular views. Also, the emphasis on common ground alongside the calls for listening to difference add further mystery to whether and how participants reconcile attention to difference with the pervasive pull of unity.

The descriptions of civic dialogue on race suggest that this form of public talk may actually enable listening to difference. Given such an image—an image that runs against the grain of American political culture and much empirical research on what civic life and intergroup conflict needs—why do communities choose to do it? In the following chapter, I take up this question.

CHAPTER FOUR

The Community Choice to Pursue Interracial Dialogue

Cities throughout the United States face the challenge of governing in contexts of heightened racial diversity and new intergroup tensions due to recent waves of immigration. These developments have complicated coalition building, increased the range of competing demands, and complicated decision-makers' perceptions of community priorities. Why is it that in many places communities have responded with the strategy of talk? Whose concerns and interests do these choices reflect?

There are many reasons to view intergroup dialogue programs on race as an important public good and thus as an unsurprising policy choice. Face-to-face interaction can reduce conflict among members of opposing racial groups[1] and dispel stereotypes.[2] Intercultural contact can also foster bridging social capital that can increase the capacity to collectively address future public problems or prevent conflict from occurring.[3] Dialogues may help spur collective action.[4] Dialogue among residents might also be considered an essential feature of a healthy community or a route to self-enhancement.

Despite these many ways in which talk might function as a public good, there are many reasons to expect that communities would *not* choose "more talk." Whether the goal is improved race relations or not, many local officials (not to mention political scientists) are leery of opening up governance to the broader public. They expect that doing so invites inefficiency and anti-majoritarianism.[5] Also, the history of urban politics offers numerous examples of public officials providing talk as a way to preempt demands for other types of action.[6] Offering more talk may be a disingenuous way to include residents in the policy process,[7] or a way to take visible action on a difficult public problem without really doing anything at all.[8] Therefore, many may perceive organized public talk as merely a symbolic gesture.

So why is it that communities use intergroup dialogue as a way to address race relations? And why in particular do local governments use this strategy? Public officials participate in almost all community-wide dialogue programs on race, but in some cities, there is *government sponsorship:* the programs are initiated by a local government that then provides a substantial share of the funding; public officials such as elected representatives, government employees, and fire and safety officials participate alongside community residents. In other cities, the programs are only *government endorsed:* public officials express support for the groups and participate with community residents, but the program is funded and administrated by nongovernmental organizations. What motivates government sponsorship as opposed to government endorsement?

The involvement of governments in these public talk programs is of particular concern to scholars of deliberative democracy because of Habermasian notions of the public sphere. Such theories posit that democracies need a figurative space in which citizens discuss current policy and form opinions about its effectiveness and the shape of needed reforms; thus there are reasons to be wary of public officials' control over this forum.[9] On the other hand, if we take the public sphere as a space in which people forge relationships, government involvement may be necessary. Justifications of school desegregation policy, for example, have rested partly on the presumed democratic benefits of interracial interaction. With respect to dialogue programs, public officials' involvement may signal a direct pipeline to policy change and therefore motivate some people to participate who might not otherwise. In this way, providing for local-level dialogues is one way that governments can bring citizens into the conversation that democracy presumably requires.[10]

Because these programs are often about race, we have additional reason to investigate what motivates governments to be involved. Sponsoring a forum for public talk might be considered a controversial use of public funds, regardless of the topic. Sponsoring dialogue about race raises a set of uniquely controversial issues. When it comes to race, there is a fundamental divide in American political culture over whether or not we should even focus on it. Thus, the government choice to foster dialogue about race is a contentious issue in and of itself.

This chapter focuses on this choice to make three types of contributions. It illuminates community-level choice, examining the characteristics that influence *whether* a community will provide this type of public good as well as the factors that influence *who* provides the good: governments or nonprofits. Second, it focuses on a policy choice that matters greatly to democratic theorists but has seldom been addressed by empirical political science—the promotion of discussion about difficult social and political topics by people who are otherwise unlikely to talk with one another. And third, it examines when cities take on the particular and important issue of race through fostering intergroup dialogue.

I make these contributions through a large-N analysis, to set the stage for analyses using the more intensive method of in-depth interviewing in chapter 5. If we want to know why people choose to use interracial dialogue to improve race relations, we can ask them directly, as I do in the next chapter. However, those responses are by definition subjective. They have the clear benefit of providing information on the way in which these activists think about the role of interracial dialogue, but they run the risk of representing inaccurate or incomplete reasons for the programs. In addition, as with all data analysis, interpreting such self-reports is a subjective enterprise, but does not have the advantage of quantitative analysis of enabling a numeric estimation of confidence in the conclusions I reach.

I therefore begin to assess how race dialogues come into being by using objective indicators. In this chapter, I use theories of urban public policy to conceptualize dialogue programs on race as community strategies oriented toward different race-related goals, and I examine the causal relationships between objective city characteristics related to these goals and the presence of race dialogue programs.

Ultimately, it is not a community that decides whether to implement a civic dialogue program. Such choices are made by individuals. However, understanding how public talk comes into being is not just a matter of individual perceptions. It is also a matter of illuminating the conditions under which deliberative democracy can exist. Knowing the conditions under which it can exist helps us understand what it can achieve.

In subsequent chapters, I expand on the relationships we see here by listening directly to participants and to the people responsible for the existence of dialogue programs in particular cities.

Urban Politics and Program Presence

The urban politics literature suggests several basic models for understanding why some cities adopt racial dialogue programs and others do not. Several of these models correspond to two common and opposing beliefs about the existence of race dialogues: one, that race dialogues are all about talk and self-fulfillment; or two, that these dialogues are not only talk but are action oriented toward social justice. Each model can be understood as a set of specific hypotheses.

Postmaterialism and the Desire for Self-Actualization

The first model stresses the *dialogue* aspect of race dialogues and centers on the values and priorities of a community. This model is suggested by theories of urban policy that identify economic development as the overriding goal of city leaders.[11] Insofar as the quality of race relations influences whether people perceive a metropolitan area as a "hot" city, or as a city undergoing revitalization and attracting business investment, communities may seek to implement visible programs to improve race relations.[12] In addition, dialogue programs might be part of a strategy that aims to attract new businesses, professionals with technological and creative expertise, business meetings, and tourism through enhancing cultural awareness and appreciation.[13]

Considered this way, we might expect civic dialogue to be pursued by relatively affluent cities whose development priorities have centered on high-tech and other creative industries. Such contexts have been described as "new political cultures" or "postmaterial cultures," cultures that are secure enough materially to value attention to lifestyle concerns. Theories of such cultures argue that in response to postindustrial economies, new technologies, and globalization,[14] individual affluence and concern for private wealth now coincide with concern for particular types of public issues, such as "environmentalism, growth management, feminism and abortion, gay rights, and other consumption and lifestyle concerns."[15] Concern with such issues is expected to have replaced politics centered on class and race,[16] and political participation in postmaterial contexts is supposedly structured more through individual motivation than through voluntary groups.[17] Such contexts are expected to exist in places that have younger, more educated, and more affluent populations,[18] and in cities that have relatively small black populations.[19]

Theories of postmaterialism expect that the big political project in such contexts is managing personal identity:

> The psychological energy *(cathexis)* people once devoted to the grand political projects of economic integration and nation-building in industrial democracies is now increasingly directed toward personal projects of managing and expressing complex identities in a fragmenting society. The political attitudes and actions resulting from this emotional work stay much closer to home, and are much less likely to be focused on government.[20]

In such political cultures, civic dialogue programs might provide a way for people to pursue the personal project of figuring out where one fits in the globalized, increasingly complex world. Thus this model explains the existence of interracial dialogue programs by emphasizing the *dialogue* more than the racial aspect of the discussions. Such a model suggests that local governments would choose to support dialogue programs on race to enhance the city's image and meet residents' desires to live in a community that facilitates engaged talk with other residents. And because many liberal citizen lobbying groups have shifted toward postmaterial concerns,[21] we could expect nonprofit organizations to pursue such programs because doing so is consistent with their values.

If civic dialogue is best understood as an activity that expresses the *postmaterialist values* of new generations of relatively affluent residents, then dialogue programs should be more likely in cities with:

- Higher levels of median household income among whites;
- Larger proportions of whites holding bachelor's degrees; and
- A lower median age.

A Desire for Social Justice

A second model for explaining the presence of dialogue programs alternatively stresses the *racial* aspect of racial dialogues. Rather than conceptualizing these programs as quality-of-life policies, we can think of them as redistributive policy.[22] Perhaps these programs are more common in places with less affluence and more inequality, and are rooted in the traditional conflict dimensions of class and race rather than postmaterial concerns.[23] That is, maybe they reflect a concern with social justice more than self-actualization.

If this is the case, we might expect dialogue programs on race to occur in places where there is a large store of racial power resources. Previous work suggests that we should expect policies to reflect the interests of marginalized racial groups only in the presence of relatively strong political and economic resources among members of such groups—organizations and capital that enable racially marginalized groups to organize and articulate their desires to government.[24] Karnig and Welch argue that such crucial "black resources" can be indicated by median levels of black income and education, a majority black population, a large number of civil rights groups, black financial institutions and black-owned media, and are also associated with civil disturbances on the part of members of the black community.[25] In this investigation, I examine the presence of most of these resources among blacks and Latinos. I also include an additional predictor: the recent rate of growth in the nonwhite population, because the changing demographic composition of U.S. cities has been an impetus for policy innovation that addresses these changes.[26]

Given that some work on participatory democracy suggests that nonwhites view deliberative efforts as "[u]nappealingly moralistic, self-indulgent, and white,"[27] why should we expect that racial resources have a positive relationship with the presence of civic dialogue? One answer is that some contemporary urban activism among people of color actually uses talk as an *integral* part of organizing. The Industrial Areas Foundation helps generate issues for action and relationships among broad co-alitions of people through storytelling, one-on-one contacting, and house meetings.[28] In addition, relationships between whites and members of marginalized racial groups serve as a form of power that may be a necessary precondition for securing redistributive policy.[29]

Thus we can derive a clear set of hypotheses from a second model that identifies civic intergroup dialogue programs as responses to desires for *social justice*. In this model, we should expect programs to arise in the presence of racial resources and in contexts of greater group-based economic inequalities.[30] Dialogue groups should be pursued more often where we find:

- Larger gaps between the median household incomes of non-Hispanic whites and blacks and Latinos.[31]
- Larger percentages of nonwhites holding bachelor's degrees;
- Higher percentages of nonwhites within the city population;
- Larger recent increases in the nonwhite population;
- The presence of a civil rights group; and
- The presence of a media outlet targeted to nonwhites.

Government Form

Beyond these two major models for the types of concerns generating dialogue programs on race, we can also derive a third set of hypotheses related to *government form*, because these programs constitute a particular form of linkage between residents and public officials. Regardless of whether postmaterial values or concerns for social justice drive the desire for these programs, the dialogues put public officials and residents in direct contact. Therefore, we might expect that local governments and nonprofits will be more likely to pursue these strategies in communities in which more substantial—less hierarchical—linkages between local leaders and residents are already in existence. For example, a city commissioner in

Dayton, Ohio, Dean Lovelace, explained that his city's dialogue program seemed to mesh well with a long history of citizen input through community priority boards in his city.[32] Local government forms such as district elections, an elected mayor rather than a hired (nonelected) city manager or city administrator, a smaller ratio of residents per council member, and links between civic organizations (such as neighborhood associations) and local government are all indicators of less hierarchical linkages because they increase opportunities for public participation and conduits of representation.[33] Yet another indicator of such linkages is district elections (as opposed to at-large elections), because they have been shown to produce more direct representation of the concerns of marginalized racial groups, in the form of more representatives of color.[34]

Thus, a third set of hypotheses related to *government form* predicts that civic dialogue programs on race are more likely to emerge in contexts of greater resident-government linkages. That is, we should expect dialogue on race to be more likely in cities with:

- District elections;
- A mayor as chief operating officer;
- A smaller number of residents per council member; and
- Links to neighborhood associations on the local government web page.

Southern Distinctiveness and Diffusion of Policy through Organizations

In addition to these primary hypotheses reflecting different views of the nature of civic dialogue, I explore several other hypotheses that have the potential to broaden our understanding of policy choice and the choice to pursue talk as a route toward improving race relations. First, because the history of racial conflict in particular communities likely affects the strategies that communities pursue, we might expect that cities in southern states, with their distinctive histories as former slave states, constitute a special case.[35] Are communities in this region more or less likely than cities in other parts of the country to implement dialogue programs? Do choices to promote racial dialogue reflect a different set of underlying forces in the South?

Second, are cities more likely to adopt dialogue programs if they are located in a state where a nonprofit or government agency such as the state League of Women Voters or the state human relations commission has decided to promote dialogue groups across the state? Such professional organizations (and entrepreneurs within them) can actively facilitate the spread of policy innovations like civic dialogue[36] and are sometimes cited as an infrastructure promoting the spread of civic engagement.[37] Accordingly, I expect dialogue programs to emerge more often in states in which a statewide government agency or nonprofit organization promoted the use of these programs.

Postmaterialism in Wealthy Cities, Social Justice in Lower-Income Places?

It is possible that all of these models offer insight into local decisions to promote dialogue groups but that the models operate in different ways in different types of cities. The postmaterialist model predicts that dialogue will be used in areas of greater affluence, where residents are focused on higher-order needs, while the social justice model suggests it is communities of lower affluence, inequality, and a large store of racial resources that will turn to dialogue to address longstanding conflicts. In-depth interviews with administrators and public officials that I analyze in detail in the next chapter, as well as observations of the Madison program during the early stages of this project suggested that the postmaterialist and the social justice models may fit in different contexts. For example, people in Madison as well as media coverage of the program often referred to it as yet another program for "Madison liberals"—a pejorative term implying left-leaning, intellectual people who seem to talk more than act. And yet elected officials and employees of the local government in other cities such as Dayton, Ohio, talked about the program as an absolutely necessary part of combating social injustice.

In other words, in more affluent cities like Madison, civic dialogue programs seem to arise in response to well-educated residents' desires for greater self-development. In less affluent cities with more diverse populations, like Dayton, they seem to arise as one strategy in an array of attempts to reduce inequality. Thus, in order to understand the conditions that give rise to civic dialogue, we need to test for the possibility that different patterns of influence produce dialogue programs in low-income versus high-income cities.

Therefore, I hypothesize that:

- In higher-income communities, the use of dialogue will be more associated with variables linked to postmaterial values, while in lower-income communities, it will be more associated with variables associated with inequality and racial resources.

My fieldwork informed these analyses in yet another way. I had expected the main causes of interracial dialogue programs to have been triggering events such as civil unrest related to a racial issue, a prominent case of racial profiling, or the release of a report detailing a racial achievement gap in the public schools. In interview after interview, however, I found this not to be the case, as I explain in the following chapter. I do not include an indicator of triggering events in these models for this reason, but also because the intent of these analyses is to test competing explanations for the existence of race dialogue programs with the most objective indicators possible. What constitutes a triggering event is a subjective judgment, particularly with respect to those cities that did not implement a program. It was easy to notice a significant event in the few cases in which such an event had preceded the start of a dialogue program (e.g., racial profiling incidents followed by a city-commissioned task force on race relations in the Madison context), but what constitutes a comparable event in a city that did not have a program is much less clear.

Government Sponsored vs. Government Endorsed

Finally, to this point I have lumped decisions by local governments and nonprofit organizations together when considering a community's choice to use dialogue. There is an important difference, however, between actions undertaken through government and through civil society. Because government involvement in the public sphere may either be regarded skeptically or welcomed as a necessary component of these race dialogues, it is important to investigate whether the conditions that give rise to government-sponsored programs differ from those motivating merely government-endorsed programs (programs sponsored by nonprofits). To understand how we get dialogue groups, and what we might expect them to achieve, we need to uncover the conditions under which local governments as opposed to nonprofit organizations choose to implement dialogue. Accordingly, I test the hypothesis that:

- The types of conditions that produce government-sponsored dialogue programs differ significantly from the conditions that produce mere government endorsement.[38]

Investigating the Models

To test the hypotheses outlined above, I collected data on medium-sized Census-designated central cities in a sample of eighteen states representative of the entire United States. Central cities are the economic and residential centers of a metropolitan area, designated as such by the U.S. Office of Management and Budget if they meet a threshold of population density and employment centrality. Often these are the core cities surrounded by suburbs, but in large metropolitan areas there can be multiple central cities, some of which began as suburbs outlying a larger city.[39] I chose to focus on them because of their comparability in terms of residential and economic centrality. As noted in chapter 1, I chose to focus on medium cities, those with populations between 50,000 and 250,000. Focusing on medium-sized cities limits my ability to generalize these results to urban political processes in larger and smaller cities. However, medium-sized cities constitute important sites of population growth and demographic change. Understanding the conditions that may lead such communities to choose to address race relations through dialogue programs serves as a step toward understanding the role of deliberation in urban civic life.[40]

The sample of eighteen states was constructed by randomly choosing two states from each of the nine Census-designated regions. All medium-sized Census-designated central cities in these states were included in the study.[41] Research assistants and I then conducted Internet searches, text-searches of local newspapers, and called city clerks, newspaper city editors, civil rights organizations, and local human rights commissions to determine whether a community-wide dialogue program on race relations had taken place in each of these 141 cities within the past fifteen years. I chose a fifteen year time-span to capture the time period in which community-based interracial dialogue programs in their contemporary form have flourished around the country, as explained in chapter 3. However, the vast majority of programs have come into being since 1996, as the national umbrella organizations promoting these programs were in their early stages of development in the early 1990s. I defined a community-wide dialogue program as a program in which (1) volunteers from across the community (not just public officials) had been recruited to participate in (2) face-to-face conversations about (3) intergroup relations (including race, ethnicity, and immigration), (4) over more than one session within a three-month span.[42]

When gathering this information, I determined whether a local government such as the city government (including a city agency such as a civil rights department) or a county government (including an agency such as a human relations commission) administered the program, or whether it was conducted by a nonprofit organization. In all but three cases in which the program was not administered by a local government, public officials participated alongside residents.[43]

Information on the independent variables was gathered from U.S. Census data, searches of Internet and newspaper resources, and extensive calls to local officials and activists. Details are included in the methods appendix.[44]

Talk Driven by Concern with Social Justice

Of the 141 cities investigated in this study, sixty-eight (48 percent) had an intergroup dialogue program within the last fifteen years, sponsored by either a local government or nonprofit organization, in which volunteers from the community and public officials discussed race relations over a period of several weeks or months. In thirty-three of these cities (23 percent of the whole sample), the programs were sponsored in whole or in part by a local government through financial support or administrative assistance.

To assess the conditions that have shaped local choice, as well as differences in the types of factors at work in different types of cities, I begin with two tables of simple bivariate analyses. Although the bivariate results do not allow us to draw causal conclusions, they describe and help us understand the types of communities that are pursuing dialogue. For example, even if levels of median household income do not exert a significant influence when controlling for other relevant factors, it is still important to note whether dialogue programs exist primarily in places with high median incomes. Such a pattern would have implications for our understanding of the nature of civic dialogue and its availability to Americans living in different types of cities.

In table 4.1, I compare the characteristics of cities with and without dialogue programs—in all cities, in low-income cities (cities with household incomes below the median of $36,774), and in high-income cities (cities with household incomes above the median). The results suggest that cities with and without programs differ in several respects. Notably, overall community wealth is not one of them. The first row in the first two columns shows that, in the sample as a whole, there is no significant difference between the median household incomes of cities with and without programs. In other words, it is not the case that the choice to conduct interracial dialogue on race varies by community wealth. Reading down these first two columns reveals that civic dialogues on race are more common in cities with higher levels of white and nonwhite education, higher racial income gaps, media targeted to marginalized racial groups, stronger resident-government linkages, and in cities located in the South.[45]

Many of these differences persist when cities are split by median household income (last four columns). However, several characteristics emerge

TABLE 4.1: Characteristics of cities with civic intergroup dialogue programs, by city wealth

	All cities		Low-income cities		High-income cities	
	No program	Program	No program	Program	No program	Program
City wealth						
Median household income	39,038	40,103	32,783	31,570	44,200	**50,287**
Postmaterialist variables						
White median household income	42,675	44,273	36,757	35,803	47,558	**54,383**
White education	28	**35**	24	**30**	31	**40**
(pct. bachelor's degree)						
Average age	32.9	33.8	32.5	33.0	33.2	**34.7**
Social justice variables						
Pct. nonwhite in 2000	36	35	40	38	34	32
Racial income gap	10,998	**14,003**	10,302	**12,443**	11,573	**15,865**
Pct. change in nonwhite population	77	66	66	52	85	82
Nonwhite education	14	**20**	11	**17**	18	**23**
(pct. bachelor's degree)						
Civil rights organization	60	63	70	59	53	68
(pct. of cities)						
Nonwhite media (pct. of cities)	15	**26**	15	30	15	23

as distinctive of high-income cities with programs or of low-income cities with programs. It is only among high-income cities that higher income levels (overall and specifically with respect to whites), higher average age, and location in the South significantly distinguish cities with programs. At the same time, two characteristics significantly distinguish cities with programs only among low-income cities: city web page links to neighborhood associations, and location in a state in which some organization has promoted intergroup dialogue statewide.

When we examine what characterizes cities with government-sponsored as opposed to government-endorsed programs, how do these patterns fare? Table 4.2 displays bivariate results arranged by income level and type of program. Tests of significance in this table are all relative to the baseline reported in the "no program" column for a specified income level. The results suggest that, at least at a descriptive level, "postmaterialist conditions" are most clearly associated with *government-sponsored* programs in *high-income* places. By contrast, "social justice conditions" seem to apply more broadly. Larger racial income inequality distinguishes cities with government-sponsored programs in both low- and high-income cities. Higher nonwhite education distinguishes cities with either government-sponsored or government-endorsed programs in low-income cities. Contrary to expectations, government-sponsored programs are associated with cities that experienced a *smaller* racial demographic shift between 1990 and 2000, particularly in low-income areas. The relative supply of resident-government linkages seems to matter most for government-endorsed programs in high-income places. Finally, statewide promotion of programs seems particularly important for government-sponsored programs in low-income cities.

With these descriptive patterns in hand, we may now turn to multivariate models to test (1) the power of the various models predicting community choices to pursue dialogue, (2) whether the constellation of conditions driving such choices differs across high- and low-income cities, and (3) whether different conditions explain the pursuit of government-sponsored as opposed to government-endorsed programs.

Turning to the first two questions, table 4.3 presents a binary logit model predicting the presence or absence of a racial dialogue program (either government sponsored or government endorsed) using the full range of hypotheses outlined earlier as well as a full set of interaction terms capturing differences in effects for high- versus low-income cities.[46] Analyses of this fully interactive model suggested that a subset of these effects differed significantly for high-income cities.[47] Thus the reduced model, displayed in table 4.4, includes interactions for these conditions.

TABLE 4.2: Characteristics of cities with gov't-endorsed and gov't-sponsored programs, by city wealth

	Low income			High income		
	No program	Gov't endorsed	Gov't sponsored	No program	Gov't endorsed	Gov't sponsored
City wealth						
Median household income	32,783	31,248	31,949	44,200	47,033	**53,338**
Postmaterialist variables						
White median household income	36,757	35,352	36,332	47,558	51,272	**57,300**
White education (pct. bachelor's degree)	24	**30**	**30**	31	35	**44**
Average age	32.5	33.2	32.8	33.2	**35.2**	34.3
Social justice variables						
Pct. nonwhite in 2000	39.7	37.7	**37.8**	33.5	29.1	34.7
Racial income gap	10,302	11,691	**13,327**	11,573	14,799	**16,865**
Pct. change in nonwhite population	66	72	28	85	96	70
Nonwhite education (pct. bachelor's degree)	11	**17**	**16**	18	18	**29**
Civil rights organization (pct. of cities)	69.7	60.0	58.8	52.5	73.3	62.5
Nonwhite media (pct. of cities)	15	35	24	15	7	38

(continued)

TABLE 4.2: (continued)

	Low income			High income		
	No program	Gov't endorsed	Gov't sponsored	No program	Gov't endorsed	Gov't sponsored
Resident-gov't linkages						
District elections (pct. of cities)	61	80	71	45	**73**	44
Mayor as C.O.O. (pct. of cities)	24	35	29	25	**40**	31
Residents per council member	16,254	17,973	15,139	16,701	**12,713**	**22,535**
City web page link to neighborhood associations (pct. of cities)	15	**45**	**53**	18	20	**44**
Contextual variables						
Southern state (pct. of cities)	48	50	59	10	20	31
Statewide promotion of programs (pct. of cities)	33	50	**59**	60	67	63
N	33	20	17	40	15	16

Note: Cells contain mean values for cities within each column. See methods appendix for variable construction. Results in bold indicate that a difference of means test between cities in that column versus cities in the "No program" column for that income level yielded a p-value less than or equal to .05, using a one-tailed test, not assuming equal variances.

TABLE 4.3: Full model, predicting the presence of civic dialogue programs on race

Postmaterialist variables	
White income	−.38 (.12)
White education	−6.72 (5.56)
Average age	.28 (.13)
Social justice variables	
Change in nonwhite population	−.34 (.40)
Racial income gap	.36 (.15)
Nonwhite education	42.68 (10.73)
Pct. nonwhite in 2000	8.68 (3.15)
Civil rights organization	−2.19 (1.22)
Nonwhite media	1.23 (.85)
Resident-government linkages (scale)	1.56 (.58)
Contextual variables	
Southern state	1.10 (1.19)
Statewide promotion of programs	−.05 (1.13)
City income and interactions	
High-income city	−3.28 (1.78)
White income*high income	.58 (.15)
White education*high income	−.46 (7.65)
Average age*high income	−.07 (.19)
Change in nonwhite population*high income	.81 (.83)
Racial income gap*high income	−.27 (.16)
Nonwhite education*high income	−41.37 (11.42)
Pct. nonwhite*high income	−11.82 (4.44)
Civil rights organization*high income	4.97 (1.85)
Nonwhite media*high income	−.97 (1.15)
Resident-government linkages*high income	−.92 (.69)
Southern state*high income	−.12 (1.52)
Statewide promotion*high income	.09 (1.46)
Constant	−8.80 (6.63)
N	140
Wald Chi²	43.96

Note: Entries are logit coefficients, robust standard errors in parentheses. Bold results are significant at p < .05, one-tailed test.

The results in table 4.4 reveal that the models that fit in low-income cities differ from those that explain adoption in high-income cities. The results include six significant interaction terms, indicating a variety of discernible differences between the processes at work in high- and low-income communities. For the variables used in the interaction terms, the

TABLE 4.4: Predicting the presence of civic dialogue programs on race

	Total effect, high-income cities	
Postmaterialist variables		
White income	−.35 (.13)	
White education	−7.43 (4.06)	
Average age	.21 (.09)	
Social justice variables		
Change in nonwhite population	−.17 (.28)	
Racial income inequality	.36 (.14)	
Nonwhite education	38.95 (10.03)	
Pct. nonwhite in 2000	7.79 (2.54)	
Civil rights organization	−1.83 (.93)	
Nonwhite media	.74 (.57)	
Resident-gov't linkages	1.44 (.41)	
Contextual variables		
Southern state	1.06 (.69)	
Statewide promotion of programs	.14 (.69)	
City income and interactions		
High-income city	−3.23 (1.51)	
White income*high income	.57 (.16)	.22 (.08)
Racial income gap*high income	−.30 (.14)	.06 (.06)
Nonwhite education*high income	−38.45 (10.10)	.50 (3.74)
Pct. nonwhite*high income	−12.79 (3.61)	−5.00 (2.53)
Civil rights organization*high income	4.45 (1.58)	2.62 (1.13)
Resident-gov't linkages*high income	−.82 (.48)	.62 (.35)
Constant	−6.46 (4.87)	
N	140	
Wald Chi²	39.76	
Pct. correctly classified	80.00%	

Note: Entries are logit coefficients, robust standard errors in parentheses. Entries in the right-hand column reflect the combined effect of each variable and its interaction with "high-income city." Significance tests in this column are relative to a null hypothesis of $b = 0$ in a high-income city. Bold results are significant at $p < .05$, one-tailed test.

main-effect coefficients indicate the relationship between a city characteristic and the adoption of a dialogue program in low-income cities. The
interaction terms indicate how effects for a given variable differ in high-
versus low-income cities. The right-hand column displays the overall effect
of a given variable in high-income cities (the sum of the main effect plus
the interaction term).

Table 4.4 suggests that while resident-government linkages appear to be an important determinant of program adoption across all cities, the social justice and postmaterialist models fit differently in low- and high-income cities. In low-income cities, the data support the social justice explanation. In high-income cities, there is only weak support for the social justice explanation, but the postmaterialist model receives some support.[48] That is, interracial dialogue may be motivated by a desire for self-actualization in high-income contexts, but these objective characteristics suggest it is more akin to a response to desires to address social justice.

In detail, in low-income cities, communities are more likely to adopt dialogue programs under conditions that are the *opposite* of those predicted by the postmaterialist model: lower white incomes, less educated whites, and older populations. There is support for the social justice model in the form of positive coefficients for racial income inequality, nonwhite education, and nonwhite population percentage. Contrary evidence comes from the negative coefficient for the presence of civil rights organizations.[49]

Among high-income cities, the social justice model receives mixed support: there is a significant predicted coefficient only for the presence of civil rights organizations, and the coefficient is significant in the wrong direction for the proportion of the population that is nonwhite. In contrast to what I find among low-income cities, there is some support among high-income cities for the postmaterialist model, in the form of a positive and significant overall effect for white income.[50]

These results appear to support the expectation that the structure of relationships that lead to the pursuit of dialogue programs differs significantly across high- and low-income cities. A joint test of the interaction terms and the main effect for high- versus low-income city confirms that this is the case.[51]

A final comparison will demonstrate the differences in conditions related to race dialogues across high- and low-income cities. High-income cities with a relatively low racial income gap between non-Hispanic whites and African Americans and Hispanics of $10,000 (with all other variables set to their means) have a probability of adopting a dialogue program of just 9.15 percent. Low-income cities with that same size racial income gap have the much higher probability of adopting a program of 62.60 percent. Even when we compare high- and low-income cities that have equally high racial income gaps of $20,000, we find that the probability of adopting a program is 67.16 percent among high-income cities, but is a noticeably larger 96.88 percent among low-income cities.[52]

Uniqueness of Government Sponsorship?

The conditions underlying dialogue programs on race differ for low- versus high-income cities, but are different forces at work in cities where local governments *sponsor* these programs—partially or entirely funding them and providing administrative support and participation of public officials—as opposed to just endorsing them verbally and through officials' participation? To pursue this question, I employ a multinomial logit analysis that makes it possible to simultaneously and separately test the conditions that predict adoption of government-sponsored and government-endorsed dialogue programs. This model allows coefficients for each variable to differ according to governments' level of involvement. It also makes it possible to test whether the entire structure of relationships, or possibly just individual coefficients, differ significantly across equations. For each equation, I employ the same model reported in table 4.4, including interaction terms.

Table 4.5 displays the results of this analysis. The interaction terms again allow us to see how the conditions supporting dialogue groups vary across low- and high-income cities. Turning to the main comparison in table 4.5, across levels of government involvement, we find a clear pattern in regard to the overall structure of relationships. The relationships associated with each type of government involvement are very similar, as confirmed by the mostly insignificant Chi^2 tests for differences between individual coefficients across equations and by a test for difference in the overall structure of relationships in the two equations (see last column).

Nevertheless, several coefficients do differ significantly across the two types of involvement. Older populations encourage local adoption of government-endorsed programs but not government-sponsored programs. By contrast, location in the South and smaller increases in the nonwhite population both encourage government-sponsored programs while having no effect on adoption of government-endorsed programs. Finally, focusing on the effects of nonwhite education, we find that the difference in effects across high- and low-income cities is greater where city governments have endorsed dialogue programs than where city governments have sponsored these programs.

These isolated differences may signal some meaningful points of divergence in the political processes underlying government sponsorship versus endorsement. For example, consider the fact that location in the South significantly increases the odds that a city government will sponsor a dialogue program on race, but that there is no parallel effect of southern location for nonprofit sponsorship. This pattern raises the possibility that perhaps

TABLE 4.5: Predicting presence of dialogue programs, by government involvement

	Gov't endorsed	Gov't sponsored	Test of difference (Chi²)
Postmaterialist variables			
White income	−.36 (.14)	−.33 (.15)	.05
White education	−4.99 (4.82)	−10.38 (5.22)	1.00
Average age	.28 (.11)	.03 (.11)	4.01
Social justice variables			
Change in nonwhite population	.15 (.35)	−1.73 (.83)	5.02
Racial income gap	.28 (.16)	.48 (.17)	1.33
Nonwhite education	41.67 (11.17)	38.57 (11.77)	.21
Pct. nonwhite in 2000	8.70 (2.58)	5.97 (3.62)	.70
Civil rights organization	−1.74 (1.10)	−2.23 (1.00)	.27
Nonwhite media	1.04 (.77)	.51 (.58)	.51
Resident-gov't linkages	1.30 (.43)	1.90 (.46)	2.51
Contextual variables			
Southern state	.48 (.87)	2.44 (.81)	4.49
Statewide promotion of programs	.01 (.74)	1.03 (.72)	2.37
City income, interactions			
High-income city	−3.90 (1.60)	−2.50 (1.84)	.82
White income*high income	.59 (.16)	.58 (.19)	.01
Racial income gap*high income	-.21 (.16)	−.48 (.18)	2.31
Nonwhite education*high income	−49.57 (12.44)	−32.57 (10.94)	4.11
Pct. nonwhite* high income	−15.88 (4.34)	−12.15 (4.37)	.71
Civil rights organization *high income	4.43 (1.52)	4.70 (1.97)	.03
Resident-gov't linkages*high income	−.50 (.53)	−1.20 (.57)	1.65
Constant	−9.18 (5.78)	−2.93 (5.24)	
N		140	
Wald Chi²		75.32	
Chi² test of differences in two structures			19.85 (p=.404)

Note: Entries in first two columns are multinomial logit coefficients, robust standard errors in parentheses. Bold results are significant at $p < .05$, one-tailed test.

in this region of the country, officials are turning to dialogue as a way to avoid taking more radical action about race relations. Or alternatively, they may feel forced to step in more often because civil society actors do not.

However, such findings—intriguing though they may be—are clearly footnotes to the larger story of similarity. There is little here to suggest that we should distinguish sharply between "action by government" and "action through civil society" when it comes to the conditions that promote civic dialogue initiatives.

Clues from City Characteristics

This examination of the conditions under which interracial dialogue programs arise offers clues both to how they come into being and to what takes place within them. The evidence gives little support to claims that this form of public talk is an expression of affluent residents' desires for self-actualization or their concern with lifestyle issues. Instead, explanations that center on social justice about race—that suggest civic dialogues on race will arise in cities with high levels of inequality and large stores of racial resources—receive more support. This is especially the case in low-income cities. In addition, I find that civic dialogue programs are more likely where there are more direct institutionalized linkages between local leaders and the public, supporting the idea that these programs are an additional means of communication between residents and their government. Finally, I find that many of the social, economic, and political conditions that promote dialogue groups *do* vary significantly across high- and low-income cities, but *do not* vary nearly so much across cities with government-sponsored programs versus nonprofit-sponsored programs.

Taken together, these results suggest that civic dialogue programs on race are driven by the needs of a community's marginalized racial groups just as much if not more than by the desires of affluent community members. Such a result challenges complaints that civic dialogue programs are "all talk and no action" or that members of marginalized communities see little utility in deliberative democracy. Postmaterialist explanations center on the dialogue aspect of these programs. Social justice explanations center on race. The results here suggest that these programs are about race more than in name only.

These results also speak to the relationships between governments, race, and public talk. While it is possible that dialogue programs are attractive to some public officials as a politically expedient way to merely appear to do something about race relations, such a perception can not explain the widespread existence of government-sponsored programs. The conditions that give rise to programs sponsored by governments are almost indistinguishable from the conditions that give rise to programs sponsored by social justice organizations. In other words, these data support the notion that governments pursue dialogue programs on race under the same conditions as organizations that openly pursue social justice.

These results do not tell us about the motivations of all public officials involved in these programs. It is very possible that some politicians get involved for opportunistic reasons. And it is possible that these programs are approved by city councils for partly symbolic reasons. However, the data are inconsistent with the idea that these programs are *merely* symbolic gestures, on the community level. Governments' pursuit of these programs does not seem to be an avoidance of the demands of marginalized racial groups: we observe a positive relationship between government sponsorship and some racial resources. Although some individuals may support these programs for symbolic reasons, they do not arise under conditions that suggest they are inconsistent with the pursuit of social justice.

If these programs arise in response to demands from members of marginalized racial groups, how is the representation of these concerns occurring? Through elected officials? Although elected officials are occasionally on the forefront of promoting these programs as the following chapter will elaborate, the evidence in this chapter suggests that, instead, nonelected members of the government are the crucial actors. Out of the thirty-three cities with government-sponsored programs, in only two cases, Owensboro, Kentucky, and Eau Claire, Wisconsin, was the proportion of nonwhite elected officials larger than the proportion nonwhite in the population, challenging the perception that the programs arise in response to concerns among nonwhites through an electoral connection.

My fieldwork suggests that, instead, calls for attention to race relations among communities of color are heeded through government agencies. In Waterloo and Sioux City, Iowa, for example, two cities in that state that have had an ongoing race dialogue program, the initiatives were started by the cities' Human Rights Departments. Likewise in Camden, New Jersey, the city's dialogue program was administered by the county Human Relations Commission. These are just a few examples of the many cities in which human relations departments or commissions, equal opportunities departments, and affirmative action departments are on the forefront of implementing dialogue programs on race. These programs often receive support from elected officials, but in many cities, entrepreneurs within civil rights departments and commissions have implemented the programs *in spite of* opposition from the city council. Corroborating evidence that civil rights commissions are a main source of these programs comes from the fact that among the 141 cities analyzed in this chapter, there is a significant correlation between the presence of a civil rights department or agency and a city-sponsored dialogue program.[53] In addition, most city-sponsored programs in those cities are in fact administered through a civil rights department or commission (twenty-four of thirty-three).

Thus these results suggest a rethinking of the relationship between bureaucrats and representation. Previous work on community choice has suggested that the preferences of elected officials more closely correspond to what the public wants than do the preferences of local bureaucrats.[54] But civil rights departments appear to be an important conduit for representing the concerns of residents who are concerned about racial justice. Although many bureaucrats may disdain greater citizen involvement in local governance,[55] employees of civil rights departments are an important exception.

To what extent do these programs represent a desire for a greater openness of the local government? Table 4.4 shows that dialogue programs are more likely in places that already have strong linkages between residents and the local government, and table 4.5 shows that city-sponsored programs arise in places that are no different in this respect than in places that have merely city-endorsed programs. Therefore it appears that programs arise in places in which local governments are already relatively open. One implication is that using listening as a strategy seems to require the existence of some structures—perhaps some individuals—within the existing government that already welcome open communication with the public.

This chapter has challenged the assumption that race dialogues are all talk and no action by showing that intergroup dialogue programs are more closely tied to desires for social justice than desires for self-development. But how do individuals explain these programs? Do the people behind these programs perceive them as a form of social justice action? And if individuals' conceptions do suggest that the programs are geared toward social justice, they raise the specter of another daunting doubt about public talk on race: that these programs are a multicultural enterprise that focus more on things that divide communities than on the things that unite them. The following chapter pursues this and other questions in detail, through analysis of interviews with people responsible for implementing these programs.

CHAPTER FIVE

Choosing the Action of Talk

Communities across the United States appear to turn to intergroup dialogue programs on race out of a need to pursue social justice as well as, if not more than, out of a desire to foster individual self-actualization. The previous chapter revealed this through an analysis of objective community-level indicators rather than of individuals' subjective perceptions. But do individuals' explanations for these programs support the conclusion that civic dialogue on race stems from a desire for social justice? Also, what do their conceptions tell us about what we might expect participants to do with the opportunity to have face-to-face interracial conversations about race?

If people are intent on promoting social justice, it is a bit of a mystery why they pursue civic dialogue as a strategy. The politics of unity would predict that instead of *talking* about race relations, people would choose to build bridging social capital by working together on a common project, in a cooperative, not combative fashion.[1] Talking about conflict directly might exacerbate tensions, but working on a common project supposedly diverts attention away from conflict.

Pursuing talk about race is also a bit of a mystery because public talk is not easy.[2] It seems antithetical to most American's preference for democracy that requires only their occasional interest, not their active participation,[3] and it seems contrary to the widespread desire to avoid conflict[4] and conversation with people who hold opposing political opinions.[5] More to the point, public talk *particularly about race* is notoriously difficult. It runs the risk of dwelling on one's own role in perpetuating intergroup conflict and discrimination. It has the potential to bring painful memories to the surface. It also creates a space for people to say out loud damaging stereotypes—thereby possibly legitimating racist talk.[6] Many people seem to prefer to avoid the topic of race because "the issue is simply too complex and painful."[7]

Pursuing talk about race is also surprising because members of marginalized groups often regard deliberation as unproductive.[8] As difference democrats assert, deliberative approaches have the tendency to perpetuate domination. This, combined with the common perception that dialogues are "all talk and no action," makes it particularly surprising that anyone, let alone advocates of social justice, would devote resources to pursuing dialogues about race.

There is yet another layer to the mystery of why people choose to implement dialogue programs on race. Pursuing these programs—programs that purportedly involve paying attention to racial difference—on its surface would seem to be an act that is consistent with an identity or set of values that survey-based studies have suggested is uncommon and commonly denigrated. In the context of a political culture that reveres unity and regards multiculturalism as divisive, why would any public official—especially an elected public official—choose to do this? Even though difference democrats and some social psychologists insist that difference-focused talk is necessary to overcome prejudice and achieve social justice, it is not at all clear why a politician, government employee, or even a citizen in the community would engage in this politically risky form of communication. Why do people, in communities throughout the country, make this choice?[9]

This chapter examines why individuals choose to implement dialogue groups and analyzes what their reasons suggest about the functions and uses of such groups. I help demystify this complex political act by listening to the explanations individuals offer during in-depth interviews. I turn to Joe Soss's work on participation in the U.S. welfare system for a model of such an analysis. Building on Murray Edelman's work on symbolic politics,[10] Soss investigated the reasons people gave to explain their decision to apply for welfare benefits. He noted that "like other forms of political action, welfare claiming has both instrumental and expressive dimensions" and that understanding these actions requires attention to their outcomes but also to "what [these actions] mean for individuals in particular social settings."[11]

I follow Soss's lead and pay attention to this second, little understood dimension—the meaning people in particular social settings ascribe to their political actions. We value public talk as the enactment of public life, but what do people *mean* by it? In other words, the purpose of this chapter is not to reveal what actually causes people to pursue intergroup dialogue programs but to understand and give coherence to the explanations people offer for pursuing this form of public talk. I listen to the reasons people give and take these reasons for what they are—subjective understandings of oneself and the value of a particular action.[12] The reasons people give for their actions—their "vocabularies of motive"—reveal what is meaningful to them. They can therefore help us understand what active citizens believe are sufficient justifications for public talk and therefore help us make sense of a surprising form of political action that is valued in democracies but little understood.

There are a variety of common assumptions about the choice to pursue talk as a strategy for addressing public problems that I have touched on at various points in this book. For one, it is commonly assumed that dialogue fills a higher-order individual need such as self-development or self-actualization. Talk that emphasizes listening is perceived as "touchy-feely" or "therapeutic." Second, interracial dialogue about race is expected to be multiculturalist, reifying subgroup categories over the common good, and is expected to be promoted particularly by intellectuals. Third, insofar as talk is justified as a form of action, it is a way to appease people, a kind of compromise, a strategy that people rely on because no others are feasible. Listening as action is widely perceived as not radical or intended to bring about social justice, but as passive. Fourth, if dialogue is explained as related to political action, it is used as a way to forge common ground, a common identity, or shared concerns, or another form of unity in the sense of similarity. Finally, we expect that people pursue talk as a means of addressing public problems when the situation is amenable to talk—when it is not adversarial or saturated with longstanding conflicts.[13] And if it is implemented in order to contest the status quo, we expect it to be pursued by activists, not government employees.

The following analyses scrutinize these assumptions through the use of interviews with administrators of intergroup dialogue programs on race. Specifically, I interviewed fifty-five state and local government officials and nonprofit organization employees in thirty-eight medium-sized Census-designated central cities, and ten such people in nine larger metropolitan areas. These were people whom I identified while gathering data for the analyses in the previous chapter. They were selected to represent medium-sized cities in states throughout the continental United States, and represent programs that vary in type (i.e. SCRC, Honest Conversations, etc.), government sponsorship, and racial heterogeneity of the population. More details are available in the methods appendix.

I use various labels to refer to the interviewees. I use the term "practitioner" to refer to people who were administering dialogue programs, regardless of whether they were employed by an NGO or a government. To refer to employees of NGOs, I use the term "activist" or "NGO administrator." I use the term "public official" to refer to government employees and elected officials. (I specify when I am referring specifically to nonelected government employees or to elected officials.) Of the sixty-five people interviewed, five were elected officials, twenty-three were government employees but not elected officials (including four police officers), and thirty-seven were volunteers or employees of nongovernmental organizations.

Viewing the Talk as Focused on Difference

The prevailing drive toward unity in American political culture would lead us to expect that people are advocating community-wide intergroup dialogues on race as a route toward collective, overarching identities. We might expect this to be especially the case among elected officials, who have an incentive to not associate themselves with programs that could be perceived as exacerbating racial divides. However, interviews with dialogue practitioners in specific communities around the country revealed that in fact they tend to think of this *as difference-focused talk.* Most people did not describe these programs as talk that tries to get beyond group differences by emphasizing people as individuals or by emphasizing overarching categories.

In the interviews, I asked respondents whether they expected these dialogues to focus on either common ground or difference. Was I asking a leading question, prompting people to say "difference"? The responses suggest that if anything, the interviewees thought I was looking for them to say "common ground." For example:

> *What comes closest, dialogue is valuable because it helps us recognize things we have in common, or because it helps us become aware of difference?*
>
> Well, both. But I think you want me to say the first.
>
> *Well, no, there is no right answer.*
>
> Well, both are important . . .

The socially desirable response seemed to be "common ground," or overarching identities. Taking into account this anti-difference bias in the responses, it is remarkable that among sixty-five dialogue practitioners sampled from forty-seven cities from across the United States, just fourteen of them said that they hoped the programs would encourage people to focus on people as individuals (rather than as members of social groups), and only thirteen talked about dialogue as a route toward common ground.

Some practitioners, fourteen in all, seemed to strive for unity (in the form of common identities, values, or cultures) as well as attention to racial group difference. However, the most common conception of dialogue across all of these practitioners was a privileging of group difference rather than unity. Twenty-eight of the sixty-five program administrators claimed that the main value of dialogue was its ability to help people understand difference, and did not also mention its potential to recognize or create similarity.[14]

For example, I asked a white woman running a dialogue program through a local government in Colorado whether "what is most necessary in your community is a place for people to come together to realize how they are all alike in the end, or a place for people to air their differences?" She responded: "You know, I guess I wouldn't say at the end to really say that we have got so much in common. I think to me it is more embracing the differences."

Rooting the Choice in Personal History

When I asked administrators about the history of their programs, what they thought their programs would achieve, why in particular they had turned to talk as a way of improving race relations in their city, and what other strategies they had considered, I expected to hear that they had turned to dialogue programs when other tactics had failed. But most of my interviewees did not consider dialogue programs to be a strategy of last resort. Most of them had been active in civil rights issues all of their lives. And they repeatedly said to me that *they had always advocated and tried to foster interracial dialogue.* Almost all of the practitioners could retell the story of how their particular program came into being, but they did not talk about it as an option they chose over others.[15] Instead, they talked about it as part of their overall conception of a healthy civic life. They tended to root their desire for interracial interaction deeply in their sense of self, in their personal histories.

A few examples will illustrate. Roseann Mason is a white woman who has implemented a study circles program in the Racine and Kenosha area of Wisconsin. She works for the Center for Community Partnerships at the University of Wisconsin-Extension and in that position runs a race dialogue program for people on her campus and in the community, including inmates in a nearby prison. One evening in the spring of 2005, I accompanied her to several community events. The manner in which she interacted with people at those events and the stories she told to me about how her daily life exuded a passion for racial justice displayed that she was deeply embedded in networks of activists with similar concerns.

In the mid-1990s she volunteered with an organization called Sustainable Racine that was focused on enhancing civic life and social justice in the city. At one of the organization's earliest goal-setting sessions, organizers invited Mason and other attendees to write their concerns about the community on pieces of paper, tape them to a wall, and then congregate around the topics they wished to work on. One woman wrote "racism," and Mason chose to stand beneath that sign. "That was really the beginning," she said. She had heard about study circles, and she and the others who expressed interest in racism that night decided to conduct a pilot round.

I asked Mason why she had chosen to stand beneath the "racism" sign that night and why she had decided to pursue a race dialogue program. She said that she had grown up in Racine, historically one of the most diverse cities in Wisconsin. She attended a Catholic high school in the 1960s, where she met a nun who sparked her interest in interracial interaction. The nun had started a local club with several other activists that was designed to promote interracial interaction among youth. Through that club, Mason developed lasting interracial relationships and a lifetime commitment to fostering interracial understanding.

Such lifelong commitments were not unique to the white practitioners I interviewed. For example, Belinda Cronin, an African-American woman who has been involved in Mason's program as a facilitator, similarly attributed her attempts to implement dialogue to a desire for interracial interaction that stemmed from her youth:

> In the small town that I came from in Tennessee, whites and blacks knew each other. . . . When I look at my life, that's what I have known. Interaction with other people, with whites, is a part of my life.

She recounted a desire for interracial relationships and antidiscrimination activism that continued into her adulthood and professional life as a middle-school teacher and assistant principal. She described her desire to improve race relations via interracial interaction as "something that was so branded in me. It was like part of the DNA that I came here with."

I found that many elected officials and employees of local government agencies also explained their choice to pursue race dialogues as one decision in a string of many to promote interracial interaction. For example, Dean Lovelace is an African-American man who is an elected city commissioner in Dayton, Ohio. He decided to implement a race dialogue program with the help of several local leaders when tension between blacks and the police department came to a head in the late 1990s. After months of impasse, Lovelace said they declared, "*Time out! Let's talk* a little bit here!" Those attempts at interracial dialogue grew into a community-wide program that continued for over six years, to the time of this writing.

I asked him what in his own experience had led him to pursue a dialogue program as a way to reduce racial tension and racism in his city. He said that he had attended a predominantly white school and had many white friends. When he was in the seventh grade, he went to a neighbor's house with some playmates, "and they would not let me in their yard or the house, saying, 'We don't allow niggers in here.'" But the friends he was with stood by him and said:

> "Ok, well, we're niggers, too, and we're never gonna play with you again." And I said, ok, these guys stood up . . . From that moment, I said there are going to be people in my life that are willing to take a stand to integrate. And I really respected them for that . . . I played on a football team, we played a lot of white teams and they were often disparaging us, you know, and I grew up in that kind of environment and felt that hey, hey, hey! We gotta get *through* this at some point in time. I am a person who has always kind of confronted and talked about it versus kind of hide and shove it under the rug and I have tried to be a person to say, "We have to find ways to get to know each other as a people."

So from early on, you thought a way of improving race relations was to talk to one another?

Yeah, yeah, so we could find the commonalities, even though we may be different, and we can celebrate our differences, as either African Americans or Asian Americans or Native Americans. We should celebrate that without saying, "We should all just kind of melt down into one common race." Celebrate our differences and find a way to help reduce those gaps. That's the kind of tip I'm going on these days. I see the disparities between different ethnic groups and it is not acceptable to me. And I am always looking for ways to reduce gaps between blacks and whites.

But some people might say, well in order to reduce those gaps, let's not spend time talking, let's work on economic development or some other strategy that is totally different from talking. What do you say to that?

Folks simply wouldn't believe it! I think people . . . My white friends may be stuck on the illusion of progress for African Americans. But if they, in fact, drill down, remove the Tiger Woods, and the Oprah Winfreys and Colin Powell and look at the regular brothers and sisters, you see how people are struggling. You look at the big picture and say, "Like WHOA! Look at the wealth gap!" . . . When you look at the quality of housing, the homeownership rates, the health care rates, the uninsured—When you start looking at that then you start saying, "Ok, we have some more work to do here."

When I pressed dialogue practitioners on why they decided to begin their program, several, like Lovelace, pointed to heightened tension around a particular event or series of events, but this was actually a very rare response. Much more often, their choice to pursue the particular race dialogue program reflected the policy streams model put forth by John Kingdon in his study of congressional agenda setting.[16] In Kingdon's model, policies gain prominence on an agenda when several streams come together simultaneously: a problem, a policy solution, and fertile political conditions. Likewise, intergroup dialogue programs seemed to arise in situations that were ready for such an innovation, when the following three conditions coincided: long-brewing tense race relations and racial injustice, local leaders' (entrepreneurs') desire for a solution to this tension, and an influx of information about the use of intergroup dialogue programs in similar cities.

A Necessary Complement to Action

The way practitioners including Lovelace, Cronin, and Mason talked about their choice to pursue dialogue suggests that they did not arrive at this decision through a maximization process. They were not weighing the pros and cons of dialogue against other possible strategies. It was not a compromise, or a strategy of last resort. No one I interviewed expected that dialogue was a panacea, or that it alone would eliminate racism and hostile race relations. But contrary to the common perception that public talk is unwieldy and that it impedes action, these practitioners commonly conceptualized dialogue as *integral* to action.

Some practitioners did emphasize talk as distinct from action, and talked about the program's nonpartisan and nonpolitical affiliation as an asset. Mary Jane Hollis, executive director of the Aurora [Illinois] Community Study Circles, talked about her program as a "neutral container," a place where people would feel safe talking openly about their feelings and experiences with race relations precisely because the program did not aim to advocate any particular type of outcome.

However, other practitioners envisioned the program as one component of pursuing social justice action. Some emphasized the act of listening to difference during dialogue and cited the need to "deal with the dirt first" before focusing on "harmony" or other forms of unity. Others talked about the need to listen to one another to "completely define the situation—have all of those underlying factors that formulate people's opinions on the table so that you know what they're talking about and you know what's underneath it" before deciding what the problem is and planning action steps to address it. Some described this as identifying the issues in the community "that need healing."

Yet others saw race dialogue as a way to give people a "better understanding of their own role in the problem." Walter Reed, an African-American man who was the executive director of the Waterloo Human Rights Commission at the time of my first interview with him,[17] said that recognizing racism was particularly important even among the so-called "choir" that had self-selected themselves into the program:

> The one thing I do know is that if we're going to address issues of race, diversity, we've got to address people who do these things. And they are often times what I categorize as good people. You know—jerks, we see them coming. But those good people who are the silent people, who can say something or do something and make a difference, we needed a way for them to come out. Now racism, and the practice of racism, is by a group of good folks. They go to church, they are philanthropic, they are right, they do all of these things that are wonderful, but they'll get behind—or get in a session, get with a group of their friends, and they will make a decision that is not based on anything but a hostile racist view. And sometimes they've done it so much that it is normal. And sometimes you just have to point those things out to them.

Even practitioners who were more conservative about the extent of racism said recognizing racist acts is an important step in improving race relations. A fire department official who had helped facilitate a program in Iowa claimed that racism was less of a concern to most people than jobs and the economy, and was the only person of the eight interviewed in his city to disagree that neighborhoods there could be characterized by race and/or class composition. Nevertheless, he argued that in order to improve relationships in his community, whites needed to talk with people of different racial backgrounds to recognize "how privileged they are" and how things are "stacked in their favor."

Many people who said dialogue was necessary in order to become aware of the extent of racism specifically mentioned the importance of having a forum in which people of color could watch whites recognize just how naïve they had been about discrimination in their community. They recounted examples of so-called racially tolerant whites expressing surprise at the possibility that they had themselves perpetuated racism in their everyday lives. Practitioners claimed that many whites had listened to the experiences of people of color, and realized that they did not in fact know enough about what it is like to experience racial discrimination to speak on behalf of members of marginalized groups. Practitioners claimed that the act of witnessing that transformation made people more likely to seek collaboration with their white community members.

Often, practitioners claimed that dialogue about race was a necessary part of social justice because of the history of their particular city. They sensed a need to finally address head-on long-simmering racial tension. This was especially the case among practitioners who were working in cities with histories of civil unrest that had been labeled "riots": Tulsa, Oklahoma; Camden, New Jersey; Richmond, Virginia; Springfield, Illinois; and Waterloo, Iowa. Public officials as well as activists made these arguments.

These practitioners' insistence that race dialogues are a necessary part of social justice action flies in the face of evidence that exposure to alternative views may actually stifle political participation by inducing ambivalence or encouraging avoidance of further controversy.[18] The communication that these practitioners were advocating was not just about exposure to different perspectives and a hope that people would gain understanding of those perspectives. They viewed this interaction as a way to open up communication, to foster relationships that would allow collective action to take place. They said that confronting public problems in a way that bridged major lines of social difference simply required exposure to difference.

In addition, at the same time that practitioners commonly viewed talk as necessary for social justice action, they also viewed action toward social justice as necessary for public talk. Many people talked about intergroup dialogue as a kind of action that all healthy communities ought to have on an ongoing basis, to counteract the common tendency to avoid interaction across group divides.[19] That is, like Habermas, Dewey, and Arendt, they valued the existence of talk in and of itself. However, rarely did they treat talk as action without referring to its connection to other forms of participation.

We can understand these conceptions more thoroughly by revisiting for a moment the work of political theorist Danielle Allen. Allen argues that in the post-*Brown v. Board of Education* era, people live in a democracy that purports to treat all people equally and in a society in which all members exist in the same civic space. In order for that to work, she argues, we need to learn to "talk to strangers":

> In their daily activities, citizens can interact with strangers according to the norms of political friendship and begin to develop reservoirs of trust to sustain political reciprocity, but this nascent interpersonal trust will never mature into full-blown political friendship unless it is given serious political work to do.[20]

In this conception of citizenship, people value talk and action in combination, not talk as a substitute for action. Race dialogue practitioners commonly articulated a similar vision of civic life. They viewed talking to strangers as meaningful and effective when it was intertwined with other forms of "serious political work."

Not all of the practitioners I interviewed conceptualized talk as an integral part of social justice action. For example, the mayor of Madison, Wisconsin, from 1997 to 2003 was a strong advocate of her city's race dialogue program but did not intend for her city's program to lead to political action. Mayor Susan Bauman, a white woman, had assembled a city race-relations task force of elected and nonelected officials and community members in the wake of heightened concern with race relations and racial profiling. The task force had suggested a variety of actions that the city could take to improve race relations, including the dialogue program. An African-American man who was head of the city's Equal Opportunities Commission was an outspoken proponent of the program. However, local activists criticized it as the least proactive strategy the city could have adopted among the task force's recommendations. When I interviewed Bauman, she said that one of her main goals for the program was to overcome the apathy that existed among many residents in Madison about race relations:

Do you have hopes about any kind of policy change that might come out of the Study Circles?

I keep wondering what exactly is the point of an action forum [a name commonly given to a study circles session in which participants decide which actions to engage in after participating in the dialogues]. I really would like to see attitude change. I mean that's really where . . . We've passed all the laws that say that we shouldn't discriminate because . . . based on gender, based on the color of your skin, national origin, you know, sexual orientation. You name it, you shall not discriminate. Well, fine. Now how do I internalize that?

She stated that one of the biggest accomplishments of the program was that the dialogues "have kept the issue of race relations, and of celebrating the diversity of the community, right in the forefront."

At a potluck meeting for the program's steering committee several months after our interview, Hedi Rudd, the woman coordinating the program (a multiracial employee of the mayor's office), voiced concerns about the lack of support for the program among some members of the city council. She said they needed to demonstrate to the council and to the public that the circles were productive, and said that a good way to do so would be to demonstrate that the discussions led to some visible forms of action. Mayor Bauman responded, "I strongly disagree" and said the focus should be on generating more circles, rather than getting current participants involved in action.[21]

Again, this avoidance of linking talk to action was atypical among people who promoted these programs. One way to see this is to notice that my interviewees saw personal growth as integral to, not separate from, social justice action. For example, Belinda Cronin, the African-American activist in Racine, talked about dialogue primarily as a route to self-actualization. But personal transformation was the route she conceived as essential for widespread and profound social change. She said it was relationships with people of other racial backgrounds that allowed her to overcome fear and figure out how she could best contribute to the goal of social justice. "It's not that everybody needs a project. Everybody needs a *consciousness*." She emphasized the need for empathy and argued that relationships are an important form of civic action. This may sound like a nonradical perspective on social justice, but her comments were situated in a sense of urgency. "We either band together or divide like fools [at this point in history]. . . . People are bitter. You've got pockets boiling over and it is going to *explode!*"

Cronin's views exemplify the perception that self-understanding is part of the project of social justice, not tangential to it. Her views recall those of John Dewey and of Hanna Pitkin's reading of Arendt, who in various ways argued that deliberative democracy is an integral part of democracy both for its positive effects on individual development as well as on community progress.[22] Susan Bickford explains that because acts of democratic citizenship that combine speaking and listening take courage, a consciousness of one's relation to others, and a willingness to reconsider one's beliefs, participation in such acts involves self-development.[23]

Carol Hardy-Fanta's work on Latina activists in Boston helps further illuminate this intertwining of self-development and social justice. She identifies a tendency among these female activists to conceptualize politics in terms of connections or relationships. Such a focus puts a premium on communication that gives as well as takes, and it creates a politics that nourishes not only the community but the individual who engages in action.[24]

Public Officials and the Pursuit of Dialogue

The comments of the former mayor of Madison, above, raise the possibility that elected officials are pursuing race dialogues as merely an expedient way to appear to do something about race relations. My interview data do not generalize to the population of all elected officials pursuing race dialogues around the country, nor do they tell us the true individual-level motivations underlying this choice. However, my interviewees did reveal the justifications for dialogue that elected officials perceive are publicly appropriate—at least to the public of a university researcher.

I found that public officials' conceptions of race dialogues were very similar to those of community activists. This corroborates the result from chapter 4 that, on the community level, the conditions underlying programs sponsored by governments are very similar to those underlying programs sponsored by nonprofits.

Many elected officials, like activists, justified their choice to pursue dialogue as one driven by a practical need to deal with racism and to address the changing nature of their communities. For example, John Crews, mayor of Cedar Falls, Iowa, and a white man, participated in and facilitated some of the study circles in Waterloo, a neighboring city.[25] The way he justified his choice to support the race dialogues suggested that he saw it as necessary for pursuing social justice in the Waterloo-Cedar Falls area, and also for simply doing his job as mayor. When asked how he justified spending his time working on such a program, he said that demographic trends toward an increasingly racially diverse society meant that "you could say it is just totally self-interest." As a mayor, "You've gotta, you should, deal with it and you've gotta deal with it whether you want to or not. . . . You should morally and . . . you just need to adjust."

Lovelace, the city commissioner in Dayton, also declared that interracial dialogue is a route toward substantial social change. He did not describe his choice to pursue these dialogues as a way to draw attention away from the problem but instead as a way to set the stage for social action:

I want to know how it works—the kinds of things you imagine coming about because of these conversations.

One thing we should be doing is helping to increase and maximize human relations in a sense, especially in a city that is so racially divided. . . . The issue of how we in effect promote integrated neighborhoods, those are things that I think that are kind of policy agenda items, that I certainly have stayed close to and now at least we have a mechanism to at least air those points of view through this group here.

So you say that through the dialogue you can bring out those issues, and have people talk about them—it is a way for the city government to engage the citizens in discussion.

Uh huh.

The reason I put it that way is that sometimes, it seems that some locations . . . try to [maintain their programs] as much as possible as a kind of neutral container

. . . [and are] very careful to not try to portray it as an arm of policy or some kind of advocacy. And so is it different here?

Yeah, yeah. There is something that is going to sort of bubble up in those dialogues that needs action, that is why we say, "From dialogue to action."

And so you expect that is going to happen?

Oh yeah! And it *has* happened, through these dialogues or through an awareness that this is going on, there has to be a way to translate into action, whether it is we need to organize suburban mayors and managers about how they in effect look at integrated neighborhoods, and if they have some zoning restrictions that maybe bar folks from certain kinds of lot sizes that tend to inhibit people often times who are low income or people of color, you know from living in these neighborhoods. . . . So it is a power perspective. The notion of having an integrated police force and workforce is a policy agenda.

He went on to explain that he uses the dialogues as feedback, as a way to become aware of the public's concerns. In 2002, he was using the dialogues to gauge disenfranchisement—among whites. Shortly before I interviewed him for the first time, the city had elected a black mayor and an additional black member to the city commission. This meant that 80 percent of the elected city officials were African American. "I think some folks are worrying about how our white friends are processing this black power, this kind of new black power over here."

But his intention was not to use the dialogues to appease whites. Instead, he said he wished to improve communication between African Americans and city hall, as well as among African Americans and whites in the community:

You've got to have a way for folks to talk to each other, otherwise I think you get the Cincinnatis. [The previous spring, civil unrest had erupted in Cincinnati.] If you don't talk about power relationships and ways to improve your economic lot, ways to deal with the barriers, from you maybe moving to another community because you are African American, something like that. . . . Sometimes you've got to kind of talk through that stuff. Then you can convince somebody—folks in power can change the policies. . . . And if nothing is not there, then they say, "Ok then I'm going to get you next time." That's how people vote. But you're not the right elected official if you're not willing to think about some of the policies people are thinking about changing right here in this town. And that's the issue with Cincinnati . . . they are like, "Don't worry, just trust us!" But how can you trust without meaningful dialogue? "Here's what we're going to do, here's what we've done." Hopefully they will value that. Some folks are so angry, and they are going to be angry. They want tangible real things, not hope and faith, looking for some real tangible things.

Lovelace's passion for the dialogues stemmed from his sense of duty to pursue public policy oriented toward racial justice.

His conception of dialogue is not necessarily representative of all officials who publicly supported race dialogue programs. In fact, in some cities, the programs seemed to exist in spite of elected officials. For example, the programs in Waterloo and Sioux City, Iowa, seemed to have arisen despite opposition from within the local government. In both places, elected officials had lent financial and verbal support to the programs, but there are signs that they had done so unenthusiastically. People affiliated with the Waterloo program lamented that although mayors of nearby cities had participated in the dialogues, their own mayor had not. Also, in July 2003, the council voted to eliminate funding for the Human Rights Commission's temporary employee responsible for administering the program. In Sioux City, the council considered eliminating the entire HRC staff. That program was administered by a nonprofit offshoot of the HRC, and thus this was not necessarily a sign of lack of support for the program. Nevertheless, community activists affiliated with the program claimed that the council had initially funded it in order to quiet the executive director's demands for more expensive and visible policy changes.

Many public officials did openly support these programs as a step toward policy change. One example that the SCRC commonly cites is (former) Mayor Karen Hasara in Springfield, Illinois. When Hasara was mayor, she visibly pursued and backed Springfield's study circles program and pledged to implement the recommendations the dialogue groups devised. As a result, the city changed its hiring policies and attempted to diversify its police department.[26] Other examples include the campaign for race dialogues by Bob Knight, a former mayor of Wichita, Kansas, while President of the National League of Cities, mentioned in chapter 3.

Perhaps ironically, the perception that civic deliberation, or intergroup dialogue specifically, is "all talk and no action" may actually enable action to occur in places that elected officials or others in the community do not think are "ready" for it. In such circumstances, the reputation of intergroup dialogue as a harmless activity, not associated with substantial change, may work to its advantage. But the way that it actually is conceptualized by others with a more direct role in implementing the dialogue suggests that it is commonly used as a springboard for action oriented toward altering public policy and basic processes in a community's civic life.[27]

Using Dialogue To Confront

Even though some public officials conceptualized dialogues on race as an integral part of action, they surely did not want them to serve as an arena for bringing conflict to the surface, did they? The prevailing politics of unity would suggest such a goal is dangerous to the public good. However, even though pamphlets promoting intergroup dialogues called this an opportunity to "dialogue, not debate," many practitioners expected people to use these conversations to confront one another. Some practitioners, like Lovelace, the Dayton city commissioner, advocated attention to conflict and said diverting attention away from conflict would be quickly derided as artificial.

Granted, not all practitioners hoped that dialogue programs would serve as an arena for confronting conflict. Some attempted to structure their program to avoid current controversial topics in order to get more people to participate, particularly political leaders.

Nevertheless, in some communities the use of dialogue programs was clearly intended to serve as a means of directly confronting powerholders. This view is exemplified in the comments of activists in the NCCJ in Des Moines, Iowa. In July 2002, I interviewed Rudy Simms, an African American man who was Executive Director of the Iowa NCCJ, and Jesse Villalobos, a Latino man who was the Program Director for the Des Moines Regional NCCJ, at a 4-H camp north of Des Moines, where they were running a weeklong camp for middle-school students from central Iowa. They said that dialogue was an important part of many of the programs they conducted because it "gives people a chance to express themselves, share opinions, feelings, hopefully respect people" (Simms) and "gives folks an opportunity to hear other people, which typically doesn't happen, typically isolated. And especially with the subject matter that we bring to the table, it's taboo" (Villalobos). Simms considered dialogue to be risky, not escapist, because people who participate "may end up changing their views, their values, their perspectives on the world even, from hearing of others' experience." Villalobos elaborated:

> And to be challenged. . . . [Our approach] is very much action-oriented and very dedicated to providing the means of skill-building and team-building so that there's an action at the end that promotes institutional change.

Later on in the interview, he added:

> I think communities—being a lifelong Iowan—communities do have pockets of people who really do care about these issues, who want to get them

out there, who want to provide more information, more opportunity for dialogue, but typically that's where it stops. And we can do all the talking in the world, but the fact is we got folks out there suffering and dying and being stepped on every day because of these things and honestly we even support it through our tax dollars and through our governments and through our agencies and institutions through things like education and health care, law enforcement. And that's just not going to fly. And an organization like ours that is dedicated to fighting bias, all kinds of bias and bigotry—that's our job to disarm.

An emphasis on action and contestation pervaded their comments about dialogue. They intended to use interracial dialogue as one way of fundamentally challenging existing structures of power in their community. When I asked, *Why are "Honest Conversations" necessary in Des Moines?*, Villalobos responded:

There is a history of racial segregation, police brutality, a lot of tension that is still boxed up in [Des Moines] and a lot of that for the city the size of Des Moines. . . . If we can really engage leadership and bring them to the task and hold them accountable [by involving them in the dialogue program], when it comes to these types of issues and policies, then they can demand that from their institutions. And if we can change institutions, then we can change communities.

Simms's and Villalobos's thoughts suggest that part of some individuals' pursuit of race dialogues stems from their perception that this form of public talk can challenge existing power structures. Such perceptions were not restricted to people working with NGOs. Reed, the African-American executive director of the Waterloo Human Rights Commission, was an outspoken proponent of intergroup dialogue and had implemented a program in his city that had lasted for eight years at the time of this writing. He talked about dialogue as a way to open up local power structures to members of marginalized communities.

Waterloo has a long history with racial tension, and Reed had been a civil rights activist in that community throughout his life. Waterloo has had a significant African-American community since the early 1900s, when the Illinois Central Railroad recruited strikebreakers from African-American communities in Mississippi to complete construction of a rail link between Minneapolis and St. Louis. In 2000, 13.9 percent of the population was black.

When I met with Reed, race relations had been tense for decades. In 1955, the Iowa State Teachers College in nearby Cedar Falls produced a report that documented these conflicts.[28] At that time, deed restrictions, loan refusals, and targeted housing ads perpetuated severe patterns of housing segregation.[29] The report also noted a small number of black professionals, job discrimination in the form of sorting African Americans into the dirtiest and hottest jobs in the local Rath meat packing plant and the John Deere tractor factory, and discrimination in local hotels and restaurants.[30] Segregation and discrimination were pervasive in the local schools, with all but one or two of the high-school-aged black students attending East High, and only one African-American teacher in the district. Echoing novelist Alan Paton's often-repeated claim,[31] the report noted that churches were the most segregated local institution.

Forty-eight years later, when I first visited Waterloo, there were many signs of change, from integrated diners to public librarians using old card catalog cards—from the former "segregated" or "East Library"—as scrap paper. But problems persisted in Waterloo, and these were readily apparent, too. Reed cited numerous examples, all of which were easily verifiable. He mentioned an achievement gap in the local schools,[32] racially motivated vandalism,[33] and discrimination in real estate and local business.[34] He also spoke of a history of African-American disenfranchisement. This, too, was evident, even to a visitor. Driving around Waterloo, I noticed an open letter posted outside the Cedar Valley Boxing Club in the predominantly African-American part of town. The letter, posted on three panels of one-story-tall plywood read:

> PUBLIC NOTICE. To inform the community that the Waterloo City Council and Waterloo Chamber of Commerce Does Not Support this Small Business or the Free Cedar Valley Youth Program this Business Support Financially. On August 12, 2002, the Mayor and City Council passed an ordinance to prohibit parking along the east side of the 600 block of East Fourth Street, which directly effects the businesses in that block, community and the free youth program these businesses financially support. . . . This decision is against the interest of the community, this business and the free youth program we have established together. The Waterloo Chamber of Commerce, Waterloo Mayor, and City Council are responsible. As a community we need to select our city officials more carefully. We will be putting a petition out against the Waterloo Mayor and City Council's decision, to abolish the illegal no parking ordinance and to restore commerce. This will allow us to continue serving the community and supporting our youth program. THANK YOU FOR YOUR SUPPORT.

It was this context that Reed invoked when explaining his decision to pursue a race dialogue program:

I think that it's necessary here—I think it's necessary a lot of places, because as we grow and as we face community challenges, we need to begin to practice doing that together. The day of putting together a community strategy and leaving a group of people out doesn't work because after people get tired of being treated like second-class citizens, or being treated as if their opinion doesn't matter, then they start to act out. And you know I just think we have not reached our full productive capacity as a community because we don't collaborate enough. And having a, being on the side where we have not—I know what Have Not is. And I just—I'm tired of being there. And seeing people there on purpose. I'm like, "Oh no. That's— we don't want that. I don't want that. Why do I want to raise a family here and I know you're constantly spending your time trying to keep me down instead of working with me to make this community better?" Seeing that we have a contribution to make, not bringing that kind of energy to the table to help find solutions I think is a, is . . . is . . . is . . . is a sin. And that's why, I think circles are important. I think people need to be brought into the process, instead of being used as puppets all over the place. I've grown through all of that. I have seen a lot of stuff happen here, and I don't like it. And since I've chosen to be here, I choose to try to make it better, as a good use of my time.

His explanation for the program did not frame it as a way to avoid intergroup tension. Quite the contrary. He portrayed it as a means of confronting simmering hostility and a way to set the stage for serious action.[35]

Moreover, Reed saw these programs as a way to focus specifically on the enduring issue of race. Part of Reed's frustration with African Americans' status quo in Waterloo seemed to stem from the ways in which local public officials had directed their attention toward Latinos and Bosnians (the latter had arrived in the 1990s) in the community. A newspaper article about the treatment of the newly arrived Bosnians quoted him as lamenting the lack of attention to local blacks in contrast to the open welcome the community was extending to the recent Bosnian immigrants.[36]

When talking about his decision to try intergroup dialogue, he emphasized the need to talk, directly and frankly, about race:

We're not trying to be all things to all people. . . . I want us to address race. Diversity is fine. All of those other things are fine, but what ails us is what we feel about the issue of race. We're going to set race right in the middle of the table [places his styrofoam coffee cup there] and I don't care how you come in, that's what we're focused on. And so for the five years that I've been here [as head of the HRC], we're focused on race. . . .

[A few minutes later, he continues on this path]:

I've been sort of the task master in that I don't let the program go off into a thousand different directions. That has made some people upset, but I'm like, deal with it. This is where we are. This is where we are going to stay, until we get to a certain point, then we can move away from that. But the point we start at is always going to be a matter of race. And I am telling you, Kathy, every single time we go off, we can deal with everything else, but there will be something happen, where race is a factor.

In the community, something will come up?

Something will come up, a hate crime, or decision made by local government, or just some foolish act in the community or something will come up where race is a factor. Well if that's always the factor, if we are always back to this, then let's deal with it.

Reed's insistence that his community focus specifically on race is notable because that conception of the purpose of dialogue might in and of itself cause us to conclude that these programs were primarily about calling attention to difference. Reed wanted to confront intergroup conflict specifically about race. But he faced these programs with a politics that was sensitive to the desire for unity as well. Notice what Reed had to say in the midst of this statement. Inserted into the portion of the conversation marked by the note "[A few minutes later . . .]" above, Reed said the following:

People want to talk about race without getting their head blown off, or chewed off, or just because this way I've gotta feel small. No. What you say is important, we want to hear that. And what we've found is that when you really look at the issue of race and start talking about this thing, that we have more in common than we have different. And so we are finding the commonalities and what I try to do is celebrate those when we find them. And then where we really have differences, you really find out that it is really small, but that is where you can work. This is where work needs to take place. But let's celebrate family, let's celebrate whatever it is that you do, I mean I'm learning in the process about different cultures and different things like that, but I also know that white parents feel the same way as black parents—they want their kids to succeed and be successful, and they want safe environments and they want this and want that. How do we know these things if we don't talk to each other?

Reed is a person who came of age in the Civil Rights movement, participated in sit-ins in high school and has devoted his life to working for racial justice. He supports multiculturalism vigorously in his comments. He asserts that attention to race is absolutely necessary, and that it ought to be the job of government to give attention to the demands of racial groups. But he does so in a way that is not totally about difference. His conception challenges our notion of people who call attention to difference as those who seek to place racial divides above considerations of what binds a community together.

In fact, many of the interviewees (whites as well as people of color) talked about attention to difference not in contrast to the concerns of the community as a whole or that of whites, but as a practical necessity, an essential part of conducting one's job and furthering the project of addressing racial divides. This is a contrast to the assumption that addressing intergroup conflict or forging bridging social capital is best achieved by focusing on similarities.

I found that even among people who perceived dialogues were valuable for their potential to uncover or create unity, there was nevertheless a belief that listening to difference was important. Walter Rooff, the mayor of Waterloo, is a case in point. It was under his administration that the race dialogue program in Waterloo began. Rooff, a white man, claimed that the program began when he asked Reed to implement such a program. Others in the community were less convinced of Rooff's support or responsibility for the program, and pointed to the fact that he had declined to participate in the program. When I asked Rooff why he believed the dialogues were a good idea, he said "until we sit down and break bread and learn about one another—and I do that through churches—you really can never find out that there is more that we have in common than difference."

Despite placing a value on unity in this respect, later in the interview Rooff discussed the importance of becoming aware of others' experiences:

So what exactly do you think the programs can achieve? What do you expect a program like Study Circles to do?

Well I think it can not only cross racial barriers, I think it can cross age barriers, . . . [and] there is an area of prejudice because of poverty. I grew up in a poor neighborhood and I went back to a reunion of two schools that were in this poor area of our city. And as I talked with these people—I went to Lowell school, and I was just two blocks from them, from where their homes were. And I said, "But you went to Riverview and Nelly Garvey" [two other elementary schools]. I said, "Why?" I said, "We all lived in the same area." And they said, "Your parents had more money." And I said, "You know I never realized that." And then I asked a woman who was a little bit older than I how she was treated at the high school level and—this has got to be back in the '50s and '60s—and she said that she was told by the assistant principal that he didn't "want any trouble out of you people." And they were white, they were poor, and the only prejudice that was caused there was because of their poverty. And I guess I never realized that. You know I'm 58 years old and I've been mayor for 10 years, and in politics for 17 and I'm saying, "my God I never realized that there was that poverty bias." I just didn't—never dawned on me. That's sad that I didn't realize that, that that was the case.

In this story, Rooff suggests the importance of conversation for opening up one's eyes to the experiences of others in the community. He asserts that dialogue helps identify similarities, but nevertheless notes the power of talk in making himself aware of difference.

Other people were more clear about the need to focus on difference, and this included people we might least expect to exhibit multiculturalist attitudes, such as fire and police officers in Midwestern states. One example comes from Lieutenant John Daws of the Waterloo police department, who is white. He talked about dialogue as a necessary part of modern-day policing in his city. At the time that we talked, the police department was in the process of incorporating a version of a study circle program in its officer training. His involvement in the program stemmed directly from his role as a police lieutenant, and he was attempting to establish an ongoing program in which members of the community and officers would dialogue over repeated sessions.

Daws argued that this was a preventative and proactive program that, if effective, would reduce the cost of policing in the future. He said that establishing personal relationships through these dialogues increases understanding across racial and ethnic backgrounds, makes members of minority communities less afraid of police officers, makes minority youth in the community more likely to choose law enforcement as a career, and ultimately reduces the time and resources necessary to solve crimes:

> What's your first reaction, you know if I pulled you over today in your car? [I shudder.] See! You'd be scared. Why? When I get pulled over, I mean you don't see no halo over my head, when I get pulled over, I am the same way, I have the same reaction. I'm scared because, "What did I do wrong?" . . . [But] if I pulled you over, and you and I have had a social life for a period of time, your first reaction is, "Well I might have done something wrong, but it's John Daws! He still might give me a ticket, but I know this guy. And I know that I'm OK." I mean, mentally safe. . . .
>
> As a school resource officer, I was [in a public school] for five years and in that five years, I taught 1,500 sixth graders. I have a young man that is at Lo-

ras College over in Dubuque, that walked in my door the other day . . . and he says, "I want to do my internship here." He's getting a degree in police science, and "I want to do my internship here and I want to be a Waterloo cop." See how this works? If I back up to '79—I was the high school liaison officer at West High, and now I see people your age or higher and they have their kids and they introduce me as Officer Daws. . . . You can't put a value on that. That's worth a million dollars. And that—it's worth a million dollars in that I have an i.d., but what's it worth when that person calls me and says, "Hey Billy Bob is the guy that killed that woman or killed that man in that robbery"?

Now if we put all of our officers in a [race dialogue], you know you put two officers at a table of six or eight citizens, and students, and . . . we do this for let's just say we do this for eight or ten hours, over a two-hour or a three hour class, over a five or six week period, you've now established—when you're done there, you're gonna have six friends, and they're gonna have two friends, and you can't put a value on that.

We spend fifteen, eighteen to twenty thousand [dollars] on a homicide in overtime. . . . That's just the first five days. . . . So the more contacts or the more folks we have that can befriend us or let us know—Let's not talk dollars. I don't care if we spend eighteen thousand dollars to solve a homicide, if you take that murder suspect off the street in the first twelve hours, what have you done to the community? You've made them feel safe. You've told the community, hey this is my town, this is our town and we don't want a murder suspect running around out there.

Daws remarked that establishing police-community relationships through dialogue programs can result in better, cheaper policing, and safer communities. In his conception, this was a strategy that he and other officers advocated not as a way to appease community members, but as simply a practical way of conducting modern-day policing.

Dialogue as a Way To Be Who They Are

Why do people choose to improve race relations through intergroup dialogue programs? The reasons we have encountered in this chapter stress the role of personal history and a perspective on civic life that values relationships and stresses dialogue as a necessary complement to other forms of action. These lay theories of dialogue challenge many scholars' conceptions of the place of talk in everyday democracy.

For one thing, practitioners' conceptions do not suggest that listening-focused talk is primarily about self-development or self-actualization. They talk about it as serving a political function: action. They tend not to talk about it as a passive action, a compromise strategy, or a strategy they turned to because they knew it would pass approval. Instead, they treat it as an integral component of eliminating racism, attaining racial equality, and doing their jobs. Many practitioners rooted their conceptions in a lifetime of concern with social justice in which talk and action were intertwined.

These conceptions have credibility because if these practitioners were pursuing this talk as primarily a means of self-development, postmaterialist theory suggests that they would readily say so. Postmaterialism holds that people *value* self-development and self-actualization. Therefore, if postmaterialism were at work, social desirability would bias their remarks in favor of emphasizing self-actualization.

Although many practitioners talked about recognizing difference as an essential part of moving their communities forward, their words and behaviors seldom fit the common stereotypes of multiculturalism. As noted in chapter 2, public opinion research suggests that multiculturalism is supported by only a small portion of the public, feeding claims that privileging racial group differences is elitist. But it would be incorrect to say that civic dialogue is a function of just a fringe element in these communities. It is true that just a small minority of people in a given community participate in these programs (with a few rare exceptions).[37] However, the rosters of people involved do not support the idea that this form of public talk is pursued by people with extremist political agendas. Participants include elected officials, city government department heads, government employees, fire and safety officials, librarians, public school teachers, local business leaders, maintenance workers, retirees, full-time parents, and other ordinary citizens. Moreover, even those who assert the most intense injunctions to focus on difference commonly also talked about the need to identify similarities.

And contrary to some treatments, the perceptions among people conducting dialogue do not support the idea that contexts have to be sufficiently unitary, in the sense of consensus over interests, for public talk to be feasible.[38] The question that concerns these practitioners is not whether we have enough in common or sufficient friendship for *deliberation* to work, but whether or not we have the right kind of communication in place for *democracy* to work.

Also, the justifications for the choice to engage in dialogue that center on the necessity of dealing with conflict stand in contrast to prescriptions of contact hypothesis research that fruitful intergroup contact involves working on common projects together in a noncompetitive manner. Dialogue practitioners suggest that if the people who are attempting to forge productive relationships are embedded in a context of longstanding conflict, people need to confront that conflict head-on, not avoid it.[39]

Finally, it is not just activists who advocate contestation. We see it among government employees, and even elected officials. The way these officials as well as NGO practitioners are conceptualizing talk is at odds with a belief that when public talk is used to contest the status quo, public officials will distance themselves from it.

As a practical answer to the challenges these people face in doing their jobs and improving race relations, their conceptions of these programs reveal some weaknesses. In some contexts, it seems that dialogue was allowed because it was perceived to be innocuous. Others explicitly say that they do not wish for it to be connected to action. And yet others talk about wanting to focus specifically on race, implying that attention to related issues such as immigration detracts from the job they perceive they need to do.

The conceptions of race dialogue uncovered in this chapter are further illuminated by a comparison to the study of "concord organizations," conducted by Barbara Nelson, Linda Kaboolian, and Kathryn Carver. These organizations "bring together people with fundamentally opposing views or identities for the purpose of promoting civil society while recognizing group differences."[40] Nelson, Kaboolian, and Carver investigated "how people with profound differences agree to work together, especially how they form organizations that explicitly bring them together across deep divides of history and values."[41] They focused on concord organizations in the United States and in countries with more intense group divides: Ireland and South Africa. Through site visits and interviews, they examined over one hundred organizations that incorporated dialogue, either as the primary function of the organization or as a preliminary step toward other types of actions.

Nelson, Kaboolian, and Carver propose an "investment theory" of collective action to explain the emergence of concord organizations. In contrast to conventional conceptions of collective action, in which actors' choices are understood as a function of a cost-benefit analysis, they find that individuals behaved as though they were investors. The "goods" involved seemed to be values-based rather than economics-based; the conflicts were about identities and beliefs, and thus were not solvable by dividing up the goods among the groups in conflict. Instead, what people valued was watching the relationships and the trust they established through their investment ripple out to positively influence community life and future conflicts.

The interviews and site visits I conducted support many of the claims of this investment theory. People who founded programs in their communities often did conceptualize the need for dialogue as arising from values-based conflicts. They simultaneously had concerns with economic, social, and political inequality alongside a perception that fundamental intergroup misunderstandings needed to be resolved. No one emphasized economic benefits over social ones, and no one expected dialogue would be a quick remedy. Many expected—and believed that they achieved—ripple effects in the sense that graduates from the program would behave differently. They expected participants would use their newfound courage to stop everyday discriminatory behavior, such as racist jokes and discrimination in workplace hiring practices.

However, one aspect of practitioners' explanations for why they chose to do this work is not encompassed by the investment theory. When people explained their involvement, they did not describe it as a choice, or as one alternative among many in which they decided to invest their resources. They talked about it as the obvious thing to do. They explained it as a necessary part of *any* action toward improved race relations or social justice.

Nelson and colleagues mention that founders of concord organizations perceive that it is necessary to form these organizations, but they explain this necessity in terms of opportunity costs. They argue that founders perceive that they would pay a high price if they did not immediately take action, given the status quo and a current window of opportunity. In contrast, I find that when practitioners express a sense of necessity, they do so as a function of identity. In other words, their claims that race dialogues are necessary are rooted in the overall perspectives from which they view the world and in their sense of the kind of people that they are.

This aspect of the choice—or perhaps it is best to say "the act"—of implementing a dialogue program is not necessarily at odds with the investment theory of concord organizations. However, it deserves further attention because it is an alternative way of conceptualizing political behavior that opens up our understanding of the pursuit of public talk. Again, people pursuing intergroup dialogue talked about this not as a choice but as an act that allowed them to be the kind of citizens they saw themselves as being. Rather than conceptualize the decision to pursue bridging social capital as *whether* to do so, they talked about it as the question of *how can I NOT pursue this?*[42]

This is an aspect of political behavior that is not unique to the act of implementing intergroup dialogue. Recognizing that people pursue certain political behaviors because doing so is consistent with their identities helps explain some of the most confounding political acts. Kristen Monroe has shown in detail that altruistic behavior—the willingness to risk one's life for the sake of others and in the absence of any immediate benefits to oneself—is explained in large part by the concept of identity.[43] People engage in altruistic behavior because acting in that fashion is consistent with their sense of self. Soss identified similar patterns among women choosing to apply for welfare benefits.[44] From the outside, behaviors may appear to be a choice, but the words of people actually performing these acts suggests that the path they follow is the only one they are aware of that does not clash with their identity.

Conceptualizing political behavior in this way can help us understand the link between motivations and behavior. Resource-based models of political participation argue that the costs of participation are high. Given this, we expect that people are only likely to engage in political and civic acts if they are motivated to do so.[45] Joanne Miller has examined the link between an array of political acts and five types of motivations: value expression, social, ego defensive, self-interest, and collective interest. She finds that value expression and collective interest have a significant, positive effect on the willingness to participate in a wide array of political acts besides voting.[46] Acting on the basis of the motivation of "value expression" is synonymous with the act of behaving in a manner consistent with one's identity. Unraveling what motivates these acts requires understanding individuals' perceptions of their place in the world.

We have seen in this chapter that the motivation to do interracial dialogue is embedded in personal histories, conceptualized not as an expedient way to deal with a pressing public issue but as part of individuals' identities. When individuals come together, all with particular identities, some with attachments to dominant racial groups and others with identities as members of marginalized racial groups, how do they negotiate the balance between unity and difference? The following chapter pursues this puzzle in detail.

CHAPTER SIX

Negotiating Unity and Difference

How do participants in race dialogue programs negotiate issues of unity vs. difference? In chapter 3, we saw that promotional pamphlets and facilitator guidebooks on civic intergroup dialogue programs portray these discussions as a place in the deliberative system for people of different racial backgrounds to listen to their differences *and* find common ground. Chapter 5 demonstrated that NGO and government practitioners alike make similar claims. These pieces of evidence tell us that civic intergroup dialogues are a space in which people are expected to negotiate a balance between unity and difference, but how do they do this? How do people collectively work out *whether* they should communicate in ways that pay attention to difference, and *how* do they make sense of themselves as members of the same community and yet people who identify with particular social groups?

Their task is greatly complicated because of the political culture in which they are embedded. As explained in chapter 2, research on public opinion shows that unity exerts a powerful pull in American political culture. Few members of the public support extreme unity in the form of an ethnocultural conception of national identity, but most people value unity to some degree. At the same time, very few people support extreme attention to difference, or "hard multiculturalism."[1] Instead, most people seem to support an incorporationist view, in which there is a mix of unity and difference.[2]

Perhaps the best way of describing how Americans feel about the proper way to reconcile unity and diversity is that they are very ambivalent about it.[3] Ambivalence over competing principles pervades American public opinion,[4] particularly attitudes related to race and ethnicity.[5] When given the chance to reconcile the polar forces of unity and diversity, how do people do it?

Thanks to Richard Merelman, Greg Streich, and Paul Martin, we know something about what goes on. These scholars studied the content of the National Endowment for the Humanities dialogues on American pluralism, specifically the content of twenty-one of the dialogues in the upper Midwest. They found that the conversations cycled back and forth between an emphasis on unity in the form of American national identity and on diversity in the form of ethnic and racial pluralism. Seven of these dialogues used a Study Circles format in which the participants met more than once. In five of these series, Merelman and colleagues observed that the later sessions emphasized national identity more than the first sessions, but these emphases on national identity were not typically positive.[6]

The dialogues Merelman and colleagues studied were about pluralism, but the groups were not encouraged to discuss race or institutional racism, and many rarely did so.[7] Thus several questions remain. What generates the cycling back and forth between unity and diversity when that pattern occurs? And in groups in which people are assembled for the purposes of talking about race relations—a more explicit call for attention to difference—what do these patterns look like? The questions are important because if movement toward unity occurs as a function of whites dominating the discussion, then difference democrats who critique deliberative practices will gain little solace from knowing dialogue is a part of the overall deliberative system. If conversations move toward an emphasis on racial and ethnic identity without attention to unity as well, then critics of multiculturalism will likely dismiss dialogue as divisive. And if the modal pattern is cycling, knowing how people collectively negotiate attention to both unity and difference will help illuminate the capacity of the deliberative system to give due attention to both of these polar forces. In other words, knowing that groups of people express ambivalence in the course of civic dialogue is important, but the next step is understanding how the process of reconciling competing considerations works.

Listening In on Race Dialogue Groups

To examine what goes on within civic interracial dialogues, I participated and observed the repeated discussions of six groups that met in four cities. The observation of the first group was a pilot study, and it consisted of observations of a ten-week city-sponsored study circle in Madison, Wisconsin, that met in the fall of 2000. I was not allowed to record these conversations, and I therefore rely primarily on the other five groups in the analyses below. These other groups met for four- or five-week sessions, and each of them met within the same six-week period in April and

May 2005.[8] In the methods appendix, I explain my case selection, procedures for gaining access, and other aspects of the participant observation
method in greater detail.

I chose these programs because they occurred in cities that were close
to one another, could be classified as medium-sized,[9] and because the
groups met concurrently and used the same Study Circles Resource Center curriculum, *The Busy Citizen's Discussion Guide: Facing the Challenge of
Racism and Race Relations*.[10] These similarities allowed me to examine how
the content of the conversation varied with the composition of the group
and the local context. The groups differed in important ways, including
the diversity of the groups, the participation of public officials, the time of
day during which they met, and the facilitators' styles.[11]

I intentionally chose to observe multiple groups in two of the cities
to probe the way conversations varied depending on the composition of
the group as opposed to the local context. Finally, I also chose these cases
to represent communities with varying degrees of racial and economic
diversity.

These criteria resulted in the following cases: two groups in Aurora,
Illinois, two in a "central Wisconsin" city, and one in a "southern Wisconsin" city. I refer to Madison and Aurora by name, but pledged a higher degree of confidentiality to the participants in the other cities, and therefore
refer to them only by their approximate location ("Southern Wisconsin"
and "Central Wisconsin").

Aurora was the most diverse city in the sample (52.1 percent non-
Hispanic white), and was distinctive in its large Hispanic population
(32 percent), which traced its origins back to a Mexican community that
started in the 1920s during the growth of the railroad industry.[12] The city
is economically very diverse, with both high-income neighborhoods and a
large amount of public housing.

Both Aurora and the southern Wisconsin city had reputations as cities
with high crime rates. The southern Wisconsin city had some of the high-
est unemployment in Wisconsin. Each city had at least one college within
its limits, but Madison was by far the most university-type town. It is also
a state capital.

Politically, Madison was the most liberal, as indicated by the partisanship of state and local officials elected from these cities, and the balance
of the presidential vote in 2004. The central Wisconsin city was the most
conservative by the same measures. The abundance of Bush/Cheney bum-
per stickers in town, and a billboard announcing "3 million unborn children who won't . . . pay social security taxes" near the entrance to the city
signified this leaning.

The methods appendix lists the pseudonyms and racial backgrounds of the participants of each of the groups, but a brief overview will illuminate the nature of these groups. The two groups that met in Aurora were quite different from each other. One group met on Monday nights at a local college and was facilitated by an African-American woman. It contained eleven members (including the facilitator and myself), four (36 percent) of whom were people of color. The facilitator's style differed markedly from the other facilitators in my sample. She repeatedly said that we were not restricted to the SCRC curriculum, and insisted that the conversation follow its own path. She never instructed us to read from the SCRC booklet during the sessions, in contrast to the other groups in which we would regularly read portions of the book aloud to one another. Whereas the discussion guide stated that facilitators should be neutral,[13] the facilitator in this group debated many of the participants' comments. Several of the group members were not comfortable with her style; two said so publicly in the group, and two said so in private conversations with me. Because the discussion in this group was more akin to debate than dialogue, it serves as a useful point of contrast to the processes that occurred in the other groups.

The second Aurora group met on Tuesday mornings. It included nine members, two of whom were people of color. The facilitator was a white woman. She contributed her own personal stories at times, but treated her role as one of moving the conversation along rather than of instructing participants when their perceptions did not resonate with her own.

The group in southern Wisconsin was the least diverse, although the city itself was racially heterogeneous (between 60 and 65 percent non-Hispanic white). It met on Thursday nights in a downtown church. It consisted of twelve members, three (25 percent) of whom were people of color.

The central Wisconsin city was the least diverse (between 90 and 95 percent non-Hispanic white). One of the two groups I observed in that city met on Wednesday mornings at the public library and was co-facilitated by a young white woman and a Mexican-American woman. There were eleven group members, three (27 percent) of whom were people of color. Two of the members, an African-American man and woman, were a married couple.

The other central Wisconsin group met on Thursday afternoons. The facilitator was a Hispanic woman who had an unusual and energizing style of walking around the table as the rest of us talked. There were nineteen participants, eight (42 percent) of whom were people of color. The African-American couple participated in this group as well.[14]

What Brought People to The Dialogues?

Typical mechanisms of political recruitment bring volunteers to the dialogues—word of mouth, local media, and organizations. Responses to the surveys given to Madison and Aurora participants demonstrated this, as did the introductions each participant made in the first session of the groups I observed.[15] Interviews with practitioners suggested that newer programs rely more on local media to recruit, while older programs had an ample supply of volunteers recruited through their large network of alumni.[16] Recruitment through media was done primarily through announcements attached to related articles in newspapers, particularly weeklies targeted to people of color and readers interested in civil rights.[17]

In the surveys and during the dialogues, many participants explained their choice to volunteer as a desire to improve race relations combined with a desire to think about one's own racial background. For example, many people cited a need to think about issues that had come up around their own multiracial identity, parenthood or grandparenthood of a child of a different racial background, an interracial marriage, living in an increasingly multiracial neighborhood, or suddenly moving to a homogenous white city from a more diverse place. Many people said they were spurred to volunteer by increasing diversity in their workplace.

A few people seemed to join because they were skeptical of the program, were concerned about the use of city resources or the way local activists expend their energy, and thus wanted to examine it from the inside.

Several people seemed to enroll in the dialogues merely as a way to pass their time. Some retirees said friends had suggested it as an interesting way to interact with other people. Christine from the Aurora Monday night group went so far as to say she had volunteered quite blindly: "I had no idea what this was about, didn't even know it was on racism, but I am in a book club and someone suggested that I would enjoy it."

Of the six groups I observed, approximately ten people had previously participated in a discussion group in their city's program. The majority of these people were people of color, one symptom of the programs' relative difficulty recruiting people who were not non-Hispanic white.

Only one person was required to participate, a woman in the southern Wisconsin group who was assigned to attend by supervisors at her corporation. They were considering using the program as part of their own human resources programming. Participants who were city employees were not required to attend. However, most of them were strongly encouraged to attend by supervisors and were allowed to do so during their normal working hours, as extra incentive. Besides pay for city employees, participants were not compensated for their attendance other than with snacks during the discussions, certificates, and in some programs commemorative pins upon graduation.

Most of the participants expressed a longstanding interest in intergroup relations or in people of other cultures. Their curiosity about other cultures or their desire to improve social justice had led them to self-select into neighborhoods, family environments, or occupations characterized by interracial relationships. Thus they are much akin to the activists who implement the programs. That is, it seemed that when the opportunity to engage in organized interracial dialogues arose, it resonated with their interests and conformed with other activities they enjoyed or valued, and so they volunteered.

In every type of race dialogue forum that I observed, from the six groups that met a minimum of four sessions to the one-shot PBS/Urban League forums for viewing and discussing documentaries related to race relations, at least one of the participants (aside from the facilitators) raised the question of "how are we going to move this into action?" Some people may have been involved for the sake of talking alone, but that seemed to be far from a universal motivation.[18]

The Structure of the Discussions

The Study Circles curriculum guide structures the sessions so that the discussions progress across the following topics:

Session 1:   "Race relations and racism: Experience, perceptions and beliefs"

Session 2:   "Dealing with race: What is the nature of the problem?"

Session 3:   "What should we do to make progress on race relations?"

Session 4:   "What kinds of public policies will help us deal with race relations?"

Session 5:   "How can we move from words to action in our community?"

There were several exceptions to this. In the central Wisconsin city, all of the groups that met during the same month held their fifth session together as an "action forum." The Aurora Monday night group did not follow the discussion guide and did not follow this progression of topics, although it did discuss some of the themes addressed by the other groups, as I examine below.

In the analyses in this chapter I study the dynamics of these various groups in detail, but I will briefly characterize here what the interaction was like. Each of the groups either sat in a circle around one big table or arranged several tables into a circle. The one exception was in Madison, in which we arranged our chairs into a circle with no table between us. Facilitators set a tone of hospitality by pointing out the nearest rest rooms at the start of the first session and often provided snacks and coffee or water. All of the sessions were two hours in length. The Aurora Tuesday morning group occasionally took a break during the session. In the other groups, individuals were invited to take a break when necessary.

The practice of sitting in circles and taking breaks as we wished exemplified an atmosphere of voluntary participation unified by a common purpose that characterized these groups. Those people who did not want to be there simply did not return after the first or second sessions. The sense of common purpose was reinforced by facilitators frequently asking participants to read portions of the curriculum aloud to get us all focused on the same topics and questions.

One of the remarkable things about these dialogues is that for as much as people avoid talking about race across racial lines, and as uncomfortable as the conversations can be, people readily took to it. Talking about race is a difficult and unfamiliar task even for the people who volunteer for these programs. But they jumped in, seizing the opportunity. As we will see in detail in chapter 8, some people were more outspoken than others, but it seemed like a very normal thing to be doing on, say, a Wednesday morning.[19] As soon as the facilitators asked us for initial introductions, the task at hand did not seem unusual. People readily talked about their own stereotypes and experiences with racism. The norm in all of the groups was to let people finish talking before contributing to the conversation, but people did occasionally interrupt one another. There was never any shouting, although several people did raise their voices in a way that conveyed frustration or particular passion on a topic. Only two people, in separate groups, shed tears (briefly).

Participants asked each other questions easily, and did not often wait for the facilitator to direct the conversation. At times, the facilitators would break us into pairs or smaller groups to talk over some of the viewpoints presented in the book and then reconvene the larger group to compare notes. There were silences at times, but these were pensive silences, not awkward ones. More commonly, several people wanted to talk at once, and the conversations had to be cut off at the end of the two hours despite participants' frequent desires to continue. This varied by facilitator and mix of participants—some conversations were more energized than others. However, even in two groups that got off to a slow start (the Aurora evening group and the southern Wisconsin group), by the fifth session, the talk flowed easily with all members of the group readily participating.

There was some initial mystery regarding the goal of the programs. Several participants asked pointed questions about what the purpose of the program was and what types of actions we would be taking afterwards, and one woman admitted that she had some hesitation about the political goals of the national sponsoring organization. But even these people stated in the last session that they had valued the experience.

Participants would often linger a bit afterward to talk with one another, especially after the later sessions. I noticed an atmosphere of friendship around each of these groups, although some personalities did clash. One example of this friendliness comes from the central Wisconsin Wednesday group. The group members shifted from strangers to friendly acquaintances within the first ten minutes of their first meeting. At the start of the session, I explained my purpose to the participants, passed out consent forms, and then left the room while the participants discussed whether or not to allow me to participate in and observe their group. When they called me back in approximately five minutes later, I noticed that the group members were already joking with one another and offering to serve each other coffee.

I tape-recorded and transcribed all of the sessions except for those in the Madison group, the Action Forum of the central Wisconsin groups, and the third session of the southern Wisconsin group, which I was unable to attend. In the excerpts below, I refer to the participants with pseudonyms. I insert my own clarifying statements in brackets, but present the conversations as they occurred verbatim. When a portion of the conversation has been omitted to condense it for presentation, I use the symbol "[. . .]." I use the symbol "==" to indicate interruptions.

Initial Statements Focus on Unity

I sought to learn whether the members of the groups focused on unity or difference, how they negotiated how to reconcile the two, and how they collectively figured out which lines of difference to pay attention to. The definition of unity I used in these analyses was a recognition or forging of shared membership in a given category or a shared identity, recognition of shared understandings or interpretations of events or issues, recognition of shared experience, or recognition of shared traditions. In this way, the unity I was looking for was a focus on similarity and overarching categories. I conceived of this as a contrast to a focus on difference, which I defined as attention to subgroup—particularly, racial group—distinctions. I expected that a focus on difference would take the form of talk about membership in or identity with social group categories (more specific than categories that included all of the participants), talk about variations in experiences across group members, or talk about variations in cultural traditions across group members.

As an initial step in my analysis, I coded my fieldnotes and transcriptions for evidence of unity and difference according to these definitions, and then examined how unity or difference arose over the course of each group's meetings. I then compared these patterns across groups to examine whether and how the process of balancing these competing influences varied.

Because the topic of these dialogues is race relations, we might expect that the people who volunteer for them come to the table ready to focus on difference. But this, notably, was not the case. The group discussions conveyed a great deal of ambivalence about the proper balance of unity and diversity, and surprisingly, there was a good bit of discussion about whether it is appropriate to focus on diversity at all. Many people began their initial sessions with strong presumptions about how to reconcile unity and diversity. And oftentimes the answer people tended toward was a privileging of unity.

This was particularly evident in the way participants introduced themselves. In each of the groups, at the beginning of the first session, the facilitators asked the participants to say a few words about why they had chosen to participate. In several groups, some of the participants expressed the desire to "better understand," but none of the participants introduced themselves as wanting to "celebrate difference" or "diversity." A far more common theme was the desire to "get beyond race," a desire for a "colorblind" society, or a belief that "underneath it all, we really are the same." This was expressed by people of color as well as whites. In addition to many people asserting a desire to recognize common memberships, many people (most frequently, but not exclusively, whites) *disdained* attention to racial categories. They talked about recognizing racial difference as a negative thing, not a step toward a more just democracy.

This attention to unity continued to appear periodically throughout the remaining meetings. One way it emerged was when the facilitators asked us to discuss definitions of race in the second session (except in the evening Aurora group). Commonly, when defining race people would offer up definitions that mentioned physical characteristics, primarily skin color, but would back away and say the only type of race we ought to focus on is "the human race." And again, it was not only whites who did this. In the first session of the Aurora group that met during the day, both the African-American and the Mexican-American members of the group offered up a colorblind ideal when talking about their early experiences with discrimination:

STEVE [African American]: [When I was growing up] there were two or three different communities that were outlined for blacks and we lived in that community. My parents from the time I can remember hearing them speak, they would instill in me that people are—it doesn't matter what color you are—people are just people. . . . My parents just instilled in me—people are people regardless of what color they are, don't let that be the basis for your judgment.

CILIA [Mexican American]: Mine is like Steve—we were brought up, too: "People are people." No color, no nothing, and we did live a lot in different projects. I remember one time in Jericho Circle [a housing development] and the majority of the people there are black. I always thought I was black in kindergarten, my mother put the braids on me and the beads, couple of my best friends were black and one day in an argument they told me I wasn't black. To me that was like, "What do you mean I am not black? I mean I eat with you, I sit with you!"

Wariness of privileging race was ubiquitous in these conversations. Surprisingly, these participants were not devout multiculturalists. In fact, the participants were often suspicious of multiculturalism at the same time that they were sympathetic to some of its aims. They seldom used the rhetoric of multiculturalism, rarely using terms like "multiculturalism," "difference" (in terms of race or ethnicity), or even "diversity." Instead, terms like "colorblindness" and the "human race" were more common. In addition, most participants seemed unfamiliar with common multicultural metaphors.

For example, in the central Wisconsin group that met in the public library, during the third session, the facilitators organized us into pairs. My partner was Samuel, an African-American male. In neither of the previous two sessions had anyone mentioned the terms "difference" or "multiculturalism." "Diversity" was mentioned only twice. We were asked to discuss our thoughts on "working together on common projects" as a way to "make progress on race relations." Part of this viewpoint read, "Shared projects—a park clean-up, for example—remind us of the things we have in common." I used the opportunity to ask Samuel for his thoughts on the politics of difference. I said, "I am questioning how much we should focus on common ground—I worry that that focus overlooks individuals' identities." In response, Samuel, said "I see what you are saying. That is so true. . . ."

When we reported back to the group as a whole, I said the following:

> We thought that working on common projects is a great way to connect people and build bridges. . . . But we actually spent a lot of time talking about the weaknesses. . . . We worried that sometimes this talk about consensus and coming together is not about "let's all contribute each equally," but "let's have people of color kind of give up some of their own subgroup identities to become a part of the mainstream."

At this point, Tizo, the Mexican-American facilitator, began nodding her head visibly, in contrast to her typical neutral stance. Samuel continued on by reciting a fable about an elephant and giraffe, frequently used in diversity training to illustrate how building relationships fails to work when people of different backgrounds expect others to adopt their own practices.[20] Tizo then referred us to the back cover of our guide which displayed a painting of a melting pot in drab colors and a salad bowl in bright colors. The point of the illustration was to portray the salad bowl (sometimes referred to as a "mosaic" by multiculturalists) as a positive alternative to the "melting" of all cultures into one.

Though Samuel had edged toward supporting a multicultural view, he continued by saying that we do not want one or the other of these models—we want a blend of both:

SAMUEL: By accepting new standards guess what? We create new norms, and by creating new norms, guess what? The other stuff just drops off, because we are working as a team, and we are doing it together, and it is not offensive because guess what? We are working together to bring change.
TIZO: So instead of the melting pot, you have the salad bowl like on the back [cover of our booklets].
SAMUEL: Well, well, it is a blend of both! Because we got a salad bowl, but also we melting off the old! But we are not forcing you to do it. You're doing it voluntarily by coming together in a group. So that makes it nonthreatening.

Samuel resisted the multicultural metaphor, and no one ever mentioned it again in that group. In the other central Wisconsin group, in which he also participated, Samuel again mentioned his vision of blending by melting off prejudices the next day. Ginger, an African-American woman expressed discomfort with the term:

GINGER: We don't see enough of cultures blending together.
SAMUEL: "Blending" is a good one.
GINGER: I don't know if that's the right word I want to use—but, we socialize, we don't come together. If there is something going on [like a cultural

event], that brings us all together. But still, you'll see everybody in their little clique-y group.

When the Aurora daytime group discussed that same part of the curriculum, that facilitator also brought up the salad bowl metaphor. Our conversation went as follows:

JUDY [facilitator, white]: Pretend you are a committee, have to decide where to focus school policy—look at the back of the book [pointing out that painting to us]. Do we work toward a total melting pot or toward the analogy of a salad, as a whole you end up with something that is greater than its individual parts?

WAYNE [white]: [Not directly answering her] View five [which states "People of color need to find strength in their own values and traditions"]. The mere fact that it is in this book does not mean that it is good to me. I read this and obviously this can not be positive. "We should strive to build cultural social political and economic institutions [that appreciate and emphasize the richness of our own cultures]." We've already done that [referring to racially exclusive clubs in town]. I don't believe in that. . . . That melting pot I believe is how we are going to succeed. . . . We can't have a Spanish section in the school and black section in the school and white section in the school—we have got to bring these children together so that generations can learn to live together and not listen to us parents that are still racist.

JUDY: So you want to put the emphasis on everyone coming together?

WAYNE: Melting pot . . . not saying that because you're Spanish you have to become white or Americanized, but bring your culture into ours and blend, and food can maybe connect us.

[. . .]

CILIA [Latina]: They use the Cinco de Mayo now. Schools *do* emphasize, learn the traditions. We have an assembly, and on Cinco de Mayo they have their dishes brought in, so I know there was one time [at one of the schools]—they even had a Chinese or Vietnamese day, and the kids learned from that.

[. . .]

KATHY [white]: So is that salad bowl or melting pot, like when the schools do that, and have a certain, like a Vietnamese day or whatever?

WAYNE: I think that is melting pot.

SARA (white): No way. They are keeping their==

WAYNE: Allowing the other cultures to see==

SARA: But then "to see IT." "It" is isolated, alone, like a carrot or a cucumber.

RACHEL: But then you make it into the salad.

The participants did not readily use multicultural terminology. Although race dialogue programs have been developed by people who are familiar with the scholarship of difference democrats, the people participating in the dialogues I observed did not come to the discussions with the politics of difference readily in mind. They seemed more familiar and at ease with the language of melting-pot assimilation.

There are even signs that the participants generally disparaged what Citrin and colleagues have called "hard multiculturalism."[21] During the third session of the central Wisconsin Thursday group, the facilitator asked the group to discuss the view that "People of color need to find strength in their own values and traditions." The group immediately pounced:

AL [white]: Isn't this [segregation] what we used to have?
Multiple people in the group say things like "yes" and "you are so right."
JOHN [white]: Makes no sense to even talk about it—that's why we're here.
[. . .]
A few seconds later in the conversation, an African-American woman says:
ADALINE: [This view] creates separatism, pessimism, because it says educating racist people is not the best use. It assumes you can not educate them. . . . But there is not anything wrong with having African-American businesses that cater to African Americans. Nothing wrong with that.
But a white woman in the group repudiates this:
JULIE: But you can't have it both ways, though. You can't have an all white place==
ADALINE: I'm talking about you have shops that can not cut African-American hair. Where are we going? We gonna have to go to Milwaukee. If there is a barber shop==
JULIE: But if I would come in, they couldn't say==
ADALINE: Yeah—Many times, they have to go to white schools to learn, so they can usually cut all hair [implying that they *could* cut Julie's hair].
JULIE: You can't have it both ways.
ADALINE: Just like you go into a Chinese neighborhood, there is a Chinese restaurant, sells Chinese food. It is OK to have cultural types of businesses.
JULIE: As long as anybody can go there—so it's not an all Chinese==
ADALINE: No—I'm talking about—No, No, No [realizing that Judy thought she was advocating businesses that would only serve African Americans]— It's a business that is *owned* by African Americans.

These participants objected to hard multiculturalism, or the idea that subgroup memberships and identities should take precedence over overarching categories. Contrary to what we might expect, that kind of a politics of difference was not at work in these dialogues.

The participants in these programs also defy expectations with respect to political ideology. At that same time that they were not in general avowed multiculturalists, they were not radical liberals. As the comments above convey, many of their comments were quite conservative, claiming that racism is either not pervasive, not a prominent problem, or not the result of institutionalized racism.[22] A few additional excerpts illustrate.

A white woman in a group in a central Wisconsin city, talking about how we ought to make progress on race relations:

> Right, and that goes to the feeling that things are owed—that they are still owed something. Let's just take today and what we have today, and if your education isn't where it should be, then just like me or anyone else, you have to improve on that to make it better. It doesn't matter what happened yesterday, we only have today. So if you're not where you want to be, we only have to give the same effort to get there.

A white man in the group in the southern Wisconsin city, denying that we ought to focus on race:

> I hear these things [stories of racial discrimination], I have no reason to believe that that's not occurring. But I'm worrying two things. What can we do about it—we are here but we're not the kind to perpetate those things hopefully, but what else can you do to change someone else's attitude? And I come back—I don't think that just people of race have to deal with the similar type of problem—probably old people, young people, heavy people, everyone is judged, discriminated against based on physical characteristics that have nothing to do with their character. I wonder if we dwell on it too much. If someone doesn't like me because I'm short, I can't do anything about it. If I lose a job, maybe I have to try harder or whatever. What can be done? Can anything be done about someone else's attitude? As sad or unfortunate as the stories are.

And a white woman in a group in Aurora, Illinois:

> My philosophy: we are the product of what we choose for ourselves. Granted, some people start out with a little more than others, but it is up to us. What I put in my mouth, what I put in my head—my reaction to things.

These comments are remarkable not because they were atypical in these discussions but because they did not generate responses. They fit in with the flow. The central tendency of the participants was without a doubt on the liberal end of the political ideology spectrum, but the variance was rather wide.[23]

Observers of other civic dialogue programs similarly find that participants in civic dialogue programs tend to include a range of people, not just
multiculturalists or liberals. In their study of the NEH National Conversations on American Pluralism and Identity, Merelman, Streich, and Martin
found that the 32 percent of participants who returned evaluation surveys
tended to be politically liberal and supportive of multiculturalism, but the
authors note a likely liberal bias among those who chose to respond to
their questionnaire.[24] Also, they found a good deal of ambivalence about
multiculturalism in the course of the discussions.[25] Matt Leighninger, a
former senior associate with the SCRC who became executive director of
the Deliberative Democracy Consortium in 2006, has been a practitioner
of civic deliberation, including dialogue programs on race, for over a de-
cade. He similarly observes that people implementing and volunteering
for these programs address the issue of difference from conservative as
well as liberal perspectives.[26] Also, Jacobs, Delli Carpini, and Cook note
that participants in face-to-face deliberation in general do seem to be a
biased reflection of the communities in which they meet, but are not as
unrepresentative as many critics of deliberation assert.[27]

Negotiating a Focus on Difference

Listening long enough to notice that participants in these programs
are not necessarily devout multiculturalists opens the way for analyzing the complex processes at work in these groups. It is not the case that
people simply come together to focus on difference. Instead, they arrive
at these groups with their feet firmly grounded in a unity-centered political culture. Do they, then, actually pay attention to difference, and if
so, how?

The reflections that people make at the end of their round of sessions
suggest that they do in fact pay attention to difference in these groups.
During the last sessions, it was common for participants to remark that
their "eyes had been opened." Participants in a variety of groups in Madison and Aurora besides those I observed made similar claims, as noted in
the evaluation surveys I conducted. An open-ended question revealed that
very few people perceived that their dialogues had achieved consensus or
common ground.[28] Instead, the most common response was that the dialogues achieved awareness of difference.[29]

In the course of the observations, I witnessed this understanding or
awareness of difference as whites expressing shock or surprise at the extent of discrimination in their own communities and at the barriers that
remained to people of color. But it was not only whites who expressed a

new awareness of differences. People of color expressed surprise at the perspectives held by whites, particularly at their lack of awareness of discrimination. In other words, a white person might say, "I had no idea that my African-American neighbor is followed through the store every time she shops for food." And an African American might say, "I had no idea that whites had no idea!"

The desire by many to believe that their groups were in consensus initially blinded them to the extent of conflict.[30] However, the structure of the communication enabled the talk to focus on difference. People struggled to reconcile the polar forces of unity and diversity in their political culture. Indeed, it is far more accurate to say that they struggled *to balance*, not *reconcile* the two.[31] The process was not always comfortable or admirable, but we can say that in its course, people were doing the work of giving meaning to multiculturalism, or to a conception of how people of diverse cultures ought to live together and govern one another.

Individual Investment in Unity and in Difference

One of the reasons that this process is best described as a struggle to balance rather than reconcile is that individual participants seldom showed any evidence that they actually did reconcile the tension between unity and difference. Indeed, some individuals never displayed awareness of the way in which they contradicted their support for unity with a desire to recognize difference as well.

Many of the participants came to the groups supporting some tenets of multiculturalism. For example, one of the central tenets of the politics of difference, that social group membership is correlated with experience and perspectives, seemed to be a given and a matter of common sense to many of these participants. They regularly remarked during the dialogues that having diverse groups is essential to these dialogues, for without having people of a wide variety of racial backgrounds in the group, certain perspectives would not be represented.[32]

Nevertheless, few stuck to such a storyline consistently. Liza, the African-American facilitator in the Aurora evening group, defended herself against complaints by some of the group members that she had diverged from her role as facilitator when she sought to lecture the group on how the experience of African Americans differs from that of whites. "I don't know how you expect me—or what your expectations were as to my participation. Obviously I have a thought and I am allowed to express it. Since I was the only African American here and there was no voice to speak for, hopefully I would be allowed to speak up for that." However, she had begun the dialogue round by talking about how we need to recognize how we are all the same.

This ambivalence across the statements of one person of both a desire to focus on the unifying category of all of humanity and a desire to recognize race was evident in the comments of other participants as well, sometimes within the same statement. In the other Aurora group, during the final session, the facilitator asked the African-American man for his thoughts on where he wished to target action toward improving race relations:

STEVE: Wherever there is young people involved . . . that's who's going to be leading the country. . . . I want my kids [who are biracial] to understand—I want them to know who they are—be aware of their heritage, and I try to stress to them that people are people and I think sometimes people may say—I do this a lot, talk to people on the phone and then they meet me and I can see it in the look on their face: "Oh! I didn't expect you to be black!" And it's like, why not? I mean is that supposed to be a compliment or what? Because it isn't.

KATHY [white]: Do they actually say that?

STEVE: A number have, but most of the time I can see it on their face. "This isn't quite what I expected." But why is that? Why? Why? And people will say, "You know you are a credit to your race." Well, what race? Black? Or human race? You know? And I think we need to stress that if there is a decent human being, you are a credit to the human, not Spanish, black. I guess my work would be with young people.

Later in that meeting, while talking about the kind of action he plans to take after finishing the discussions, Steve said:

Personal, just being cognizant of my own prejudices. Prejudice is just a prejudgment of someone . . . get so used to dealing with people, making assumptions, all kinds of people. Racism—it is always before me, has always been before me—whether it is because I bring it about or other people make me feel that way. Growing up, when I was four, my bus driver, school teacher, lady at the grocery store, principal, the police officer—they were all white, so I feel like I have a pretty good handle on what white people are like, but not how white people—a large black man—we are not all angry, or Malcom X.

On the surface, Steve's comments stress unity. He says that "People are people" and that people should attribute praise due him not to a particular race but to the human race. Moreover, he laments that people assume he is angry simply because he is a large black male. But his comments call for attention to difference, not avoidance of it. These are not comments that race should be ignored, but rather an assertion that it should not be used to discriminate against other human beings. These comments are part of difference-focused communication because they say, "Look, this is what it is like to live in this community as a black man."

"What the Hell Do I Call You?"

The existence of this ambivalence on the individual level made for a more powerful struggle on the collective level. The process of balancing was not simply the act of multiculturalists locking horns with liberal individualists. The groups never drew such distinct lines. Many of the participants were simultaneously invested in the tenets of multiculturalism and the politics of unity.

The struggle took place on an unsteady platform of little solid unity. Despite the common rhetoric of unity in the use of terms and phrases like "colorblindness," few people actually identified a source of similarity across people. The topic of universal norms of behavior (such as abhorring murder) or universal values (such as valuing happiness) did not arise in any of the groups. Nor did people talk about how certain life experiences (e.g., parenthood, marriage, death of a loved one) are common to many people. And despite claims by people of all races in these groups that "people are people," the only way in which this was explained in detail was, ironically, through talk about the common tendency among human beings to categorize others into groups. When participants did identify common experiences, this took two forms: (1) shared recollections of television shows, and (2) recognition of the similar experience of hearing racist statements made by relatives. (These latter similarities were only acknowledged among white participants.)

Did the groups balance unity and diversity by focusing on overarching categories other than humanity as a whole? This occurred only in one group, the Aurora daytime group. One participant talked about the need to foster an overarching identity with the city as a whole:

CILIA [Latina]: More like a community thing, it is not the East Side of Aurora. It is Aurora. Not the West Side of Aurora. It is Aurora. The town, we are creating it. We're getting bigger, we have to make it a community thing, not just an East Side thing. Let's get the East Side [the less affluent side of town]. I do see a lot of groups are going out there—a lot of neighborhoods are doing their own groups to get rid of crime, take care of their areas, but . . . it is our city we're living in here. We don't want to be known as the "almost Chicago" with all the murders, gangs. We want to be known for something else. And I think it is just more community involvement and everything.

This statement was not commented upon by any of the other participants, in this or subsequent sessions.

Identity as Americans did indeed come up, but these discussions were about whether or not people ought to refer to others as members of particular racial or ethnic categories or simply as "Americans." Although the groups were not asked to discuss what labels to use to refer to different racial groups, every group talked about this topic. And rather than these conversations serving as a way to recognize or produce unity, they stopped the advance of unity in its tracks and forced the groups to confront the balance of unity and difference.

For example, in the Aurora daytime group, in the second session when discussing the definition of "race," Wayne brought up racial categories commonly used on government forms such as the Census. The Hispanic woman in the group said:

CILIA: In my time, Caucasian was the white, Hispanic or Latin—anybody from Latin race.
WAYNE [white]: What is "Latin"?
CILIA: Mexican.
WAYNE: You are using a term that seriously I don't recognize. Latin is a language.
CILIA: Yeah . . .
WAYNE: Where does "Latin" come from?
RACHEL [white]: You could ask Dan Quayle, he was going to go to Mexico and learn Latin [laughter].
WAYNE: OK, "Latin America" meaning that section of the world.
STEVE [African American]: Latinos—Latin language is something different.
WAYNE: OK then, "Hispanic." What does that mean?
SARA [white]: From Hispania.
RACHEL: Hispaniola.
SARA: It's a geographic connotation.
WAYNE: There's a Hispania?
JUDY [facilitator, white]: The Caribbean.
RACHEL: So I would just go with the flow, didn't make any difference to me—I would go with this group, maybe I didn't see or didn't want to see the differences?
WAYNE: I apologize [laughing].
CILIA: No it's good [to discuss it].
WAYNE: My father-in-law . . . said, "I am Mexican, I am not Hispanic, not Latino, I come from Mexico (he would say 'mehico') and nothing to be ashamed of." Pretty sharp man. Don't have to be Hispanic to be accepted.

Later on in the conversation:

RACHEL: Funny because the Puerto Ricans don't like to be called Mexican. A guy got insulted when I thought he was Mexican.

ELNOR (white): When is the term "Latino" correct, "Hispanic" correct?

CILIA: Well to me Latino means South American, Colombian . . . people from that area. Maybe I am understanding that wrong, too.

JUDY: My general understanding is that when I hear Latin America, I think South America, but from past participants, even in groups there is a lot of disagreements about what to call people, and that makes it all the more difficult for those of us who are not in the group. In the white group, in the African-American group there are differences.

STEVE: Absolutely. I say black, because that is what I grew up with, am comfortable with. But there are blacks who would rather be referred to as African Americans, which is not an issue for me, but that is the way it is. And it has changed. It has changed in our lifetime.

And the topic of the definition of different labels came up again during our break, when Sara asked about the meaning of "Chicano."[33]

This discussion is typical of the conversations about racial labels because it took the form of information-gathering and expressions of uncertainty over the appropriate labels to use. But sometimes conversations about racial labels would go further. People would talk about why it was necessary to use a subgroup label at all. The conversations would then become an open debate about the appropriate balance of unity and diversity.

This occurred in the central Wisconsin group that met on Thursdays. For example:

DON [white]: I have a question. Why do we hyphenate certain names? Why do we call ourselves African-American, Scottish-American? We are American. And I am confused as to what do I refer to when I am speaking about your particular race [looking at the African-American people at the table]. Are you African American? Are you black? Are you negro? Are you people of color? We have heard all those things come out. What the hell do I call you? [People giggle a bit as it is clear he is partly joking.] You can call *me* an American.

In the following, I relay the way this conversation progressed. The remarks illustrate that in these discussions the clash of perspectives *did* get attention, despite the desire of many to stick to unity. In particular, it is the comments of members of marginalized groups that encouraged whites to notice why labels matter. This basic pattern appeared across all of the groups.

In response to Don's question, the facilitator called on Ginger, an African-American woman in the group:

GINGER: First you can call me by my name [laughter]. Whether one individual of color wants to be called African American, [or] black—It is your time frame in life. It is what your struggle has already been up until this point. My mom, you know she may prefer to be called black==

BERNITA [Ginger's mom, an African American, smiling]: Colored.

GINGER: [concedes, laughing a bit] Or colored. Probably my *grandmother* wouldn't have minded colored. To me, when you—it is a label, you're right. We're all Americans, but when I am called colored it brings back a negative history. It reminds me of things I don't want to be reminded of. We have moved past that. I prefer African American, because that is a more positive label and it shows that we have come a long way but we're not where we should be in society and everything else. So when you say such labels as "African American" the time frame makes me think of—you know, I remember back when people were called colored and it was the civil rights and they were sickin' dogs on us, they was beating us and I don't prefer that.

Several minutes later, Samuel sounds a theme of unity:

SAMUEL [African American]: I'll be honest with you, since I was a kid, haven't labeled myself anything but American. But I got in a lot of trouble with that from both sides of the line [later he explains that he means from whites as well as from blacks]. I had to be something. Definitely not white. Definitely not Italian. But generation to come, we are going to get to the point that we are going to see people as Americans. [Several in the group say "uh huh."] And I'll be glad to see that.

MARIA [Latina facilitator]: That's your point, right Don?

DON: That s right.

ADALINE [African American]: And also, Don, I think—they identified us, because they tried to strip us of our heritage. But to say African American—hey it's "now I have some roots" and so that is probably the best term to use, but it doesn't hurt to ask, "Do you mind? Are you African American? Or would you prefer to be called something else?" But finally we belong because they tried to strip us of everything we had.

To this point in the conversation, a theme of unity and belonging to an overarching group remains strong. But when a white person starts to talk about unity in a way that denies difference, Samuel, an African American, pulls him back, as the following comments show. The conversation followed Adaline's comment (above) with the following:

JOHN [white]: When I was in Milwaukee back in the '60s, some friends and work-related people were black. When we had a discussion, that was another person. Color was nothing. It was just another person. To me, the Green Bay Packers are a team—they have to be that way, can't be a team if they look at each others' difference.

And in response to this last remark, Samuel, who had seconds ago mentioned the overarching category Americans, makes a call to recognize difference:

SAMUEL: Can I say something, John? And I don't mean to be abrasive, but for us blacks, we hear white people say that all the time to us.
MARIA [Latina, facilitator]: Say what, Samuel?
SAMUEL: Say that, ah, "It don't make a difference—my best friend is black, color don't mean anything." We hear that all the time, but in reality it *do* make a difference.
ADALINE: When push comes to shove.
SAMUEL: When push comes to shove, it makes a difference.

In this conversation there is not only a push and pull of unity and diversity, but an airing of viewpoints among African Americans. In a comment later in this session, Bill, a white man, acknowledges that hearing these perspectives matters for his own interpretation:

One thing you said though—Samuel and Adaline—that struck a chord—when someone categorizes you as a term, African American, part of the problem you have is you look back into a vacuum, don't have a foundation, positive association because you've been demeaned. But on the other hand for a white person, you don't have that experience. We are somewhat creatures of our own history.

What Bill claimed to have heard seems different than the intention behind Adaline's earlier statement. However, his statement that it "struck a chord" is an important signal: it signals that some listening was going on, that something in their experience rang true with him.

Importantly, this listening often took the form of whites attending to the perspectives of people of color. When the groups discussed the definition of race and whether we ought to pay attention to racial subgroup categories, both whites and people of color mentioned the desire to treat all people as humans. But when these claims were challenged, *in all cases* these challenges came from racial minorities. For example, when the central Wisconsin group that met on Wednesdays in the public library discussed the definition of race, and various group members tried to focus on "the human race" rather than race, an African American and the Mexican-American co-facilitator challenged this trajectory:

TOZI [Mexican-American co-facilitator]: What is race?

MIKE [white]: The human race, I think that would be a nice goal, to just have the human race, to just have people at some point choose to differentiate based on other things. Their skin color is the primary one that I am aware of.

[But then, the African-American male in the group challenges this leaning toward unity.]

SAMUEL [African American]: Well like I said before, it is a group of people that have the same kind of—blacks got their thing, whites got their thing—their culture, blacks eat soul food, things they have, things that they identify with.

VALERIE [white co-facilitator]: . . . If you have a black parent or a Hispanic parent and you ask that family what is the child—and they would say this child is Hispanic and this child looks pretty African American to me. . . . So is race a choice?

JOHN [white]: It almost is. You check it yourself. If you are talking about an application or what you would consider, the Census, you check what you want. . . .

[Then the Mexican-American facilitator asks him to reconsider.]

TOZI: So say someone is here and you needed to explain to them that they needed to—you know race is—what would your definition be, how would you explain that to them?

KATHY [white]: If we would explain to an outsider, an alien, I think it would not so much be a choice, but something that is forced on people—not forced, but something that society has developed—so we have a sense of what a black person is, or a sense of what a Latino is or Hispanic person is or Asian American is—so I think it is choice and also the way society kind of creates a definition of the categories that matter.

JOHN [agreeing a bit that race is socially constructed]: I think that is kind of—there is an American view of what it is, and then there is what the rest of—people in Brazil who have a little darker skin tone, that someone who is pure white, they consider themselves white [but] in this country they probably wouldn't be considered white.

ADALINE [African-American]: That's right.

JOHN: So I think it depends on your context.

MARY [white]: I think we should put a question mark! I don't think there is anything . . .

MARGARET [white]: We should pull the Census figures and just write down human.

[. . .]

TOZI: I think that is the lovely way of saying that—"the human race," but we need to know what that is in order to break it down as to why there is racism.

JOHN: Well I think that some people consider people different—they aren't quite human, as human as a white person might be. I mean that is the basis of it.

TOZI: So are we getting down to skin color?

[Group members say "Yeah, yeah," and laugh.]

In the end, Tozi, the Mexican-American facilitator, encourages the whites in the group to not avoid defining race but instead to recognize that much of the popular meaning of race hinges on color. When people of color made these kinds of challenges, their remarks alerted people to the relevance of race in contemporary life, despite the group members' desires to not use racial categories to distinguish people.

These group discussions were heavy with statements desiring to see "people as people." But the mix of participants in these groups prevented that from happening. The comments of Samuel and Tozi above exemplify a general pattern: when one or more people sounded a theme of unity, people of color in the groups would make a plea or insert a story that asked their fellow members to listen and pay attention to difference.

"Why Is Culture Important?"

Even though people of color would commonly challenge assertions that the groups ought to focus on unity, the conversations did not necessarily shift to a sustained attention to difference. The process of negotiating whether to focus on difference was an ongoing task.

The following series of conversations serves as an example. The conversations took place over several meetings of the evening Aurora group. In the first excerpt, we see a clash between the multicultural perspective of Lucy, a young Puerto Rican woman, and Christine, an older white woman. Liza, the African-American facilitator, demonstrates her own ambivalence on the proper balance between unity and diversity as she supports Lucy's insistence that subgroup identity matters, and yet bristles when she perceives that Christine is denying that identity prevents her from qualifying as an American. In addition, although Christine insists that subgroup identities should not be important, she takes umbrage with too much focus on unity in the form of nationalism. In this and the subsequent conversations excerpted below we see people struggling as a group to negotiate "the" proper balance between subgroup and overarching categories.

Although this group did not stick to the study guide, they spent much of the second session talking about racial group labels, just as the other groups did. At the beginning of the second session, Liza, the facilitator, started off by asking, "Will there ever come a time when we will be rid of racism?"

BETH [white]: Yes ! Yes! When we all intermarry and we are all the same color.

CHRISTINE [white]: But there are many, many other "isms," racisms. . . .

[. . .]

LUCY [Puerto Rican]: I was getting a blood test done. . . . It was really out of the blue, so didn't get it, thought it was just, "So hey where are you from?" Just like in conversation, and I said, "Oh, I am Puerto Rican," and she looked really confused, looked at her papers, and came back to me and said, "So I think I have to put you down as Pacific Islander?" [in questioning tone]. [The group laughs.] I didn't get that, "Oh, you needed to check a box." I explained that it was part of the United States.

To this point in the conversations in this group, much attention had been paid to the perspective of marginalized groups, especially to the viewpoint of African Americans, as represented by the facilitator. But shortly after this story, Christine, a white woman, starts to argue that recognizing subgroups is detrimental:

BETH: So in other words, that is the first thing we have to learn about people, is how to identify them.

CHRISTINE: Why do we have to?

LUCY: Why do we have to?!! Because look at where we are today, because we are ignorant, and we are about this part of the globe (puts thumb and index finger together) and the rest of the globe on that world map—we are just sort of like, "OK, you can learn it if you want to earn extra credit." . . . Even when teaching about our culture, it is from a very particular perspective, very particular view, when talking about our own history. . . .

[. . .]

CHRISTINE: Why is culture important?

LUCY: To me?

CHRISTINE: To anyone. You can only comment on what it means to you.

LUCY: Ummm. Mine is important because it defines who I am, where I come from, it helps me to understand how I got to be here and understanding other people's cultures is important. It will help me to understand what makes them come to the decisions they come to, especially living in this country when there are people from other cultures that come to this country. . . .

CHRISTINE: ==I just think it is divisive. You know I don't think we're ever going to get rid of racism until we stop having such emphasis on being the ethnic part or—I guess because I don't have any [laughs to herself]. . . .

BETH: But there are certain qualities that are instilled in people==

CHRISTINE: So get over it!

BETH: I mean like if you are doing business with somebody from China or Japan, they are very reserved and very formal, and when you are doing business with them you really have to sort of adjust to their mold.

CHRISTINE: If they are from the orient, but if they are here second generation, I think they should be assimilated by now. . . . [. . .] I can understand all that—wanting to know what other cultures are about, but why you have to assume that that's who you are is amazing to me. I guess I had a grandfather that—didn't know what he was. And I got such a mixture of blood in me that I have never claimed any one thing as being responsible for my behavior, and it is just==

BETH: Well I don't think of it in terms of behavior, it identifies who she is.

LUCY: There are certain types of music that I am drawn to, drawn to it. Don't know why that is, maybe because I grew up with it, but I will hear it in other types of music that you know, it is interesting to me, there are certain types of foods that, um, certain smells that just taste good to me, some things that don't. My culture has affected how I think and how—and when I see people, if I am meeting somebody new who is within my family, especially another Puerto Rican, I greet that person differently. We are very touchy-feely, hug and kiss, we greet each other differently, and that is part of who I am and it has everything to do with my culture.

BETH: I think we should celebrate diversity myself. I think this would be a very boring world if we were all homogenous.

[. . .]

LIZA [African-American, facilitator]: . . . Goes back to another point that Lucy raised, how she is being referred to, and how each person could possibly refer to themselves and it is how you see yourself. And how you accept what is ascribed to you, that becomes a label. . . . At the base of our very beginning, we are attracted to things, and we have to kind of find out why we are attracted to them, certain sounds, certain smells, certain tastes. . . . And other people take that and put that label on a whole group of people. . . . Just let me give you an example. . . . Because it may not be acceptable at that time, or because there is a different interpretation, I am labeled an "angry woman," and then I can walk around with that label. . . . My whole point is, do you see how we bear labels that other people put on us? It doesn't have to be so.

Later on in the conversation, Christine fervently opposes nationalism and ethnocentrism. A white man, Matt, had mentioned flag waving after 9/11, and Christine jumps in:

CHRISTINE: That is what I saw flag-waving as. An exclusive group that—you weren't patriotic or you weren't an American if you weren't pro-war and you put a flag on your car on wherever, on your chest, to prove that you were the patriot. . . . I wore a "no war" button with an American flag under it, so I don't know where you would put me there.

AMAAL [Arab American]: That's wonderful. That's different. Because we are forced to make this dichotomy. Why do we have to choose either?

LIZA [shifting the topic a bit]: Does anybody think about the people who wave their flags and occasionally wear sheets and white hoods?

CHRISTINE: I had a grandfather who did that.

LIZA: Oh do you?

KATHY [white]: Wow.

CHRISTINE: I was very, very little, didn't even know. My grandmother said "give me that." But later, I had the flashback that I had found this hood.

[. . .]

BETH: Seems to me a lot of people when they get round in their fifties about, that's when they seem to start to need to find out where they came from.

LUCY: Well, it was a lot earlier for me. [To Christine:] I'm really curious why you don't have that interest at all.

CHRISTINE: Because I think we are all children of God and I start with that. And I believe that's the commonality and our differences can be fun and they can be interesting, but I don't think they should divide us and I think when you hang onto them, they tend to, that diversity is divisive to me.

Then, Beth says, "In college, two of my best friends were black" and proceeds to explain that she and her college friends had learned a great deal from each other. This starts a ten-minute instruction from Elic and Liza to Beth about how it is inappropriate to refer to the race of her friends and how, if she had said that in any other context, African Americans present would assume she had "issues" with race.[34]

Later on in the conversation the question of labels reemerges:

CHRISTINE: So how do you define yourself if you are mixed blood? How do you see yourself?

LUCY: You are "other."

CHRISTINE: I mean internally.

LIZA: How do I see myself?

ELIC [African American]: Well, no, as a person.

LUCY [turning to Christine]: Well, it would be a more interesting question to pose to you. How do *you*?

ELIC: No. I think it is a legitimate question [to ask Liza].

LIZA: I don't mind answering that question at all. I just see myself as a person, as a human being, I identify more closely with the African American culture. I'm like Lucy, you know there are certain sounds that attract my attention more than others, certain smells, certain tastes, that attract me more than others, and I think that—I hope certainly, because I work at it as a life goal that I see myself enough as a person that wherever I am planted that I can accept my fellow man and try to function in that environment as a whole person.

CHRISTINE: Well that would be the end of racism if we could all do that. But I don't think that works. I think that everybody takes on an identity from their culture.

LIZA: And I don't have any problem with that because—there is nothing in my culture that makes me ashamed of who I am.

LUCY: And aren't we driven to—I mean I don't know how you get away from that. I think we are driven to understand ourselves. There is sort of this need to. And you say you don't have that.

CHRISTINE: No I don't.

LUCY: That is fascinating to me. I think you are the only person I have ever met==

CHRISTINE: Really?

LUCY: ==that absolutely does not.

CHRISTINE: Well there's so many, I've got so much mixed blood that I don't know what to blame anything on [she chuckles]. I'm not typical anything, I was raised as an American.

LIZA: Well so was I, Christine, but ==

CHRISTINE: There isn't any culture that I could trace to—my father, yeah he made sauerkraut. [A few people laugh.]

And then early in the next session of this group, Adam, one of the white male participants, says the following while arguing with Liza, the facilitator, about the intention of one of his statements about public schooling:

The biggest issue—I mean I think we all want the same thing in this room, to just be honest—what you would call a colorblind society or an ethnically blind society, the issue is how you get from point A to point B. That's why I come to these discussions to find out ideas about how you get—you know this is my third one and I haven't encountered too many crackers along the way, so I think we are generally in agreement that society would be better off if people would accept each other as individuals and not objectify each other.

His statement is met with nods.

Across these sessions, there was considerable ambivalence in the group about whether to prefer a society in which race is recognized versus one in which race is overcome. Perhaps Christine was just being difficult. But whatever motivated her comments, they were taken seriously by the others in the group. They fueled the others' struggle with the proper place of cultural difference.

Two sessions later, in the final session, there was a long pause near the beginning of the session, and I took the opportunity to ask the group directly if what they wanted was a colorblind society, as Adam had asserted in the previous session:

KATHY: I have a question . . . and tell me if I am getting off track. But to what extent do we want a colorblind society?

ADAM [white]: Well, there's a colorblind colorful society, because actually I wouldn't want us all to intermarry and all look the same. . . . We shouldn't all be the same, but it should be colorblind—discrimination free, not colorblind.

BETH: Well, we want to be unique in some way, this is our identity. And I agree that we just have to overlook whatever—not overlook, there just shouldn't be barriers between—should treat everybody alike.

[. . .]

LUCY: Like Christine, who isn't here today, but she talked about how, towards the beginning [of our meetings (referring to the conversation quoted above)], I may not be getting this right, but she said something like, "You know, the more people want to define themselves as a particular way or hold on to what ever these differences are, the more that um that it separates people." And not only that, but, "It shouldn't matter, because we are all God's children." She doesn't want to identify herself as any one particular—because she has so many different types of people in her family that she doesn't want to identify as one or the other, it shouldn't matter because we are all just God's children. And that is kind of the same question that you are asking.

KATHY: Yeah—so what do you think?

LUCY: I don't think so. I was—I think when she said that I was—I didn't get it, I was surprised, surprised that someone would think that way because, you know—but I think it's, um, I think that is just a really dangerous way to look at people. I think it is just an easy way to say, "I don't even want to be bothered to learn about your culture. I don't want to be bothered to learn where you're from. It really doesn't matter because we are all God's children." But the reality is, you know, if I'm not a Christian, I am not your God's child, and if I'm not—if that were the case, you know, to be told, "We're all God's children," I think that would be really patronizing to a lot of people.

BETH: I think the difference is between noticing and judging. I think it is OK to notice the person's skin color, but when you follow it with judgment, that's—that's the division.

[. . .]

ELIC: Your statement about colorblind [to me], from my perspective, I think what people want to say is, "I do not associate with certain colors, certain characteristics." So like colorblind in that sense because when you see a person that looks different from the mainstream, certain images come up, and the images are negative and if you are a thoughtful person, you will reject those negative images that go along with it. That's a good person. . . .

AMAAL: My reflection on that, Kathy, is that there is a fine line—can be a fine line between desiring to celebrate our culture or our otherness, wherever we are you know, on the periphery of things, and then we want to celebrate it in a way that doesn't dampen the voice of others. And so sometimes when people are not open to that, I think maybe they feel that in other people celebrating their differentness, or their otherness, they felt their voice was dampened. And maybe that happened. But I think it is very important to enjoy differences and learn from each other. . . . We have mainstream society at the center and we have these people that are on the periphery . . . the ones that really haven't even been named . . . there has not even been acknowledgement . . . that they are being treated unjustly. . . . And they have to celebrate to be able to come in, and then it's important that when people come in, they don't dampen the voices of people on the periphery. . . . I think we should all be watching who is on the periphery. . . . if we want to be socially responsible toward one another.

LIZA: . . . Whether or not we want a colorblind society may not be of our choosing. It probably is just going to be something that is just going to evolve. And it has already begun, with our young people. . . . I think the more in this society that that particular age group blends and blends and blends, we will see more intermarriages, like Beth expressed, that intermarriage is going to bring a shade of color. It is just going to happen. I don't care. So we may not have a whole lot of choice about color. We do about culture. Because you can still do that and maintain your own culture, even in an intensely personal interpersonal relationship like marriage.

Near the end of the session, Dolores returns to this theme:

DOLORES [white]: It kind of goes back to Christine's comment—I heard that a little bit differently, too. I heard her saying that in her mind we are all equal, that we all have dignity and worth and that we should respect that. That's what I heard . . . but I am not denying that it could sound different to different people. That's what I heard. And I don't think that we are ever going to make any changes anywhere unless we take that approach that everybody has dignity and worth and is worthy of respect. It just seems really basic. A lot hinges on it.

Even when Christine was absent in this last session, these group members tried to sort out the proper balance between unity and difference. Across the discussions of this group we see various people groping for unity or a society where color does not matter. But continually, people of color in particular asserted the value of cultural diversity and questioned whether we wish to ignore difference. Participants did use unity as a fallback in these conversations, as the polite route. And yet the structure of these dialogues allowed for people to challenge the mainstream frame of common ground. In the context of this alternative form of communication, it becomes acceptable for members of marginalized groups to articulate their perspectives.

The pattern is more complex than whites asserting unity and people of color tugging them back with assertions of diversity. People of color strive for unity at times, as seen in Liza's remarks that she disdains being labeled an "angry woman." And whites at times assert the value of recognizing diversity. *Collectively,* these groups consider the trade-offs. They are neither hard multiculturalists nor people unaware of the power of subgroup categories in social and political life or in self-esteem. Instead, they are ordinary citizens, using the opportunity to find a balance that makes sense in their community.

It is interesting that these people do consider the trade-offs between unity and diversity as well as they do, given the volatility of the topic and, in particular, given that years of experiment-based research has suggested that intergroup contact is inherently precarious. From work on the contact hypothesis, we have learned that reducing prejudice through intergroup interaction requires careful control of the characteristics of that interaction. As noted in chapter 2, some of this recent scholarship prescribes an emphasis on overarching as well as subgroup categories. Such an emphasis might seem unlikely for people in a discussion group to achieve, particularly a group that follows no set curriculum, given the strong pull toward unity in the political culture. However, we can see people in this Aurora group considering both overarching and subgroup categories, even without much structure. They do not have a protocol of an experiment or a university course syllabus to guide them. These participants were raising the trade-offs of their own accord.

Perhaps most notable in this respect is the way that they consider both cultural pride and the dangers of nationalism. Christine disagrees that racial identity ought to be emphasized, but at the same time disdains jingoistic patriotism. In the course of the second session, she and others in the group readily acknowledge that the denial of subgroup categories can be taken to extremes in the form of nationalism. Although the logic of unity "turns the merely different into the absolutely other,"[35] this group follows a different path. They seem to distinguish positive or prideful patriotism from negative patriotism or nationalism.[36]

In these struggles we see the way in which this difference-focused talk is not just about recognizing group differences or identities. It is often about the struggle over whose voice gets heard. Who labels is an expression of who has power. Allowing members of subgroups to name themselves is empowering because it enables people who identify with that category to have some control over its meaning.[37] Asserting what one is to be called by others is an important exercise of autonomy and accomplishment of recognition.[38] Thus debates over labeling conveyed curiosity at times, but they also conveyed a struggle over power, a dynamic I explore more deeply in chapter 8.

Listening and Accepting

Did these contributions to the dialogue really cause people to listen and rethink their perceptions? In the parlance of a leading model of public opinion, did people not only receive the messages they encountered in these groups but accept them into the range of considerations stored in their minds as well?[39] The content of the dialogues suggest that many people did use what they heard to achieve a different understanding.

It is obvious that Lucy listened to what Christine said—that a person of color paid attention to what was said by a white—and heard that some people see little utility in paying attention to subgroup identity. But do these conversations challenge the assumption among critics of deliberation that, in public talk, members of dominant groups do not listen and members of marginalized groups do not have the opportunity to voice their views? Yes. Christine may not have changed her mind about the value of subgroup identity, but she engages the claim directly, face-to-face, with someone who articulately defends the importance of ethnic identity. The fact that this conversation happened—not its effect—is in itself a democratic value. And the conversation is itself action and a part of civic life.

In addition, the conversations in the other groups display that whites listened to people of color. To illustrate, I focus on conversations centering around one white man in the central Wisconsin Thursday group, Don. His remarks throughout these sessions conveyed frustration and an active attempt to figure things out—he called this, simply, "confusion."

In the first session, he introduces himself as the son of southern European immigrants and notes that he himself had experienced several cases of severe discrimination in town. People of color around the table then contribute numerous stories of their experiences with discrimination in this central Wisconsin city. When the group reconvenes a week later, he wonders aloud if it is a bad thing that blacks live together, given that this is a pattern that immigrants to the United States, such as members of his family, have exhibited throughout history. Several people in the group, including a white male and an African-American woman, respond that the segregation experienced by early European immigrants is different than that experienced by blacks today. Don responds in a way that suggests he is listening to these stories: "I hear what you are saying: You may have the ability to move anywhere you want, but the acceptance may not be there."

Later in the conversation, he comments that separatist practices such as Miss Black America pageants are problematic. He pulls out a newspaper clipping about a police department hiring case in Milwaukee and calls this and several other cases reverse discrimination. At this point, the Mexican-American facilitator stops him and asks him to consider what he is hearing at the table—not about what is going on in other communities.

He does not respond, but later on makes a statement that suggests, again, that he is hearing some of the stories of people of color at the table:

> I probably had very little discrimination against me, but there has been some. But I can't imagine, can't even come close to imagining how you must have felt [looking at the African Americans at the table], how you must feel every day. I can't. And until we can, I don't want to be negative about this—we've got a hell of a job on our hands.

In the fourth session, the last time the group meets as a whole (before the fifth and final "action forum" session with the other groups in their city), the participants are discussing six different views on the "kinds of public policies [that] will help us deal with race relations." Ginger, an African-American woman, settles on one policy in particular and notes how the people of color in the group have brought unique perspectives to the discussions.

> The viewpoint in number five—we just "review our policies, take the racism out"—that hit the nail on the head. These sessions here—a lot of times, I think if you have not been in the midst of certain situations, the way minorities have, it is hard for you to get an understanding. Because I have heard around the table that even from the most simplest thing like living in a community but you've gotta go out of the community to get your hair done. I mean *the most simplest thing.* And I think these circles help individuals who don't come in contact with these types of situations to get more of an understanding and a grasp. That viewpoint is right on the money. . . . It would be hard for people of color to understand that some of these things do take place also, but we have been through it. And we know it is there.

And Don again remarks that the stories he has been hearing have surprised him:

> How do you do it? I'm sitting here thinking I must be the most naïve sixty-nine year old man in the world. I can't imagine.

Several moments later, another African-American woman in the group refers to some of Don's earlier claims that existing laws, if properly enforced, would be sufficient to improve race relations.

ADALINE: I want to mention—about Don saying we are supposed to enforce things . . . and everything would be perfect—that stuff is illegal, that is true, but it still happens.

DON [muttering]: Going to hell in a hand basket.

MARIA [Latina facilitator]: What do you mean by that, Don?

DON: I'm very confused.

MARIA: This is a good thing I think.

DON: We have a law that does not protect you. That confuses me. I am confused by many of the things we have talked about in the past, but today has been the most confusing for me overall. I get a feeling that we are all still, after all this time, kinda hedging around what we really want to say.

Don's comments convey the uncomfortable nature of this talk and also the possibility that it only skims the surface of what people actually want to say. It is quite likely the case that even after four sessions and in this "safe" format people were guarded in their remarks. But looking across all of the sessions, Don's comments suggest that even if people were not revealing their most private thoughts in these dialogues, they were causing each other to reconsider their preconceptions. The fact that people quite likely are somewhat guarded in these dialogues makes it all the more remarkable that signs of listening and shock and awareness were ubiquitous. Even if people were holding back, the stories they told opened the eyes of other participants, as Don himself indicated.

Don's remarks within the conference room in which the group met demonstrated some "acceptance" of the messages of difference he was hearing, but it was actually his interactions with one of the African-American group members across the course of the sessions that most alerted me to this transformation. He and Elihue did not know each other before participating, but by the end of the session they were chatting with one another before and after the group, and outside the building in which we met. The remarkable thing was that the two made visible, difficult attempts to strike up a friendship. Many people volunteer for these groups to meet others of a different racial background. And yet common awareness of this makes any attempt to strike up a friendship awkward and risky. Don's vocal skepticism that unity could ever be achieved was set against a gradual attempt to forge it. At the end of the second session, he ventured this:

DON [to the group]: Let's get together and call each other up. Now this is being negative, I don't like to be negative but sometimes you have to be to get to the positive. Is there anybody who would hear as though my saying, um, Elihue right? [Making sure he has his name right.] "Let's go and have a beer when we get out of here." You know what I'm saying? Can we get past that feeling that if I do that [to himself, getting up the courage:] OK, I am going to say this—if I do that, won't people look at me and say, "He's playing tokenism" or whatever? You know what I'm getting at? Even you might say that to yourself? [Looking to Elihue.]

JENN [white]: You can't win, yeah.

[...]

GINGER [African American]: I don't know if—I wouldn't think that generally people would off the bat think that. Now once you go together with these few beers and you start talking, you can spot a phony.

ADALINE [African American]: Yes you can.

SAMUEL [African American]: That's right.

GINGER: So I got to get to know you and talk—that's what we should do. We shouldn't have these preconceived notions, or prejudices, but once I got to talking to you and found that out, then I'd leave you with the bill.

[laughter]

DON: I'm not talking about your perception, I'm talking about the perception of others around—

MARIA [Latina facilitator]: We've got to bring this to a close. . . .

[. . .]

DON: Trust. If I say to you, "Let's go have a beer after we leave here," do you trust me that I am just saying it to you as you? [pause] Answer that.

ELIHUE [African American]: Well, I wouldn't go with you because I don't drink beer.

[Raucous laughter]

JOHN [WHITE]: He doesn't want to be stuck with the bill.

DON: Come on! I'm serious. Would you, would you trust my intentions?

ELIHUE: I would.

It seemed as though this was the first time that Don had invited a person of color on a social outing (admittedly a rare experience for many people, including participants in these groups). It signaled to me a shift that was caused in part by listening. In the first two sessions Elihue had spoken openly about his experiences with discrimination at the hands of local law enforcement officers, employers, and school officials. Don had expressed skepticism that such different experiences existed across members of his community, and skepticism that any attention to difference was appropriate. However, his overture to Elihue and the way they lingered together before and after the sessions conveyed that he had developed or at least given in to a desire to listen.

Was this just a desire to get to know Elihue and not necessarily a desire to listen to the experiences of an African American? These discussions demonstrated time and again that as much as people, particularly whites, wanted to believe that "people are people" and that it is possible to "not see color," that many *wanted* others to see color, to notice their racial identity, and to notice that race matters. Elihue's repeated remarks to that effect suggest that when Don sought to spend more time with Elihue, he was respecting and acknowledging such a view. Don's overture to Elihue is significant because he made it in a context in which difference is recognized rather than ignored.[40]

Difference-focused, Yet Not Hard Multiculturalism

The fact that part of what people did in these dialogues was listen to difference might cause some to discount these conversations as a practice obsessed with separation rather than unity. But such criticisms are not well founded. Ordinary citizens were using these opportunities for difference-focused talk to understand the experiences and perspectives of people of different racial backgrounds, and they were doing so in contexts in which people were trying to connect with one another rather than build higher walls of separation.

How can it be that these people were doing difference-focused communication yet not necessarily approaching dialogue through a multiculturalist ideology? Recent scholarship on national identity provides guidance. In chapter 2, I discussed Deborah Schildkraut's work on national identity and language policy, which identifies multiculturalism as one approach to national identity. In her study, she used focus groups to examine the way people use various models of national identity when talking about language policy. This work shows that individuals are neither ethnoculturalists, nor liberals, nor civic republicans, nor incorporationists (a category that includes multiculturalists). Instead, people express ambivalence about these models and attempt to fashion national identity that is a hybrid of several of them. She concludes that "multiculturalist" is not so much a label for a person but an orientation to policy.

I rely on Schildkraut's analyses to shed some light on how the communication in these groups paid attention to difference, but did so through orientations other than multiculturalism. Schildkraut analyzed the way people use different models of national identity in their discussions about English-only language policy. I replicate that analysis here. I identified all of the conversations related to language policy that took place in the five groups that I recorded, and coded them for the different models. Following her procedures and using her code frame, I coded each "completed thought" pertaining to language policy.[41] As I elaborate further in chapter 8, the southern Wisconsin group did not discuss language policy and is therefore excluded from this analysis. Schildkraut's code frame specified the types of comments that qualify as one of the four primary models of national identity, as well as hybrid visions that combine two of these models.[42] See the last section of the methods appendix for this frame, along with additional subitems I added for this analysis and a specification of the types of comments that qualified as hybrids.

Following this procedure, I find that even though people in these dialogues were participating in difference-focused talk, they used a multiculturalist lens less than a quarter of the time in any given group, and in an average of just 21 percent of the completed thoughts across all groups. Table 6.1 displays these results by discussion group. The multiculturalist lens was indeed important for these groups. In two of them, it was the model of national identity that people most often invoked. Moreover, it seemed to be used more often in these dialogue groups than in Schildkraut's focus

TABLE 6.1: National identity frames and language policy discussions

	Cent. Wisc. Wed.	Cent. Wisc. Thurs.	Aurora Mon.	Aurora Tues.	All Groups
Liberalism	.17	.08	.10	.15	.12
Civic republicanism	.30	.15	.07	.15	.17
Ethnoculturalism (rejection of)	.00	.15	.17	.11	.11
Ethnoculturalism (acceptance of)	.04	.00	.17	.05	.07
Incorporationism (multicultural)	.22	.23	.20	.19	.21
Incorporationism (melting pot assimilation)	.13	.31	.20	.16	.20
Hybrid including multicultural incorporationism	.00	.00	.07	.03	.02
Hybrid excluding multicultural incorporationism	.09	.00	.03	.11	.06
Unclassified	.04	.08	.00	.07	.05
Total N codable completed thoughts	23	13	30	75	141

Note: Entries are the percentage of codable completed thoughts classified in each category. The southern Wisconsin discussions were not included in these analyses since none of the four discussions recorded contained mentions of language policy.

groups.[43] However, this does not overshadow the result that this perspective accounts for just a minority of the statements made about language policy.

How is it possible that people can do difference-focused communication and yet not through a multiculturalist perspective? An example from the dialogues will illustrate. When the Aurora daytime group first discussed language policy, during their first session, Steve, the African-American man, expressed his opinions on it, and then turned to Cilia, the Hispanic woman, and asked her for her direct experience and perspective on the issue. His turning to her constitutes difference-focused communication. But his comments were not made through a multicultural lens. Here is what he said, with insertions underlined indicating the national identity frame these statements convey:

> Talking about language and being able to understand people—you've gotta be able to understand [civic republicanism]. I've had people get angry at me, Hispanics. People get angry at me because I don't speak their language, and that—that—that bothered me, like *wait a second!* When I was in the Middle East in the military I learned to speak some Arabic because I wanted to communicate with these people for my own sake. I think

at some point—you know—in our school systems, I think we enable the Hispanic community sometimes when we have Spanish-speaking-only classes. And I don't know— [turning to Cilia] I don't know how you feel about that, but that bothers me, but when I am teaching in a class and I can not communicate with children because our schools aren't teaching them the English language. . . . I don't know—maybe you have never experienced this but you go to McDonald's and you can't communicate with the guy in the drive-through because he doesn't speak English. It is our own fault, when we don't speak English in the early years in our own grade school [hybrid: ethnoculturalism and melting pot incorporationism]. So I guess I have never really spoken with a Spanish speaking-person, how they feel about that. And I guess—what are your thoughts on that?

Steve turns to Cilia to listen to her perspective, but his viewpoints are closer to civic republicanism, ethnoculturalism, and melting pot incorporationism than multiculturalism.

"Wholeness," Not "Oneness"

In these civic dialogue programs on race, we see people becoming aware of the manner in which racial identity matters in their communities. And this happens for both whites and people of color. Whites express surprise or a newfound alertness to the extent to which race matters in everyday life. People of color proclaim that through the sessions, they become aware of how little the whites in their community understand the extent of racism. In other words, both whites and people of color gain a greater awareness of *how* race matters in everyday life in their city.[44]

We might conclude that people of different races get different things from these conversations. But listening to the content of these conversations challenges assumptions that the utility of these conversations for whites is in gaining understanding, and for people of color is primarily in being heard. Participants of *all* racial backgrounds seem to gain understanding, *and* convey a need to have their concerns heard in the rare context of an interracial group.

These conversations serve as a window to the processes that go on in actual, practical politics when community members try to confront race through talk. In contrast to work on intergroup conflict that emphasizes that intergroup contact is most productive for reducing prejudice when it focuses on overarching identities, we see people participating in interracial dialogues taking a different route. They seldom talk about themselves as members of a common community. Rather than clarify a shared identity, they tend to undertake the task of clarifying a complex identity of people who desire the noninterference of color as well as an awareness and respect for racial differences.

Even though the participants do not talk about a shared community, they nevertheless seem to strive for a type of unity. Here, a desire for unity appears as a striving for improved connections or relationships among people. But this is more akin to unity in the sense of "wholeness" rather than "oneness," to borrow Danielle Allen's terms.[45] Even though some of the participants declare that they prefer to think about the human race rather than racial categories, the conversations do not dwell on similarity. A common conclusion, stated out loud and conveyed through the behavior of the participants, is that making progress on race relations requires paying attention to race and acknowledging the way in which racial categories continue to matter, even if people desire a world in which discrimination no longer exists. Also, some who assert that they seek a "colorblind" world, when pressed state that they do not really wish for a world in which race is not noticed but wish for one in which race is no longer a source of discrimination.

How is it, then, that people negotiate whether to go beyond the claim that "people are people"? And how do they reason about how to draw such lines? Three elements summarize what this chapter has revealed: the group nature of these discussions, listening, and ambivalence. First, the group nature of these discussions refers to the fact that people worked out whether to go beyond unity claims because the groups included a mix of perspectives. Individuals entered the discussions with preconceptions about how to balance unity and difference, but were challenged by alternative perspectives on the form this balance should take. Secondly, listening made it possible for people to nudge one another away from the blinders of unity and also away from the spiral of difference. It was the willingness to listen that made this collective struggle possible.

Finally, ambivalence mattered, too, and it mattered in ways our usual individual-level focus on political behavior might not cause us to anticipate. Historically, scholars of public opinion have viewed ambivalence over political stances or issues as a function of lack of information or of a less-than-sophisticated ideology.[46] In other words, ambivalence is often taken as cause for worrying over whether people are capable of living up to standards of good citizenship. But Jennifer Hochschild alerts us to the possibility that ambivalence is actually a cause for "cautious optimism."[47] Based on her work on citizens' lay theories of distributive justice and public opinion among middle-class blacks, she argues that the presence of ambivalence as well as disjunction, or "troublesome distinction[s] drawn between two arenas of life," provides openings for democratic progress.[48]

The presence of ambivalence and disjunction in individuals signifies awareness of, rather than obliviousness to, the complexities of the political and social context. People whose beliefs call into question common distinctions can cause others to think critically about contradictions in the political culture, too. And this state of affairs opens up opportunities for new approaches to public policy. She argues that, rather than a danger to democracy, the presence of disjunction and ambivalence is essential to it, ensuring that we have a political system that consists of people who engage in critical analysis and an openness to different perspectives.[49]

This study illuminates these arguments by showing how ambivalence at the individual level enabled group-level ambivalence. Ambivalence was indeed an asset. It fueled the task of actively negotiating a conception of citizenship in contexts of diversity. Some people entered these discussions without recognizing that it might not be appropriate to conceptualize people simply as people. However, others' ambivalence caused them to reconsider. People who made unity claims were confronted with the fact that even some of those who wanted to see all people as equal also saw a value in paying attention to difference. Thus individual-level ambivalence encouraged this struggle by making the content of the group discussions not a given, nor simply a bastion of multiculturalism, and by adding credibility to claims that attention to difference is necessary.

There is at least one alternative way to read these conversations. It is possible that these people were not struggling with unity and difference but were simply appearing to do so. Maybe conventions of appropriate Midwestern behavior dictate that people listen politely to others. In addition, maybe the participants simply tuned out what they heard. Maybe they weren't actually listening to each other and maybe what was said had little effect on the individual participants' attitudes. For example, if steeped in a culture of unity, perhaps whites who expressed a preference for colorblindness reverted to such a focus upon leaving these discussions.

I find such readings implausible for several reasons. First, the body language, the intensity of the comments made, and the expressions of surprise strongly suggest that these were more than polite exchanges. I use the term *struggle* because the force of the exchanges suggests that people actively engaged in the thorny issue of race and racial difference.

Second, regardless of what individuals do with this experience and how it impacted their individual preferences, the context that these groups created and the opinions expressed within them are important political facts in their own right. The views spoken in the group context formed the information environment to which each of the individuals were temporarily exposed. Recalling Habermas, Dewey, and Arendt, the public realm is something that people collectively create. This is what it looks like in practice. Regardless of whether each of these individuals would say the same thing in a different context, or whether the views expressed altered the opinions they expressed the next day, this *is* what people did with the opportunity to create a racially heterogeneous public realm.

As examples of the act of constructing the public realm, these groups hold general lessons about the practice of dialogue and deliberation. It is possible for deliberation to occur within the minds of individuals.[50] But it is the group nature of this exchange that generated the task of balancing unity and difference that we see here. Collectives produce capacity in ways that individuals can not, particularly individuals existing in a racially segregated world. These collective struggles are not always pretty. They are often awkward and at times upsetting. But these groups showed an ability to engage this difficult task and appeared to make honest attempts to do so. The conversations call into question claims that if you bring people of divergent perspectives into a forum together, the result will inevitably be heightened conflict. It is not the case that people were disgusted with this public talk process.[51] Nor is it the case that they found it to be perfectly harmonious. Allowing ourselves to set aside such presumptions allows us to see how people create citizenship through public talk like these dialogues.

CHAPTER SEVEN

Scrutinizing and Listening to Stories

People participating in civic intergroup dialogue programs struggle with the opposing forces of unity and difference. But they face another, related, task as well. They begin these programs expecting to develop relationships with other people in the community at the same time that they expect to reason through the public problem of race relations together. People promoting these programs claim that these dialogues are different from other forms of public talk because they encourage people to listen to perspectives that are often overlooked. But they also allege that these programs involve more than just dialogue—that they are *deliberative* dialogue. They claim that these programs are valuable because people use them to reason through difficult public problems together while simultaneously also paying attention to difference.[1]

How does this work? How do people use these forums to accomplish both listening and reasoning together? This chapter probes how people are using civic dialogue by paying particular attention to the forms of talk that they use. It examines the modes of talk that people put into practice and how people negotiate a balance between unity and difference as they do so.

The reader might have noticed in the previous chapter that a predominant way in which people communicate in these groups is through storytelling. To contribute to the dialogues, people offer up reports of personal experiences from their lives or from the lives of people to whom they have a personal attachment. In this way, they convey to each other their perceptions of their community.[2] Previous work has shown that storytelling pervades many forms of face-to-face public talk.[3]

Storytelling, simply put, is the act of providing a narrative about experience from one's own life, either a specific event or reference to a pattern of events. These narratives are not necessarily fully developed stories, with a plot and an elaborate series of events. In the race dialogues, as in many other examples of public talk, they are typically brief reports of personal experience.[4] Such stories do more than just relay a series of events. They make arguments, often moral arguments, about what behaviors and identities ought to be accepted.[5] Human beings tell stories to make sense of the past, relate it to the present, and control the future.[6] Narratives pervade all aspects of culture from conversations, to history, to stained glass windows.[7] Just as they show up in the "public discussion" of mass-mediated messages,[8] they show up in face-to-face public talk as well.

Although storytelling is pervasive, people also use other modes of communication during public talk. They at times refer to facts, history, the content of news stories, or abstract principles to support or illustrate the statement they wish to make. In forums in which appropriate reasons are things that all or most participants can accept,[9] stories particular to a certain individual might actually be unwelcome.

Storytelling has the potential to help people make sense of community identity and sort out what they wish to do to improve civic life. But it is not clear how people use storytelling when they are expected to not only deliberate about public problems but to dialogue with each other as well. Difference democrats assert that telling stories can insert a variety of perspectives into the deliberative system, and yet previous work suggests that in the course of public talk, people try to reconcile the presence of competing stories or frames. That is, although difference democrats hold up storytelling primarily as a mode of listening, others suggest people use it in public talk to scrutinize others' claims.

A prominent call for storytelling put forth by difference democrats as a way to produce greater attention to marginalized perspectives is made by Iris Marion Young.[10] Storytelling can help people understand the experience of those who occupy other social locations or positions in the constellation of social groups and status structures in society;[11] communicate the basis of values and cultural meanings held by those others;[12] and communicate experience in a way that enables listeners to notice their own positions in others' lives and how they might be viewed in a manner different than they had previously considered.[13] Elaborating on this last point, Young writes:

> Inclusive democratic communication assumes that all participants have something to teach the public about the society in which they dwell together and its problems. It assumes as well that all participants are ignorant of some aspects of the social or natural world, and that everyone comes to a political conflict with some biases, prejudices, blind spots, or stereotypes.

Frequently in situations of political disagreement, one faction assumes that they know what it is like for others, or that they can put themselves in the place of others, or that they are really just like the others. Especially in mass society, where knowledge of others may be largely mediated by statistical generalities, there may be little understanding of lived need or interest across groups. A norm of political communication under these conditions is that everyone should aim to enlarge their social understanding by learning about the specific experience and meanings attending other social locations. Narrative makes this easier and sometimes an adventure.[14]

Difference democrats such as Young expect that storytelling is a mode of speech that gets members of dominant groups to stop, listen, and understand the perspectives of people whom the deliberative system typically silences.[15]

However, alternative or competing stories are often viewed as a threat or an obstacle to be overcome, not an asset to be embraced.[16] Previous work on public talk suggests that when participants are confronted with a story that challenges dominant understandings, we should not expect them to notice its inherent value but should instead anticipate that they will scrutinize it and attempt to reconcile it with dominant modes of understanding. Because the fault lines of power inequalities in a community often coincide with divisions among racial groups, stories that suggest a particular experience among members of a given racial group might be perceived as a threat to the turf of another group rather than simply an invitation to expand one's horizons.

Moreover, there is evidence that even when the topic is not specifically race, people seem to frequently use narrative for rational tasks like interpreting issues rather than relational tasks such as listening to difference.[17] David Ryfe, in an analysis of videotapes of five National Issues Forums, shows that people use storytelling to make sense of an issue when they lack expertise on the topic,[18] to convey sincerity and trustworthiness,[19] and to engage in argumentation while still being civil and polite.[20] Even when the use of storytelling takes on a more dialogue-like or relational cast, it appears people use it primarily for the sake of forging unity, not paying attention to difference. Ryfe argues that people "tell stories to establish an identity appropriate for the context at hand" and that storytelling can also enable the development of a collective frame.[21] In fact, Ryfe argues that the main contribution of storytelling is that it allows people to build on one another's experience and develop a kind of consensus about what the issue is about and what the group has achieved. He shows that when a contrary situation arises—when group members use stories to articulate competing rather than shared frames—a sense of frustration pervades the conversation.[22]

Other studies similarly provide evidence that storytelling's main contribution is to establish unity, not listen to difference. Marian Barnes, in a study of forums designed to engage older people and public officials in discussions about social care services in the United Kingdom, concludes: "From this process of story telling common concerns emerged."[23] Analyses of informal deliberation in small group conversations likewise show that participants build upon the stories of others to clarify and reinforce shared interpretations and identity and create contexts in which certain perspectives are acceptable.[24] In addition, an analysis by Dan Bar-On and Fatma Kassem of an oral history project by Israeli and Palestinian students found that through storytelling people make claims about what is appropriate. Through building on each others' stories, they collectively craft a group perspective, group identity, or build a collective moral sense.[25] In other words, various scholars have concluded that storytelling often works not to lend attention to difference but to build unity in the form of shared perspectives and identities.[26] In fact, major studies of the role of storytelling in civic deliberation have been pursued as investigations of whether this mode of talk can lead to consensus and compromise.[27]

And yet it is possible that storytelling does provide attention to difference. There is some evidence from online public talk that people who perceive their views are in the minority are more likely than others to participate by telling stories.[28] Various empirical scholars have asserted that narrative can contest dominant cultural narratives,[29] expose people to internal group differences,[30] and help people "construct a more complex image of the 'other' than the one usually conveyed through the media."[31] And we can see this dynamic at work even in situations that others have described as tending toward unity. For example, even though Barnes concludes that people use stories to identify common concerns, her evidence also suggests that storytelling alerted public officials to some unique perspectives. The officials, or service providers, initially discounted older citizens' stories expressed in the forums as mere "anecdotes" but gradually came to recognize that these perspectives were valuable for reforming policy.[32]

Archon Fung argues that civic deliberation geared toward community policing and public schools avoids some of the dominating effects of deliberation because it does tend to include both narrative and rational modes of speech. Meetings about local problems tend to focus on concrete needs rather than democratic principles, he asserts. Because the goal is to solve problems rather than have one's vision of democracy prevail, it requires only "tentative agreements about effective solutions rather than an enduring consensus on values or goods."[33] Because the consensus required for civic deliberation to proceed is not as demanding as more formal modes of deliberation, we might expect that storytelling in these contexts would lend itself in part to attention to difference.

Therefore we have reason to expect that even in contexts in which participants are expected to listen and strive to understand one another as well as reason through public problems, storytelling would work to give attention to difference as well as perhaps serve as a mode of forging unity. But, again, how does this work? How do people use storytelling in the service of these different tasks? Asking these questions not only moves us closer to understanding how people negotiate unity and difference in the course of these dialogues; it also expands our understanding of the use of storytelling in civic life and enlarges our conceptions of the limits and contributions of relational and rational modes of communication in the deliberative system more broadly.

The Multiple Functions of Storytelling

The previous chapter contained a variety of examples of people using storytelling in intergroup dialogues, and that is indeed indicative of the communication that took place. As in ordinary conversation, one person relaying events from his or her own life commonly presented the opportunity to others.[34] Often the communication took this form because the curriculum called for it. In the first session of these groups, the guidebook suggested that all participants talk about their first experiences with racism.[35] The format of the discussions encouraged storytelling in other ways as well. The conversation guidebooks encouraged people to "Value one another's experiences. Think about how your own experiences have contributed to your thinking."[36] The perception that the dialogues were intended to increase understanding and foster relationships also presupposed that people would share information about their own lives.

The extent of storytelling varied across groups, as previous research would suggest. Ryfe argues that storytelling is more likely when the conversations are less structured, in terms of facilitation and overall format. Under "strong" facilitation, when the facilitator is performing much of the task of managing the conversation by regularly interjecting and summarizing others' thoughts, people are less likely to use stories to communicate.[37] In addition, storytelling seems less common when there is a more rigid agenda, such as in citizens' juries,[38] or in formal committee meetings.[39] In contrast, small group situations without any facilitation or agenda commonly involve the telling of stories.[40]

Consistent with these findings, stronger facilitation and more structure seemed to hinder storytelling in the civic dialogue groups I observed. Groups whose facilitators urged them to stick closely to the curriculum told fewer stories to one another. And in the first several sessions of the Aurora evening group, when Liza, the facilitator, was frequently interjecting comments into the discussion, group members told fewer stories than in later sessions, when she spoke less often.

The use of storytelling confirmed yet other conclusions from Ryfe's study. People used stories like evidence, often in cases in which it seemed they lacked more specific information or expertise on a particular issue. At times a person would tell a story in order to contradict a claim someone had just made, but to do so in a relatively polite way that skirted direct confrontation. A brief example comes from the Aurora Tuesday (daytime) group. Judy, a white woman, told a story about a neighbor's perceptions of Hispanics, and Cilia, the one Hispanic in the group, challenged the claim with a general reference to her childhood:

JUDY: Our neighborhood a few years ago, we had—pretty, pretty mixed. Had a Hispanic family move in across the street and I said to my neighbors, who are Hispanic, "I can't speak [Spanish] but can you just go over there and greet them and welcome them?" And they said, "Well Hispanics don't do that."

CILIA: That's funny because you know, to me I think that we are the ones who trust more people. That's the way I was brought up. Always offer people a plate, a cup of water—don't let a passerby go by without feeding them.

This use of storytelling seems to serve a dual purpose—communicating different personal experience, and also reasoning through the issue at hand. It was common that people would offer up a story after someone else had done so in order to contrast with, rather than corroborate, the other's experience.

In other forums I observed that involved dialogue but did not meet over repeated sessions, storytelling was also common but seemed geared more toward listening. In Madison, the local PBS affiliate and the local Urban League branch periodically sponsored events open to the community that included the screening of a documentary related to race relations followed by group dialogue. During these events, I observed difference-focused communication that entailed a good deal of listening. The ground rules displayed were similar to those suggested by the SCRC, and the style of facilitation was consistently oriented toward enabling all who wanted to speak to contribute to the discussion, rather than toward settling on a consensual interpretation of the film or current events. In these contexts, participants often relayed personal stories, and they were seldom challenged by the other participants. When others asked questions, it was to elicit more of the narrative a person was telling rather than to contest it. In other words, the communication participants engaged in was more akin to testimony rather than to reasoning through public problems together. They seemed to listen, but not argue.

This was particularly the case following the viewing of a film about three Cambodian-American young men who returned to Cambodia to visit relatives. Organizers of the event had invited people of Cambodian heritage in the Madison area. Approximately thirty-five people attended, eight of whom were Cambodian. (Approximately five of the attendees were African American, and one woman was Latina.) When the facilitator asked if anyone wanted to speak, many of the Cambodian participants recalled their own experiences as immigrants or children of immigrants living in the Madison area. The others present were so intrigued by what they had to say that rather than break into small discussion groups, all of the people present arranged their chairs into one large circle. I noted in my fieldnotes that the white attendees seemed to listen—not one of them spoke during the discussion.

Storytelling in these one-meeting forums served the purpose of conferring attention to the typically excluded perspectives of racial and ethnic minorities. But in the multi-session intergroup dialogue programs, in which the structure was more clearly geared toward working through public problems together, storytelling did serve both relational and rational roles.

The curriculum called for this. In the first session and at the beginning of each individual session, people were asked to talk about their experiences in an attempt to achieve dialogue, such as their first experience with racism. At other times, participants were given five or six views to discuss on topics such as "the nature of the problem [of race]," "what should we do to make progress on race relations," and "what kinds of public policies will help us deal with race relations." The guide asked participants to talk about the merits of the different views, imagine what would be important to someone who supported each of the views, and why they personally would choose one over the other. Although participants were asked to keep an open mind, listen, and strive to understand others' positions throughout their sessions, when discussing these views, the talk often resembled debate more than dialogue. Storytelling was commonly the vehicle through which people accomplished this.

For example, in the central Wisconsin Wednesday group, Tizo, one of the facilitators, asked us to define institutional racism:

MIKE [white]: . . . After we graduated eighth grade, we went into high school, and all the kids I mentioned [students of color]—most of them got put into the technical high school. Other people went into the college prep program. . . . I don't know if that still happens today, but that is what I perceive as institutional racism. And you know the counselors may have thought this is the best we can do for these people, but that isn't really. It should have been up to that person—you are defined by your race or ethnic group.

TIZO [Latina, co-facilitator]: So it [institutional racism] would be policies that are set. . . .

[. . .]

SAMUEL [African American]: I'll give you an example. Our constitution says we are all created equal. Is that true? No. They say that we are, but we are not created equal and we don't have the rights that a lot of people have. It says we have the rights, but those rights are not carried out. I can walk in on the job and have the same credentials—I'll give you an example. I worked for the [name withheld] company. This job I had was supposed to have a certain amount of education, but this person had no education at all, he got the job because he was Caucasian, color of his skin. Things like that.

MARK [white]: That all enters into it, you know. But also let's keep in mind— imagine that it was just a homogenous society and everybody was of the same race or something. People are born unequal because some people are genetically predisposed to be more intelligent than other people. I don't know—right out of the crib, whatever your aptitudes happen to be—also separate people other than just race.

SAMUEL: That's true.

MARK: So it is not just race. But race can be an inhibiting factor into it. Some cases are there. But "we want to present"—they want to set forth an institution, promote the people that are most sellable to the public. In that sense then you leave the other people that are not—you know what I mean?

Samuel offers up his personal story to try to define institutional racism. Again we see storytelling work to facilitate listening—it communicates a different experience—but it is also used in the process of argumentation. Stories served as offerings to individual attempts to better understand, but they also served as fodder for group debate.

Inserting Stories of Difference

If storytelling served the purposes of scrutinizing as well as listening, how did it lend itself to the negotiation of unity and difference? Storytelling was ubiquitous, and a wide range of people contributed stories to the discussions. But stories told by people of color seemed to carry a different weight. Their stories of experiences with discrimination frequently alarmed the whites in the groups. They told stories about discrimination in employment, criminal justice, education, and housing as well as incidents that occurred in everyday interactions with other community members. Bernita, an older African-American woman in the central Wisconsin Thursday group, recalled her experiences with Jim Crow laws while growing up in the South. Elic, an African-American man in the Aurora Monday night group, talked about clerks in a local store accusing him of shoplifting. Elihue, a black man in the central Wisconsin Thursday group, told a story about police claiming that his son's car had been recently used in a crime, although the car had been on blocks for years. Several black people in different cities talked about landlords telling them apartments had been rented as soon as the landlord saw the color of their skin for the first time.

The reports of personal experiences by people of color produced shifts in the conversation. Sometimes these stories would slip by, apparently unnoticed. But evidence that they snagged as they did so, and caused people to ponder, manifested later in the conversation or after several weeks. For example, in the second session of the Aurora daytime group, a white woman was discussing institutional racism. Early in the conversation she had remarked that such racism is a thing of the past. But as the conversation progressed and people of color offered up personal examples, she openly rethought that point of view:

SARA [white]: I remember my cousins growing up in Pensacola, drank from a "white" fountain. But now institutional racism has to be more financial because there is no segregation anymore, they actually bus kids to the nonwhite schools, take Chinese kids and dump them in the north side schools because too many white kids there. I can hardly think of institutional racism being blatant nowadays.

STEVE [African American]: Oh I would—some things in the police department, probably seven or eight years ago where officers were eating lunch or dinner at these private clubs around town, well minority officers weren't allowed to eat there—weren't allowed membership—Irish Club, Phoenix Club, all of these little clubs—Tiger club—some still don't. And the chief said you are not allowed to eat at these places while you are on duty.

WAYNE [white]: I took my whole gang (work crew), all seven or eight of us, took us to the Tiger Club, and one of them is Spanish [Hispanic] and the bartender wasn't going to serve me.

Later in that session, Sara reconsidered her views:

SARA: Now that I said that I feel stupid, that I said there wasn't blatant racism out there. Because now there are lots of things that are coming to mind, that could be probably racism.

RACHEL [white]: There still are. Every day and we just aren't aware of it.

Another example illustrates how stories worked to generate listening to difference. In the central Wisconsin Thursday group, during the first session, two Hmong men who had come to the United States in the early 1980s as refugees talked about how their neighbors believed that they were going to steal their dog and eat it. The story received a lot of laughs when they told it, but two sessions later, one of the white women in the group remarked that she had "thought they *did* eat dog" until she heard their stories.

Sometimes people of color used narrative to draw attention to difference in a way that contributed to the process of scrutinizing others' claims. They would tell stories that directly contradicted whites' denial of racism. Their stories challenged these denials by simply conveying, "Look, I have experienced it personally." For example, in the second session of the central Wisconsin Thursday group, the group discussed the meaning of institutionalized racism. A white man said:

SCOTT: In this city, I don't see it. I see racism at my level, usually at night, but I don't see it as purposely keeping someone in a particular neighborhood.

MARIA [Latina facilitator]: What do you see?

SCOTT: More problems with our Hmong refugees right now where people beat them up or tease them—but I don't see it—I really can't see anybody holding anybody down [systematically]. . . . Yeah, like in Milwaukee where aldermen say you can't cross this line or—can't really see—[a black man next to him, Elihue, is visibly disagreeing]. Maybe Elihue . . .

ELIHUE: You probably won't see it, because you know—but I can assure you there is a lot of it. A lot of racism.

Later on in the session, during a discussion of the definition of racism, this white man, Scott, responded to a story by a black person by saying, "See that's good to hear because we don't see that perspective. Not good to hear that that's happening, but good to hear about it."

In the next session (the third of five), Elihue again talked about the kind of everyday racism he faces in town:

ELIHUE: Sometimes I'm in a store—people look around—grab their purse, grab their child.

MARIA: You actually witness that?

DON [white]: Grab their child?!

ELIHUE: Yeah!

And later on, one of the white men, Stan, openly remarked how surprised he was to hear such stories: "I guess it is a real eye-opener to me, Elihue, to hear you talk about your son in the schools and people clutching their purses in the stores and that, I guess, I just don't know how you feel about that."

Elihue provided yet another reality check when the conversation turned to the criminal justice system during the fourth session. The group was discussing the viewpoint that "We should review our policies for the racist assumptions they contain, and take that racism out" when John said:

JOHN [white]: I think this whole viewpoint is based on larger cities. I don't see this happening in [this city]. I see judges being fair. Some of the judges we have in [this city] right now will put you on probation before they put you in jail.

MARIA: OK. Well, there you have a viewpoint. Elihue?

[Many people in the group laugh because by this session we had become aware that Elihue felt mistreated by local law enforcement on numerous occasions.]

ELIHUE: It happens. It happens a lot, you know. It just—there are ways of— especially with judges [in this city], ways of going around it, so it won't make it seem so racist. I mean, you can tell—you can tell the differences. Thinking about myself, in [a nearby city]. I felt more comfortable in that courtroom in [that city] than I do over here. Here, you are—you get the feeling that no matter what you say, you have already been judged. That's what I feel. I might be wrong.

Although people would at times contribute stories to indicate that they had similar experiences to others in the group, often people of color would use this form of communication to insert attention to difference. These contributions usually took the form of, "Actually, I have first hand experience with that. I am one of the targets of the policy/act/sentiment that you are talking about and I have a story that suggests a different perspective."

At times whites in the groups would challenge the validity of a claim that a person of color made and ask for further justification, a dynamic I investigate more fully in chapter 8. But this was most common when a person was relaying a second-hand story, or reciting a fact from news media. In other words, narratives of personal experience, particularly of first-hand experience with bearing the burden of discrimination, held a special authority in these groups.

In fact, the manner in which whites told stories displayed that they perceived that part of their job as participants in the dialogue was to listen to the stories of people of color. They would regularly tell second-hand stories of discrimination, to supplement the views of people of color. This worked in several ways. Sometimes, when people of color would tell a story, it would cause whites in the group to recall an additional experience with racial discrimination, one that they had witnessed themselves. In the large central Wisconsin group, one man talked about being refused service when taking his son and his son's African-American friend to restaurants. Another man in that group talked about getting hostile stares from supposed friends when taking a famous black musician who was visiting into a local club.

People also used second-hand stories when few people of color were present to represent narratives themselves. In those cases, whites and other people of color would strive to bring in marginalized voices. For example, the southern Wisconsin group was the least diverse group in the sample. When no people of color attended the second session except for the Arab-American co-facilitator, she stated that she was stepping down from her role of facilitator in order to contribute her own stories. And in that same session, she tried to represent the views of African Americans by relaying reports of personal experience that African-American participants had told in previous groups that she had facilitated. In another instance of the use of second-hand stories, when discussing reparations for slavery, the white facilitator relayed the views of black inmates from a different dialogue group. Also, throughout the southern Wisconsin group's sessions, various participants mentioned a story about discrimination told by a black woman who had only attended the first session. And after the Arab-American woman stopped facilitating (after the second session), the white male facilitator continually referred back to her experiences with racial profiling.

"Dialogue, Not Debate"

Participants used storytelling both to listen to difference as well as to reason together. This intertwining of these different modes of communication arose in part because participants conferred a special role on the stories of people of color. And yet the insertion of stories of difference did not *reconcile* unity and difference but instead seemed to feed the ongoing opposition between these polar forces.

The conflict between the simultaneous goals of paying attention to difference and yet forging a common understanding of public problems manifested itself in an ongoing tension between dialogue and debate. Although the relational or dialogical nature of these programs helped legitimize attention to the perspectives and experiences of people of color, it was continually in tension with the larger collective project the participants were engaging in—the rational task of reasoning together about what they wished their communities to be like.

To illustrate, I draw on the central Wisconsin Thursday group. The facilitator of this group had a particularly tricky task. There were nineteen people in the group, many of whom were rather outspoken and several of whom tended to speak at length. She clearly sought to follow the curriculum guide's instruction to keep the discussions focused on dialogue and not debate, reminding the group of this often.

At the beginning of the second session, she asked us to discuss what we had learned in school about the history of race relations.[41] After forty minutes on this, the discussion turned to assimilation. One white man said that it was an inevitable pattern that we "lose our ethnicity" after immigrating to the United States. Then, Colleen, a white woman responded:

COLLEEN: I think it is kind of unfortunate that you said that we are losing our heritage and our history. I think everybody needs to have kind of a sense of who they are and where they came from and their parents and grandparents and trials and struggles that they've gone through no matter what your heritage is and also bring your heritage out and educate other people who aren't German or Irish or black or Hmong as to what your culture is and what we have to offer other people. . . . [. . .] You kind of have to still retain where you came from and then pass that along to people that you meet from other cultures.

[. . .]

SAMUEL [African American]: I like what she said about the history—I am going to say something here that may be a little harsh, but I'm going to say it softly.

MARIA [Latina facilitator]: Dialogue not debate.

SAMUEL: Not going to debate. We as black people really don't have a history because we were pulled here against our will. Can't trace back to Africa—we were raised here—forced to work for nothing, our babies raped—I mean our wives raped, and when we didn't comply with what they wanted, they sold us, so we are still trying to find out who we are.

MARIA: I am sad to say this also happened to the Native American population.

SAMUEL: Not trying to put anything on anybody, but we don't know.

MARIA: Thanks—Don?

DON [white]: Devil's advocate—

MARIA: This is not debate now.

DON: OK. I got this down—wrote it down earlier. [Looking at his notes.] First of all, we are different. We are absolutely different.

MARIA: Hmm mm and that's OK.

DON: Baloney out there about we're all the same. We are NOT the same. You're smarter than I am, you're taller than I am, you know—we are different.

At this point, Don launches into his question about "why do we hyphenate certain names" and "what the hell do I call you?" discussed in the previous chapter. Later on in the session, Don again raises a provocative point: "Could we talk about reverse discrimination?" Maria responds, "Sure we can. But remember—dialogue, not debate." The group proceeds to talk about affirmative action. Don pulls out a newspaper column that discusses a case of alleged reverse discrimination in New Orleans:

DON: Here are two black people in positions of authority who used race as a tool to hire people. And where is the outcry? There isn't any outcry at all!! Fifty-five white people were denied positions and black people were hired in their place—all you get is a little piece in a newspaper!!! No awareness.

MARIA: I think we are moving a little into the debate, not dialogue—but your point is well taken—I might ask you to think about it this way. Not knowing what the article says. Let's say the company has two thousand white people and now they hire fifty-five black people. Does that give some perspective?

DON: Does give some perspective, but it's not the case.

SAMUEL: What I would like to do, I would like to throw something else in there.

MARIA: OK now, we're not going to debate. I am going to be vigilant.

SAMUEL: OK—group discussion: Can blacks, on the definition [of racism] that Bruce shared with us,[42] can a black actually be racist?

JOHN [white]: Absolutely—human being . . .

STAN [white]: Yeah, I've been the recipient of that . . .

[. . .]

ADALINE [African American]: . . . But we forget the definition that was put out there—"Racism is perpetrated by a majority group that has power and control." From that definition . . . it indicates that people of color can't be racist, but they can be discriminatory, can't be racist.

[. . .]

BILL [white]: I'm curious, why is it so important as a group to split hairs on the definition of racism? Why for example, Adaline, do you feel that—Do you feel empowered by your perception that you [as an African American] can't be racist?

MARIA: Now when you say "why," you're not being judgmental.

BILL: No, not being judgmental—why split hairs? The definition isn't ridding the behavior—it is a descriptive word, and I am curious why you are so reluctant to ascribe that word to you.

ADALINE: You know why? Because it is a reality. I felt the social economic structure, the political structure and how they control because I have continually had to fight against racism all of my life from first grade all the way up until now, and the last five years since we moved to [this city].

Throughout this one session, Maria, the facilitator, admonishes the participants to engage in "dialogue not debate." However, the participants continually push against this constraint. And it is when they do so that some of the most seemingly productive parts of the conversations occur. When Don overstepped the dialogue/debate bound and said, "What the hell do I call you?" a conversation that exposed a wide array of perspectives and stories ensued. These stories were not offered up just as testimony, in which it would have been difficult to tell whether participants had listened to the narratives or not. Instead, people used the stories to argue, reason, and make sense together of the balance between unity and difference.

One might wonder whether the facilitators in a way welcomed debate. As members of the communities in which these forums took place, and as volunteers for a program focused on race relations, didn't they want some debate to happen? I saw little evidence to support such a view. It seemed to me that usually the people who had been recruited to facilitate these programs (as well as the one-evening events sponsored by PBS and the Urban League) had been chosen because of their ability to maintain decorum, to dissuade people from confronting one another, and to insert some type of distraction or conflict-quelling strategy when debate erupted.

Although guidebooks and facilitators tried to maintain a mode of communication that was dialogue and not debate, it was the use of debate within the context of dialogue that enabled participants to convey sincerity. If participants had simply listened and not engaged in the often combative task of reasoning through topics together, they would not have had a chance to demonstrate that their desire to understand was genuine. Because these participants asked each other difficult questions when it might have been easier to avoid conflict, they conveyed that they were taking each other seriously. Without challenging each other, they might not have created connections amongst themselves. When a person communicated a different perspective through telling a story, and someone in the group challenged that perspective, we know that a connection was opened up in the sense of a flow of information. It is as if participants said, "I have listened to you and taken your view seriously enough to be threatened by it, confused by it, or find some aspect of it to disagree with."

Typically, these intergroup dialogues are expected to elicit more honest contributions than other forms of public talk because they take place in a context of safety and openness rather than a situation in which people are strategizing to enable their view to win. The phrase "dialogue not debate" is intended to create safe spaces that enable open conversations to occur.

But some of the boldest flashes of honesty came through when people had the courage to directly confront one another. One example comes from the most direct confrontation I witnessed in these dialogues. As in many of the groups, in the southern Wisconsin group we would take turns reading alternative viewpoints on the causes and solutions for racial discrimination in the discussion guide and then discuss them. The African-American man in that group would read in a labored fashion and frequently mispronounce words. This went unacknowledged for several occasions until the man stated that he had been mispronouncing words intentionally to provide an opportunity to alert the European Americans in the group to their own discrimination and to bring their racism to light:

LUKE: I was in [a local leadership training program]—we were taught this, and I, I often do it, quite often, I likes to do it—to tell us about the European Americans. You see an African American make a mistake and you *know* he made it, and will not correct him. That's a form of discrimination, right there. You *know* he missed. And I have done it here. By reading. Mispronounced the words. And *no one* would say anything about that word or correct it.

[*A white man in the group immediately responds:*]

BOB: That's just being polite, though!

DEB [white, agreeing with Bob and reacting to Luke's statement with shock]: Yeahhhh!

BOB: That is just being polite. I wouldn't *think* of interrupting!

DEB [again agreeing with Bob]: Yeahh.

LUKE: That's not==

DEB: Did you *expect* us to butt in and correct?!!!

LUKE: Not butt in==

DEB: WHA????????!!!

LUKE: See—this is the reason people can't come close together, because we are afraid of one another. We afraid that we would hurt one another.

His challenge to all of us definitely caught our attention. Rather than engage this conflict and address it directly, the group quickly negotiated a way of avoiding it. A few seconds later, Laura, a white woman says, over Deb's retorts and (as the facilitator is trying to intervene):

> I agree. I agree with [Luke]. Just as an example, and I agree—just to give you an example—teaching, I think that if I have a diverse group and I am more gentle with my African-American students, they will quickly pick up on it. And rightfully resent it because basically what they are getting is—in my perspective—they are not getting the same type of attention from me if I don't interact with them. So I think it is a pretty good point.

And then the facilitator reminds us that we can use the word "ouch" at any point to signify that we have been offended and calls for a quick break. Notably, in the next session, when Luke again mispronounced words, no one corrected him, and he did not make a remark about it.

This was an incredibly uncomfortable moment, and the not surprising response by all of us was to avoid allowing it to spiral into an even larger conflict. But even though the participants did not engage this issue further, its brief emergence served a purpose. Luke made his point loud and clear, and got our attention. Even this small amount of directly scrutinizing one another seemed to bring about more attention to a different perspective than merely listening to one another could on its own.

There is another layer to this conversation that speaks to the productive tension between dialogue and debate. What Luke is asking for is to be treated equally, not simply to be listened to. He wants to be heard, but also challenged as if he were white. The other group members' strong sense of appropriate behavior—at least in the social circles they normally inhabit—clash against this desire. Their unchanged behavior in subsequent weeks suggests that Luke did not change their minds. However, they may never have been privy to this glimpse into the experience of racial discrimination if Luke had not chosen to debate rather than dialogue in that moment. Dialogue can open up the deliberative system to the stories of people whose voices are not normally heard, but debate can demonstrate equality among the storytellers.

But doesn't debate exacerbate conflict? Not necessarily. In particular, when whites challenged people of color in these dialogues, this provided an opportunity for people of color to raise awareness at the same time that it ran the risk of inserting divisiveness into the conversations. The central Wisconsin Thursday group provides an example in a discussion that spanned the group's third and fourth sessions. In the third session, the group is talking about one of the members' experiences with employment discrimination. Julie, a white woman, says:

JULIE: You can't always say, though, that happened because she's black. You don't know if that happened. That could happen to me. I could have a master's degree in education [and not get hired for a teaching job]—You can't always assume it is because of race.

[. . .]

GINGER [African American]: Julie is right. It is not always about race. Sometimes they just don't like you.

JULIE: Maybe it really wasn't==

GINGER: I am sure there are instances where it is not about race. But let's be realistic. We know our history in America, in this country, it is probably more times that it is race than it is not.

ADALINE [African American]: That's right.

MARIA [Latina facilitator]: And being on the receiving end—the grey area, not knowing—

JULIE: Maybe it's because they just don't like you, you know what I'm saying?

The topic changes. But at the end of the session, Ginger returns to it:

GINGER: When I say stepping out of your box—If you don't have any friends of different cultures, you would never know that this sort of thing exists. Julie just wasn't aware—it happens and I think [saying this to Julie]—It goes back to getting to know cultures, educating yourself about different cultures and different people, and I think if you understood better that these things do take place, you would accept it more. Not to pick on you, but yeah, sometimes it's not about race. But you know, I don't know, um if you have neighbors or different, or people at work or friends that are other than Caucasian==

JULIE: But the problem is the community doesn't have many yet.

GINGER [looking around the table to the African Americans present that day]: Well, you got four! [laughter]

JULIE: Honestly, I don't see people of color.

GINGER: Well, after next week [when the discussions are over] you can't say that. But I think if we had better relations of people of different cultures—when they tell you their story you'll be more accepting. You can say, well my friend went through the same things. It's like socializing, educating, stepping up. There is like so much to do.

[laughter]

JULIE: No, I really believe that that does happen. That you don't get hired, but you always can't==

MARIA [to Julie]: Do you feel like you're hearing [what Ginger is saying]?

JULIE: Sometimes they maybe use that as an excuse.

GINGER: Well, that would go under the term of "playing the race card." It probably does happen. But the instances that I know, friends and family, it has been genuine. I'm sure people play the race card for their own gain, but that should not overshadow the point that sometimes it *is* about race.

And then in the fourth and final session, Ginger again returns to this theme:

GINGER: If something is not a part of your everyday experience, it is not that you don't understand it, but it has never been an option to think that someone—that someone like me would ever have problems in a community where everything should be OK, equal.

JULIE [conceding]: Don't think of it because it was never right there in my face.

These conversations illustrate how a challenge raised by a white person, here Julie, did not dissolve the dialogue into bedlam but provided an opportunity for the further communication of difference. Like Ginger in the above example, people of color often used scrutiny as an opening to tell stories, facilitate awareness, and disconfirm stereotypes.

The fact that these direct confrontations did not erupt into debilitating conflict reflects both positive and negative aspects of these dialogues. The willingness of these participants to engage in civil communication helped a group return to dialogue when debate occurred, enabling the conversations to continue over the course of several weeks. But this mix of civility and debate also meant that direct challenges to one another were rare. The exchange with Luke about the mispronunciation of words is remarkable for what it produced, but also for the fact that it was a singular experience across the course of my observations. Also, without repeated interactions, groups would most likely not have had the dose of civility that enabled debate to occur. Debate was less rare during first sessions while people were still getting comfortable with one another. On the upside, people did not become more hostile to each other in the last sessions, when the shadow of future meetings was lifted. Perhaps they anticipated crossing each other's paths again in the community.

Mutual Intelligibility through Scrutinizing Stories

The kinds of communication at work in civic intergroup dialogues challenge prevailing notions of deliberation in several ways. First, difference democrats hope that storytelling inserts the voices of marginalized groups into public talk as objects for dominant group members (whites in this case) to listen to. Although the use of narrative served this purpose, it also worked in the opposite direction, in ways that difference democrats might describe as perpetuating domination: people of color listened to the stories of whites. In addition, people did more than just listen to these stories. They used them as objects of debate and scrutiny, even when facilitators constantly reminded them to "dialogue and not debate."

Second, contrary to previous work on storytelling, these narratives did not work primarily to facilitate unity. Stories served to insert difference into the conversation and alerted participants to divergent perspectives. And people did not use storytelling to focus on common identities or common experiences.

Because listening to difference, as well as listening to dominant views, happens in these dialogues, this form of public talk may contribute to the quality of the public sphere and the quality of civic engagement. The inclusion of attention to difference may motivate some people to participate, that is, people who would be reluctant to participate in other forms of public talk because they perceive (and perhaps have experienced) that their views will be ignored. And for those who are used to dominating discussions, participating in public talk that emphasizes listening may force them to become aware of insights they might otherwise not hear. The nature of these dialogues is such that people tell stories that they likely do not tell in other interracial settings, if they have the opportunity to talk in such settings at all.

This potential for dialogue to bring out unrecognized perspectives is part of the reason that conflict resolution strategies often incorporate dialogue. Typically we think of political conflict as something to be reconciled. We tend to turn to either debate or voting to come to a resolution. Debate can subject alternatives to the cold, hard light of day to uncover the best choice. Or, if conflict over the alternatives is intractable, we can use voting.[43] But dialogue is yet another alternative. Dialogue might open up consideration of a problem to new options that can move a conflict forward and reveal unforeseen ways of getting around an impasse. Perhaps its greatest potential is in conflicts between particularly distinct cultures, as in the realm of international relations.

One might argue that claims that dialogue and storytelling can alert people to new perspectives are illogical. If an individual's social location influences how he or she interprets information, as difference democrats assert, then do narratives really communicate information about differences in perspectives and experiences? Won't listeners interpret the stories and the views they hear through their own lenses? Undoubtedly some of this goes on.[44] However, the fact that dialogue conveys experience through the mouth of someone who has actually lived that experience means that these stories do have the potential to create moments of awareness and newfound understanding. The information conveyed in a story could be conveyed in different forms—in a more factual manner, as second-hand information, etc. But the fact that a human being says, "Look, this experience happened to *me*, someone whom you have established a bond with by engaging in face-to-face interaction in this room" means that the information likely takes on a different weight. Even though people interpret narratives through their own particular lenses, the information may carry a different impact than if it had been received in a less personal form.

Alongside the potential benefits of storytelling, there are downsides as well. When considering the rational purposes of public talk, personal reports of experience may actually cause us to give undue weight to some considerations. Personal reports of experience may be *too* convincing. When people relate events from their lives, they often dwell on those experiences that were unusual or particularly vivid or striking.[45] One might argue that these narratives are therefore misrepresentative of an individual's overall experience in a community. When people talk about the frequency of particular experiences in their lives, do these things really occur "often"?[46]

The fact that storytelling in these dialogues often involved more than listening—collective reasoning as well—suggests that part of what people got out of them was a better understanding of the connection between broad public issues and their own community. When someone would mention an international, national, or state issue, or an issue in a nearby town or city, typically the discussion would continue as people brought up related experiences from their own lives or that they had heard second hand. In this way, storytelling not only played the role of exposing people to the experiences and perspectives of others, but was a way for a group of people to make sense of an issue as well as to call into question those statements they found hard to believe. They interpreted issues and events, and reasoned through them in light of their own lives and their own community.[47]

This work of storytelling may help explain why participating in intergroup dialogues on race is related to greater awareness of racism in one's local community. In a recent study of a public screening of the PBS documentary, *The Two Towns of Jasper,* Hernando Rojas and colleagues demonstrate that a random sample of people who watched the video on their own, as well as a random sample of people invited to attend the public screening and facilitated small-group dialogues afterward, showed increased willingness to talk about race relations and also an increased willingness to participate in action related to improving race relations.[48] However, only the people who attended the screening *and* participated in the dialogues afterward also exhibited an increased awareness of racism in their community. The dialogues observed for the present study suggest that it is partly the act of localizing the issue of racism through stories that opens participants' eyes to the extent of racism.[49]

Telling stories that overlap in their relevance to local affairs is a way of building shared perspectives. But there is much in these discussions to challenge our notions of the place of unity or similarity in the deliberative system. Much of deliberative theory expects that in order for deliberation to proceed, participants need to tap into common understandings and shared language. But we see that in these dialogues people are often presenting information that is quite alien to the experience of others in the group. Rather than make appeals based on widely acceptable reasons or widely shared experiences, people told stories that highlighted difference. They started from the presumption that the reasons behind their beliefs might not stretch across racial lines.

The participants nevertheless attempted to tap into a different type of common tool of understanding. These attempts center not on shared language or experience, but on geographic space. Part of what storytelling in these dialogues does is convey information about events that happen in the physical communities that people share. The stories often took the form of, "You won't understand this, but look—it happens right here, in this geographic community that we live in together."

Thus one power of narratives is that they help communicate alternative perspectives among people who share a political community in fact but not in practice. Even if the stories are alien to listeners' experience, and even if the listeners do not agree on the evidence presented within the stories, they can serve as a basis for discussion. In this way they may not produce mutual *understanding* in the sense of similarity of understanding, but they can bring about "mutual intelligibility" or the ability for people to communicate their perspectives to one another.[50] And storytelling within these race dialogues may in fact build consensus in the form of agreement about the ubiquity of discrimination in the community. But notice: even if they do achieve this form of unity, they do so through paying attention to difference.

Ryfe's work alerts us to the potential that when a group does not settle on shared narrative or consensus, the participants will experience a sense of frustration.[51] However, I seldom observed frustration in these groups, despite the fact that participants commonly told stories that clashed with or challenged the preconceptions of others in the groups.

It may be that when participants know that the purpose of public talk is partly to listen to others, hearing different stories is less likely to lead to frustration. People seemed instead to value the exposure to these stories of difference, as in comments like, "See that's good to hear because we don't see that perspective." The participants did not necessarily find the experience of listening to stories to be a pleasant one, but their earnestness and commitment suggest they nonetheless found it worthwhile.

The particular structure of these dialogues mattered for the use of storytelling within them in other respects as well. In her study of storytelling in online deliberation, Francesca Polletta concludes that the setting matters a great deal for storytelling. Who tells stories and when depends on whether storytelling is perceived as appropriate for a particular context and speaker. In her analysis of discussion following the AmericaSpeaks deliberations over the future of Ground Zero, Polletta found that storytelling was used less often when the conversations turned to policy.[52] However, in the race dialogue groups, storytelling was often used in the context of discussions over policy, perhaps because the structure of the dialogues encouraged this behavior. In addition, public officials as well as community residents told stories, as we shall see in chapter 9, perhaps increasing the legitimacy of this mode of talk in the dialogues.

CHAPTER EIGHT

Authority and Legitimacy in Dialogue

Difference democrats propose dialogue as an antidote to the dominating tendencies of deliberation. However, the previous two chapters suggest that in the practice of civic dialogue, it is not simply the case that members of marginalized groups talk and members of dominant groups listen. This corner of the deliberative system involves the dual tasks of listening and argumentation, and we have seen people of a variety of racial backgrounds engage in both of these acts. If that is the case, do these programs actually shake up typical patterns of who has power in public talk? Do these dialogues attain a freedom from power that other aspects of deliberation seem unable to achieve?

The politics of difference and the politics of unity give us different expectations about what occurs. A politics-of-difference view leads us to expect that dialogue allows people to challenge dominant conceptions, resist emerging consensus, and question standard notions of power. But this does not necessarily happen. Opening up the deliberative system to alternative modes of communication like storytelling might merely create new forms of hierarchy rather than achieve freedom from the power dynamics of the broader society.[1] Also, acknowledging the pull of the politics of unity might lead us to expect that the group dynamics would encourage people to set aside their racial group attachments in order to enable the group to forge consensus.

Civic intergroup dialogue programs exude a self-consciousness about power imbalances that suggest these conversations involve an active questioning of assumptions about whose ideas are worthy contributions to public talk. How do people in these dialogues negotiate whose voice is a legitimate contribution—that is, a genuine, credible, and authentic one—and who therefore has authority or power over the topics of discussion and the perspectives through which they are discussed? Understanding how this works is essential to understanding what these conversations can achieve and what deliberative democracy contributes to the ongoing task of creating the public's sense of itself.

Thus this chapter probes how people negotiate power over the conversation in these contexts of dialogue that supposedly question conventional standards of authority and legitimacy. It also asks how this process bears on the simultaneous process of negotiating consensus or disagreement. Whereas the previous chapter examined how different modes of communication work in these dialogues, this chapter examines more closely how power works, particularly how racial identity matters for the give and take of power in these conversations.

To investigate, I used the observations of dialogues to analyze all conversations related to four race-related policies. I analyzed the conversations in the groups that allowed me to tape record their full conversations: the two groups in the central Wisconsin city, the group in the southern Wisconsin city, and the two groups that met in Aurora, Illinois. (Please see chapter 6 for an overview). I chose two of the policies, affirmative action and reparations for slavery, because the discussion guidebook instructed participants to discuss these issues (and therefore I knew that the observations provided some data on the content of talk about these issues in each of the groups). I chose the other two policies, immigration policy and language policy, because these were salient national issues with respect to race and ethnic relations at the time that I conducted this study, but were not prominent topics in the discussion guide.[2] This enabled me to examine how people negotiated which topics were acceptable for discussion. In addition, the fact that the Aurora evening group did not follow the discussion guide provides a useful point of comparison.

This approach is a contrast to the strategy William Gamson used in his influential study on political understanding. In *Talking Politics*, Gamson assembled focus groups and asked people to discuss four prominent public issues. In my approach, I did not assemble the groups, choose the topics for the discussion guide, nor attempt to influence which issues participants brought up of their own accord. Instead, I observed which issues arose and how the group members negotiated the place of these issues on the agenda. Thus, in contrast to Gamson's approach, I was able to observe *how* people negotiated attention to particular issues.

These analyses also therefore extend previous attempts to observe how people interpret political issues in the context of authentic interaction. Previous studies have investigated how people make sense of politics in interpersonal talk that they themselves have created in segregated settings such as racially homogenous groups in neighborhood corner stores and barbershops,[3] but this study provides an inside look at authentic talk in an interracial group.

Legitimate Topics, Legitimate Views

Which issues did the participants allow onto the agenda, and how did they negotiate attention to these issues?

The groups that followed the discussion guide were asked to discuss reparations and affirmative action. The manner in which the groups treated reparations demonstrates that participants were not consistently using the dialogue to engage in contentious discussion. There were some topics that no one seemed to want to debate or challenge dominant opinions about. Reparations for slavery was clearly one of these. Across all of the groups, the tendency was to try to avoid this issue. No one talked about it until the curriculum specifically asked them to do so, and once they had passed this section of the guide, they did not mention it again. And when the guide suggested they discuss it, the facilitators and participants approached the topic with trepidation. In a telling demonstration of this, the group that did not follow the guide (the Aurora evening group) never addressed the issue.

Perhaps because of the sensitive nature of the topic of reparations, when the guidebook put it on the agenda, all of the groups showed signs of groping for consensus rather than engaging in talk about subgroup differences. Sometimes group members pointed out agreement on the policy. In all of these cases, that agreement was opposition to reparations. In the one group in which someone made a strong statement in favor of reparations (the southern Wisconsin group, articulated by a white woman), no one disagreed with her and the conversation quickly turned to another topic.[4]

All five groups discussed the two topics the guide instructed them to talk about—affirmative action and reparations for slavery—except for the Aurora evening group, which as stated above did not discuss reparations. Talk, or lack of it, about the two issues not prominently featured in the guide—immigration policy and language policy—provide clues as to what drove the groups' agendas. The two Aurora groups discussed both topics. Of the three Wisconsin groups, only the central Wisconsin Wednesday group turned its attention, briefly, to immigration policy. That group also discussed language policy, as did the central Wisconsin Thursday group, briefly. The southern Wisconsin group discussed neither.

When the guide did not specifically encourage discussion of a topic, what conditions seemed to encourage participants to take it up? It appears that the topics groups took up were driven partly by the composition of the groups and local current events. It was the Aurora groups that were more likely to talk about both immigration and language policy than the groups in the Wisconsin cities. This is not surprising, given that Aurora has a larger Hispanic population (see table A.1 in methods appendix). Although many Hispanic people in Aurora are not actually immigrants, the whites in the discussions tended to categorize all Hispanics together and classified both immigration and language policy as "Hispanic issues." Also, the prominence of the Hispanic community is apparent even in a brief visit to the city. Several blocks from the building in which the Aurora evening group met is a large supermarket whose signs are almost entirely in Spanish. I stopped by one Monday evening and noticed that I was the only non-Hispanic person inside. Mexican music played on the intercom. I overheard only Spanish as I listened to the other customers and the clerks. Earlier in the evening, I had spent some time in the public library and overheard a group of teenagers chatting, switching back and forth between English and Spanish as they did so. I went downtown to a restaurant and a bakery, and heard the clerks and customers speaking only Spanish in both places.

Another reason that it is not surprising that the Aurora groups discussed immigration and language policy issues more than the other groups is that it was only in these groups that Latinos were participants (a Latina in each group). There were Latinas in both of the central Wisconsin groups as well, but they were facilitators and they stuck closely to the guidelines that asked for facilitators to "remain neutral."

When the facilitator in the Thursday central Wisconsin group did try to insert disagreement, she did so by urging those who were overlooking dissent to listen more closely. For example, when discussing reparations, several whites, including Don, made comments opposing the policy, using arguments of "I never had slaves. You folks were never slaves." Samuel and Ginger, two African Americans, stated that they did not necessarily agree with reparations, but believe that history needs to be recognized. Don responded:

> Anybody who is alive who doesn't know that slavery was a horrible thing has got to be a robot. You don't have to be a Democrat to be a jackass. . . . Apologies are only good when they are heartfelt. Making an apology would be hypocritical. Because I don't know what I am sorry for. I didn't do that. I may be sorry for what you had to go through, what your people had to go through, what the Native Americans had to go through. Native Americans do have it pretty nice, they have reservations, have nice casinos, they are not hurting at all. . . . Accept the fact that it happened, it happened to you, them, whoever. But let's get on with it.

Maria, the facilitator, tried to shift attention to alternative views by asking Don to recall the stories he had heard:

MARIA [Latina]: But then what about the day-to-day stuff that's happening, Don?

DON: The day-to-day stuff, it's going to happen, and I think that each and every one who really has any compassion for each other has gotta step forward when you see these things happening like that. You know, you apply for a job, qualified, and didn't feel that the law was going to protect you. That's frightening. That's alarming that something like that could happen today.

By emphasizing that the views of people of color are legitimate and credible contributions to the discussion, Maria exerted authority over the discussion and got Don to acknowledge the views he had been overlooking.

Liza, the African-American facilitator in the Aurora evening group, pursued a more active interpretation of her role. Indeed, she was an aggressive facilitator whose style many of the participants perceived to be overbearing and inappropriate. Like Maria, she influenced which views and topics people brought into the discussion, but she did so by questioning rather than validating the legitimacy of these contributions. In chapter 6, we saw that tension arose in this group over whether or not even to discuss the issue of immigration policy. In more detail, white participants in the group alluded to immigration briefly in the first three sessions. Each time, Liza changed the topic to focus either on American Indians or African Americans. In the third session, she brought up the topic of "loose borders," but did so in order to argue that the government had ignored immigration enforcement so that cocaine could be transported across the borders in order to further oppress African Americans through the drug trade. When she did this, others in the group jumped at the chance to talk about immigration policy. She quickly changed the topic.

In the fourth session, Adam blatantly stated that he wished our conversations had focused more on Hispanics and she reacted abruptly:

ADAM [white]: I would like to see the study circles concentrate somewhat more on bridging the gap between the Hispanic community and the European community you know==

LIZA [abruptly]: I will pass that along to Connecticut [meaning the Study Circles Resource Center, despite the fact that she had repeatedly stated that we need not stick to the published curriculum].

ADAM: Hmm [chuckling to himself]. Maybe Mary Jane [Hollis, the director of the Aurora Community Study Circles] would be more local perhaps. That's the overriding issue I think in Aurora.

LIZA: That is where it would have to go because it would change the whole platform [pointing to her book, which is titled, *Facing the Challenge of Racism and Race Relations*].

The group continued to talk about Hispanic immigration, particularly employment, and in a few minutes, Liza interjected:

LIZA: This is not a new pattern.
CHRISTINE [white]: I don't remember our government looking the other way and allowing==
LIZA: It goes back not to immigrants but to people who were already here. . . . What is happening to the Mexican Americans or illegals—there is not a thing that the African-American community has not experienced. Work from sun up to sun down. Did work that nobody else wanted to do. Paid nothing, sometimes not paid at all. Had six, seven, eight, nine, ten, twelve people to a house. Just to have a roof. None of this is new to the African American.[5]

Liza commonly deflected attention away from Hispanics or other social groups by calling attention to the relative oppression of African Americans. That pattern showed up in other groups as well. For example, during a discussion of affirmative action, the African-American man in the southern Wisconsin group redirected the conversation by questioning whether it was appropriate to categorize women as minorities. He said that paying attention to gender took away from a focus on race.

Liza's style was unique among the facilitators I observed in these groups, and the comments of participants in her group who had previously been members of other study circles in Aurora indicate it was unique among other facilitators in the Aurora program. She often steered the course of the discussion and dictated which issues and racial groups were worthy of attention. Her behavior might cause us to pay less attention to what occurred in this group because of its atypicality. But I take the group instead as a valuable opportunity to examine what goes on in these conversations when the ground rule of equal participation and the norm of civility are less respected.

Who Represents Diversity?

The conversations in all of the groups were struggles over which topics were legitimate, but they were also struggles over which participants were legitimate representatives of marginalized views. This was perhaps most clear in conversations about the diversity of the dialogue groups. In the central Wisconsin group that met in the library, the Mexican-American facilitator made a rare mention (for her) of a story from her own life and acknowledged her identity as a Latina. She told about a time in which a police officer gave her a warning for speeding and marked her race as "white." She said she was surprised by this. In response, the African-American man in the group said, in a way that conveyed he truly did not know how she identified herself racially, *"Are you white?"*

Similarly in the contentious Aurora group (the evening group), when one of the participants confronted Liza about her combative facilitation style at the beginning of the second session, she defended herself with the argument that she had been trying to represent the perspective of African Americans. A discussion of whether or not the group is "diverse" ensued:

LIZA: This, in all fairness, is not what we have come to know as a diverse group.

MATT [white]: Well it wasn't last week, but it is more diverse now. [Including the facilitator, that night the group included one white man, three white women, an African-American woman, an African-American man, a Puerto-Rican woman, and an Arab-American woman.]

LIZA: I suppose if you want to call it more diverse, it is OK.

MATT: In terms of race, I think it is.

LIZA [questioning the validity of this claim]: You have one Hispanic and if I am not to be a participant you have one NaBAB [Elic, the African-American man, had introduced himself as "a NaBAB, a Native Born American Black"].

MATT: Right.

BETH [white, interjecting]: Well she's Puerto Rican [pointing to Lucy], and you are—Amaal? What is your?

AMAAL [Arab American]: Arabic.

BETH: So . . .

LIZA [turning to Amaal]: But to the outside world, is that how you function? [She is questioning whether we should consider Amaal a contribution to the "diversity" of the group.]

AMAAL [somewhat shocked]: Of course.

LIZA: When people go and see you, do they see you as Arabic or do they see you as a white person?

AMAAL: Many people don't know what Arabic people look like, but I am Arabic to me.

LIZA: Yeah to you, you are, and because I know you, you are to me.

BETH: And the name is definitely Arabic.

LIZA: But I mean to live and function, I don't know that it is viewed exactly that way.

Later in that session, Elic, the African-American male participant, articulated some misgivings about attention to categories other than African American, as he explained why he disliked the term "diversity":

> I used to be at diversity meetings at [a university]. It was all whites and Japanese-Americans and I asked where were the blacks and Mexicans and they said, "This is about cultures, not race." People use diversity in different ways, they use it as a euphemism to exclude race.

In the third session of this group, Elic, similar to Liza's remarks in the second session, denied that Arab Americans deserve attention as a marginalized group. In talking about attempts to improve race relations through education, I mentioned that in teaching a public opinion course, I had struggled to include survey studies on people other than whites, and an Arab-American student had confronted me about the lack of attention to the views of Arab-Americans in the course. To this, Elic responded:

ELIC: But Kathy, these other people can blend in. I can't blend in unless I become like Michael Jackson and wear hair extensions.

KATHY [white]: I don't know . . .

ELIC: Oh yeah they do! They do! I mean I have seen whites and Arabs—they dissolve, nobody blinks an eye. It is their ability to blend in, period.

ADAM [white]: No==

ELIC: Let me finish. Also they come from a strong culture. So they are businessmen from way back, I mean the Arabs I know are well educated, they are well off, so they can afford to come—but they can also choose to. I can't do that.

KATHY: I don't know . . .

ELIC: I can't do that.

KATHY: Well the comments that were said to me certainly made it seem as though they felt as though they weren't blending in, at least on campus. But you know, it is hard for me to say.

ELIC: It certainly may seem at least on their part, yeah, especially after 9/11 you see==

ADAM: Well I used to teach high school in Chicago for one year. A class I taught for eight weeks was an Arab bilingual class. And they can't blend in. They were Palestinians, Kuwaitis, and they definitely did not blend in. And then definitely when they go to city hall, they definitely got the same looks that African-American kids complained about getting. So you can say that about the Irish—they were able to overcome it, because you can't tell—but I'm with Kathy—Arabs are definitely as shunned as African Americans can be.

Liza then changed the topic.

In the last session, Dolores, a white woman, brought up a concern that attention to Hispanics and immigration draws away attention from African Americans. She also mentioned that she was disappointed in the diversity of the group. The program director, who sat in on the end of that session, remarked that this group was fortunate to include the views of a wide range of ethnic groups. Again, Liza retorted. "Of the ten people who were registered for the group, seven of them were Caucasian, one Puerto Rican, one African and one undeclared [referring to Amaal], but who in networking in the community probably would be viewed as a white person, I don't know." [6]

These exchanges underscore that not all identities counted equally in these discussions. Just as people struggled to balance unity and difference in terms of how to conceptualize racial diversity, they also struggled with who had power to speak and to be listened to. Although all the groups I observed held the black/white divide at the top of their agenda, they each were meeting in communities that were struggling with a broader array of differences, even beyond race. The fact that these groups did not give all dimensions of race consideration, much less equal consideration, speaks to the fact that these discussions were not just about sharing and listening to the stories of whomever wanted to talk. Participants were actively negotiating whose views were legitimate contributions.

At the same time that the participants negotiated over who rightly represented the perspective of a person of color, they also struggled with who had legitimacy on particular issues. These struggles were more common in the more contentious groups such as the Aurora evening group and the central Wisconsin Thursday group. For example, in the Aurora evening group, the tone that Liza set led to a continual questioning of the appropriateness of certain topics on the agenda and who ought to address them. They used the dialogues for more than listening. This was particularly apparent around the issue of language policy. In the first session, Liza vehemently defended Ebonics and set a tone that dampened any sustained consideration of language policy. One of her statements from that conversation was as follows:

> We never called it Ebonics. It was a way of communicating with our great grandparents, our grandparents, and our parents, who did not have learning opportunities in every case, but in every case they were crystal clear in what they said. There was no mistaking about it. And you understood it because understanding is with the heart. It is not always with the intellect.

Part of that conversation involved an argument with a white woman in the group, who taught English as a second language at a nearby college. This woman, Beth, asserted that Ebonics "came from American English and African language blended together," which Liza disagreed with abruptly, saying:

LIZA: No it doesn't.
BETH: Yeah, I have the book at home.
LIZA: Trust me. I'm black. I know. I grew up in it. That is not where it comes from. It comes from a group of people who were brought here who were not permitted to speak their own tongue.

This stark assertion that there is only one valid perspective on the issue—Liza's—dampened the debate that night. Rather than engaging the topic and inviting sustained consideration of Liza's and others' experience with Black English, the group stumbled uncomfortably to other topics.

Later sessions continued to include a struggle over whose views were legitimate contributions to the dialogues. In the second session, Beth raised the topic of Ebonics and defended her position with the book she had mentioned in hand. Elic had just joined the group, and he showed impatience with the topic:

> I would also like to say that we really shouldn't spend our time discussing languages. What we are here for is to deal with issues dealing with barriers.

In the third session, it was clear that he objected to residents of Aurora not speaking English. He explicitly silenced Lucy, the Puerto Rican in the group. Liza asked, "So how do we deal with our local issues?" After a few remarks, the conversation proceeded:

ADAM [white]: Hispanic versus Anglo issue here in Aurora, that's a problem.
LIZA: That's a problem?
ADAM: Yeah! I mean there is a lack of communication between the two groups.
CHRISTINE [white]: Who are the racists?
ELIC: Suppose I were to say Hispanics?
ADAM: I'd say you've got a problem out there. I'd ask you why.
ELIC: Ohhhhhh, language. Lack of language.
ADAM: What about the language?
ELIC: Nobody understands it.
LUCY [Puerto Rican]: I understand it!
ELIC: But you're not in this conversation.

ADAM: I say a lot of people I hang around with have lived in Aurora their entire life, and that's part of the problem, and again, that's part of the Hispanics' problem. They're not looking outside their own ethnic group on certain issues. We drive down parts of Chicago, all the signs are in Polish, in Korean, in Chinatown—all in Chinese. So people in Aurora tend to think that the Hispanics are the only group who comes here who don't lose their language, but that's false on two levels. Other groups *do* come, and the Hispanics *do* learn English. [Turning to Elic] So you really don't like Hispanics? Or are you just . . .

ELIC: No no no no—just stimulating conversation.

Elic's retort to Lucy that "you're not in this conversation" blatantly underscores that, by making assertions about whose voice is a valid contribution, participants at times prevented consideration of alternative views. Elic shut Lucy out of this discussion completely, even though objectively she had authentic, relevant experiences to add.

The fourth session of this group presented a reprieve from this pattern of repeatedly contesting who had authority. We were a slightly smaller group that night. Lucy, the Puerto Rican woman, Matt, a white man, and Elic, the African-American man, were absent. We sat in a more intimate arrangement than the other nights, tightly fitting around one small table. In such close proximity we had what one person remarked afterward was a "real dialogue." It was less contentious and the facilitator did not interrupt other participants as often. The discussion contained more attention to issues and views that Liza and Elic had previously deemed illegitimate. Liza and Amaal, the Arab-American woman, were the only people of color present that night.

It was in that context that a sustained discussion of illegal immigration emerged. It was peppered with prefacing statements that signaled the group members were afraid of sounding racist. It took on a consensual tone as the three white people with experience with immigrants in the workplace talked about their beliefs that illegal immigration depresses wages and causes people to overlook African Americans. At the same time, they made comments that having Hispanic immigrants in general is "good for the neighborhood," downtown development, and crime rates. They encouraged each other to talk about immigration and made remarks that it is acceptable to oppose illegal immigration. As they did so, they also acknowledged—by talking about inflammatory letters to the editor—that opposition to immigration is often racist.

These discussions underscore a trade-off. When participants perceived that they were doing "real dialogue," a wider range of views was allowed into the discussion, and the content was less contentious. That is, greater civility meant less questioning of legitimacy and authority. When all views are equal and welcome, discussions are more likely to include often-overlooked perspectives. However, such a norm of courtesy means that contesting the views expressed is less appropriate.

At the same time that participants sought public talk that did not trample minority views, many of them wanted the talk to do more than merely "not trample." We can see this in the evidence in chapters 4 and 5 that these programs are implemented not just for self-development but for the pursuit of social justice. Many people sought for this talk to produce some type of change, and taking action to achieve that presumably involves some scrutinizing of alternative paths to take. The struggles over legitimacy suggest that in the practice of public talk the desire for inclusivity and the desire for action are continually in tension.

Using Legitimacy to Struggle with Consensus

Tension over whose concerns are valid representations of racial oppression demonstrates how people struggled over legitimacy. But an additional dimension of power dynamics in these groups centers on how people used claims to legitimacy to exert authority over the path of the conversation and in particular to sort out whether the conversation tended toward consensus or toward disagreement.

The conversations on reparations demonstrate that sometimes people would assert legitimacy to insert alternative views, even though they were in basic agreement with the apparent consensus in a group. On this controversial topic, the pull of unity was strong, but African Americans nevertheless asserted some authority and encouraged the other participants to consider why someone might favor reparations. The central Wisconsin Thursday group provides an example. Initially, whites in the group expressed opposition to and skepticism about reparations. But then Samuel, the African-American man in the group, asked the group members to think about the issue from an alternative point of view:

> I understand where you're coming from but *let's take this from another angle* [emphasis added]. When I heard Jesse Jackson talk about this here it opened up some understanding to me. What we gotta realize is that we were forced over here to this country and we were made to live a lifestyle that was not conductive to our culture, so we need restitution.

Shortly after, Samuel enabled the group to turn its attention back toward consensus by agreeing that "we would probably have a civil war in this country over" reparations, and that it seemed like such a policy would be difficult to implement.

On other topics, Samuel and others were more reluctant to let the group tend toward consensus. At the beginning of the second session, it was clear that at least one member of the group had been mulling over the group's conversation about affirmative action from the previous week. This person, Mike, a white man, said that he was personally ambivalent about the policy:

> I wanted to ask others about—I was reminded of an old saying, heard it was attributed to Lincoln: "You can't make a poor man rich by making a rich man poor." Thinking of it in terms of our discussion about trying to outreach and trying to hire a bilingual person into the library system, the flip side of that being someone who is equally qualified and didn't get it because they weren't [bilingual]. Some days when I think about that, I come down on the side of the library, but in other days, I wonder—I wonder what other people's thoughts are. The broad context is affirmative action. I have wanted to and had to practice affirmative action in certain ways and to a certain degree, but wondered what people thought about it. Where does it stop being good and start being punitive to other groups?

Someone changed the topic when he raised this question, but later in the conversation, when defining the term "reverse discrimination," the following exchange occurred:

MARY [white]: Reverse discrimination gets us into what Mike was talking about—affirmative action—Michigan and California are the two schools I've been reading about in which they tried to institute affirmative action. . . . But you know I think until it probably affects each one of us individually, you know you can sit here and say we need affirmative action and we need it now and it should be everywhere and what have you, but if you are the one that has the daughter or you're the one that has the sister or the brother that didn't get the job because they put another person in it because of affirmative action, probably look at it a whole different way. . . .

ADALINE [African American]: *Well, let me give you some examples of institutional racism so that it is kind of clear to people* [emphasis added]—I had been in the corporate world for a long time, and I was in banking and it was just pretty clear that there was institutional racism because across the board, even though our neighborhood was made up of—a big portion of the neighborhood had African Americans, when you went into a bank, that the bank itself hardly had any African Americans to service that community when there was plenty, including myself, African Americans that were qualified—just as qualified as anyone else. Even here in [this city], you know I came with good *gobs* of experience, masters degrees and everything else, and I could not even get a teller's job initially when we got here five years ago.

SAMUEL [African American]: Still don't have a decent job.

ADALINE: And that is a horrible institutional racism. They would not, they just would not hire, based upon the color of my skin. Regardless of my credentials. Sometimes they would look at my credentials and say "Whoa!" And say, "Come on in!" They want to interview you, then all of a sudden it changed because of the color of my skin.

The conversation turned to racial profiling, and the members expressed general agreement that profiling goes on—at least in other cities. Then some of the whites started to bring in stories of witnessing discrimination, building the case for sustained attention to the experiences of people in particular racial groups:

MARK [white]: When I sold my house [in another state], the city was maybe one third African American. The realtor, regardless, he can't say, "We don't want to sell it to blacks." But my neighbor, who I always thought was not prejudiced—a school teacher—we had some black people come though the house. The next day he came over and said, "Are you going to sell to *those people*?" Well I think he was looking at it economically, because his property—you know the old block-buster deal . . . it's racism. But people that ordinarily are not racist==

[*Various people comment that that behavior is racist.*]

PATRICIA [white]: Mark, when you lived [there], did you see a lot less institutional racism in a place like [that city]?

MARK: I believe I did, yes.

PATRICIA: Yeah.

MARK: Because we had so many different ethnic groups there.

PATRICIA: See, that is what I am feeling, too. Where I moved from this was just *finished.*

MIKE: Other places, like big university towns like Madison, have a more cosmopolitan atmosphere. These things are less—people are less prejudiced.

KATHY [white]: Well, we still have it, though.

PATRICIA: Talk about that. I'm curious, because that's like the bastion of the progressive. . . .

I talked about various forms of discrimination that occur in Madison. Moments later as people began to talk about quotas and reverse discrimination as it relates to colleges and universities, Samuel made yet another plea to the group to listen to the stories of people of color:

> But you also got to look at that political power structure, because they want to control, and they don't want too many of this group, and this and that there. *See you all got to understand it, because you haven't been through that, haven't been exposed to that* [emphasis added]. When I went to college. . . . I was getting straight As on my tests. I'll never forget this: A professor said, "There are some students in here getting As who are straight D students." So I stood up, "Are you referring to me sir?" He turned red. I said, "Well, I *am* college material. I *am* getting As so who are you referring to?" . . . I think a lot of this is because of the system, the way they view us, think we are taking something away from them, this and that there, but this is not the case.

When Samuel says, "See you all got to understand it, because you haven't been through that, haven't been exposed to that" and when Adaline says "Well, let me give you some examples of institutional racism so that it is kind of clear to people," they are asserting legitimacy, asserting that their contributions are authentic. Samuel states that he wants the participants to "look at that political power structure." He invokes his credibility on the topic of job discrimination to urge the other participants to question their understanding of and preferences on affirmative action. Their assertions do more than insert stories of difference or bring recognition to the fact that discrimination occurs. Their personal experience functions as a kind of expertise that is not necessarily a substitute for lack of factual information, but it has a unique claim to credibility that gives them authority. By emphasizing that they have unique claims to the topic at hand, they exert authority over the conversation and shift it away from the emerging consensus that affirmative action is detrimental.

The Riskiness of Asserting Authenticity

Claims to legitimacy at times conferred authority on a speaker but also at times resulted in a special burden. Speakers who sought to be regarded as legitimate or credible representatives of people who had experienced racial discrimination were at times asked to speak on behalf of entire racial groups.

At the end of the first session in the groups that followed the printed curriculum, participants were asked to discuss several scenarios related to discrimination, which they chose from a list. In the central Wisconsin Wednesday group, a white woman immediately latched on to an

affirmative action example because of a recent event in nearby Milwaukee. Seventeen white police officers had just won a court case in which
they had sued the city and the former police chief, an African American.
The court had decided that the chief had promoted less qualified black
and female officers to the position of captain over the white officers. The
conversation quickly turned to whether or not the local police department
had any people of color. The white facilitator noted that the city was actively recruiting people of color, and a white man supported this, noting
"they should be representative of the community." Others agreed, and this
tending toward consensus continued as Samuel talked about his employers discriminating against him. But then Mary, a white woman, started to
voice her concerns:

> You want a diverse workforce. You want your community to employ people,
> what have you, but when you get to a certain job or a job that demands a
> qualifying exam or qualifications and you don't have a minority who meets
> those qualifications, how—that's the crux of the matter there. Do you then
> pick the less qualified minority, or do you pick the most qualified person
> according to, you know . . . ?

The conversation continued for a few moments until Adaline, the African-
American woman in the group, argued that if "you want to represent your
community, and you want to make sure that you are showing that you
are diverse and you do offer equal opportunities," you have to go out and
recruit people. Several comments later Samuel remarked that part of the
obstacle is changing the community so that it is welcoming to people of
color:

> If they can not be accepted, then they are not going to stay long. You can
> give them a job, you can bring them in, but they've got to be accepted, they
> gotta be treated like individuals. Um, because um, I know in fact that we
> have people here right now working in [this city] and they hate it because
> they are not getting treated right.

In response, Mark, a white man, turned to him, and said the following:

> Is part of the problem on the other side of the coin, Samuel, do you think
> because I think ah you know it is your ethnic group you're talking about,
> they have a right and share their heritage and their subculture and you
> know—and that is good—and maybe they don't have that as accessible to
> them here in [this city] and maybe not that they are not accepted by the
> general—but they don't have the pocket of people that they can identify
> with.

Notice how Mark asks Samuel to speak on behalf of African Americans. This example underscores a risk people of color took in asserting legitimacy by announcing that they had authentic experience as victims of discrimination and as targets of policies designed to remedy such discrimination. Sometimes, when people asserted that they were credible representatives of people who had experienced racial discrimination, whites took this as an invitation to ask them to speak on behalf of entire racial and ethnic groups. People of color were generally quite patient with such requests. But their visible discomfort at times underscored that claims to legitimacy came at a cost.

Language Policy and Resistance to Authority Claims

People were often willing to concede authority in these dialogues, but not unconditionally. Matters of language seemed to be one policy area in which people resisted allowing attention to difference to upset a bedrock source of unity: shared language. As Schildkraut demonstrates, the idea that shared language is a necessary part of a healthy polity pervades many aspects of national identity, not just liberal individualism. Even civic republicanism asserts that people need a common language in order to engage in civic life together.[7] Throughout these discussions, there was a pervasive belief that a vibrant civic life and a vibrant economy require that people speak English. Even though these discussions gave some attention to alternative points of view, and even though some people attempted to frame a contribution to the discussion as a particularly authentic or credible statement on bilingualism, these dialogues did little to alter the insistence that people learn English.

In the Aurora daytime group (not the evening group with Liza), one of the participants was a Mexican-American woman with personal experience with bilingualism. On the first day this group met, the woman, Cilia, talked about how she has "a problem with Rs, when I roll them," something that a teacher commented on when she was in grade school and about which she continued to be sensitive. Later in the conversation, one of the older white women, Ruby, said delicately that she expects people to learn English:

> I think there is a place to be yourself and have pride in your roots and let your children know about your heritage, but I also think there is a dividing line. I think out in the business world, if you want to be a receptionist, you had better know how to speak correctly. I find myself—I like to think that I am broad-minded but I find myself resenting people from other cultures

that have chosen to live here but want to keep their identity so separate. . . . In your own home, I don't care what you do, but out in the public, and if you choose to live in this country, then I think you have to know the language and you have to go along with what is going on here. Is that coming out like a bigot? Does anybody want to shout "ouch"?

A few comments later, Steve, the black man in the group, agreed with Ruby, but then turned to Cilia to ask her, "what are your thoughts on that?"[8] Cilia responded by stating that her native culture does not put a premium on education, so it is difficult for Hispanics to learn English when they come to the United States. But then she continued by telling a personal story that emphasized the value of bilingual education:

CILIA: I know what you are talking about because when I put my daughter in school, we spoke Spanish at home, and I tend to speak both languages. My husband was more Spanish-speaking at home. . . . I thought the bilingual program was helping her learn English, not emphasizing the Spanish language itself. So actually she learned the Spanish language until she was in the second grade. And I thought, "Oh no. When she gets in third grade she's going to have a difficult time" because they were going to release her to the English program. But it *did* benefit her. My son, I didn't put him in that program. I went ahead and put him in the regular English program, and he actually—now he doesn't speak or write the Spanish language, but my daughter is now dominant in both the English and Spanish.

STEVE: That's interesting.

CILIA: So she actually corrects me in my spelling and my Spanish, but my son is at a disadvantage. But it is also that we don't educate ourselves, we think about coming over here and making money whichever way we want because over there in Mexico—poverty, you know, it is so bad. You are lucky if you have electricity in whatever little town you live. But I think it is educating—when you come over here learn, be willing to learn because it is there.

Steve seemed to learn something from hearing Cilia's point of view when he remarked, "that's interesting." But when the group reconvened for the second session, it seemed to be Cilia who was most affected by the conversation. She said the conversations "got me thinking a lot," and had led her to clarify her previous opinions. She told a story about how the conversations had led to a "dialogue with my brother-in-law and his wife— trying to explain to him that he is Mexican. But he resisted that, said he was American. . . . He is totally against teaching his kids their Mexican background . . . doesn't want them to learn Spanish."

Moments later, our entire group witnessed the utility of bilingualism and its presence in everyday life in Aurora. As Cilia spoke, several of us noticed a Hispanic-woman and a young girl in the doorway behind her. We waved her in and she asked in Spanish if anyone speaks the language. Cilia then spoke with her in Spanish and realized that the woman was looking for her daughter. Cilia went to help her locate her daughter, who was presumably somewhere in the building. None of the group members remarked about this incident, during this or the subsequent sessions. The fact that it *was* unremarkable is perhaps an indicator of the familiarity people in the group had with similar incidents, and their ambivalence about the need for bilingualism.

Later in that session, several people in the group acknowledged that there is a great deal of resentment among non-Hispanics in Aurora about Spanish-speaking businesses. They did so in a second-hand fashion, referring to the opinions of other people or whites in general. Both Ruby and Sara conveyed that they have positive attitudes toward their Spanish-speaking neighbors and wished to communicate with them. However, in the third session, Sara displayed clear distaste for speaking Spanish rather than English by referring to an incident "years ago":

> There was this woman who was going to sue a beauty parlor because the women were speaking Spanish. That was rude to do that in front of a white customer. There ought to be a law to regulate those people from speaking Spanish in front of white customers. When you are at work you should speak English.

Cilia responds with her personal experience:

CILIA: But there is a company I worked for—when I went in there, I didn't know—but that was the problem they had—majority working there were Hispanic, getting paid very little, conditions very hot, could not speak Spanish during working hours. How can they communicate with these people? It was a big thing—they had labor relations in there—I would not be able to tell Spanish people who came there that I couldn't give them an application because they didn't speak English. *Do you know how I felt?* [emphasis added] Because they are looking at me like, "You're Hispanic!" And I was like, "I am sorry. You need to speak English to be able to . . ." "But you know Spanish, don't you?" Sometimes I would just make an excuse, excuse myself because that was very hard. Personally, I just think we have to respect who is around us. If, Sara, you come up to me==

SARA [white]: But if I'm paying to get my hair cut and they are like chit chit chit chit chit [imitating high pitched, rapid Spanish] I am paying them, they are my slave for the hour.

RACHEL [white]: OHHHHHH!
[Others say "ohhhhhh" and make audible objections to Sara's statement.]
CILIA: But are you going in there because the Hispanic lady is going to charge you ten dollars for a haircut or if you go to a fancier place they are going to charge you thirty for the same haircut?

The discussion showed no resolution—Cilia and Sara continued to disagree, although Sara apologized profusely for her use of the term "slave." And later in the session Ruby reiterated her stance that people ought to learn English and said, "I think we water things down in protecting everybody's rights and everything to where some of our traditional values have been lost."

In the next session, only Cilia conveyed that she had been considering alternative perspectives. The facilitator asked her to discuss an approach to improving race relations stated in our discussion guides as follows: "We should review our policies for the racist assumptions they contain and take the racism out." Cilia discussed this view by saying that the conversations had led her to recognize that some people may feel discriminated against if a job advertisement states that bilingual skills are required, not just preferred.

Discussions of language policy spanned all five sessions of this group. When Cilia was present, her contributions inserted attention to the targets of this policy. But the other group members showed no signs that her authentic contributions had changed their minds about language issues.

When taken together with the conversations about language policy in the other groups, it seems that views on this issue are particularly resistant to enlargement through attending to difference. Although this form of public talk enables people to balance unity and difference, there are limits on just how far participants were willing to interrupt the pull of unity. Some differences seemed more threatening than others, and languages other than English seemed to be one of them. Even when faced with powerful stories of first-hand experience with bilingualism, others continued to assert that speaking something other than English was too divisive and too much of a threat to the fabric of their community to heed authoritative views to the contrary.

Tracking Patterns of Power

If this form of communication that welcomed attention to difference did not necessarily confer authority on members of marginalized racial groups, did it challenge the power dynamics that plague other forms of deliberation? Or do civic intergroup dialogues exhibit the same kind of processes that difference democrats lament?

In the course of public talk, people rely on the scripts and codes they use in other encounters, and they look to status markers from the society as a whole for clues about whom to defer to, listen to, and take seriously.[9] This, of course, is the worry of difference democrats—that these tools of communication learned in other settings perpetuate inequality in the course of deliberation, or public talk more generally.

Civic dialogue has the potential to interrupt the dominating effects of social status. In these programs, it is not automatically clear that those with power in the community are assumed to also have power over the conversation. Perhaps civic dialogue on race turns these assumptions around and leads people to expect that it is instead members of marginalized racial groups who have the most valuable statements to contribute. All forms of public talk are sufficiently unfamiliar to the people involved to force people to create new norms for interacting.[10] Intergroup dialogue programs on race—in which many participants are talking about race with people of a different racial background for the *first time in their lives*—are a particularly novel kind of public talk. Thus we should expect that participating in them would be likely to develop new norms for interacting, including revised notions of what kinds of people ought to be listened to.

In this and the previous chapter, we have seen that people *do* actually listen across lines of racial difference and do express that they have reconsidered their preconceptions. This is an influence on a particular kind of power, framing, or control over the interpretations or perspectives that are allowed to dominate. The evidence that people of color pulled their group discussions back from unity is one piece of evidence that these groups did not simply reproduce patterns of power that exist in the larger society. Not only did members of marginalized groups alert people to experiences they had never heard about or had never listened to in detail, they also had the power to present alternative perspectives on public issues that were not consistent with the dominant, consensual interpretations. Moreover, through discussions about racial labels and categories, people of color exerted power over the definition of categories imposed upon them.

I do not mean to imply that these discussions completely challenged prevailing notions of power. People *did* rely on familiar cultural scripts to communicate with one another, and these scripts likely perpetuated existing power inequalities. Based on their manner of dress, their life experience, and occupations, almost all of the participants were of middle-class as opposed to, say, working-class or upper-middle-class backgrounds. They may, for example, have been less likely to challenge perspectives that perpetuated existing class structures.

In addition, many participants often relied on the familiar script of "student," which automatically conferred power on the facilitators. Participants regularly referred to these groups as a "class" and when in doubt about how to participate would refer back to behavior they had learned in school: they would sometimes raise their hands if they wanted to take a turn. They would commonly direct their comments to the facilitator as opposed to other "class" members, unless the facilitator directed them to do otherwise.

To probe further the patterns of power that emerged in these groups, I examine these dialogues with respect to two particular aspects of power. These can be understood as agenda-setting, that is, who speaks, listens, and gets listened to, and justification, or who is forced to provide justification for his or her claims.

The political science literature readily acknowledges three faces of power. The first, outright persuasion or causing someone to reach a decision they otherwise would not, is the first face of power.[11] The second face of power is agenda setting, or power over which issues get considered.[12] John Gaventa, building on the work of Steven Lukes, identifies a third face of power, the power over how a situation is interpreted, which I considered earlier with the concept of framing.[13] Molly Patterson alerts us to another aspect of power operating in deliberative forums: who in a deliberative setting has to provide justification for his or her remarks.[14]

We can examine agenda setting in several ways. First, we can examine how much group members participated. Did whites speak more than people of color? A count of the number of turns group members took, excluding myself and the facilitators, showed that typically whites in each group did speak more often. Tables 8.1 through 8.5 display these results. In thirteen of the twenty-two sessions (59 percent), the average number of turns among whites was higher than the average number of turns among people of color. Also, even when the average number of turns taken by whites and people of color were similar, in all of the groups, whites were a majority of the participants. Thus the perspective of whites was likely still most prominent in the discussions.

It is notable, however, that these results do not show outright dominance by whites. For example, in the central Wisconsin groups, in three-quarters of the sessions people of color tended to speak more often than whites.[15] This result is informed by evidence visited earlier that whites as well as people of color regularly claimed that participating in the dialogues had allowed them to learn and gain awareness. Both whites and people of

TABLE 8.1: Speaking turns by participant, southern Wisconsin group

Pseudonym	Race	Gender	Session 1	Session 2	Session 4	Session 5
Facilitators and investigator						
Sandra	White	Female	48	.	.	.
Amna	Arab-Am.	Female	8	23	.	.
Fred	White	Male	.	47	60	70
Kathy	White	Female	5	26	15	9
Group members						
Luke	Afr.-Am.	Male	12	.	26	21
Frank	White	Male	19	46	.	.
Lois	Afr.-Am.	Female	19	.	.	.
Rosemary	White	Female	7	.	36	27
Laura	White	Female	12	41	39	36
Bob	White	Male	8	4	18	13
Barb	White	Female	7	.	.	.
Deb	White	Female	.	.	50	31
Averages						
Whites			10.60	30.33	31.00	25.33
People of color			15.50	23.00	26.00	21.00
Men			13.00	25.00	22.00	17.00
Women			11.25	41.00	37.5	31.50

Note: Cell entries include counts of number of turns taken by each participant. Averages do not include turns taken by facilitators or investigator, except for second session in which Amna participated as a group member, not a facilitator. Missing values denote an absent participant. Data are not available for the third session.

color commonly remarked that their "eyes had been opened" to issues of discrimination and to alternative experiences. It does not seem to be the case that listening was unidirectional or that whites consistently held center stage. Such evidence suggests that in this aspect of the deliberative system, people of color exerted authority that they may not have had access to in other aspects of life in their communities.

As for an additional dimension of power—justification—I analyzed the transcriptions to determine whether who asks for justifications and who is asked to justify their claims varies systematically with respect to race.[16] As tables 8.6 and 8.7 display, I found that demands for justification took place most commonly in groups characterized by more contentiousness. This is likely due in large part to the facilitators' styles,[17] but it may also be due to the size of the group, the diversity of the group, and the communication

TABLE 8.2: Speaking turns by participant, Aurora Monday (evening) group

Pseudonym	Race	Gender	Session 1	Session 2	Session 3	Session 4	Session 5
Facilitator and investigator							
Liza	Afr.-Am.	Female	57	76	89	64	47
Kathy	White	Female	1	5	12	4	18
Group members							
Christine	White	Female	14	55	53	81	.
Lucy	Puerto Rican	Female	5	23	14	.	19
Amaal	Arab-Am.	Female	7	19	21	18	14
Rebecca	White	Female	3	.	.	.	.
Adam	White	Male	35	.	76	73	41
Dolores	White	Female	14	.	16	36	29
Matt	White	Male	16	41	25	.	.
Beth	White	Female	16	65	19	7	23
Elic	Afr.-Am.	Male	.	59	20	.	11
Averages							
Whites			16.33	53.67	37.80	49.25	31.00
People of color			6.00	33.67	41.67	18.00	14.67
Men			25.50	50.00	63.67	73.00	26.00
Women			9.83	40.50	24.60	35.00	21.25

Note: Cell entries include counts of number of turns taken by each participant. Averages do not include turns taken by facilitators or investigator. Missing values denote an absent participant.

styles of the people within the group. The rates of justification did not change in any obvious way across the sessions of each group, except that participants made fewer demands in the first sessions.[18]

Some important racial patterns emerge from this analysis. People of color, particularly African Americans, were asked to justify just as much, if not more than, were whites (proportionate to their number in the group). However, African Americans tended to make more requests than whites. In other words, in these forums people of color may be held to a higher standard of evidence, as tends to be the case in other settings of public talk. But the nature of these dialogues enables African Americans in particular to demand information and reasons from others, and they apparently made use of this opportunity. In addition, signs that participants commonly asked people of color to justify what they had said may be

TABLE 8.3: Speaking turns by participant, Aurora Tuesday group

Pseudonym	Race	Gender	Session 1	Session 2	Session 3	Session 4	Session 5
Facilitator and investigator							
Judy	White	Female	16	47	30	41	37
Kathy	White	Female	3	16	8	14	16
Group members							
Wayne	White	Male	17	61	26	33	15
Cilia	Latina	Female	6	16	14	13	.
Steve	Afr.-Am.	Male	6	28	10	21	29
Ruby	White	Female	8	16	8	15	.
Rachel	White	Female	8	33	13	23	29
Sara	White	Female	10	66	23	.	31
Elnor	White	Female	2	4	5	4	3
Averages							
Whites			9.00	36.00	15.00	18.75	19.50
People of color			6.00	27.00	12.00	17.00	29.00
Men			11.50	49.50	18.00	27.00	22.00
Women			6.80	27.00	12.60	13.75	21.00

Note: Cell entries include counts of number of turns taken by each participant. Averages do not include turns taken by facilitators or investigator. Missing values denote an absent participant.

a sign that whites were listening to the contributions that African Americans and other people of color were making.[19]

An Opening to the Closed Circle of Deliberation?

This chapter has investigated how people negotiate power and struggle over who has legitimacy and authority in civic dialogue programs on race. In chapter 6, we saw how people use these dialogues to struggle with the balance between unity and difference. Investigating the exercise of power in the dialogues further reveals that the format of these programs enables attention to difference. Members of marginalized racial groups were able to insert their views because of the way in which these discussions interrupted conventional notions of authority.

This chapter also further illuminates the power of storytelling, discussed in chapter 7. We see here that people were able to establish legitimacy through reference to their own specific personal experiences—storytelling.

TABLE 8.4: Speaking turns by participant, central Wisconsin Wednesday group

Pseudonym	Race	Gender	Session 1	Session 2	Session 3	Session 4
Facilitators and investigator						
Tozi	Latina	Female	85	46	22	19
Valerie	White	Female	48	30	29	30
Kathy	White	Female	23	12	11	10
Group members						
Mark	White	Male	53	54	20	26
Mike	White	Male	28	55	36	.
Lisa	White	Female	19	16	9	4
Adaline	Afr.-Am.	Female	46	48	22	19
Patricia	White	Female	28	37	7	19
Mary	White	Female	71	39	24	31
Margaret	White	Female	21	12	14	.
Samuel	Afr.-Am.	Male	80	58	38	39
Averages						
Whites			36.67	35.50	18.33	20.00
People of color			63.00	53.00	30.00	29.00
Men			53.67	55.67	31.33	32.50
Women			37.00	30.40	15.20	18.25

Note: Cell entries include counts of number of turns taken by each participant. Averages do not include turns taken by facilitators or investigator. Missing values denote an absent participant.

People of color tried other strategies to exert legitimacy, but these seemed less persuasive. For example, occasionally people of color would bring in news clippings or printouts from Internet sites (as would whites) to provide credibility to their statements. However, these contributions were more often challenged than were personal stories of past experiences. Group members would question the accuracy of the news or Internet reports, but personal stories were taken at face value.

The struggle over legitimacy and authority revealed in this chapter further speaks to the question of which forms of communication people use in these civic dialogues. When people struggled to balance consensus and disagreement, it was the mix of forms of communication—listening and scrutiny—that allowed this negotiation to occur. Whereas we might think that scrutinizing others' claims is the source of disagreement, the focus on listening in these programs allowed participants to notice alternative

TABLE 8.5: Speaking turns by participant, central Wisconsin Thursday group

Pseudonym	Race	Gender	Session 1	Session 2	Session 3	Session 4
Facilitators and investigator						
Maria	Latina	Female	33	93	70	85
Kathy	White	Female	5	6	4	1
Group members						
Julie	White	Female	7	7	18	10
John	White	Male	4	19	26	20
Al	White	Male	16	10	31	34
Bill	White	Male	10	29	.	.
Colleen	White	Female	8	16	9	9
Bernita	Afr.-Am.	Female	3	5	.	.
Ginger	Afr.-Am.	Female	2	30	26	11
Don	White	Male	13	38	25	28
Jenn	White	Female	4	17	.	16
Paul	Asian-Am.	Male	4	.	.	.
Leng	Asian-Am.	Male	3	.	.	.
Adaline	Afr.-Am.	Female	6	33	29	26
Samuel	Afr.-Am.	Male	10	49	40	38
Elihue	Afr.-Am.	Male	2	21	29	2
Bruce	White	Male	.	20	.	.
Scott	White	Male	.	18	9	11
Stan	White	Male	.	11	11	10
Averages						
Whites			10.13	18.60	19.86	18.25
People of color			4.29	27.60	31.00	19.25
Men			7.75	23.89	24.43	20.43
Women			5.00	19.00	20.50	14.40

Note: Cell entries include counts of number of turns taken by each participant. Averages do not include turns taken by facilitators or investigator. Missing values denote an absent participant.

views when they had previously presumed consensus. The content of these dialogues suggests that civic intergroup dialogue is not immune to the patterns of domination that are present in other forms of deliberation. However, bringing in listening makes it possible for people who do not normally have power to make claims to legitimacy and to exert some authority over the conversation. Contrary to the assumption that domination of already marginalized groups is inevitable in deliberative democracy, a

TABLE 8.6: Average Number of times participants were asked to justify statements

	African American	Latina	Arab American	White
Central Wisconsin Wednesday	N = 2	N = 1 (Mexican-American facilitator)	N = 0	N = 8
Session 1				.13
Session 2	2.0			.25
Session 3				.13
Session 4	.50			
Central Wisconsin Thursday	N = 5	N = 1 (Mexican-American facilitator)	N = 0	N = 11
Session 1				
Session 2	.60			
Session 3	.40			.38
Session 4	.20			.56
Aurora Monday (Evening)	N = 2 (including 1 facilitator)	N = 1 (Puerto Rican)	N = 1 (Iraqi American)	N = 7
Session 1		1.0	2.0	1.0
Session 2	2.0	2.0	1.0	1.0
Session 3	1.5		1.0	1.33

	N = 1	N = 1 (Mexican American)	N = 0	N = 7
Session 4				.60
Session 5				.20

Aurora Tuesday	N = 1	N = 1 (Mexican American)	N = 0	N = 7
Session 1				
Session 2				
Session 3				.14
Session 4				
Session 5				

Southern Wisconsin	N = 2	N = 0	N = 1 (Kuwaiti)	N = 8
Session 1				.14
Session 2				.33
Session 3				
Session 4				.33
Session 5				

Note: Entries represent the average number of justifications asked of participants within each racial category who were present for a particular session. Justifications asked of the group as a whole are not represented. The central Wisconsin Thursday group also included two Hmong men in the first session, but they did not ask for justifications nor were they asked for justifications. Whites includes author.

TABLE 8.7: Average number of times participants asked others to justify statements

	African American	Latina	Arab American	White
Central Wisconsin Wednesday	N = 2	N = 1 (Mexican-American facilitator)	N = 0	N = 8
Session 1				
Session 2	.50	2.0		.50
Session 3	.50			
Session 4				.17
Central Wisconsin Thursday	N = 5	N = 1 (Mexican-American facilitator)	N = 0	N = 11
Session 1				.36
Session 2				.50
Session 3	.75			.33
Session 4	.25	2.0		
Aurora Monday (Evening)	N = 2 (including 1 facilitator)	N = 1 (Puerto Rican)	N = 1 (Iraqi American)	N = 7
Session 1	6.0			.57
Session 2	2.0	1.0		1.25

Session 3	3.5	1.0		1.17
Session 4	3.0			
Session 5	.50			.40

Aurora Tuesday	N = 1	N = 1 (Mexican American)	N = 0	N = 7
Session 1				
Session 2				
Session 3		1.0		
Session 4				
Session 5				

Southern Wisconsin	N = 2	N = 0	N = 1 (Kuwaiti)	N = 8
Session 1	.50			.14
Session 2				.67
Session 3	NA		NA	NA
Session 4				.33
Session 5				

Note: Entries represent the average number of justifications requested by the participants within each racial category who were present for a particular session. Justifications asked of group as a whole are not represented. The central Wisconsin Thursday group also included two Hmong men in the first session, but they did not ask for justifications nor were they asked for justifications. Whites includes author.

slight shift in the purpose of the deliberation to include listening as well as scrutiny can apparently open up public talk to excluded views. And contrary to assumptions that listening will mean divisiveness and privileging of antimajoritarian views, we see people collectively reasoning and struggling with which views to privilege.

Difference democrats have suggested that interracial public talk is especially likely to produce struggles over legitimacy and authority. And previous empirical research suggests that these struggles make interracial public talk not feasible. Does the present study alter this conclusion? To consider, I briefly review a study of town meetings about school desegregation in New Jersey, conducted by Tali Mendelberg and John Oleske. In that study, the authors call into question whether deliberation can ever be effective in contexts of racial misunderstanding. They analyze the content of two town meetings, one in a white town and one in an integrated town, and conclude that interracial deliberation is an ineffective way to resolve conflict, produce decisions focused on the common good, or increase understanding of others' perspectives.

Mendelberg and Oleske reach their conclusion through a careful analysis of the content of statements made during the meetings. They identify phrases that participants commonly used and judge whether these are genuine, reasoned appeals to the common good. They find that in the meeting in the predominantly white town, participants made claims that appealed to the community rather than to self-interest. However, the authors argue that on closer inspection, these claims have racist undertones and ignore or manufacture facts. In the integrated setting, others present scrutinized these very claims and denounced them as racist. But rather than advancing the deliberation, the effect of such scrutiny was to squelch it.

The authors conclude that the participants did not start the deliberation with shared meaning. Moreover, the atmosphere of dishonesty and hidden motives prevented the participants from building a shared sense of community that would enable deliberation to proceed. This poses a major dilemma for interracial deliberation, the authors assert:

> Subordinate groups cannot rely on deliberation to secure equality and build a community with dominant groups, because deliberation must have equality and community as preconditions to succeed. The situation is a closed circle. One cannot get what one needs when the process of obtaining it is itself tainted by the lack of what one needs.[20]

How can people in diverse communities break this closed circle? The authors suggest that one solution is "to make sure that those who deliberate lead their lives in common."[21] But most U.S. cities do not consist of contexts in which people of different racial backgrounds live integrated lives. Thus, barring radical social and political change, deliberation seems an impossible mechanism for improving race relations.

They suggest, however, that "deliberative solutions . . . can also have a place" if they follow the instructions of Allport's contact hypothesis. Reflecting the most common interpretation of this hypothesis, the authors state that contact "must be carefully structured so that the line of demarcation between people becomes less salient to them (e.g., selecting neutral discussion sites)."[22] In other words, the solution these authors propose is to either pursue institutional change rather than deliberation, or to pursue deliberation that draws attention away from conflict.

But notice how this conclusion contrasts with the practice of civic intergroup dialogue programs. These programs are an attempt to use a form of public talk to address race relations, and they go against the grain of the typical interpretation of the contact hypothesis. Rather than draw attention away from conflict, they enable its direct confrontation. And rather than draw attention away from racial divides and subgroup identities, they bring those attachments front and center.

Does this solution, which diverges from what Mendelberg and Oleske propose, break the closed circle of deliberation? Does public talk that incorporates listening allow participants to produce shared meaning? It is not clear from the Mendelberg and Oleske analysis what constitutes talk that occurs through shared meaning, but the authors clarify what it is not: It is *not* language that has a racist undertone, has hidden motives, is said without a willingness to be scrutinized by listeners, and does not "acknowledge the validity of the other side's interpretation of language."[23] In other words, the authors do not assert that talk in these interracial forums needs to consist of shared meaning in the sense of identical interpretations of statements. Instead, what interracial public talk requires is a willingness to take others' views seriously, a willingness to reconsider one's own views, and a willingness to have those views scrutinized by others.

In the conversations analyzed above and in the previous chapters, we see evidence that these requirements are being met occasionally. We see people reconsidering their claims that racism is not pervasive, and they are doing so after listening intently to the claims made by people with different understandings. The dialogues do not take place on the back of shared understandings in the sense of identical interpretations. They start from the presumption that many understandings are *not* shared. Rather than an emphasis on conflict, they begin with the intention of listening. When statements verge toward an assumption of shared identity or verge toward an assumption of consensus, people of color offer up stories to the contrary, and the groups often respond by considering alternatives.

The implication is that it is not shared meaning across racial lines that is necessary to open the closed circle of deliberation. Instead, what is required is a shared willingness to scrutinize each others' contributions and question each others' claims to power over the discussion.

The investigations of intergroup dialogue in this study nevertheless present reasons to be cautious about how useful deliberative approaches can be in the realm of race relations. Even in these dialogues, not all participants are scrutinized to the same degree. These dialogues are a site in which conventional notions of authority are contested, but they seem at times to confer legitimacy on people of color without simultaneously requiring whites to assume an equal role in the exchange. In order for these dialogues to serve as a site in which motives and perceptions are open to scrutiny by listeners, everyone needs to contribute—people of dominant racial categories as well as people from marginalized racial groups. As suggested in the previous chapter, if whites mainly listen and only people of color speak, then the dialogues are not actually an exchange or a collective attempt to move a community forward.[24] If only members of marginalized racial groups take on the role of speaker and are seldom in the role of listener, this may not constitute power over the conversation so much as a peculiar status. In such a situation, only their views—not the views of members of dominant racial groups—are subject to scrutiny. This reduces the potential of this public talk to serve as community- and action-producing discussion. As Susan Bickford explains,

> Exempting some from listening (either implicitly or explicitly) can stifle the vitality of political interaction, and could also result in a kind of patronizing hierarchy of citizenship: certain citizens cannot be expected to exercise certain responsibilities and thus are somehow lacking, not wholly mature citizens. . . . If I regard you as exempted from listening because of your oppression, I certainly am not regarding you as a partner in political action. It is as though I am doing something *for* you, rather than our acting together—or on a collective level, as though *we* are letting *them* into *our* public, rather than creating one together through speaking and listening.[25]

Intergroup dialogue needs to be civil enough for people to talk and share views. But for it to constitute a joint project, a credible joint attempt by people to understand their community and take steps to improve it, it has to involve the scrutiny of all participants.

When these dialogues did manage to inspect the views of whites as well as people of color, they did so because the topic was specifically about race. Because these groups began their discussions with the understanding that the discussions would address racial categories—though not necessarily with a shared understanding that this focus was appropriate as a matter of public policy—it was possible for people to make claims that consideration of racial divides in public policy is appropriate. Doing so allowed people to alert each other to the fact of race, and perhaps most importantly, the fact of whiteness and the power that appearing to be white holds in everyday American life. It is because these discussions were about race that this mode of communication was able to overcome some of the ways deliberation perpetuates racial inequality. Civic dialogue in and of itself might very well exhibit the dominating tendencies of public talk in general. But when combined with explicit attention to categories of inequality, it opens up the possibility for people to challenge conventional patterns of authority.

CHAPTER NINE

Public Officials and Residents in Dialogue

Public talk is public because it is discussion among members of a community about public problems. But civic intergroup dialogue programs are public in yet another sense: they involve, along with ordinary members of the public, public officials, whom I define as policymakers (elected and nonelected officials) as well as street-level bureaucrats such as members of the police department and librarians.

Activities that are part of the fabric of civic life need not involve public officials, but there is no doubt that civil society and government are intertwined. Government policies have *shaped* the character of civil society. Political parties and the U.S. postal system fostered civic associations in the early United States, the Civil War gave rise to networks and relationships that entrepreneurs turned into postwar associations, and during World War I, the federal government nourished the growth of organizations like the Red Cross in order to provide services to troops.[1] Also, we expect to see government actors taking part in civic life. In events like community celebrations such as fairs and parades we expect that elected representatives and government employees like members of the fire and police departments will be a part of the proceedings.

Despite the intertwining of government and civil society, in the contemporary United States the public can feel that government is quite distant from them. If government actors listen to the public, it seems that they do so primarily through "listening" to election returns. This is cause for concern. Since World War II, the manner in which services and policies are administered has changed dramatically, placing new information demands on both government actors and members of the public that actually require more government-public interaction. In the last five decades, governments have shifted from providing services and administering policies on their own to doing so through public-private collaborations. The government increasingly relies on third parties like social service agencies, commercial banks, private hospitals, universities, and day-care centers "to deliver publicly financed services and pursue publicly authorized purposes."[2] Lester Salamon explains that what was once easily referred to as "government" is now a complex and elaborate process of "governance."[3]

This "new governance" complicates the job of both citizens and officials. It is now even more difficult for members of the public to make sense of public policy and government action. Some of the tools that are now used to administer publicly financed services and policies are invisible to the public, never appearing on budgets.[4] Public officials, in turn, face the challenges of dealing with these new administrative mechanisms and also a new necessity to relate to their publics. Because policies are now commonly administered in collaboration with members of the public, government actors have to have the capacity to communicate with the people they are collaborating with and the people they are providing services to.[5]

Moreover, because this shift in administrative form is occurring in a context of increased racial and ethnic diversity, the new governance requires more than technical expertise and mechanisms for providing information. It requires mechanisms of understanding. In the cultural diversity that characterizes contemporary U.S. cities, it is often the case that administrators and citizens view public problems from different perspectives and approach the act of communication itself with culturally different scripts and codes.[6] And on top of these barriers to understanding, there is yet another: a widespread belief among people of color in particular that government is not responsive to their needs.[7]

The new governance provides opportunities to remedy some of these divides. The prevalence of public-private partnerships means that there are now more opportunities to build stronger connections between the government and the public.[8] However, depending on how they are handled, these partnerships may actually alienate citizens. Steven Rathgeb Smith and Helen Ingram argue that in order to prevent further damage to the tenuous bonds that exist between government and citizens, this new governance needs to foster a deliberative component that engages the concerns of members of the public.[9]

On the local level in particular, the nature of government-resident communication is of concern for reasons above and beyond the new governance. The surge of public-private collaborations is layered on top of Progressive-era reforms which distanced the public from policy processes. These changes included replacing ward-based with at-large council representation, replacing mayors with hired city managers to serve as chief operating officers of local governments, and replacing partisan with non-partisan elections. These forms of government persist in many cities and create barriers between local government and citizens because they promote the perception that local policymakers are specialized experts and hinder residents' ability to know whom to contact or to hold accountable.[10]

Citizens' perceptions that officials are unresponsive have some merit. Many local public officials report reluctance to open up governing processes to greater public input for fear of inefficiency, direct criticism, and lack of control.[11] In addition, those who seek to make local governance more collaborative with residents have to deal with a legacy of promises of enhanced citizen participation that were largely empty gestures. The federal government required "maximum feasible participation" of neighborhoods affected by Community Action legislation of the 1960s (and similar requirements were made under the Model Cities act), but citizens were often excluded from holding decision-making power in practice.[12] Also, such provisions for collaboration were soured by claims that the designers of the legislation did not actually intend to involve citizens in the policy process.[13]

Most cities have institutionalized government-resident deliberation. Public hearings, for example, are a longstanding and common fixture in U.S. communities. According to a 1995 survey of city managers and chief administrative officers in cities over 50,000 in population, 97.5 percent of cities regularly use public hearings.[14] Citizen committees or boards, collaborative forums sponsored by governments, and forums sponsored and administered primarily by NGOs likewise provide opportunities for government-resident communication.[15]

But these forums can take many forms, and the typical model is not to put public officials and residents on equal footing. Public-government forums vary in who participates and how participants are chosen (from self-selection, recruitment, random selection as in Citizen Juries and Deliberative Polls, to the inclusion of volunteer or professional stakeholders); what communication role citizens play (i.e., listening to officials, expressing preferences, exploring perspectives, bargaining, deliberating, or deferring to officials); and the connection between these forums and political action or policy change.[16] They also vary in who sponsors the communication and whom it is intended to influence.[17]

The common form is a forum sponsored by the government in which citizens participate as listeners. Usually, the purpose is to inform the public or get the public's tacit stamp of approval for policy already formed.[18] That is, the typical form is for a one-way exchange of information in which public officials sit at the front, and community residents sit in the crowd. Such a set-up is symptomatic of the strong presumption that when it comes to

public policy, ordinary citizens are not experts and lack the capacity to provide valuable input.[19] In those cases in which citizens participate in public
talk more than as passive listeners, the role they adopt is often one of angry
dissenters pushing the forum into what John Gastil aptly calls "bedlam."[20]

Entrepreneurs both in and outside of government have innovated newer,
collaborative forms of public deliberation.[21] But many of these forums do
not necessarily alter the official-as-expert paradigm and do not create contexts conducive to questioning officials' perspectives. Button and Mattson
observed seven deliberation forums, some of which contained interaction
between public officials and citizens. They concluded that all of these
forums—including the ones among officials and residents—tended toward
consensus, not toward participants challenging one another.[22] Moreover,
Button and Mattson found that these discussions were expert-driven. The
members of the public would defer to the legislators present rather than
exchange in a conversation as equals. Frank Bryan has observed similar
dynamics with school officials in his extensive studies of Vermont town
meetings.[23] Indeed, public hearings commonly perpetuate the citizen-as-
consumer model, suggesting that we should not readily expect public officials to relinquish their status as experts in deliberative settings.[24]

The Unique Potential of Civic Dialogue

The race dialogue programs that communities are conducting around the
country are perhaps an exception. They may create a new type of context
for citizen-government interaction. In the vast majority of programs, residents and public officials engage in these dialogues together. Even when
local governments are merely endorsing the programs, not sponsoring
them, officials from police officers to mayors participate as members of the
same conversation. Unlike town hall meetings or public hearings, dialogue
programs encourage citizens and officials to listen to and speak with one
another as fellow members of the same community, not as actors located
on different levels of a power hierarchy.[25] Residents and public officials
sit in the same circle rather than in a speaker/audience format. Citizens
do not just step up to the microphone, give testimony, and hope that public officials will listen.[26] Both city residents and public officials tell stories
and are expected to listen to one another. In short, these forums present a
fundamental rethinking of political roles. Rather than presuming officials
have the expertise, the set-up of these dialogues regards the experiences
of community residents as valuable information. This is not one-way communication, but communication that is expected to influence *both* officials
and residents.[27]

An important precedent, and one that is often interwoven with civic dialogue programs, is community policing. Community policing is an approach to law enforcement in which the goal is to communicate with neighborhood residents to identify local problems and help them solve problems—rather than impose policy experts' solutions on neighborhood residents. It emerged from a reaction against Progressive-era reforms that had shifted policing from patronage jobs to a bureaucratized profession. Although such reforms "cleaned up" policing, they also distanced it from the public. They created an expert-centered model of law enforcement that proved damaging to relationships between police and the poor and people of color, and left law enforcement ill-equipped to deal with urban unrest in the late 1960s and early 1970s.[28]

Thus community policing attempts to reform policing into a function of the community, rather than a force imposed on it. It represents a fundamental rethinking of government-resident communication with the potential to alter the quality of public life. Under community policing, residents likely encounter a law enforcement officer on the street while walking about. This creates a very different public life than if residents were only to encounter an officer while being charged with breaking a law.

The effect of face-to-face contact with public officials on neutral turf applies to interactions with officials besides police. Richard Fenno's study of members' of Congress behavior in their home districts suggested something qualitatively different about meeting up with representatives while taking part in community festivals or the mundane events of civic life versus contacting them through more formal means of calling, writing, or scheduling an office visit.[29] Walking up to one's representative and shaking hands before football games, after parades, or during corn roasts alters the quality of representation and the character of citizenship.

Communication between residents and public officials is a public good.[30] But these examples demonstrate that the way people constitute it together can take a variety of forms. What form does it take in civic dialogues on race? How do people negotiate who has authority in these conversations and whether people listen to marginalized perspectives? In the remainder of this chapter I make use of the observations of race dialogues to investigate these questions. I look at the discussions that included public officials and compare these against the dialogues that took place just among members of the public.

The Unremarkableness of Officials' Participation

Among the six dialogue groups that I observed directly, three included public officials. The remarkable thing about the discussions that included both members of the public and public officials is their unremarkableness. In many respects the content of the dialogues was no different when officials were involved. In fact, readers who have read the preceding three chapters are already familiar with their discussions and have encountered exchanges between citizens and officials without even knowing it. Public officials participated in both the Aurora Tuesday group and the central Wisconsin Wednesday group. And the central Wisconsin Thursday group was organized specifically to bring local officials and members of marginalized racial groups in the community together.

More specifically, the participants of the groups can be categorized into three types: people who were not public officials, street-level bureaucrats (public officials who were not policymakers), and policymakers (both elected and nonelected). No public officials participated in the southern Wisconsin group, although two of the members had either held or run for elected office in the past. In the Aurora evening group, two women were street-level bureaucrats, employees of a county health department. In the other Aurora group, there were also street-level bureaucrats: Steve, the African-American man, was a police officer, Wayne, the white male member of the group, was an employee of the city public works department, and Cilia, the Mexican-American woman, was an employee of the city public relations department. In the central Wisconsin Wednesday group which met in the public library, there were two street-level bureaucrats and one policymaker: Mary and Lisa were both librarians in that library, and Mike was a department head in the city government. Finally, most of the central Wisconsin Thursday group were public officials, and the group met in the police station. Some of the participants were street-level bureaucrats: Colleen was a librarian; Julie worked with the senior center; Jenn worked in the city attorney's office; and Scott was a firefighter. The group also included many policymakers: Don and John were (elected) members of the city council; Bill, Al, and Stan were each heads of city departments; and Bruce was the city manager.

In retrospect this may be surprising. The comments these public officials made most likely did not seem markedly different from other members of their groups on first reading. They listened to people in their groups just as the other residents did. Also, they challenged the residents in the groups, and the residents challenged them. For example, in the conversations about reparations discussed in chapter 8, we saw officials challenging residents. Don, a city councilperson, asked one of his African-American constituents pointedly: "I never had slaves. You folks were never slaves. Who would make reparations for slavery?" Other requests for input were less sharp. Mike in the central Wisconsin Wednesday group asked for the members' thoughts on affirmative action, a policy that he was hired to implement. Kevin, the police officer in the Aurora daytime group, turned to another city employee, Cilia, to ask her for her first-hand experience with language policy. I underscore these examples to demonstrate that public officials were not just showing up for these dialogues, nor were they behaving in ways that suggested mere pandering to the participants. They used these opportunities to challenge and listen to members of the community.

And there are signs that residents learned from officials. In the Aurora Tuesday group, we saw Sara change her mind about the ubiquity of discrimination after hearing Steve's story about African-American police officers being denied service in local clubs. Likewise, officials seemed to learn from residents. Scott, the firefighter in the central Wisconsin Thursday group, said "See, that's good to hear because we don't see that perspective" in response to the stories being told by the African-American residents. Stan, a head of a city department, expressed shock in response to Elihue's testimony that people clutch their purses when they see him in a store.

I intentionally did not identify the public officials in the preceding chapters in order to emphasize the fact that they were participants alongside the other community residents. They sat in the same circle, answered the same questions, obeyed the same ground rules, and were asked to participate on an equal basis with the other participants.

But did these people actually treat each other as equals and did they behave as equals? The other participants recognized that the public officials were public officials, in slightly varying degrees. They clearly recognized policymakers, elected officials, heads of city departments, and public safety officers as representatives of the local government. The public safety officers were recognizable because of their uniforms and also because they had to respond to calls via pagers and cell phones, sometimes by abruptly running out of the room during the dialogues. Other street-level bureaucrats who wore uniforms, such as Cilia (city public relations) and Wayne (city maintenance) in the Aurora Tuesday group were visibly distinct as well. The public health employees, librarians, and the senior center administrator may not have been considered officials by any of the participants but me.

In the central Wisconsin Thursday group, the members of the group knew that they were convened as part of a group for public officials, and the city employees knew one another. At the start of the first session, each of the participants stated their occupation. Several of the policymakers simply said, "I work for the city." If anyone was not immediately clear what positions these participants held, it was me, the outsider to the community.[31]

An Exchange through Listening

From the analyses of conversations in the preceding three chapters it should be clear that people did not seek to avoid controversy or talk about differences in perspectives simply because public officials were in the room. In fact, the central Wisconsin Thursday group that consisted of ten public officials and eight community residents was one of the more contentious among those I observed. Don, an elected city councilman, directly confronted the residents in attendance, and Adaline, Samuel, Ginger, and Elihue took up his challenges.

Don and others openly questioned the utility of recognizing racial groups and racial identity. The fact that conversations took place about "what do I call you people?" and how race actually matters in the local criminal justice system are signs that officials, like residents, were using the dialogues to negotiate a balance between a desire for a more cohesive community and recognition of marginalized perspectives. These discussions served as forums in which the roles of expert and citizen were relaxed and at times reversed. It was not a given that public officials, particularly policymakers, had authority over the conversations. Indeed the situation called for them to listen.

A quick look at how much public officials and ordinary residents spoke shows that public officials, policymakers as well as street-level bureaucrats, did not clearly dominate these conversations. In tables 9.1 through 9.3, I reproduce the analyses presented in chapter 8 for the three groups with substantial numbers of public officials in them, but this time denote which group members were residents, street-level bureaucrats, and policymakers and show averages for each of these groups as well as for public officials overall.

We can see that in the Aurora Tuesday group and the central Wisconsin Wednesday group, public officials did tend to speak more than ordinary residents. But in the central Wisconsin Thursday group (table 9.3), the group with the largest crowd of public officials, residents spoke more often than the average public official on three of the days, and on two of those days residents spoke more often on average than both street-level bureaucrats and policymakers.

These analyses only scratch the surface of what went on in these groups, however. To explain in greater detail how group members negotiated whether and how to confer deference toward public officials, I turn to the central Wisconsin Wednesday group. Participants in these dialogues did at times turn toward public officials to ask them to share their expertise, and this dynamic was particularly evident in this group in which Mike, a

TABLE 9.1: Speaking turns by participant, Aurora Tuesday group

Pseudonym	Race	Position	Session 1	Session 2	Session 3	Session 4	Session 5
Facilitator and investigator							
Judy	White		16	47	30	41	37
Kathy	White		3	16	8	14	16
Group members							
Wayne	White	Public works	17	61	26	33	15
Cilia	Latina	Public relations	6	16	14	13	.
Steve	Afr.-Am.	Police officer	6	28	10	21	29
Ruby	White		8	16	8	15	.
Rachel	White		8	33	13	23	29
Sara	White		10	66	23	.	31
Elnor	White		2	4	5	4	3
Averages							
Street-level bureaucrats			9.67	38.33	16.67	22.33	22.00
Residents			7.00	29.75	12.25	14.00	21.00

Note: Cell entries in the top portion of the table contain counts of number of turns taken by each participant. Averages do not include turns taken by facilitators or investigator. Missing values denote an absent participant. Names in bold are nonelected public officials.

TABLE 9.2: Speaking turns by participant, Central Wisconsin Wednesday group

Pseudonym	Race	Position	Session 1	Session 2	Session 3	Session 4
Facilitators and investigator						
Tozi	Latina		85	46	22	19
Valerie	White		48	30	29	30
Kathy	White		23	12	11	10
Group members						
Mark	White		53	54	20	26
Mike	White	Dept. head	28	55	36	—
Lisa	White	Librarian	19	16	9	4
Adaline	Afr.-Am.		46	48	22	19
Patricia	White		28	37	7	19
Mary	White	Librarian	71	39	24	31
Margaret	White		21	12	14	—
Samuel	Afr.-Am.		80	58	38	39
Averages						
Public officials (all)			39.3	36.67	23.00	17.5
Street-level bureaucrats			45	27.5	16.5	17.5
Policymaker			28	55	36	—
Residents			45.6	25.33	15.00	11.50

Note: Cell entries in the top portion of the table contain counts of number of turns taken by each participant. Averages do not include turns taken by facilitators or investigator. Missing values denote an absent participant. Names in bold are non-elected public officials. Names in bold and italics are policymakers.

policymaker in the position of a head of a city department, participated. But the conversations in this group also show that technical expertise did not automatically result in authority in these groups.

In the previous chapter, I noted how Mike had asked the other participants what they thought about affirmative action. In the second session, Tizo, a facilitator, asks us to define reverse discrimination. John responds:

Well, I had made some comments earlier about what is the difference between affirmative action and reverse discrimination being a bad thing, and we have had some examples lately for example in the Milwaukee police department. There was a case there. My experience in terms of affirmative action when we try to give out government contracts, we do some

TABLE 9.3: Speaking turns by participant, Central Wisconsin Thursday group

Pseudonym	Race	Position	Session 1	Session 2	Session 3	Session 4
Facilitators and investigator						
Maria	Latina		33	93	70	85
Kathy	White		5	6	4	1
Group members						
Julie	White	Senior center executive	7	7	18	10
John	White	City council member	4	19	26	20
Al	White	Dept. head	16	10	31	· 34
Bill	White	Dept. head	10	29	·	·
Colleen	White	Librarian	8	16	9	9
Bernita	Afr.-Am.		3	5	·	·
Ginger	Afr.-Am.		2	30	26	11
Don	White	City council member	13	38 ·	25	28
Jenn	White	City attorney's office	4	17	·	16
Paul	Asian-Am.		4	·	·	·
Leng	Asian-Am.		3	·	·	·
Adaline	Afr.-Am.		6	33	29	26
Samuel	Afr.-Am.		10	49	40	38
Elihue	Afr.-Am.		2	21	29	2
Bruce	White	City manager	·	20	·	·
Scott	White	Fireman	·	18	9	11
Stan	White	Dept. head	·	11	11	10
Averages						
Public officials (all)			8.85	18.50	18.43	17.25
Street-level bureaucrats			6.33	14.50	12.00	11.50
Policymaker			10.75	21.17	23.25	23.00
Residents			4.29	27.60	31.00	19.25

Note: Cell entries in the top portion of the table contain counts of number of turns taken by each participant. Averages do not include turns taken by facilitators or investigator. Missing values denote an absent participant. Names in bold are nonelected public officials. Names in bold and italics are policymakers.

outreach, try to find minority contracts. I don't have any qualms about that. I think that is what it is and clearly should be. But when there are set-asides, then I start to think about whether there ought to be set-asides for a particular group. That I guess is the quandary, and I am interested in hearing people's thoughts. Does it promote some sort of backlash? And there have been some different thoughts about that. I think I heard Jesse Jackson say something about affirmative action: "Mend it, don't end it." I think he was beginning to recognize some issues, you know? Bill Cosby's kids—should they be able to go to a certain school simply because of their race or something like that? In his case, he is a multimillionaire—should he be able to go over someone who isn't a minority, who is coming out of Appalachia and has really had a hard life, too? And I think that is what they have been trying to mend rather than end, those are the kinds of thoughts I'm trying to go through in my mind—how to make affirmative action work for a broader context, not view it as just a minority program— a racial/ethnic minority program.

As the conversation starts to turn toward opposing affirmative action, Samuel brings in a reality check from personal experience, the common pattern noted in the previous chapters:

But ah, let's look at it this way—be optimistic about it—what if we took away all of those guidelines? Everyone who can come can come. Now do you think they are going to be fair, when they see African Americans come through that door and want to apply for college?

A similar pattern happens in the session the following week, when the group talks about affirmative action again. Samuel and Adaline, the married couple, talk about personal experience in the workplace as African Americans, and they take it a step further to demonstrate how all white people are implicated by bringing up the concept of white privilege. Mike is again a part of this conversation, but this time people are not turning to him for information, but are instead directly challenging him on the city's handling of diversity and hiring:

SAMUEL: I have something that I want to share. [Reads from his notes:] "White privilege is more than a set of attitudes or individual opinions. It is an overarching comprehensive framework of policy practices, institutions, and cultural norms that undergird every aspect of our society. Too often discussion of discrimination focuses solidly on the effect of those who are oppressed as their oppressors are beneficiaries." Because people benefit from these systems that are set up, you know.

ADALINE: What I thought was interesting about that [statement in the discussion guide]—it said "racism maintains the power and wealth." Sure. But also, it benefits even the poor white people because they are able—that is a privilege, when you see them you don't know they are poor, but because they are white, they still may get a privilege because of those few white rich people who establish that echelon in the power and the wealth. Me and my husband witnessed that. We did a lot of work in an Appalachian community in Ohio. And even there, people of color were seen as less— even though they were poor and living in shacks, they still thought they were better than me and my husband. Still a mindset.

PATRICIA [white]: I think that when Adaline talks about institutions taking the forefront and I think there is a real promising result from that. They are the one group that can cause the most discrimination, but they are also the savior. You get the most for your dollar when you have those sorts of programs in a company.

MIKE [white]: My question to that is, why aren't they doing that already? It's been around for a while, there must be some resistance or something.

ADALINE: Well, I could ask *you* that, Mike. Why hasn't the city done it?

[pause]

MIKE: "Why hasn't the city?" We *have* an affirmative action plan.

ADALINE: No. I mean diversity training.

MIKE: Yeah?

ADALINE: That's what she's talking about—the education. Bringing programs in—going amongst the groups and making sure the employees are trained.

MIKE: I don't think they thought it was a priority, and that's kind of the point of my question was—why would they do—I guess I am saying I think it is a good recommendation, I just don't know why someone would jump in and start doing it now just because we (as a study circle) made a recommendation.

This conversation demonstrates that although participants did turn to public officials for their expertise, they did not always do so with deference. Instead, they used the opportunity to hold members of the government accountable. Here we see Adaline's claim to legitimacy as a person with direct experience with discrimination exert authority over Mike.

The other central Wisconsin group provided even more opportunity for African Americans to hold members of the local government accountable, given the large number of officials in that group. People made use of it. To demonstrate, I analyze their discussions of affirmative action.

To set the stage, it is helpful to realize that most of the public officials in this group had little prior interaction with African Americans, like many of the residents of this central Wisconsin city. For example, when John, a council member and a white man, introduced himself to the group he said:

> I am about as German as you can get. My great grandfather was one of the first people to settle in [his village in Wisconsin]. And I grew up on the homestead with my mom and dad. That was 66 yrs ago. I went to a small Catholic school. Where I came from, it was all white German people until I got to high school. Then I went to—ran into Italians, French, you name it, but I went to school back in the '50s, we were still a white high school and in the '60s we started with the folks here moving into [this city]. . . . The very first black man [who lived in the city in recent decades]—and I knew him personally, worked at Sears Roebuck when I worked downtown—I believe that was the first black man we ever had in [this city] and I got to know him very well. Because I was in retail, and he was too. I was about age 18.

Other people in the group recognized the name of this "first black man,"[32] indicating just how homogenous this place was. Some of the other city employees expressed more experience with people of different racial backgrounds while growing up. Not all of them had grown up in the city, but all but Don were raised in Wisconsin. Given that background, it is likely that these discussions were a rare opportunity for many of them to have conversations with people of color in the community about race.

Below, I first present much of this group's conversations on affirmative action and then discuss the implications of this for our understanding of official-citizen communication. These conversations demonstrate several things. To anticipate a few, they show that the conversations were not dominated by the public officials in the group. Members of the community tell public officials to listen, both directly and through offering up stories, and the officials claim that they have in fact listened and have in fact learned something. Also, we see policymakers and street-level bureaucrats listening to and learning from each other.

In the first session, the group considered affirmative action only implicitly, when Samuel refers in passing to the difficulty that he had finding a job when he first moved to the area. In the second session, the city manager attends. An hour into the session, the group is talking about local examples of discrimination. Don, the white city-council member, asks, "Could we talk about reverse discrimination?"

MARIA [Latina facilitator]: Sure we can . . . but remember—dialogue not debate.

SAMUEL [to Don]: Ok, give us a definition.

DON: Sure—reverse discrimination is that that excludes others for various reasons such as race, religion, gender, sexual stance for political reasons.

That's the definition I came up with for reverse discrimination. . . . There is all kinds of reverse discrimination, but what is reverse discrimination in race relations? What happens if we would have a Miss White American contest? There would be such a turmoil—what if we had a Miss Black American contest?

BRUCE [white, city manager]: They do!

DON: And they do. See, I think this causes a problem.

But then Bruce raises a different perspective.

BRUCE: Isn't reverse discrimination more along the lines of being a member of the power structure, the dominant race?

SAMUEL AND ADALINE [together]: There you go, that's right.

BRUCE: Because of antidiscrimination laws or whatever prohibited from . . .

MARIA: Give us an example.

BRUCE: Well I went to law school, the Bakke case, the guy didn't get into medical school at the University of Michigan, he was white and didn't get in, even though he had higher scores. He sued for reverse discrimination and won the case, and got in. . . . That was the big case, Hispanics, Native Americans, got in ahead of me. I was discriminated against, but I didn't see it as reverse discrimination. I think that may be the great American fairy tale. Claiming reverse discrimination may be something to make me as a white person feel good when I fail.

In the next session, the third of four, the group picks up the topic of affirmative action again. The theme for the day is "What should we do to make progress on race relations?" When the group discusses "View 1," that "We must fight prejudice, and build interracial understanding," people talk about their experiences reaching out to people of different racial backgrounds and how to make this central Wisconsin town more welcoming to people of color. Samuel offers a perspective that Al, a head of a city department, says is new to him:

SAMUEL: Some of the blacks we reach out to—they won't come out here because they are scared at night. It makes them feel uncomfortable. They will call up and say they want to come visit . . . but they won't come out here. They are afraid at night, especially coming from Milwaukee.

ADALINE [African American community member]: They've got an idea that it is very racist up here.

AL [white, city department head]: Are they afraid of the police or are they afraid of all of us?

ADALINE: Both.

SAMUEL: Both, especially the police.

AL: So it's not just the police? . . . *I never thought of that.* I'm afraid to go into parts of Milwaukee at night, but I never thought anybody would be afraid to come out here. [emphasis added]

MARIA: You've never heard this?

AL: Never heard it.

Later in the session, Maria asks the group to discuss "View 3," that "We need to address institutional racism." Colleen, a white employee of the public library, remarks that she was surprised that there were no people of color in the police or fire departments:

JOHN [white, council member]: Well from the inside, nobody is applying to it—goes back to the thing that nobody wants to move to [this city].

SAMUEL: I don't think that's true, sir, I don't think that's true.

MARIA: Well, remember we are not debating. Need to move to dialogue . . .

JOHN: We follow the same rules, no matter the race.

MARIA: Yet we don't have any minorities.

And then the group begins an extended discussion of how hiring actually works in their city government:

AL: We have a few city employees of color and of other cultures, but I think in the police department part of what councilman [name suppressed, referring to John] might be saying, and I have heard the police chief say that you can't get—they have all these rigid tests—there are qualified applicants, but no qualified applicants to date have been willing to take a job in [this city]. I don't know that for a fact, but that's what I've been told. *I don't know why, but I'm starting to get an idea* [referring to the stories about fear of coming to the city told earlier in this session; emphasis added].

[laughter]

JOHN: You said last week—people won't come out to see you because you're living in the country—a part of it is true, like you said, Al—don't want to accept a job in a white community . . .

MARIA: Because of the fear . . .

JOHN: Right.

[. . .]

STAN [white, city department head]: Working with the city, we have tried to reach out to do the recruitments in Milwaukee or Racine, and that is what we get is that they would rather work in Milwaukee or Racine or a community that has an African-American population. We have tried to get qualified applicants to come out here and we just don't get any.

MARIA: So we are talking about a willingness to get out of the comfort zone and come to a community.

[. . .]

SCOTT [white firefighter]: We don't really do it effectively. . . . We put an ad where there is black people that live and say we're trying to recruit black people. You don't go down to the inner city or go into Racine or Kenosha and talk to people and actively try to recruit or bring them up. Like, we really need diversity on the fire department. We have one Spanish guy now—it helps—but it's only one. We really need some Asian or some Hmong real bad right now. Because we have absolutely no ability to talk. I tried to learn that language [Hmong] and . . . really tough so, we just—we put a band aid on just to say we're taking a shot at it. [Turning to Stan.] You know Stan, if you really—I'm not picking on you specifically, but if you really want it, you have to go down—There is a way you could do, if it was true, wasn't just lip service, it could be done. You could do it, even the chief of the Madison fire department talked about how they recruited initially, how they recruited women—how they went about doing it. Um it is important—I am glad there are city councilmen here and city managers and council members because the importance of it can't be overstated. . . . I have a female on my crew at my station and it helps so much. It makes us so much better, and adaptable to any situation. . . . They have an insight you know that we don't share. This lady I remember was held captive all day and the guy was raping her and she was a hostage and a swat team broke in and then there is me and my partner, a couple of dumb asses standing there and looking at her "You OK?" She did not—we needed—really could have used—then we go to the hospital and the nurse has to give her a big hug. It was like going to a funeral with your wife—you just don't know what to say, you know, you're standing there with your hands in your pockets [laughter]. So it really is important, I mean if you're going to trust—if him and I go out on a call together [pointing to Elihue], they're going to trust him more instantly.

STAN: I think this is important to both the police and fire department and support of the city council and the support of the city administration that we attempt to do something about this.

MARIA [Sensing a heated debate coming on]: Um, remember perception—we're feeling some perception, you know, we're listening. We don't want to challenge it, we want to talk about it.

JOHN: Yes we do [want to challenge it].

AL: You know if we overwhelm Maria, we could rush her and then we could debate. [laughter]

DON [who came to the session late]: I keep hearing Scott say, "You gotta go there and get them." When I joined the service, I chose to join the service.

No one had to come and get me. When I wanted to be a teacher, I chose to become a teacher. No one had to come and recruit me. I don't understand why the perception is that we have to *go* there and *get* them.

SCOTT: Because then they==

DON: You want to be a fireman then go someplace and apply to be a fireman. Have the qualifications necessary. If it takes education, athletic ability, whatever. Apply for it. You mean somebody is saying you can't apply for that? I think we have got laws that protect us when people discriminate. . . . Apply for it, have a little assertiveness. I don't think we have to go looking for people.

MARIA: That's a very good comment—and I think you are going to have some responses.

And he does, including the following:

AL: Well actually, I learned something earlier today [before you arrived], that just blows my mind. These guys were telling us that African Americans are afraid to come up into this area especially in the countryside because they are afraid for their physical safety amongst us. [pause]

DON: I think I brought that up once a long time ago—I'm afraid to go down to certain parts of Milwaukee—

AL: Well, we were talking about that, and I don't mean to back us up [to an earlier point in the conversation]. But this is not perceived as a friendly place to African Americans. So what kind of a person—Say an African American, goes through police science school and has the qualifications and you know is of an age when he is looking for work—he or she—and there is a job in Milwaukee, and there is a job in [this city]. Which job are they going to apply for?

DON: Well if he's from Milwaukee, he's going to apply for Milwaukee.

AL: And that's how it happens. I think that's what these guys are telling us.

SAMUEL: . . . I was the first black [in a place I worked at]. They didn't know how to treat me, sabotaged me because they didn't know how to deal with me. . . . We gotta make people reach out and make people feel comfortable, especially in the workforce.

GINGER: My perception, Don [giggles]==

DON: Don't be debating now [jokingly].

GINGER: You know, what works, works. What works in City A may not work in City B. Because of the history that our country has, we have got to work at diversity. So if you gotta go get 'em, go get 'em. And the other thing is, when you advertise to try to recruit minorities to different levels of the workplace, you are advertising, "OK, come to [this city] to work." OK I know some people that they commute—they work here, but they go back to Milwaukee. OK, we need to also promote not only working in the area, but living in the area. . . . The whole city has got to come together and work in unity. . . . The whole city needs to be welcoming—if they have children, let's face it, we want to feel comfortable. Some people do work in a place where they feel comfortable, but choose to commute because they don't fit well in the community. So we have all got to get on board, make it feel welcoming to minorities. . . .

[. . .]

MARIA: So the question might be . . . why aren't there blacks, African Americans in the police force? Whey aren't there more Hispanics? Why aren't there—something has happened.

DON: Do they feel that it is a lost cause to even try to get in?

ELIHUE: All my brothers are officers. Pretty much all my first cousins are officers. I got an application for over there [to be an officer here in town], but I didn't turn it back in because I didn't feel comfortable—you know?

DON: Why not?

ELIHUE: Being the only black up here, you know? Who knows [what would happen].

DON: Somebody's got to be the first one.

ELIHUE: I don't want to be the first one.

MARIA [stopping Don]: Don, let's listen to what he is saying.

ELIHUE: And also the feeling that you're going to have someone looking over your shoulder, just waiting to get you out of there because they don't want you there. Anyway, took you this long to get the first African-American officer. What's wrong with this picture?

SCOTT: [As a person of color hired into a white department,] you would put up with way more than that. For instance, this Spanish guy we just hired— a nun came in to speak about death and dying and—it blew everybody's mind. Out of the clear blue sky she goes, "Like your people [referring to the Hispanic firefighter] are not as fast—can't understand death, harder for them to comprehend death so it takes longer." [People in the group groan.] And he made a joke, goes, "Yeah my people are a lot slower, I'm not as fast" but everybody was like, "Wow. From a nun!" And even when I moved here—being white, but not living in [this city], if you are not from here—I was here a year—people at the Y[MCA] wouldn't talk to me. . . . So I can't even imagine—I can really empathize with what you're saying.

When Maria, the facilitator, asks us to discuss "View 4: We must overcome our doubts, stop thinking of ourselves as victims, and take responsibility for our own lives," Don launches back in:

DON: Doesn't that kind of go along with what I just said earlier about going out and going after something? Rather than waiting for someone to say, "This is available to you, do you think you would be interested in it?"

SCOTT: The point is that it may not be anybody's lifelong dream down in Milwaukee to come and be a firefighter in [this city], but it is an asset to us. It benefits *us* in certain circumstances. It benefits the community to make us more adaptable to emergencies. That's why. If you would reach out—not to do somebody a favor in Milwaukee, but to do *our* community a better service I think.

MARIA: Well said, Scott.

Notice the many things going on in these conversations. Ginger, Samuel, Adaline, and Elihue all speak directly to the public officials, telling them that the perspective of African Americans in the community differs from their preconceptions, and plead with the public officials to *listen*. And in turn, various officials in the circle, particularly Al, state that in fact they have heard information that is new to them. We see these community members teaching new things to the officials, and we also see Scott the firefighter, who has had more direct experience with the implications of affirmative action than the other city employees, also asking the policymakers to listen. Much of this work is done through stories, and much of it is done through appeals to legitimacy along the lines of, "Look, I have lived this experience, therefore you ought to listen to what I have to say." These are role reversals at work as the elected officials and department heads become the listeners and those with direct experience—the residents and the street-level bureaucrats—are treated as the ones with expertise.

But such an alteration in the typical official-as-expert-paradigm does not completely explain what people did with these dialogues. Residents *did* turn to officials for their expertise and the policymakers did at times use the opportunity to instruct, give information, and explain why the demands of marginalized communities are often not heeded.

For example, in the final session of the central Wisconsin Thursday group, affirmative action arises again with the topic "What kinds of public policies will help us deal with race relations?" Al, a department head, and Scott, the firefighter, express strong support for affirmative action, while Don continues to express some skepticism. Colleen, the librarian who had earlier expressed surprise at the lack of people of color in the police and fire departments, asks the department heads directly why the city does not have an affirmative action officer.

COLLEEN [white]: Is there an affirmative action officer with the city?

AL: No.

[. . .]

AL: Human resources department does maintain affirmative action or equal opportunity policies—on everything, everywhere, including the advertisements, and they are for real. And complaints can be processed through our equal opportunity commission. And we will hire investigators if necessary. It doesn't come up very often. Occasionally we get a housing complaint and it will get investigated and go to the commission. If it determines that there is probable cause, they will forward it with recommendations to the state equal opportunities commission. So there is a process out there. Doesn't get used very often.

COLLEEN: Sounds like a lot of paperwork, though.

AL: Not a lot of paperwork on the part of the complainant, no. . . .

COLLEEN: Seems like you would want somebody vocal in that office or commission or department that is out there [emphasizing the issue].

[. . .]

AL: We don't have a person that does this, are you kidding? We haven't got the people to do half the jobs. . . . This is just a small part of the job of the human resources director, which==

COLLEEN: And do you think—I know this is off the topic, but is it something that maybe should be a separate . . . ?

AL: No. No way. Not with 220 employees.

STAN: People have got the impression that the city==

COLLEEN: Is that a lot or not many? I don't know==

STAN: is this huge organization. We are not. No. The number of people that work for the city—we are a pretty lean organization. . . . If we hire six people a year total, and it is all in police and fire. You wouldn't have a whole person just to make sure that those six people, that people of color had a chance at those slots. To have a whole position just to do that is way out of proportion, not to the size of the problem, but to the size of the organization.

In this portion of their conversation, we see policymakers explaining to street-level bureaucrats their own perspective on an affirmative-action coordinator and city hiring procedures. Al and Stan explain that it is not feasible to have a person whose entire job is devoted to minority recruitment. But this example of public officials providing information to others in the group does not overrule the general story here that these were not one-way exchanges of information. These participants seemed to teach each other.

Later in this same session, the conversation conveys that many, if not all, of the public officials in the group have a new awareness of race relations because of the discussions. When talking about the discrimination that is embedded in existing policies, Don again expresses some skepticism, but is confronted by the stories offered up by the African Americans in the group. At this point he asks the question mentioned in chapter 6, about how they can go through life facing such barriers:

DON: How do you do it? I'm sitting here thinking I must be the most naïve 69 year old man in the world. I can't imagine==

MARIA: I see a—I think it is important for me as the facilitator to point something out, and that is this. . . . We have to honor your feelings, not write them off, make sure we're honoring feelings here—I see what you are saying [to Don] you do not understand this. It is not connecting here.

DON: Nope.

MARIA: But you are keeping your ears open and you're listening. But the diversity circle is the arena or the vehicle for helping us to open yourself. And while, Don, you may walk away still not quite understanding, you've been exposed to feelings, right?

DON: Yes I have. [He is saying this with a very serious face, despite the fact that he is often joking.]

MARIA: . . . and the thoughts of other people who have—They are pretty powerful—and have experienced such things.

AL: And you can't help but walk away knowing more than—for at least those of us who were, you know—we live in [this city in], Wisconsin, we are not exposed to a lot of minorities, and we certainly haven't necessarily, at least I haven't, looked at things from the minority point of view. So it is very valuable to hear the things we're hearing.

MARIA: Thank you, Al.

AL: And if sometimes some of us find it hard to believe, you know, we were all laughing last time about [African Americans from Milwaukee] driving to [Samuel and Adaline's house in the country]—and then I get home and I read in the paper that it just happened in Oconomowoc [when a black man fishing in a lake was assaulted by two white volunteer firemen]. You know? So I gotta believe you. I gotta believe you.

MARIA: Validating isn't it?

AL: I would have believed you anyway [jokingly], but then it was right there in the paper.

Later in the session, Maria asks us whether it was worthwhile to participate in the dialogues.

AL: I was floored. When you guys talk about with um, not feeling safe in some areas, or not feeling welcome in some areas, that was a revelation to me. . . .

DON: I thought I learned some things and in the end, like Julie says it makes you think about things otherwise you might not have thought about, so to answer your question, the answer is yeah.

STAN: Well, just gives you more perspective on how we all view things— different perspectives and I guess some of the feelings that you guys have [referring to the African Americans in the group] that I guess I didn't quite realize. I always thought I was a fair-minded person and I, you know, I can say I grew up in Racine [one of Wisconsin's more diverse cities], but I guess I didn't really understand.

SCOTT: It surprised me, the level that you guys see. Surprised me that some are completely unaware of it.

These conversations demonstrate that dialogues among members of the public and members of the city government, including policymakers and street-level bureaucrats, are not necessarily about deference to public officials. Here we see ordinary citizens instead challenging public officials. The conversations show that people used these discussions to hold public officials to account. Adaline in the Wednesday group had asked Mike to justify why the city had not used diversity training. In the Thursday group, Ginger instructs Don and the other city officials to approach affirmative action in a holistic way, that is, by attempting to make the entire community more welcoming to people of color.

The stories of the African Americans in the group bring a consideration of different perspectives and experiences to this policy discussion. And the public officials show signs that they hear at least some of these views. Al, a department head, says "I was floored" with the stories that he listened to, and that he had never heard that people of color might fear for their physical safety when simply visiting the town, because of the color of their skin. Even Don, perhaps the most obstinate in the group, expresses surprise at the extent to which antidiscrimination laws may not prevent employment discrimination, after hearing Adaline's stories.

The exchange is not just from citizens to public officials but vice versa as well. In this central Wisconsin Thursday group, Al and Stan explained their perspective that it is not feasible to have an affirmative-action officer. In the Aurora daytime group, Sara told Wayne during a break that she valued the chance to hear the perspective of a city employee. "I have never really known a city employee, so I relish this," she said.

I also saw evidence that testimony was communicated from public officials to residents in the way Samuel and Adaline talked about the public officials in the Thursday group during the dialogues of the other central Wisconsin group. When Scott the firefighter first introduced himself to the Thursday (public officials') group, he said that one day, while riding in his engine with his crew, they drove by a house with African-American children playing outside. A racial epithet was scrawled on the house. They stopped and asked the childrens' mother about it, and she said that the landlord did not want her to remove it for fear of damaging the paint. Appalled, Scott and his crew painted over the graffiti for her. The next week after Scott told this story, Samuel relayed it to the other central Wisconsin group and said, "This fireman was so good—I was really impressed." In addition, Samuel remarked to me in a private conversation that he was very impressed by the public officials' level of concern with diversity.

In these various ways, these conversations enlarge the consideration of policy related to race. And they also illuminate that these discussions served as communication between street-level bureaucrats and policy-makers. When Scott the firefighter tells Stan and the other officials that diversifying the fire department is an asset to the entire community and tells Don that achieving that requires active recruitment, this is the act of a government employee communicating to other public officials and elected representatives. Colleen's asking about the lack of an affirmative action officer is an example of the same information flow.

We often think of *elected* public officials as the ones having the most direct connection to the people and therefore as the government actors who are most capable of providing representation of public concerns.[33] But here we see street-level and city hall bureaucrats providing representation. By inserting their stories about the practical need to take difference into account in governance, by directly attempting to persuade elected officials, and by pointing out to elected officials and others the importance of the stories they have heard, the bureaucrats help further insert the concerns of marginalized groups into discussions of public policy.

Contributing Expertise

If the discussions in these race dialogues involved listening between residents and officials, how is this different from the discussions that took place in the groups without public officials? The topics discussed did not differ noticeably, as suggested in the analysis in the previous chapter. However, the presence of public officials meant a qualitative difference in the nature of the conversations. For example, when discussing affirmative action, all of the groups considered stories of discrimination and various viewpoints about the merits and drawbacks of affirmative action. And often, claims would be made about what "the government" should or should not do. But when public officials were present, these claims were directed at actual human beings. We could see that, above, when Adaline asked Mike, "I could ask you that, Mike. Why hasn't the city done it [diversity training]?" or when Colleen asked why the city does not have an affirmative-action officer. When officials were in the group, people could, and did, ask them to justify their positions and local policy.

The distinction was also evident in conversations about racial profiling.

In the southern Wisconsin group, when an African-American woman told a story about security guards racially profiling her son and accusing him of shoplifting in a local mall, the conversation centered on the injustice of such incidents and the lack of recourse that young black men have in those situations. Likewise, when Samuel, the African-American man who participated in the two central Wisconsin groups, talked in both groups about police repeatedly pulling him over while driving home from work, the conversation expressed exasperation at how something like that could happen. But in the Aurora Tuesday group, the one group in my sample in which a law enforcement officer participated, conversations about racial profiling were markedly different. Steve, the African-American police officer, raised the topic in the first session and very frankly explained how it happens.

Before anyone had mentioned racial profiling, Steve asked the group to discuss the topic, when we had been asked to choose to discuss several examples from a list of scenarios involving discrimination:

STEVE: I'm looking at case eleven ["You and your date are walking to your car after seeing a late movie. You see a group of young black men coming toward you. They are wearing baggy clothes and talking loudly. Fearing a confrontation, you cross the street."] You talk about stereotyping. I guess that is actually going on there. Another type of stereotyping that the law enforcement community has been accused of is profiling and that is basically another word for stereotyping. And because of that officers in the state of Illinois are required to fill out traffic data sheets. On any traffic stop, the officer has to submit one that includes the name, what they were stopped for, whether they were searched, their color or ethnic background. I assume what the government is going to do after this two-year period is to determine whether we are profiling.

To be honest, there is a place for profiling. Example being in—let's say I don't know how familiar you are with different parts of Aurora, but if you go on the far east side, say Loucks and Grand, where it is predominantly black, high crime area, high drug area, prostitution. . . . But to see at 1 a.m. two male whites driving in a pickup truck through that neighborhood [chuckles to himself] it is like Sesame Street. "Something does not belong here." Is that stereotyping? Is that profiling? Yes. Is that wrong? Not necessarily. There is a time and a place for that. Am I going to try and stop that truck? Yes. They don't belong there. More than likely, 99 percent of the time they are going to try to pick up a prostitute or sell drugs.

You go to the other extreme where you are in Stonebridge [an affluent neighborhood] and you see two young blacks driving around in a 1982 Impala that is falling apart, loud music. You see them drive around the block two or three times. It's 11 a.m. Am I going to try to stop them? Yes, absolutely. Are they doing anything wrong? No, but my experience tells me they are probably casing houses. So I guess I just say that to—looking at case eleven where these guys look like you know—do people do that? Absolutely. Do I do that? Yeah. I'm a police officer, I carry a gun. I see people walking toward me, I look at them—not just their skin color—but I don't want to be a victim. Is every black kid wearing baggy pants going to mug you? No, absolutely not. But you have to be aware of what is going on around you. We live in a world—it is tough out there sometimes.

JUDY [white facilitator]: Anyone have any questions for Steve on that?

RUBY [white]: I agree with you so completely, because you do have to know when something looks unusual. There is a young couple across the street. Knew they were out of town. Saw a car, a guy looked kinda funny, so I called and said, "Stacey are you all right?" And she said, "Yeah, I just had a pizza delivered." . . . When things don't look right you have to check into it.

STEVE: I wish a lot more of that would happen, as far as people policing their own neighborhoods, knowing their neighbors. It would make our job so much easier.

Here, because Steve, a police officer, is present within the group, the conversation goes beyond mere allegations of racial profiling to a consideration of the perspectives that might underlie why it happens. In other portions of the dialogues, Steve's attendance means the presence of expertise that again alters the nature of the conversation. During the fourth session of that group, we were discussing the view that "We should review our policies for the racist assumptions they contain, and take that racism out." Cilia, the Mexican-American woman, tells a story, and Steve, using his knowledge of the local laws, points out that it is a case of discrimination:

CILIA: I think it also has a lot to do with knowing where you are going. I have two cousins who were raised here in Aurora. Everyone moved back down to New Mexico. And New Mexico is very hot, and they are allowed to have tinted windows. [Tinted windows are illegal in Aurora, Illinois.] If you don't, the sun is just getting into you. And about four years ago they came to visit. Their windows were tinted—like Steve had said one time, if you go to an area that is all black and you see two white people in the middle of the night, you know that is suspicious. Well, they drove to a casino late one night, when they were here. . . . Coming home, they got pulled over. It was very cold, 1 or 2 in the morning. And the officer actually stayed there until they took the tint off of the window. . . . My brother was like, "That was just racist!" And I said, "Well, no—that was not knowing the laws in Aurora."

[But Steve stops her.]

STEVE: But was the car from New Mexico?

CILIA: Yeah.

STEVE: That's not right. If it had New Mexico plates . . .

CILIA: But I said they shouldn't have been out anyway—we have to know the area we are going into. It shouldn't be that way, but you know . . .

[. . .]

WAYNE [white]: They still had the right to be wherever—those officers don't sound square to me.

STEVE: No. That doesn't sound right. Because if you're from another state . . .

Steve's expertise comes into play in this conversation, but not in a dominating fashion. He is contributing it to the group. Rather than dampen the telling of stories or the consideration of different perspectives and experiences, Steve's presence helps people recognize the event as an act of discrimination. A similar dynamic happened when the group talked about gangs. Several of the members expressed concern about gang activity in the city, and Steve was able to provide a history behind the activity and answer a variety of their questions about it.

These examples suggest that the presence of public officials meant that discussions included more than complaints about the government or musings about the motivations behind certain policies. When public officials were present, they often shared their expertise in ways that the other participants welcomed. Although there are good reasons to fear that deliberative democracy will be hijacked by experts, the above analyses are evidence that in a context that values listening, the presence of public officials can be informative rather than dominating.

The Precarious Place of Public Officials in Public Talk

It is easy, however, for a forum that purports to facilitate listening to lapse into the more familiar model of domination by experts. The City of Madison Study Circles on Race evolved over time from a community-wide dialogue program into a program that sponsored dialogues in specific neighborhoods confronting problems like heightened crime or resident-landlord conflicts. One of these forums took place in the spring of 2005 in a neighborhood that had recently experienced two drive-by shootings. The organizers publicized the forum widely and over fifty people attended. The crowd was composed mainly of older, white, long-time residents and younger African-American women and their children, who were relatively recent newcomers to the neighborhood. The neighborhood's (white) alderwoman, social service workers (three white women and one

African-American woman), and two white male police officers also attended. The participants sat in groups, eight to ten people per table, and were instructed to engage in small-group conversations for much of the forum.

I sat at the table that included both of the officers and listened to both white and African-American residents hold the officers to account. One young black woman said that she had been the one to call the police after the first recent shooting, and asked why it had taken officers so long to respond. A young white woman at the table wondered aloud about the enforcement of noise ordinances. The police officers answered these questions respectfully. But the general dynamic of the meeting was not one in which the residents were experts and the police officers were listeners. When all of the participants convened as one large group, the officers stood and addressed the crowd. They eventually moved to the front of the room and gave a presentation with the use of a large city map to argue that response times are long because the police department's resources were thinly spread. Some two-way communication did go on in this session, but it was mainly the residents who listened.

Likewise, a PBS documentary viewing/discussion forum about racial profiling in Madison featured the presence of several police officers, two of whom were on a short list for the position of police chief at the time. The forum was promoted as an opportunity for community discussion, in which the screening of a documentary would be followed by a facilitated discussion. After the screening of the film, the officers sat as a panel in the front of the room. They fielded questions, and members of the audience voiced their concerns, but it was clear from the arrangement of the tables and chairs alone who the experts were in the room. The people in this forum and in the neighborhood meeting above created qualitatively different contexts than those in the repeated race dialogues.

The contrast between the dialogues and these other forums underscores that a change in the format can switch the balance from public official as co-participant to public official as dominator of the event. This is not just a small change in format: the dialogues differed from the standard public hearing format in their emphasis on listening, their repeated sessions, and their seating arrangements. Nevertheless, intergroup dialogues might be mistakenly assumed to contain the same type of communication as other forms of public talk.

The fact that the format of this alternative form of public talk enabled challenging public officials is important because the one-shot forums demonstrated that community residents were hungry for dialogue, not just panel discussions or town hearings. For example, in another PBS forum in the series, the topic was public education since the *Brown v. Board of Education* decision. The Madison superintendent of schools attended (a white man), as did two (elected) members of the school board (one African-American man and one white woman). Much of the evening was dominated by the expertise of these officials. During the discussion portion of the evening, the participants first broke into small, facilitated discussion groups and then reconvened as a large group during which the officials sat in front as a panel. The superintendent was invited to address the crowd, and stood in front and gave a presentation that seemed to go on longer than intended. He cited many statistics and at one point groped for a way to explain racial disparities in test scores and said, "I have a really great graph to show you. I wish I had it with me." In all of these ways, he and the other officials took on the role of experts imparting information to members of the public.

However, the residents in attendance tried to use the opportunity to hold the officials accountable. They demanded answers to their questions about bussing and about their perceptions of unequal treatment of students of color. And when one attendee aimed a particularly intense allegation of racist behavior at the superintendent, a facilitator attempted to diffuse it, saying "he is our guest." But a member of the crowd said, "It is my observation that talking about race should be uncomfortable. The only way to solve this is to confront it." The organizers of the event did not allow for this confrontation to occur, but it was clear that many of the community members present wished that it had.

The attempts to contest the official line during the repeated race dialogues could have turned those conversations into bedlam, but they did not. Sitting around the same table, over repeated sessions, there seemed to be enough civility that the discussions did not teeter on chaos, and yet did include contestation. Consistent with recent work on U.S. congressional behavior, debate, confrontation, and partisanship are not the opposite of civility. In the absence of debate, it is possible to have incivility; and it is possible to have both partisanship or valuable debate in a context of civility.[34] In the dialogue groups on race, it appears that civility may have made productive debate possible.[35]

We could regard the precarious place of public officials in these discussions as evidence that it does not take much for public talk between officials and residents to revert to the official-as-expert paradigm or dissolve into bedlam. But we could take the lead of Archon Fung and see this in a more promising light. He notes that the "fragility" of government-resident deliberations means that it takes only "small perturbations of the discursive process" to bring about deliberation that has more promising outcomes.[36]

An "Empty Gesture"?

When a public official or a public safety officer is in the group, discussion of issues related to race still refer to "the government," but members of "the government" are there to respond. They engage in a two-way exchange with members of the public. They offer up their own stories, as well as explanations and expertise. Of course, these contexts could be perceived as an opportunity to avoid blame, or an opportunity to merely make an empty gesture toward the improvement of race relations.

It is quite likely the case that some public officials use these civic dialogues for precisely these purposes. Those occasions in which mayors or elected officials touted the programs but did not themselves take part seem to be cases in point. And it may also be that in larger cities policymakers are more likely to be seen and to see themselves as having a much higher status than the ordinary citizen, complicating their ability to participate as equal discussion members. But this chapter cautions against the assumption that when officials engage in public talk with residents, or public talk about race in particular, their motives must somehow be shady.

First, the behavior of public officials within these dialogues suggested that they listened and learned from what they heard. Their audible surprise at the stories they heard and the way they challenged the other participants to defend and explain their views suggests that at least some of them were participating in order to learn information that had the potential to improve their capacity to do their jobs.

Second, because these were repeated sessions and these programs were voluntary, the officials' attendance demonstrates their commitment to participating in the interactions. Despite the fact that the group members questioned them intensely at times, they continued to return for additional sessions. The one exception is the city manager in the central Wisconsin city, who attended only the second session. This, however, could be interpreted as a show of concern, rather than avoidance. He had not signed up to take part in the session, but explained that he had heard about the productiveness of the first session and wanted to catch a glimpse of the discussions. In addition, a personnel issue arose in that city government during the month our group met that the other policymakers could very well have used as an excuse to skip one or more sessions. However, even on the afternoon after a major event related to this issue, all but one of the officials attended.

Third, most of the public officials in these groups were not *elected* officials, calling into question the assumption that officials participate in order to win votes. Only Don and John in the central Wisconsin Thursday group that met in the police station had been elected. If participating in these dialogues is just a hollow attempt to curry favor, it is not clear why nonelected officials would take the time to attend. Of course, participating in these programs may have been a way for the government employees to impress their supervisors. But such a goal could have been pursued in a variety of other ways. And in this conservative, 95 percent white city, we might expect that *not* attending the dialogues would win more approval.

Finally, one of the people who *is* an elected official, John in the central Wisconsin Thursday group, demonstrated a transformation in his orientation to the dialogues across the course of the session that speaks to the sincerity behind the public officials' participation. At the beginning of the first session, after I had asked for consent from the group to participate in and tape record the conversations, Maria asked us to say "a few words about your racial or ethnic background." John responded that he wanted to pass. "I'm more here to learn about what happens here as a city official." He had not signed up for the group, and Maria was not aware that he would be there. She let him pass, but when everyone else at the table had taken a turn, she came back to him, saying, "And John, I just can't let you off the hook. You are here—you are present, and we want to hear." He proceeded to share his background about being raised on his German ancestor's homestead. From that point on, he attended as a full participant and was present at every session, including the fifth session action forum.

By the end of the second session, he appeared to no longer be a skeptic of the process. With about twenty minutes to go in the session, Maria asked us to sum up the state of race relations in the community:

DON [white]: We've got a long way to go.
JOHN [white]: But we've got a good start.
GINGER [African American]: We've started, let's keep going.
COLLEEN [white]: Keep working on it, keep going.
[People continue on, contributing specific areas to work on, then John says:]
JOHN: Did somebody say how do we get to people who aren't in this room? That's our job. It is our job to get out and say we can have these sessions fifty-two weeks a year if we had to and get more people involved.

At the action forum, Samuel remarked to John, "I was really impressed with you, you know, the first time you show up, say you are just there to observe, but I really saw some change. By the end of the thing, you were really into it." John responded with a large handshake and smile. "Well thank you very much. The first job of an elected official is to listen and then react, and I just think that is so important." Then he asked Samuel for his vote. "Next time I come up for election you just remember that, remember this name right here (pointing to his name badge)." Was part of his motivation in attending the sessions the electoral connection? Probably. But that in itself is not a sufficient explanation for his regular attendance, seemingly sincere contributions, and change in expressed attitude toward the process itself.

Even if we grant that officials' motives for participating were sincere, were they participating with an eye toward social justice, toward substantial policy change? Or did the officials who participated act as though they merely wanted to gain a better understanding? Much of the discussion did center on the desire to understand in order to administer policy more effectively, not necessarily to build capacity for a radically different approach to local policy. But insofar as these officials treated these conversations as useful for improving their ability to meet the needs of a diverse community, it seems that the dialogues worked toward a combination of self-development and social justice goals. Moreover, even if none of the officials participated to bring about policy change, it seems much less likely that, without their participation, the local government would take any steps at all to improve race relations.[37]

Co-participation, at the Table Together

Participants in these dialogues—public officials and residents alike—remarked that they encountered valuable information and saw listening happening. And what is more, this was occurring across racial lines, across longstanding barriers in these communities. It is not the case, therefore, that official-resident public talk necessarily resembles the official-as-expert paradigm. And when it takes on another form, it is not necessarily bedlam, nor a mere show of listening on the part of public officials. In these civic dialogues, policymakers, street-level bureaucrats, and community residents listened to each other.

Besides the public officials employed by city and county governments in these dialogues, there was yet another public official in the room in each of these groups: me. As an employee of the largest state university closest to each of these cities who introduced herself and passed out consent forms on university letterhead at the beginning of each session, it is likely that the participants were aware of my unique status. My experience in that position was similar to that of the other public officials. Participants turned to me with questions, at times asking about how people on my campus dealt with affirmative action. They also occasionally challenged me, asking why my campus had been unsuccessful in diversifying its student body and faculty and staff.[38]

As we have seen in this and other chapters, the negotiation of roles as both listeners and critics of others' claims was not always smooth or comfortable. It takes work for people to listen to one another and assume the risks necessary to confer equality by critiquing others' claims. It takes work on behalf of public officials to give up authority and sit at the table rather than at the front of the room. And it also takes work on behalf of community residents to communicate concerns to these power-holders. In particular, people of color have to have the patience to explain experience with discrimination to people who are otherwise unaware of it.

A major implication of this chapter is that we need to revise our notions of expertise in the deliberative system. It is not necessarily the case that participants in public talk treat technical expertise as the only useful and legitimate kind of knowledge. In these dialogues, we see residents and public officials alike remarking that stories of experience with discrimination are valuable. That is, public officials treat these stories as valuable inputs for the administration of policy, and they do not have to be cajoled into recognizing that.[39] Their participation is not merely an empty gesture but rather seems to be aimed toward solving the difficult problem of race relations. We see officials displaying the capacity to listen and we also see residents displaying the capacity to discuss reasonably, not asserting "uninformed or unrealistic demands" as an expert-centered model of deliberative democracy would expect.[40]

Observing these conversations also disconfirms the presumption that the presence of public officials mean that these dialogues are especially likely to tend toward unity and convergence around the status quo. Instead, we see little difference in the balance of unity and difference in the dialogues that included public officials compared to those just among city residents. Some justifying of present policies took place, but this did not necessarily mean the public officials were adamant in exerting their authority against potential change. When the central Wisconsin groups talked about affirmative action in the city government, even though some officials explained the lack of people of color and the impracticality of an affirmative action officer position, they engaged in prolonged questioning of current practices. Indeed, some public officials openly questioned department heads and elected officials on their lack of effort in this respect, and there were demonstrations of intent to modify these policies in response.

The results also speak to the practice of street-level bureaucracy. In order for street-level bureaucrats to do their work "smoothly" they need the consent of the people they deal with.[41] Sometimes these government workers get automatic consent because people have learned appropriate ways of interacting with street-level bureaucrats like teachers and police officers from previous interactions and from socialization in the broader culture.[42] But sometimes the authority of a bureaucrat's job title is not enough. If citizens perceive that the bureaucrat or the government in general is unresponsive—is not listening—they are less likely to give consent. These dialogues may be a way for street-level bureaucrats to convey that they are listening to both immediate participants and to the broader public, and thereby improve their ability to do their jobs.

There is another way in which observing these dialogues enlarges our understanding of the administration of street-level bureaucracy. Clients (or citizens) and bureaucrats may have misperceptions about each other which impede the administration of policy.[43] This is a two-way problem. It is not just the case that street-level bureaucrats need to understand their clients better. Clients also need to understand the job of a bureaucrat better. These dialogues provide a way for officials to explain what they do and why they do it in a non-patronizing manner.

The broader story is that this exchange of information is valuable not just for conferring sincerity on officials' desires to listen but also for the practice of representation. I use the term representation here to mean not only the acts of paying attention to citizens' needs and justifying decisions back to citizens but also the act of explaining to citizens just what it is that their government does. For citizens to hear this information, it helps if it is communicated in a context that demonstrates respect by treating them not as people on a lower rung of a hierarchy but as co-participants in the governing process.

CHAPTER TEN

Beyond Romance and Demons

The love of deliberative democracy runs deep in the United States. The Lincoln-Douglas debates and New England town meetings are icons of American democracy, examples we hold up as quintessential good citizen behavior. But these images are overly romanticized. The myth of the Lincoln-Douglas debates expresses nostalgia for a time of vigorous civic involvement that never actually occurred,[1] and romantic images of New England town meetings overlook the grittiness of the exchanges that actually take place.[2] Even intergroup dialogue programs, which are an example of people attempting to do some of the most elusive and difficult form of public talk—interracial conversations about race—display behavior that is not simply brotherly love or a striving for mutual understanding.

On the flipside of our romanticized images of public talk is our strident skepticism of it. We demonize public talk for its lack of action, its mere lip service to pressing public problems. Our skepticism of the capacity of ordinary citizens, the sincerity of public officials who supposedly engage them, and the potential for talk across racial lines in particular counter our admiration for deliberative democracy.

Perhaps it should be so, for somewhere between the romanticizing and the demonizing lies the actual practice of deliberative democracy. This book has set aside our assumptions about deliberative democracy long enough to take a look at one particular manifestation—intergroup dialogue programs on race in cities throughout the United States. Doing so has revealed a texture of a civic action that is both promising and problematic.

This study has shown that cities throughout the United States are using talk to address race relations. In these intergroup civic dialogue programs, small racially diverse groups of volunteers come together over repeated sessions to talk face-to-face about race. This is not deliberation in the sense of talk oriented toward decision making. Instead, it is dialogue that is intended to enable listening to the perspectives of others in the community as a way to improve understanding.

A skeptic might assume that these programs are a way to avoid taking action to improve race relations. However, we have seen that these conversations do not occur in conditions or proceed in ways that suggest they are all talk and no action. First, the analyses of the conditions giving rise to these programs across a sample of medium-sized cities in chapter 4 showed that civic intergroup dialogue programs do not only occur in wealthy communities as a way to enhance self-understanding. Indeed, the standard resource-based model of participation[3] does not seem to fit on the aggregate level.[4] Even in lower-income cities, and particularly in lower-income cities with substantial economic inequality, people have turned to intergroup dialogue in conditions associated with a pursuit of social justice. Also, we saw that the conditions of government sponsorship of these programs are indistinct from NGO sponsorship, suggesting that the motives for government involvement in these programs are not different from those of organizations insistent on pursuing social justice.

Probing the reasons that practitioners give for turning to dialogue, in chapter 5, revealed further evidence that the choice to pursue civic dialogues and the behavior within them do not fit the assumption that this is simply recreation for participants. Practitioners—government employees and employees of social justice organizations—explain that they consider the dialogues to be an integral part of pursuing profound change in their communities. They conceptualize their decision to implement these programs not as a choice but as a practical necessity. They talk about this not as something that they turned to as the best available strategy, or on the basis of multicultural ideology, but as something that stemmed from a lifelong belief in interracial interaction.[5] The act of people engaging in talk for the purposes of defining how they wish to live together is part of political life, just as is deciding specific courses of action.[6]

Chapters 6 though 9 examined these dialogues directly. Listening to the discussions in six groups in four cities in Wisconsin and Illinois revealed that the content does not display the dominating focus on unity that critics of deliberation demonize, nor the unimpeded attention to marginalized views that difference democrats romanticize. In these dialogues people do listen to difference. Observing them reveals listening between people of different racial backgrounds and listening between public officials and residents. And yet people collectively struggle with the proper balance between attention to racial group identities and distinctions and attention to identities of unity such as "Americans." Despite the desires of some people to "get beyond race," or to achieve a "color-blind society," and the tendency to start gravitating toward assumptions that everyone is in agreement or "underneath it all we really are all alike," people of color halted the drift toward unity, or common identity, and the drift toward consensus, or agreement on policy stances. By inserting stories of their own experiences with discrimination, they encouraged the others to pay attention to difference.

Storytelling was important here as it served to expose people to the possibility that people of different racial backgrounds could have very different experiences in everyday life—from shopping to interactions with the police—in the very same geographic community. And it was also important for its ability to alert people to the reasons that people of different racial backgrounds might have different perspectives.

But these dialogues were powerful not just because they provided an opportunity to listen to difference. Instead, they seemed to do the most work when the participants ignored facilitators' mantras to engage in "dialogue and not debate." It is when people scrutinized each other's claims that they most clearly seemed to convey respect for one another.

Chapter 9 in particular revealed that this dynamic took place even among groups composed of public officials and residents. Despite assumptions that public talk that includes officials inevitably devolves either into an expert-driven presentation or into bedlam in which members of the community shout at those in power, these dialogues revealed that public talk can actually involve two-way communication. Policymakers listened to community members, and community members listened to the expertise policymakers could provide. Moreover, policymakers listened to street-level bureaucrats who had more direct experience with racial diversity in the community. Residents, street-level bureaucrats, and policymakers challenged each other and in doing so challenged conventions of expertise that operate in many other aspects of the deliberative system. Residents' stories were treated as expertise alongside officials' technical and bureaucratic information.

This study has dealt with the general question of how a community respects difference while nevertheless seeking a way to come together. How do cities in the contemporary United States use public talk to balance unity and difference? We have seen from these programs that public talk across lines of difference *can* occur without running roughshod over the perspectives of marginalized groups.[7] Because these dialogues involve listening to difference, our tendency may be to dismiss this as multiculturalism that exacerbates divides and privileges racial identity over allegiance to the community as a whole. But the fact that people of all races scrutinize others' stories and challenge each other's claims undermines assumptions that these programs simply promote a politics of difference or multiculturalist ideology. The participants express a *range* of sentiments about the proper balance between unity and racial difference, contrary to the presumption that only folks who place difference first volunteer. People are deeply ambivalent about the tensions involved and it is this ambivalence, not the attempts of multiculturalists to indoctrinate, that opens up opportunities for listening to difference. Moreover, we see that people of color do exercise power in these dialogues by using racial identity to assert legitimacy and thereby claim authority. But again, it is because the format enabled the other participants to challenge the claims of people of color, not just defer to the primacy of racial identity, that lent these views power. The direct challenging of people of color as well as whites signaled that people of a range of views and backgrounds were taken seriously.

Multiculturalism, or the politics of difference, is often critiqued for being out of step with mainstream society and an ideology that is promoted primarily by left-leaning intellectuals. But the choice to pursue and the content of these dialogues challenge our notions that multiculturalism is elitist. The people who volunteer in these programs are elitist in the sense that they represent a narrow segment of their city. But they are not elitist in the sense of people whose values have been formed in ways distinctly different from those of the rest of their community. The practice of intergroup dialogue challenges critiques of the politics of difference that portray it as an extreme approach of leftist intellectuals, or an approach to democracy that is out of step with ordinary people. These *are* ordinary people.

People who distance themselves from left-leaning politics may not necessarily distance themselves from the actual practice of listening to difference. Recall the remark of Don, a city council person and participant in the central Wisconsin Thursday group: "You don't have to be a Democrat to be a jackass." Don was not a leftist, yet he nevertheless listened intently to the stories of people with cultural backgrounds different from his own. The people who participated in these groups were not multiculturalists for the most part. In addition to the widespread value for "getting beyond race," they did not use the terminology of multiculturalism. But in the course of these dialogues, they listened to stories of people for whom race is an everyday reality, a source of pride, and a barrier to opportunity.

This is a practical politics of difference that we do not notice when looking at attitudes about diversity in public opinion polls or one-on-one interviews. Polls show that people disdain hard multiculturalist policies. Schildkraut's focus groups show that people rely at times on an incorporationist perspective that recognizes the immigrant character of the United States to talk about American identity and public policy, but only rarely do they use a mutliculturalist perspective.[8] In-depth interviews likewise show that middle-class Americans express a "benign multiculturalism" in which they disdain bilingualism, but think diversity should be celebrated, as long as the government does not force this celebration on anyone, and as long as in supporting this celebration, they do not lend support to lefty academics. These tendencies are particularly true among whites.[9]

But this benign multiculturalism looks different when diverse groups of residents in Midwestern medium-sized cities choose to talk to one another. How people react to multiculturalist principles through opinion surveys is important, particularly because many people do not actually engage in interaction with people of different cultural backgrounds—they do not experience any direct exposure to cultural diversity *to* observe. But part of the power of public opinion is the form it would take if people encountered more or different information.[10] And its power also lies in the shape opinions might take if citizens had fundamentally new *experiences*. If attitudes toward multiculturalism are attitudes about how people of different cultures ought to live together, to fully understand the nature of public opinion on this topic it makes sense to observe what happens when people of different backgrounds actually *do* try to interact.

In this study, I have examined the choice to pursue these experiences as well as what occurs within them. This is a project that is different from conventional studies of intergroup contact in which the object of study is attitude and behavioral change. Instead, I have studied the content of the contact itself and the manner in which people create the meaning of civic life together as they try to negotiate the competing values of their political culture.[11]

My approach obviously has limitations. First, this study speaks to concerns about deliberative democracy, but it is important to notice that the public talk it investigates is public talk specifically about race. I would argue that race enters into a wide variety of public talk, but because these conversations were overtly about race, and volunteers for the programs knew this, my study does not speak to the nature of conversations about race regardless of the context in which they emerge. For example, does the pulling each other back from unity through telling stories about difference occur in contexts in which people are not expecting to talk about race? Probably not. This study speaks specifically to the processes that go on among diverse groups of people who choose to engage a relatively unfamiliar group of people about race, as well as the conditions that lead to these conversations occurring.

Second, I made the choice to focus intensively on conversations about race in a handful of particular cities. This limits the extent to which I can generalize these results to the content of conversations in similar programs around the country. Do people in communities in the South, the West, and on the coasts have different types of conversations in race dialogue programs? It is possible. That possibility doesn't devalue the importance of understanding how people use this opportunity in communities in the Midwest, places we typically refer to as the "heartland" and expect in many cases to be quintessential American cities. However, insofar as the struggle to define citizenship in the 21st century is partly done by telling stories about experiences in communities in which the conversations occur, it would be worthwhile to learn more about how people do this kind of talk in other racial and political contexts.

Finally, as I stated at the outset, my decision to study the content of these programs by observing them directly, rather than by reading others' reports of what took place, or by inferring about the processes going on by measuring changes in attitudes before and after participation is an unorthodox choice for a political scientist. Making this choice comes at the cost of potentially influencing what I observe. That is, my own perspectives may have influenced what I noticed and what I believed was important about the topic of my study. That is true of all social science analysis. Even when we use data on the attitudes and behaviors of people whom we have never met, our perspectives influence the questions we ask to obtain this information and the way we interpret our results. However, when using participant observation, particularly in an interpretivist mode, part of communicating our findings ought to be an explanation of how our expectations and viewpoints played a role in our analyses. In the methods appendix, I explain in greater detail the tactics I used to minimize my influence on the conversations, to account for my influence, and to call into question the conclusions I was reaching

With these limitations of the study in mind, we can say that what these people were doing tells us about the nature of race in the United States in the early 21st century, or at least in medium-sized cities in the heartland. Race is the elephant in the room in the civic life in these communities. It is a force that it seems illogical to try to get beyond at this point in time. In the words of Samuel, one of the group participants, "It *do* make a difference." And if the goal is for race not to matter, these dialogues suggest that moving forward requires acknowledging that it does affect the everyday experience of people in ways that are invisible to folks who have the luxury of perceiving that they are without race. Also, in this increasingly racially and ethnically diverse country, it will be progressively more necessary to face the conflicts that race presents rather than avoid them. That is not a multiculturalist's creed. It is a practical necessity.

This approach has revealed that the deliberative system *does* provide spaces for listening to difference, contrary to skeptics of deliberation, and yet the communication does not entirely shun the logic of unity. I call the communication that pays attention to difference that we see in these dialogues a practical politics of difference because it stems from practical needs rather than an ideology that places racial identity above all others. Some individuals may certainly be motivated to join or implement these dialogues due to a belief that politics should be about reinforcing, recognizing, and maintaining racial differences. But the pattern across the explanations practitioners give for choosing dialogue, as well as the nature of the conversations within the dialogues, suggest this was not the norm. Theorists may ask, what kind of communication does democracy require? Residents of these cities seemed to ask, what can I do to improve my community? In other words, they were concerned with dealing with housing and job discrimination, interacting with Spanish-speaking businesses and neighbors, and other practical realities of day-to-day life. Their solution was intergroup dialogue on race.

This melding of attention to subgroup categories in combination with an attempt to find common ground is the kind of contact that many social psychologists prescribe to reduce prejudice. But the significant thing revealed in this study is that people of their own accord chose to do this, and collectively used the opportunity to focus on difference and unity, not just unity alone. Despite the privileging of unity in the broader political culture, people encouraged each other to listen to difference in these dialogues.

The dynamics in the Aurora Monday evening group teaches us the complicated business of attending to difference. At the same time that Liza, the facilitator, called attention to difference by speaking about her experience as an African-American woman, she demanded unity by denying others' claims to legitimacy. She shut down discussion of the experience of Hispanics, thereby stifling the potential for these dialogues to fully serve as a site of listening to difference. One implication is that this practical politics of difference is not flawless, and often times it does operate under the guise of attending to cultural diversity while in fact creating other forms of hierarchy. Not all people were listened to equally in these discussions.

Another implication of the dynamics in Liza's group is that listening and scrutiny must coexist in tension. Attention to difference does not come about without us challenging each other. Although participants in these dialogues challenged each other at times, moments of intense conflict were rare, perhaps to the detriment of the productivity of these groups.

These dialogues had yet other downsides. Not everyone participates in them equally. First, lower-income people were less likely to volunteer, consistent with individual-level patterns of participation in other civic activities. This underscores why listening is so crucial in dialogues that are organized around issues of inequality.[12] Because there is some evidence that the people who participate in public talk do tend to be privileged in terms of education and income,[13] it is when people with a different perspective are present that listening to their concerns is particularly valuable to avoid public talk merely perpetuating the status quo or patterns of domination.

There was at least a second population in these communities that was not involved in these dialogues: people who were highly intolerant or disagreed that racism is a problem. Sometimes these programs are dismissed entirely for this very reason. "They are not reaching the people who most need to be here" is a common complaint. However, if the purpose of these programs truly is to make significant change with respect to race relations, this downside does not undermine the whole endeavor. Who really needs to be reached the most with these programs? Those who are the most racist, the least likely to change their perspectives about the state of race relations in their community and what should be done about it? Or is it instead those who are ambivalent, but have the desire to be active in the community? Like political strategists plotting to win elections, perhaps these organizations have decided to focus their resources not on those with immutable views but on those who might be mobilized if given a sufficient nudge.

Earlier I noted that this study has called into question the claim that civic dialogues on race are all about talk and not about action. Nevertheless, one potential downside of these programs is that they will not necessarily lead to action. Yes, it is the case that these dialogues arise in conditions that suggest they are connected to social justice action and the practitioners of the programs certainly conceptualize them that way, but it is nevertheless possible that simply engaging in these conversations will entirely satiate some participants' desires to do something about race. Not everyone who talks about race, even in these settings, will continue on to engage in some kind of direct action to change the state of race relations in their community.

What Civic Dialogue Might Bring About

But some people will—and have. Throughout the country, these programs have served as the launch pad for a variety of collective actions. Typically, participants generate myriad ideas for subsequent actions together. This was evident in the six rounds of dialogue that I observed.[14] For example, in the circle that met on Wednesdays in the central Wisconsin city, during every session the facilitators recruited a note-taker from the group to record the ideas we generated for actions to take once our formal discussions were over. Each session generated a list that took several minutes to read.

Programs around the country have already demonstrated that people do not just generate ideas in these programs, they pursue and implement them. In addition to the many reports people make of actions in their own lives such as stopping racist jokes as they occur, going out of their way to befriend a person of a different racial background, patronizing businesses in racially diverse parts of the city, and attending multicultural events, collective actions occur as well. These range from activities that celebrate diversity to activities that directly challenge power structures and local public policy.[15] One of the most common results is the formation of task forces or committees which continue to meet after the end of the dialogues to address issues ranging from promoting the dialogues to lobbying for changes in school policy.[16]

A few examples will illustrate. In Waterloo, Iowa, participants have formed several "Roundtables," which are committees that meet periodically to address issues related to race. For example, a Hate Crimes Roundtable engages in public education campaigns and mobilizes residents to support victims when a hate crime occurs. They make public statements and organize neighborhood marches in a show of solidarity with the victims of hate crimes, such as people whose garages have been painted with racial slurs, people whose cars were vandalized while parked outside an integrated church, or interracial couples who have been sent hate mail.

In Dayton, Ohio, participants decided to publicly recognize African-American World War II veterans during an annual Peace Bridge event in which people march across a bridge that spans the river that has historically divided the white and black neighborhoods in the city. Other participants in that program decided to get together for a potluck before a play on challenges facing women of color in which one of their group members was performing.[17]

In Springfield, Illinois, Mayor Karen Hasara pledged that she would pursue the action ideas that study circle participants generated, which led to attempts to diversify the police and fire departments. This resulted in the first African American, the first Hispanic, and the first female hired to the fire department in ten years.[18] In addition, a group of participants decided to form the Springfield Reconciliation Coalition to address the issue of race relations from a spiritual perspective. Their activities included holding a prayer vigil and an educational and symbolic walk that retraced the path of the race riot that occurred in that city in 1908.[19] Also, the dialogue program there led to the formation of a race relations task force. One of its functions has been to mobilize people in response to race-related incidents. When Matt Hale, a white separatist and leader of the World Church of the Creator in Peoria, decided to give a speech at the Lincoln Library in Springfield, the task force held an alternative diversity celebration, diverting attention from Hale's event.[20]

In the Burlington-Chittenden county area in Vermont, study circles participants helped pass antidiscrimination laws for the public schools.[21] In Kansas City, Kansas, participants in a dialogue program formed a neighborhood association.[22] In Fort Myers, Florida, participants negotiated to obtain a supermarket in a low income neighborhood, organized a multiracial community choir, contributed work on a Habitat for Humanity house, and published a multicultural cookbook.[23]

Lima, Ohio, has had one of the most successful civic dialogue programs to date, in terms of participation. As of 2002, over 5,000 people—out of a total population of 40,081 (in 2000)—had participated in a study circle. One outcome was the placement of a YMCA downtown. Also, the programming at the civic center has begun including more works that address interracial themes.[24]

The six circles that I observed varied in the extent to which participants wanted to pursue further actions together. Several of the Madison group members met socially after graduating from the program, and several friendships were created that continue six years later. The Aurora groups seemed to have a similar outcome: several friendships, but not a desire to continue meeting as a group. However, the southern Wisconsin group had met again as a group three times in the four months since the end of their formal dialogues, with the intent of pursuing political action together. The members of both central Wisconsin groups took part in the action forum at the end of their session and signed up with other participants to pursue activities ranging from promoting the dialogues throughout the city to promoting nondiscriminatory practices in local businesses and the public schools.

Existing research suggests that these programs matter on the individual level as well. Because the dialogues do involve attention to difference, we might expect that they would lead to a heightened awareness of the problem of racism in one's community. Indeed, the Rojas et al. study mentioned in chapter 6 demonstrated such an effect in response to participation in a public forum that involved watching the PBS documentary *The Two Towns of Jasper* and then engaging in dialogue. That study also showed that participating in civic dialogue was related to a stronger willingness to participate in antiracism actions than was watching the video in isolation.[25]

Other outcomes of race dialogues are likely. Because the communication combines a focus on difference with a desire for unity, we might expect that it generates relationships and trust in others across racial lines.[26] Because the dialogues focus on race, participants may gain a willingness to talk about race and gain greater comfort in doing so. Self-reports in program evaluation surveys typically suggest that participants graduate from the discussions perceiving that they have an enhanced awareness of the problem of race, increased understanding between people of different racial backgrounds, increased trust and respect among community members, increased comfort in talking about race relations, and increased willingness to get involved in race relations actions.[27] These evaluations typically use post-participation surveys, and sometimes use pre-tests and post-tests, but no study to date has been conducted of *civic* dialogue participation using a sufficient number of pre-tests, post-tests, and a control group to determine causality.

However, Patricia Gurin, Biren Nagda, and colleagues have conducted such studies of dialogue participants on college campuses. Their studies of students have demonstrated that participating in interracial dialogues improves views of intergroup conflict,[28] increases intercultural communication skills,[29] and results in motivation to learn about other social groups, which in turn seems to spur perceptions of greater importance and confidence in reducing prejudice and promoting diversity.[30]

The practice of these programs suggests other individual-level outcomes that deserve future research. One of the reasons that we value the existence of this form of communication in and of itself is because it is a potential antidote to political polarization. Rather than people demonizing those of a different perspective, this form of communication represents an attempt to listen to the views of others. These programs are an example of people around the country trying to address divisions within their communities in a productive fashion. These conversations are not about partisan polarization per se, but they are a more hopeful indicator of the way people are dealing with conflict than much of the rhetoric around polarization conveys. The format of this aspect of the deliberative system is designed to understand alternative views more than other forms of deliberation. It remains to be seen whether people actually achieve a greater understanding of those views.[31]

For all of these important possible outcomes we should not overlook the outcome that is visibly produced by these dialogues: the creation of a fundamentally different kind of context in public life. Public life *is* what members of the public—elected officials, government employees, and everyone else—create together. These people all were embedded in the same geographic community, and, by virtue of coming together and struggling to communicate with one another across divides of race and authority, they were altering the meaning of public life in their city.

A Place for Government in the Public Sphere

The existence of these programs is a reason to reconsider our preconceptions about the proper role of the government in the public sphere. In these dialogues, many times it is a local government that has created the opportunity for people to encounter difference. And almost always, one or more prominent public leaders are openly valuing this communication through their direct participation in it. In his classic book on the contact hypothesis, Gordon Allport discussed whether we ought to expect stateways to alter folkways, or in other words whether legislation can lead to changes in the way we treat each other in everyday life.[32] This study raises another concern: perhaps we ought to focus our attention on altering the folkways of "states" (that is, governments) as well.

Many deliberative forums that jointly involve public officials and community residents merely perpetuate power hierarchies, but this study shows that there is a potential in the deliberative system for communication that goes against this norm. We see public officials listening to residents and listening to each other. The implication is that a wider range of community members' perspectives could be incorporated into local decision-making if policy makers were to implement public talk that emphasizes listening. It is possible to incorporate the perspectives of marginalized groups through institutional changes that create incentives for public officials to appeal to these perspectives.[33] But incorporating dialogue has the potential to shift elite behavior from pandering to marginalized populations due to a need to win elections to creating public policy that is attentive to their concerns due to an ability to more fully understand them.

Thus the practice of civic dialogue challenges our notions of the proper place of government in the public sphere. As noted earlier, Habermas originally conceptualized the public sphere as a figurative space in which members of the public deliberated and formulated critiques of government. Government control of this sphere is therefore seen as dangerous and antithetical to its very purpose. This results in what Simone Chambers calls a "two-tiered view of democratic politics: One tier contains formal institutions of representation (sometimes called strong publics), and the second tier contains informal citizen deliberation (weak publics)."[34] The problem is that there is therefore little conception of how these two tiers communicate with one another.[35] If the perspectives of people in the public are to influence public policy, and if the electorate is to understand the perspectives of officials they vote in or out of office, democracies should provide spaces in which those in these seemingly separate tiers listen to one another.

Nevertheless, government involvement in the public sphere poses problems for those who seek to fundamentally alter existing power arrangements.[36] Iris Marion Young argues that an activist is rightly skeptical of deliberation with public officials, "especially deliberation with persons wielding political or economic power and official representatives of institutions that he believes perpetuate injustice or harm."[37] And yet we have seen that not only *are* governments commonly involved in intergroup dialogues that challenge mainstream conceptions and in which residents directly challenge current policy makers, but these programs are especially likely to arise in situations *of* inequality. Even if some elected officials turn to talk as a less radical manner of dealing with injustice, nonelected officials in agencies such as human rights departments explain their choice with the rhetoric of social justice. Indeed, these officials sometimes sound like activists. And activists insist on the presence of officials. Employees of the Des Moines NCCJ, for example, say that having government actors at the table is essential, that dialogue with them is a way to exert power over these leaders.[38] This is a stark contrast to the fear that bringing public officials and members of the public together automatically means domination by the officials.

There is a difference in thinking of talk as a means of competition or thinking of talk as a means of recognition. Those who want to remedy injustice may view talk with power-holders as a dangerous tactic, likely to perpetuate injustice. But those who see recognition as a route to remedying injustice see the participation of power-holders in difference-focused talk as an important step forward in the battle to end inequality.[39]

Local governments may be altering the way they conceptualize public talk in the provision of public services, particularly the place of difference-focused talk. This seems particularly evident in human rights departments. In my interviews with employees of such departments and members of human rights commissions, many remarked that they spent far too much time adjudicating claims of discrimination and would prefer to focus more resources on education and prevention. Those who had implemented dialogue programs talked about this as the wave of the future and a type of strategy that cities, by necessity, would have to adopt.

This may signal a return to a former focus of human rights commissions. In 1975, Eleanor Holmes Norton, currently the Washington, D.C., delegate to Congress, and at the time the head of New York City's Human

Rights Commission, remarked that mitigating intergroup conflict and reducing tension were tasks of the past. And fortunately, in her view, civil rights commissions had made a "rapid conversion . . . to true administrative agencies, with law enforcement as the central focus."[40] Three decades later, human rights commissions' staff members commonly *lament* the lack of resources for nourishing relations across racial lines, and the U.S. Department of Justice Community Relations Service urges commissions to focus attention on relationship-building and understanding.[41] Indeed these commissions are now often called human *relations* commissions as opposed to human *rights* commissions.

Focusing on harmony and understanding may appear to be a less action-oriented route than challenging perpetrators of discrimination. But, again, this study directly challenged that claim through evidence that the conditions under which government entities pursue dialogue programs are no different than those under which social justice organizations do, as well as through evidence that practitioners pursuing this talk had often engaged in civil rights action in the past and saw these dialogues as consistent with that lifelong pursuit of social justice.

The role of the government in the public sphere in this fashion is important for what it portends for the future of deliberation in public life, and also for its potential symbolic effects. We have much to learn about the effect of government involvement in civic deliberation. In addition to the question of how such public talk affects the shape of public policy, there are many questions to ask about its effect on psychological attachments to the government and the life of the community more generally. Do people who participate in face-to-face dialogues alongside public officials come away with higher levels of efficacy? Greater trust in government? Do they gain knowledge about local government procedures and whom to contact? Does the existence of the programs affect such attitudes among people in the broader public who have not personally participated in the dialogues? In addition, how do such programs influence the officials who participate? Do the programs result in greater policy responsiveness?

Previous work on the existence of city-wide infrastructures such as neighborhood associations that connect citizens and government has shown no special effect on the linkages between government and racial minorities.[42] But the format of these dialogues has a unique potential to improve linkages between citizens and government. Perceptions of political efficacy are largely a product of signals about who holds political power.[43] The act of government actors sitting down with members of the public may send a signal that they wish to share power with members of the public. Because public officials and residents are often talking with one another in these groups, participation might lead to greater efficacy and trust in government among residents, and greater knowledge about local politics.[44] And from the perspective of officials, participation may lead to a greater willingness to engage in dialogue with residents and desire to open up governance more generally.[45]

The outcomes are not necessarily all positive. Even if such programs increase trust in government among participants or members of the public at large, such attitude change could actually impede civic life by reducing the perceived need to participate and directly oversee what officials are up to.[46] Also, those who view talk as a waste of time or do not see racism as a problem or a priority are likely to be disturbed by the idea that public officials are taking two hours out of their workday once a week to engage in dialogue.

Rather than shy away from their choice to implement intergroup dialogue, there are reasons to suggest that public officials ought to *increase* publicity of their involvement. Behavior in these dialogues shows that many community leaders and residents, even in rather politically conservative cities, engage in listening to each other. If officials are involved in civic dialogue programs partly to improve connections with the public, especially marginalized communities, then increased publicity of the fact that public officials are engaging in dialogue with residents in which they are earnestly listening to their concerns could help achieve this outcome. Also, residents might view decisions based on the content of dialogue in which citizens and officials participated together as more legitimate than those made by officials acting in isolation, particularly if the communication is perceived as sincere and not merely lip service.[47]

The role of government in promoting public talk that includes listening is important for yet other reasons. As the assertions of public officials in chapter 5 attest, resident-official dialogue could improve the effectiveness of policy and the administration of street-level bureaucracy. In addition, when the program is directly linked to a government through government sponsorship or the participation of policymakers, it may increase the equality of participation. Here is why: because this form of public talk puts public officials on a relatively equal playing field with residents—around the same table, as opposed to in a one-way speaker-listener arrangement—residents may perceive that they have opportunities to actually gain the attention of policy makers and influence policy.[48] And when opportunities for exercising decision-making power are readily available, racial disparities in participation are reduced.[49] In this way, the involvement of government—the work of policies and institutions that promote participatory democracy—may work to reduce the socioeconomic inequalities we typically see in political participation.[50]

Unity in Struggle

This study has illuminated the importance of talk that involves listening as well as scrutinizing others' claims, or more generally, conflict. The two broad views of politics with which I began—the politics of unity and the politics of difference—value conflict, but for different purposes. The politics of unity regards conflict as a temporary challenge. It urges us to engage in debate in order to reconcile differences in opinion and help identify a common means of achieving *the* common good. The politics of difference regards conflict as a means of continually calling into question those agreements and definitions of community and the common good. In very simple terms, a unity-focused conception of democracy treats conflict as something to be gotten past, while a difference-focused conception treats ongoing conflict as a means to avoid domination.

The behaviors observed in this book do not entirely comport with either view. While the conflict that participants in these groups engage in is not accurately described as exacerbating divisions, neither is it convergence or agreement, contrary to the unity-focused model. And at the same time, we see people using conflict to scrutinize the claims of people of color, as well as those of whites, contrasting with the difference-focused ideal as well.

How should we understand this? In the practice of public life the dichotomies of unity and difference, listening and scrutiny, dialogue and debate, and consensus and disagreement do not operate as dichotomies but as elements in yin/yang relationships. Rather than reconcile these polar forces, the participants in these dialogues worked at negotiating a balance.[51]

American political culture presumes that the preferred manner of dealing with the tension between unity and difference is to get past difference and focus on unity. But participants in these programs found ways to strive for a balance of the two, rather than a reconciliation that unquestioningly privileges unity. What did they use to accomplish this? Ambivalence played a large part, as many individuals' deep ambivalence about the tension opened up the possibility for discussing various sides of the issues involved. But the other part was played by the striving for conflict. By letting in some debate, people could convey sincerity. The intertwine of dialogue and debate ensured that this was not a storytelling hour, but storytelling in the service of earnest political work.

Participants in these discussions directly challenged each other at times, and it seemed that the act of letting this conflict in made the dialogues much more than superficial talk. It was the most intense exchanges that resulted in expressions of "I didn't realize" and other indicators of newfound awareness; it was the participation of public officials in such exchanges—both as listeners and as challengers—that conferred sincerity on their presence in the room. And it may be this visible willingness to reconsider one's views when challenged that enables deliberation to function in the realm of race relations. As Mendelberg and Oleske argue, interracial public talk is likely to be intractable and unproductive unless participants exude a willingness to take others' views seriously, a willingness to reconsider one's own views, and a willingness to have those views scrutinized by others.[52] It is the exercise of contestation infused with listening that allows public talk to achieve this character.[53]

The balance between civility and scrutiny and between dialogue and debate in these conversations carries its own lessons about the feasibility of interracial public talk. The dialogues were friendly, and yet some contestation went on. But it was not so agonistic that people shook the shoulders of the people they were talking to and said "Listen! Listen for God's sake!"[54] nor did they necessarily "rupture" the other's stream of thought.[55] Instead, the communication fell somewhere between dispassionate talk that ignored the extent of divisions and contentious debate that exacerbated them. The call for communication that is openly agonistic and contentious should not be ignored. But we should also note that communication that is solely contentious has little possibility of actually engaging others in the community.

The remarkable characteristic of these civic dialogues that directly addressed the contentious issue of race relations is that people, in the process, figured out a way to pay attention to these divides and yet did so in an atmosphere of friendship. They challenged one another and asked for justification, but they did so while sitting around a relatively small circle, in repeated face-to-face sessions. It is the combination of civility and contestation that made it possible to engage particular public issues in ways that were open to new perspectives and to collectively negotiate broader issues of identity, authority, and legitimacy. Norms of civility are often criticized for perpetuating domination,[56] but they may in fact make contestation of domination possible.

Civic dialogue is imperfect. Privileging dialogue over debate has the potential to silence the confrontation that confers sincerity, the willingness to be scrutinized, and the willingness to negotiate power rather than assume it. The manner in which people struggled with the balance of authority and legitimacy across racial groups shows that participants were not always adept at considering a wide range of views.

However messy, people using civic dialogues as a practical solution to racial conflict teach us that attention to difference is not antithetical to a desire for unity. Collectively, these group members simultaneously valued common ground and similarity alongside recognition of difference. Their behavior suggests that attention to difference is necessary to bring about unity. To achieve unity in the form of cooperation (whether that means living alongside one another peacefully or engaging in collective action), it helps if people speak a common language. But cooperation may also require a level of trust that comes from recognizing others' quite different experience in the world; in other words, from recognizing difference. As a man working jointly for the NCCJ and a local government in California quoted in chapter 5 explained, police officers "understand that the most important thing to community safety is information. And how do I get information? By gaining your trust. And how do I gain your trust? Well, I gain your trust by being respectful to you, by listening to you, by acknowledging you're different." In other words, these connections are being forged not in *spite of*, but *through* difference.

Scholars of deliberation do at times grant that attention to conflict and unity in the form of solidarity can coexist and can possibly both be achieved through deliberative procedures.[57] But perhaps conflict and solidarity can not only coexist but *must* coexist. Yes, shared interests and sympathies do facilitate friendship and make deliberation easier.[58] But enduring friendships do not tune out differences; they instead respect them. If I have become friends with an Arab-American woman partly because of our shared experience as scholars, and yet act unsympathetically or with indifference to her stories dealing with discrimination as a person of color, am I really a friend? It is the act of allowing unity and difference to coexist together that makes friendship and solidarity possible.

People doing civic intergroup dialogue teach us that common ground can incorporate both a recognition of difference and the recognition of enough in common to move ahead.[59] When we take the results of the observations, interviews, and the community-level analysis together, we see that at some level these difference-focused conversations are also about unity. This is not the unity of sameness or oneness, but of wholeness, or a willingness to create a public life together.[60] In the thoughts of dialogue practitioners, in the behavior of participants during the dialogue, we see evidence that people want these dialogues to bring people together. They want to connect. People do not leave these forums talking about each other as one and the same, and yet their camaraderie suggests that they have indeed established bonds.

At some level, all visions of democracy require some type of unity—something that holds the members of a polity together. In classical liberal visions, it may be a social contract or unanimity. For proponents of the politics of difference, unity takes the form of a commitment to the practice of contesting political discourse and the procedures through which we conduct this discourse.[61] The practice of these dialogues suggests yet another definition of the unity that binds people together in civic life. The thing that seems to hold people together in the practice of confronting racial difference is the struggle. For them, it is the shared struggle that provides unity. The common desire to address race relations brings people to the table, but it is the act of creating public life together and taking on the struggles this entails that provides the connection.

In calling what people around the country are doing with intergroup dialogues on race a practical politics, I am not proposing that it is practical to expect that all people in all cities around the United States will engage in such programs. It is incontrovertible that most U.S. citizens prefer to spend their time on activities other than public affairs, and that is just one barrier to achieving such a goal. However, in many places, those ordinary citizens who are concerned about race relations in their communities have turned to a particular form of public talk to make some progress. It is a practical politics because they use what they have available—their stories, their sense of justice, and their aspirations for themselves and their communities—to make some connections among people with the potential to make change, who might otherwise go on living separate lives. This talk may not be practical in the sense that it can be practiced by everyone, but it is a more practical form of democracy than one that assumes that the issue of race in the United States will heal itself.[62]

The people in these communities were using civic dialogue to create bridging social capital, to create relationships that down the line can help cities address public problems across divisions of race and across the all-too-common divide between the people and their government. However, a bridge metaphor portrays what these people were doing as too concrete, and perhaps too meticulous in its planning and execution. The act of creating the public together is an ongoing, difficult task. This is neither the work of angels nor devils, but of ordinary people.

I. Multi-City, Aggregate-Level Analysis, Conducted in Chapter 4

Description of Independent Variables
(Dependent variables are described in detail in chapter 4.)

Low-income and high-income cities: Cities in sample were divided in half according to median household income (see below).

Median household income: 1999 income, Census 2000 summary tape file 3, P53. Expressed as thousands. All Census data in these analyses were obtained from the 2000 Census, because the vast majority of programs in this sample as well as throughout the United States began closer to 2000 than to 1990.

White income: 1999 Median household income, Census 2000 summary tape file 3, non-Hispanic whites, P152I. Expressed as thousands.

White education: Percent bachelor's degree or higher for non-Hispanic whites, Census 2000 summary tape file 3, P148I.

Racial income inequality: Census 2000 data, summary tape file 3, P152B, P152H, and P152I. Subtracted the 1999 median household income for African Americans from that of non-Hispanic whites; repeated for the income gap between Hispanics and non-Hispanic whites (with incomes expressed as thousands). Averaged those two figures by weighting each by relative proportion of population.

Nonwhite education: Percent bachelor's degree or higher among people other than non-Hispanic whites, Census 2000 summary tape file 3, P148B through P148H.

Nonwhite percent: Percent other than non-Hispanic white, Census 2000 summary tape file 3, P7.

Civil rights organizations: Dichotomous variable indicating presence of active branch of the NAACP, Urban League, or a Latino civil rights/ interests organization. Collected through telephone index and internet searches, confirmed through calls to the branch.

Nonwhite media: Dichotomous variable indicating presence of one or more media outlets targeted to nonwhites. Collected though search of *Gale Directory of Publications and Broadcast Media* (2003), and telephone calls to city clerk's offices.

Resident-government connections: A five-point (0 to 4) scale created from the following 4 variables: (1) a dichotomous variable indicating whether or not one or more seats to the city council are elected by district; (2) a dichotomous variable indicating whether city has a mayor as C.E.O. rather than a city administrator or manager; (3) a dichotomous variable indicating whether city web page includes links to neighborhood associations; (4) a dichotomous variable representing whether city fell above the sample mean in the ratio of residents per council member. This last indicator was computed by dividing total population figures from the 2000 Census by the number of seats on the city council, excluding the mayor. For Lexington and Louisville, Kentucky, and Arlington, Virginia, indicator was computed with county population, because the county board is the most local governing body in these cities. Data for all four indicators were collected through search of city web page and telephone calls to the city clerk's office.

Growth in nonwhite population: Based on total number of people identifying as some race other than non-Hispanic white in the 2000 (Summary tape file 1, P8) and 1990 Census (Summary Tape File 1, P010). Computed by subtracting the 1990 figure from the 2000 figure and dividing by the 1990 figure.

Southern state: Dichotomous variable indicating city is in a former slave state.

Statewide coordination: Dichotomous variable indicating city is located in a state in which a nonprofit or government entity promoted civic dialogue between 1990 and 2004.

Cities Included in the Analysis

California: Alameda, Bakersfield, Berkeley, Chico, Davis, Escondido, Fairfield, Hemet, Irvine, Lancaster, Lodi, Merced, Modesto, Napa, Orange, Palo Alto, Pasadena, Petaluma, Redding, Salinas, San Bernardino, San Buenaventura, Santa Barbara, Santa Clara, Santa Cruz, Santa Maria, Santa Rosa, Stockton, Sunnyvale, Temecula, Turlock, Vallejo, Visalia

Colorado: Boulder, Fort Collins, Greeley, Longmont, Pueblo

Florida: Boca Raton, Cape Coral, Clearwater, Daytona Beach, Ft. Lauderdale, Gainesville, Lakeland, Melbourne, Miami Beach, Orlando, Palm Bay, Pensacola, Port St. Lucie, Sarasota, St. Petersburg, Tallahassee, West Palm Beach

Illinois: Aurora, Bloomington, Champaign, Decatur, Elgin, Evanston, Joliet, Peoria, Rockford, Springfield

Iowa: Cedar Rapids, Council Bluffs, Davenport, Des Moines, Dubuque, Iowa City, Sioux City, Waterloo

Kentucky: Lexington, Louisville, Owensboro

Mississippi: Biloxi, Gulfport, Jackson

New Jersey: Bayonne, Camden, Jersey City, Trenton, Vineland

New York: Albany, Niagara Falls, Rochester, Schenectady, Syracuse, Utica, White Plains

North Dakota: Bismarck

Oklahoma: Lawton, Norman

Oregon: Eugene, Medford, Salem, Springfield

Rhode Island: Pawtucket, Providence, Warwick

Texas: Abilene, Amarillo, Beaumont, Killeen, Laredo, Longview, Lubbock, McAllen, Midland, Odessa, San Angelo, Tyler, Victoria, Waco, Wichita Falls

Utah: Ogden, Orem, Provo, Salt Lake City

Virginia: Alexandria, Arlington, Hampton, Lynchburg, Newport News, Norfolk, Portsmouth, Richmond, Roanoke, Suffolk

Wisconsin: Appleton, Eau Claire, Green Bay, Janesville, Kenosha, La Crosse, Madison, Oshkosh, Racine, Sheboygan, Waukesha

Note: Iowa, Wisconsin, and Illinois were chosen purposively for a pilot study for this project. Vermont was one of the eighteen states sampled for the analysis, but it does not have a census-designated city of medium-sized population as defined in this book and therefore is not represented in the analysis.

II. Interviews: Utilized Primarily in Chapters 3, 4, and 5

One source of data used in this study was interviews with people who administered intergroup dialogue programs. I conducted many of these interviews while attempting to identify cities that had implemented a community-wide dialogue program on race and ethnic relations, information used in the analysis reported in chapter 4. For a pilot study of that analysis, I conducted interviews (primarily face-to-face) with twenty-nine practitioners in fourteen cities throughout the broader Midwest (Wisconsin,

Illinois, Iowa, Ohio, Kentucky, Indiana, and Missouri). In the expanded study (of eighteen states sampled from across the United States), I interviewed either the main administrator or someone involved in the administration of the program (in several cases more than one person associated with the program) for every third program of the sixty-six identified. I also interviewed two practitioners who were planning on starting a dialogue program, two practitioners who had been involved in civic intergroup dialogue programs of a more limited duration, as well as one woman who had conducted a dialogue program that involved just religious and civic leaders, not people from the community at large. This procedure resulted in twenty-six additional interviews.

These combined procedures produced interviews with a total of fifty-five state and local government officials and nonprofit organization employees who had administered intergroup dialogue programs in thirty-eight medium-sized census-designated central cities. The individuals interviewed therefore represent programs that vary in type (i.e. SCRC, Honest Conversations, etc.), government sponsorship, and racial heterogeneity of the population. To check conclusions against programs conducted in larger cities, I interviewed an additional ten practitioners in nine larger metropolitan areas. (These cities were Tulsa and Oklahoma City, Oklahoma; Cincinnati, Ohio; Long Beach and San Jose, California; Corpus Christi and Dallas, Texas; Portland, Oregon; and St. Louis, Missouri.) These sixty-five interviews (total) ranged from fifteen minutes to two and one-half hours in length, with an average length of approximately thirty minutes. I taped and transcribed all interviews, unless otherwise noted. I refrain from using the interviewee's name in several cases in which the person did not wish to be identified by name.

III. Participant Observation: Utilized in Chapters 6 through 9

The participant observation used in this study began as a pilot study of one group that was meeting in the first round of a city-run study circles program in Madison, Wisconsin. After observing the Madison group, I focused my attention on collecting data for other portions of this project, including interviewing race dialogue practitioners around the country. Their thoughts and other information I collected led me to believe that what goes on in civic intergroup dialogues likely varies depending on the affluence and racial heterogeneity of the city in which they occur. To probe this further, I chose cases for additional observations that varied on these factors. In doing so, I assumed that the community context would influence the characteristics of the dialogue participants as well as the topics they wished to talk about.

I was unable to identify a low-income, homogenous community with a civic race dialogue program. The scarcity of race dialogue programs in such cities is not surprising, given the results of the analyses in chapter 4.

At the same time that I wanted variation in city contexts, I wanted to control as much as possible for major national current events. Therefore, I sought to observe groups meeting in different cities, but all meeting at the same time. To try to separate out the effect of group composition and facilitator from city context, I sought to observe multiple groups within at least one city. I was able to gain access to discussions occurring in three cities, within 200 miles of one another, that all took place within a time span of six weeks in April and May 2005. All of the programs were run by NGOs but had the endorsement of local officials.

Because all of these programs were located within the upper Midwest, I am limited in the extent to which I can generalize these results to dialogue programs that are held in other parts of the United States. I intentionally opted to observe dialogues located in close proximity in order to control for variations in content due to region. Although the particular issues that arose in the conversations likely vary across regions, I have no reason to expect that the basic patterns in the dynamics of the conversations or the processes of the struggles people engaged in vary across the United States, except that groups in more racially diverse areas of the country may have involved more contestation among people of color, a possibility I address in chapter 8. In addition, I used the interviews with practitioners throughout the country to verify the existence of the basic dynamics I observed in these Midwestern dialogues.

Table A.1 displays the cities I selected, their median incomes, and their racial characteristics. I provide only approximate figures for income and race for the central and southern Wisconsin cities, to protect the confidentiality of the participants.

In addition to these study circle conversations, I also conducted participant observation of several other types of race discussions, all in the Madison, Wisconsin, area. I attended two noontime discussion sessions on race sponsored by the local YWCA, a series of six sessions sponsored by the Urban League and local PBS affiliate at a community center in which a documentary related to race and ethnic relations was shown and then followed by facilitated group discussions, and a neighborhood discussion in a lower-income neighborhood in Madison that was sponsored by the "Respectful Dialogues with a Purpose," the organization that grew out of that city's Study Circles on Race.

There are several pieces of additional information pertaining to a few of the groups that may assist readers particularly interested in the

TABLE A.1: Cities included in the observations

	City	Median household income	Non-Hispanic white	Black	Hispanic
High income,[a] homogeneous	Madison, Wisconsin	$41,941	82.0%	5.8%	4.1%
	Central Wisconsin (2 groups)	Between $40,000 and $45,000	Between 90% and 95%	<5%	<5%
High income, diverse	Aurora, Illinois (2 groups)	$54,861	52.1%	11.1%	32.6%
Low income, diverse	Southern Wisconsin	Between $35,000 and $40,000	Between 60% and 65%	Between 20% and 30%	Between 10% and 20%

[a] High vs. low income was determined using the median income among the cities in the analysis in chapter 4, $36,700.

observations. Of the six groups that I observed, the Madison group was the largest, made up of nineteen people, including two facilitators. Both facilitators were women; one was African-American, and the other white. Including these women and myself, there were six black women, eight white women, one black man, and four white men among the original participants of the group.[1] Of all the groups, it had the most intellectual tone. That is, participants often talked about specific academic theories of race and race relations. Several of the group members urged the others to move past vague impressions of racism and confront structural inequalities and systematic, society-wide and global patterns in the treatment of people of different racial and ethnic backgrounds. In particular, this group talked about the concept of white privilege at length. White privilege is the idea that whites, because of the pervasiveness of racism, enjoy a variety of benefits in the course of everyday life that they often do not notice. It is a concept that requires an advanced level of introspection to consider.[2] Although the other groups touched on it,[3] only the Madison group talked about this concept in depth and on multiple occasions.

In the southern Wisconsin group, two people co-facilitated the first session: an Arab-American woman and a white woman. The group members included an older African-American man who was a longtime resident and leader in the community, a white man who owned a local business, four white women (including myself), a white man who was married to one of the white women, and an African-American woman. After the first session, however, the composition changed. The African-American woman and one of the white women did not return. The African-American woman said she had conflicts with her work schedule, and the white woman had been asked to attend by her employer to check out the program for possible use in her human resources department. She seemed uncomfortable with the process throughout the first session, rarely speaking or engaging the other participants. The facilitators of the group also changed. The white facilitator had a medical emergency and never returned, and the Arab-American moved and only facilitated one additional session. Therefore, a white man who was a longtime activist in the community facilitated sessions two through five. (He co-facilitated the second session with the Arab-American woman.)

Gaining Access and Conducting the Observations

When I introduced myself and asked for the group members' consent, I stated that I would be both a participant and an observer. In all cases except the Aurora groups, I left the room while the group members decided whether they would allow me to participate, observe, and tape-record their discussions. (The Aurora facilitators said that it would be more disruptive if I left the room than if I stayed while the group members decided if they would give their consent.)

I participated just enough to earn my keep as a member of the groups. My main intent was to observe, and my microphone in the middle of the table put this clearly on display. I was more than a recorder, however. I asked questions of others and they asked questions of me. This was an advantage, because in several cases, I was able to ask questions of the group that helped me to clarify the conclusions I was reaching.

It was essential for this project to tape record the conversations. I was not able to obtain permission to record the conversations in the Madison group, and I took copious field notes immediately after those sessions. Fortunately, the other groups allowed me to record all of their sessions. Recording was necessary because I was interested in the entire conversations, not just portions related to a particular policy or social group, and because there were as many as nineteen people involved in a conversation during a given session. Also, the slightly more formal setting in which people were meeting, and the recognition that they were coming together in order to have a structured conversation made me feel less intrusive when asking for their permission to record than I would have if the participants had been meeting informally in, for example, a neighborhood gathering place. Not all participants were completely comfortable with the presence of my recorder. However, on several occasions, people would remark that they had forgotten I was recording.

As much as I could, I tried to maintain my part in the groups in ways other than conversation. For example, in the central Wisconsin group in the public library, as soon as the facilitator suggested that someone volunteer to bring food for the second session, I volunteered. I also tried to be as polite as possible and display the microphone as unobtrusively as possible. I held my tape recorder in my hand so that if anyone wanted the tape turned off at any time, I could easily do that (and explained to all the groups that this was my intention). Holding the recorder this way also enabled me to change tapes without a great deal of disruption or interference of the conversation.

I also contributed to the groups in ways that added to the flow of the talk rather than shifted the group in a new direction. As the analyses of the amount the various participants spoke reported in chapter 8 show (see tables 8.1 through 8.5), I was one of the least talkative members of each group, intentionally. This caused some tension in the Monday night Aurora group, as Liza, the facilitator, scolded me after the second session for not participating enough. The director of the group also asked that I contribute more to help the flow of the group. I attempted to contribute enough to fulfill my role as participant, but continued to hold back in the contributions that I made.

Inserting myself into these situations altered what I observed both because the participants likely modified their behaviors due to my presence and because the relationships we developed over time may have altered my willingness to notice discrimination and racism among the participants. My presence likely stimulated more attention to issues related to colleges and universities, such as affirmative action, and more attention to the possibility that race relations are different in liberal cities such as Madison. Also, my presence seemed to spur more conversations about the history of the cities in which I was observing. I asked questions about local history and people would often offer up brief accounts, including histories of race relations, that illuminated the dynamics I was observing in the groups. One might expect that people attempted to present the best face of their city due to my presence as an outsider, but reports by several participants on the one session I was unable to attend, the third session of the southern Wisconsin group, suggested that the level of contentiousness did not differ noticeably.

I employed various strategies to ask myself "how do I know what I say I know?"[4] I wrote detailed memos about what I expected to see before I began observing. I also took careful and comprehensive fieldnotes, particularly after my first encounter with interviewees or groups. These proved invaluable later on, when I had become blinded to some of the more remarkable features of their perceptions and patterns of the discussions.[5] Because the perspectives with which we view the world color what we see, it was important for me to have my observations of these discussions informed "by a wider array of observers and screens" than just my own.[6] As a white person, I needed to remind myself constantly that my own race had undoubtedly influenced what I expected to see and what I chose to notice. Therefore, I regularly asked other participants in the dialogues for their interpretations of what occurred within them, and asked several for feedback on my analyses and drafts of this manuscript. In addition, I asked friends and family members to attend the PBS-sponsored public forums with me, to provide additional challenges to my perceptions.

I transcribed all of the sessions myself. I find transcribing to be an integral part of analysis.[7] It is an excellent way to become familiar with my data. Although it is time-intensive, I find that if I combine this task with writing memos,[8] the rewards in understanding the phenomena I observe are immense. Transcribing provides an extra layer of analysis, because the tapes convey tone and emotion that would not be obvious in a transcript. Hearing these inflections again reminded me of body language that I was then able to notate in the transcripts.

Because I was conducting observations in three different cities simultaneously, I spent a great deal of time in my car. I discovered that composing memos while driving by talking into my tape recorder allowed me to record substantial detail about the observations. It also allowed me to begin my analyses as I thought out loud en route to my next site. This may not be the safest driving practice, but I found that composing while driving allowed me to make the most of my observations. For example, I was able to record and analyze information from observations in the morning while driving to another location for an evening group. By the time I arrived, I had a clearer sense of the patterns I was observing and a sharpened sense of what I was looking for in that evening's discussion.

Finally, I found that one of the most fruitful ways of becoming familiar with the communities I observed was to spend time in grocery stores. When planning my fieldwork, I obtained maps of the cities, and onto them plotted government centers, public libraries, demographic information, and major grocery stores. I tried to visit most of the major grocery stores between 5 and 6 p.m. I paid attention to the types of cars in the lot, the apparent race of the customers and the clerks, and the manner in which they interacted. I also took note of how prominent and extensive the ethnic food offerings were. What I observed helped me understand who lived where in each of the cities, and the extent of racial and class segregation in their daily lives. It helped me compare the standard of living and demographic profiles across cities and across neighborhoods within cities. It helped me understand what people meant when they referred to particular areas of their town. I would have learned much about the nature of these places from the content of the dialogues and from background research I conducted in the local libraries. However, watching residents perform the mundane task of buying groceries and observing the nature of the place in which they did so helped me as an outsider better understand their everyday encounters with difference.

List of Participants

CENTRAL WISCONSIN, WEDNESDAY

Pseudonym	*Race/ethnicity*
Samuel	African-American
Adaline	African-American
Mary	White
Margaret	White
Lisa	White
Patricia	White
Mark	White
Mike	White
Valerie (facilitator)	White
Tozi (facilitator)	Mexican-American

CENTRAL WISCONSIN, THURSDAY

Pseudonym	*Race/ethnicity*
Samuel	African-American
Adaline	African-American
Ginger	African-American
Bernita	African-American
Elihue	African-American
Julie	White
Colleen	White
Maria (facilitator)	Hispanic

John	White
Bill	White
Al	White
Stan	White
Don	White
Jenn	White
Paul	Hmong
Leng	Hmong
Bruce	White
Scott	White

AURORA, MONDAY (EVENING)

Pseudonym	Race/ethnicity
Liza (facilitator)	African-American
Rebecca	White
Dolores	White
Christine	White
Lucy	Puerto Rican
Amaal	Arab-American
Adam	White
Matt	White
Elic	African-American
Beth	White

AURORA, TUESDAY (DAYTIME)

Pseudonym	Race/ethnicity
Judy (facilitator)	White
Wayne	White
Cilia	Mexican-American
Steve	African-American
Ruby	White
Rachel	White
Sara	White
Elnor	White

SOUTHERN WISCONSIN

Pseudonym	Race/ethnicity
Fred (facilitator)	White
Luke	African-American
Laura	White
Bob	White
Rosemary	White
Frank	White
Deb	White
Lois	African-American
Barb	White
Amna (facilitator)	Arab-American
Sandra (facilitator)	White

MADISON

Pseudonym	Race/ethnicity
Wanda	African-American
Mary	White
Bill	White
Jeanie	African-American
Diana	African-American
Fran (facilitator)	African-American
Harriet (facilitator)	White
Katie	White
Connie	White
Stacey	White
Ron	White
Melissa	African-American
Dave	White
Susan	African-American
Rachel	White
Ben	White
Dolores	White
Michael	White

IV. Participant Surveys: Referenced in Chapters 3, 6, and 10

In conjunction with program administrators, I administered surveys to participants in several different rounds in the Madison and Aurora programs: to participants in the Fall 2000, Spring-Summer 2002, Fall 2002, and Spring 2003 sessions of the Madison program, and to participants in the Fall 2002 and Winter 2003 sessions of the Aurora program. Response rates for the completion of the survey administered to participants after they completed their session ranged from 35 percent to 74 percent.

The number of respondents and response rates were as follows: Among the Madison respondents, in Fall 2000, 32 of 85 participants completed a survey, yielding a response rate of 38 percent. For the Spring-Summer 2002, 26 out of 55 potential respondents (47 percent); for the Fall 2002, 29 of 51 participants (60 percent); and for the Spring 2003, 14 of 40 participants (35 percent). In Aurora, in Fall 2002, 27 of 39 completed the survey (69 percent) and in Winter 2003, 17 of 23 did so (74 percent). Response rates are higher in Aurora because questionnaires were completed during dialogue sessions rather than as mail-back surveys. Respondents to the Madison Fall 2002 survey, and the Spring 2003 surveys were entered into a lottery for a $50 or $75 gift certificate to the local civic center.

The survey included an open-ended question asking respondents to describe what they believed the dialogues had achieved. ("What do you think your group achieved?" and "Are groups like the Study Circles likely to change the greater Madison area for the better? If 'Yes,' what specifically do you think they might change? If 'No,' why aren't these groups effective?") I coded these responses for mentions of consensus or common ground. Responses that qualified as beliefs that the dialogues help achieve unity were: "Harmony"; "Greater sense of community"; "Some consensus on different issues"; "I think we achieved a measure of community"; "Larger sense of community"; "Considerable unity in spite of some personality obstacles"; "That we are more alike than different in our wants and needs"; "After comparing 'notes,' we realized that across minority cultures, we had a lot of experiences in common—We weren't alone!"; "Awareness of other racial groups as people."

I coded the remaining responses for common categories across the surveys. I used a sample of 20 percent of the responses to develop a code frame. All responses per respondent were coded. An intercoder reliability test using 1 coder blind to the purposes of the study coding 10 percent of the pretest responses resulted in a correspondence of 71 percent. Due to this low reliability, I refined the coding categories and recoded all of the responses. An intercoder reliability test using a different coder, again blind to the purposes of the study, resulted in a satisfactory level of correspondence, 92 percent. (This was computed by counting the number of unique codes per respondent across the two coders as the denominator, the number of overlapping codes as the numerator.) Responses other than the common ground or unity responses were coded as mentioning as many of the following categories as applied: Understanding of differences across people; Understanding of issues related to race and racism; Understanding or insight, not further specified; Learning, not further specified; Learning about people; Challenged each other; Political action; Personal empowerment; More civic engagement; Comfort; Deal with racism, not further specified; Make connections with other people; Share my experiences and/or feelings with others; Want to hear what others have to say; Personal empowerment; Personal growth; Overcome stereotypes; Change attitudes; Reinforce attitudes; Encourage more talk; Candid discussion; Improved relationships; Improve the community; Change behavior; No hopes; Don't know.

The most frequent response was that these dialogues helped people understand differences or different perspectives across participants. Among the Madison respondents, 38 percent of them mentioned this category. Other common responses include understanding of issues related to race (27 percent), establishing connections among people (26 percent), sharing experiences and feelings (11 percent), challenged each other (3 percent), producing policy change (6 percent), producing civic engagement (8 percent), overcoming stereotypes (4 percent), changing attitudes (2 percent), learning how each individual can make a change (4 percent). The following are examples of explanations that were coded as better understanding of differences: "They offer understanding of different races—we can learn to understand where we come from"; "Better understanding between individuals for sure in some cases"; "Empathy"; "To cause an 'understanding' of one another."

If we take the "understand differences," "awareness of differences," and "challenge each other" responses as indicators that the talk was difference-focused communication, we find that 46 percent of the Madison respondents and 36.8 percent of the Aurora respondents felt that this is what had gone on in their dialogues. Among the Aurora high school students, 66.7 percent said that their dialogues had consisted of understanding or awareness of differences or the act of challenging one another.

V. Components of American Identity included in the Content Analysis in Chapter 6

Liberal Categories
  Civil/political rights
  Private/public distinction
  English necessary for economic success
  Obey laws
  Freedom
  Economic opportunity
  Work ethic
  Majority rule
  Individualism
  Tolerance
  U.S. as land of plenty
  Rule of law
  Free market*

Civic Republican Categories
  Language law would be exclusionary
  Isolation from the rest of the community
  Balkanization/too much diversity
  Local control over decision making
  Being able to communicate
  Responsibilities/duties of citizens
  Ceremony/ritual/myth
  Important to feel American
  Voting
  Participation/volunteerism
  Language law is divisive
  Self-governance
  Neighboring*

Ethnocultural Categories
(Acceptance of ethnoculturalism)
  Nostalgia/"good" vs. "bad" immigrants
  English as American
  Blames immigrants for their "station"
  Ascriptiveness of American identity
  Anti-immigrant sentiments
  Other ethnoculturalism or ethnocultural hybrid

(Rejection of ethnoculturalism)
  Critical of ethnocultural tendencies in America
  Need to fight ethnoculturalism
  Not American because not white and blonde
  Language law is ethnocultural

Incorporationist Categories
(Multiculturalism)
  U.S. characterized by distinct cultures
  Important to maintain differences
  Laments loss of culture
  Critical of melting pot myth
  Government to help maintain differences
(Melting pot assimilation)
  U.S. characterized by cultural assimilation
  Melting as blending/"American" as dynamic
  Vague references to the melting pot
  Government to help with assimilation

Examples of hybrid codes
  Liberal and ethnocultural: market success requires English*
  Incorporationist (multicultural) and ethnocultural (rejection of): tolerance of multiple languages, awareness of social difficulty speaking Spanish*
  Liberal and civic republican: freedom combined with obligation to learn English*

Source: Schildkraut, *Press One for English*, 97, except marked entries (*).

Choices in Secondary Schools"; Quillian and Campbell, "Beyond Black and White"). See also Walsh, *Talking about Politics,* especially 76, 78 for racial homophily in voluntary associations. Social circles typically are not interracial. The 1998 General Social Survey showed 68 percent of whites and blacks nationwide had no close black or white friends, respectively ("How many of your good friends are White/Black?"). Also, many people report feeling uneasy with interracial interaction. A December 1996 poll conducted of Chicago residents by the Metro Chicago Information Center asked whites whether they feel "comfortable or uneasy" "When dealing with African Americans." While 46 percent said comfortable, 45 percent said uneasy. Intergroup contact produces considerable anxiety (Stephan and Stephan, "The Role of Ignorance in Intergroup Relations"), more than contact with ingroup members (Gudykunst and Shapiro, "Communication in Everyday Interpersonal and Intergroup Encounters"). Even when given the opportunity, people may not "step outside their comfort zones" to cross the room to engage in conversation with people of a different racial background (Walsh, *Talking about Politics*). Talking to people of a different racial background is particularly uncommon for whites. In 1997, an ABC News/*Washington Post* poll reported that only 40 percent of whites said that *anyone* in their family had brought a black friend home for dinner *in the past few years* (ABC News/*Washington Post* poll, June 8, 1997. N=1137, national sample. "During the last few years, has anyone in your family brought a friend who was black home for dinner?"). Fifty-nine percent of blacks reported that someone had invited a white person over. Similar results were obtained the previous year in the General Social Survey. (Among non-blacks [N=951], 40.6 percent said "yes" when asked, "During the last few years, has anyone in your family brought a friend who was a [Negro/Black/African-American] home for dinner?") Even in the workplace, interracial interaction is not common for whites. The 1998 GSS revealed that 29 percent of employed adults in the United States worked in an all-white workplace (N=1268. "Are the people who work where you work all white, mostly white, about half and half, mostly black or all black?"). Interracial interaction does occur at times. In a study of residents of Detroit in 1992, approximately 80 percent of whites as well as blacks reported having interracial conversations "frequently" or "sometimes" while shopping, and approximately 70 percent of blacks and 65 percent of whites reported such conversations on the job (Welch et al., *Race and Place,* 54.) However, less than 10 percent of whites and less than 5 percent of blacks in that study reported visiting in the homes of neighbors of another race (Ibid., 52).

4. Dalton, *Racial Healing*; Tatum, *Why Are All the Black Kids Sitting Together in the Cafeteria?* Even those who say confronting conflict is beneficial usually draw the limit at confronting conflict about race (e.g., De Dreu et al., "Conflict and Performance in Groups and Organizations"). This talk is also surprising because it goes against the grain of the typical aversion to potentially conflictual talk about public issues (e.g., Finifter, "The Friendship Group as a Protective Environment for Political Deviants"; Mutz and Martin, "Facilitating Communication Across Lines of Difference"; Mutz and Mondak, "The Workplace as a Context for Cross-Cutting Political Discourse"; Mutz, *Hearing the Other Side,* chap. 2). Ethnographic studies of political conversation conclude that people avoid it (Eliasoph, *Avoiding Politics*), or engage it while policing the homogeneity of their groups (Walsh, *Talking about Politics;* see also Hibbing and Theiss-Morse, *Stealth Democracy,* 134–37 for evidence from surveys and focus groups). People are exposed to cross-cutting political opinions (Huckfeldt, Johnson, and Sprague, *Political Disagreement*), but this evidence may be overstated, and people in the United States exhibit more homoge-

neity in their informal political talk than people in the eleven other countries in the 1992 Cross National Election Project (Mutz, *Hearing*, chap 2.).

5. This estimated number of programs was calculated through merging lists of intergroup dialogue programs from the Study Circles Resource Center, the Western Justice Center Foundation, information produced by the Clinton Administration on Race (*One America*), the Network of Alliance Bridging Race and Ethnicity website (http://www .jointcenter.org/nabre), the 2002 National Conference for Dialogue and Deliberation, Du Bois and Hutson (*Bridging the Racial Divide*), pursuing all links provided by the Dialogue to Action Initiative website (www.thataway.org), and recording additional programs in the process of conducting interviews and data gathering for this study. This is a count of programs resembling the basic format described above and therefore does not include programs that do not require repeated interactions among participants. The existence of a random sample of these programs was verified through additional internet and newspaper searches and interviews with local residents.

6. Varshney, *Ethnic Conflict and Civic Life*, 293–95; Barnes "The Same Old Process?"; Bar-On and Kassem, "Storytelling as a Way to Work Through Intractable Conflicts"; Nelson, Kaboolian, and Carver, "Bridging Social Capital and an Investment Theory of Collective Action"; Burayidi, *Urban Planning in a Multicultural Society.*

7. Mansbridge, *Beyond Adversary Democracy;* Mendelberg and Oleske, "Race and Public Deliberation."

8. Barry, *Culture and Equality;* Gleason, "Sea Change in the Civic Culture in the 1960s"; Renshon, "American Character and National Identity"; Sears et al., "Cultural Diversity and Multicultural Politics," 71; Shapiro, "Enough of Deliberation," 31.

9. Dryzek, *Deliberative Democracy and Beyond;* Chambers, "Deliberative Democratic Theory."

10. For example, see Merelman, Streich, and Martin, "Unity and Diversity in American Political Culture"; Mendelberg and Oleske, "Race and Public Deliberation"; Luskin, Fishkin, and Jowell, "Considered Opinions: Deliberative Polling in Britain."

11. For example, see Gastil, *By Popular Demand;* Ryfe, "The Practice of Deliberative Democracy"; McLeod et al., "Understanding Deliberation."

12. For example, see Innes, "Planning Theory's Emerging Paradigm"; Briggs, "Culture, Power, and Communication in Community Building"; Grogan and Gusmano, "Deliberative Democracy in Theory and Practice"; see also Chambers, "Deliberative Democratic Theory," for the growth of a focus on deliberation in international relations and public law as well.

13. Delli Carpini, Cook, and Jacobs, "Public Deliberation, Discursive Participation, and Citizen Engagement"; Karpowitz, "The Deliberative Potential and Realities of Public Meetings." Cook, Delli Carpini, and Jacobs show preliminary evidence from a national sample survey study that suggests people who participate in face-to-face deliberation tend to be more educated but not significantly different from the rest of the population in terms of income, gender, and political orientation. In an expanded model, age, participation in other organizations, political efficacy, and participation in other forms of political acts are significant predictors of participation in face-to-face deliberation ("Who Deliberates?"). Karpowitz ("The Deliberative Potential") uses national sample Roper data to show that attendance at public meetings on town or school affairs dropped from almost 24 percent in 1973 to about 12 percent in 1994, with the steepest declines among the wealthiest respondents.

14. Mansbridge, "Everyday Talk in the Deliberative System."

15. These two questions correspond to the first two questions among the list that Michael Delli Carpini, Fay Lomax Cook, and Lawrence Jacobs pose as the major questions facing empirical studies of deliberative democracy ("Public Deliberation," 336). See also Ryfe, "Narrative and Deliberation in Small Group Forums"; Mendelberg and Karpowitz, "How People Deliberate about Justice"; Sanders, "Against Deliberation," 362; Merelman et al., "Unity and Diversity," 802.

16. Mill, *On Liberty*; Fishkin, *The Voice of the People*; Barabas, "How Deliberation Affects Policy Opinions"; Sturgis, Roberts, and Allum, "A Different Take on the Deliberative Poll"; Delli Carpini, Jacobs, and Cook, "Does Political Deliberation Matter?"; Gastil, *By Popular Demand*; Gastil et al., "Civic Awakening in the Jury Room"; Gastil and Dillard, "The Aims, Methods, and Effects of Deliberative Civic Education Through the National Issues Forums"; Gastil and Dillard, "Increasing Political Sophistication through Public Deliberation"; Rojas et al., "Media Dialogue"; Iyengar et al., "Facilitating Informed Public Opinion"; Luskin et al., "Considered Opinions."

17. Yin calls such a case a "revelatory" case—a case that does not commonly occur but reveals processes of interest when it does (*Case Study Research*, 40). The occurrence of intergroup dialogue in cities across the country enables us to see something we normally can not—interracial discussions about race among residents of the same community in settings and situations into which they have selected themselves.

18. Young, "Activist Challenges to Deliberative Democracy."

19. Schudson, "Why Conversation is Not the Soul of Democracy."

20. Sanders, "Against Deliberation"; Polletta, *Freedom Is an Endless Meeting*, esp. 206. Abu-Nimer, *Dialogue, Conflict Resolution, and Change.*

21. Mendelberg and Oleske, "Race and Public Deliberation"; Briggs, "Culture, Power, and Communication."

22. Reed, "Yackety-Yak about Race."

23. Polletta, *Freedom*, 206.

24. Coleman, *Foundations of Social Theory.*

25. Putnam, *Bowling Alone*, chap. 22, 22–23; Nelson et al., "Bridging Social Capital."

26. Brehm and Rahn, "Individual-Level Evidence for the Causes and Consequences of Social Capital"; see Theiss-Morse and Hibbing, "Citizenship and Civic Engagement" for overview. For a counterargument, see Stolle, "'Getting to Trust'"; and for consideration of selection effects, see also Stolle, "Bowling Together, Bowling Alone"; and Stolle and Rochon, "Are All Associations Alike?"

27. Varshney, *Ethnic Conflict.*

28. Stolle and Rochon, "Are All Associations Alike?"; Macedo et al., *Democracy at Risk*, esp. 8–9.

29. For example, see Johnson et al., "Goal Interdependence and Interpersonal Attraction in Heterogeneous Classrooms." See chapter 2 for a fuller discussion of the intergroup contact literature.

30. Grey and Woodrick, "'Latinos Have Revitalized Our Community.'"

31. Jones-Correa, "Immigrants, Blacks, and Cities"; http://www.studycircles.org/pages/pages/stories.html, accessed March 3, 2003; Du Bois and Hutson, *Bridging the Racial Divide*, 5.

32. Leighninger, *The Next Form of Democracy*, chap. 3; *One America in the Twenty-First*

Century; Leighninger and McCoy, "Mobilizing Citizens"; Reichler and Dredge, *Governing Diverse Communities,* chap. 2.

33. "Public service workers who interact directly with citizens in the course of their jobs, and who have substantial discretion in the execution of their work are called *street-level bureaucrats* in this study. . . . Typical street-level bureaucrats are teachers, police officers and other law enforcement personnel, social workers, judges, public lawyers and other courts officers, health workers, and many other public employees who grant access to government programs and provide services within them" (Lipsky, *Street-Level Bureaucracy,* 3).

34. For previous research that involves observation of civic deliberation, see Mansbridge, *Beyond Adversary Democracy;* Mendelberg and Oleske, "Race and Public Deliberation"; Fung, *Empowered Participation;* Karpowitz, "Public Hearings and the Dynamics of Deliberative Democracy"; Bryan, *Real Democracy.* For previous observations of intergroup dialogue see Merelman, Streich, and Martin, "Unity and Diversity"; Merelman, "The Mundane Experience of Political Culture."

35. Monroe, *The Hand of Compassion,* Appendix A, esp. 273–75.

36. Nisbett and Wilson, "Telling More than We Can Know."

37. Berinsky, *Silent Voices,* see especially chap. 3.

38. Mills, "Situated Actions and Vocabularies of Motive."

39. Soss, "Talking Our Way to Meaningful Explanation"; see also Lin, "Bridging Positivist and Interpretivist Approaches to Qualitative Methods."

40. Please see the methods appendix for further details.

41. The number of studies of the content of civic deliberation and civic dialogue (which excludes deliberations and dialogues on campuses) makes it impossible to cite them all, particularly when including studies by public policy and administration scholars. Some examples among political science, policy, and communications scholars include those in footnote 34 as well as: Gastil, *Democracy in Small Groups;* Bryan, *Real Democracy;* Ryfe, "Narrative and Deliberation"; Button and Mattson, "Deliberative Democracy in Practice"; Grogan and Gusmano, "Deliberative Democracy"; Hart and Jarvis, "We the People"; Dutwin, "The Character of Deliberation"; Rosenberg, "Can the People Deliberate?"

Chapter Two

1. For example, Aristotle, *Politics;* Mill, *On Liberty;* Fishkin, *Democracy and Deliberation.*

2. Habermas, *The Structural Transformation of the Public Sphere;* Habermas, *Theory of Communicative Action,* vol. 2: *Lifeworld and System.*

3. Habermas, *Theory of Communicative Action,* vol. 1: *Reason and the Rationalization of Society;* Habermas, *Philosophical Discourse of Modernity.*

4. In later work, particularly *Between Facts and Norms,* Habermas emphasizes communication that does not necessarily require face-to-face interaction in small communities (Dryzek, *Deliberative Democracy and Beyond,* 24–25), but he has nevertheless continued to emphasize that deliberation is a democratic good.

5. Dewey, *The Public and its Problems,* 143.

6. Ibid.,151–52.

7. Ibid., 152–53.

8. Ibid, 150–51.

9. *The Public*, 150. See also *Individualism, Old and New*, 71.

10. *The Public*, 154.

11. Arendt, *The Human Condition*.

12. Pitkin, "Justice: On Relating Public and Private."

13. Ibid., 333–36.

14. Ibid., 340–41.

15. Ibid., 338.

16. Ibid., 343.

17. Ibid.

18. Ibid., 346.

19. Ibid., 344.

20. Ibid., 348. See also Pitkin and Shumer, "On Participation," esp. 44.

21. A recent prominent example of a theorist valuing the existence of public talk comes in Barber's *Strong Democracy*. To wit: "But democracy understood as self-government in a social setting is not a terminus for individually held rights and values; it is their starting place. . . . Without participating in the common life that defines them and in the decision-making that shapes their social habit, women and men cannot become individuals" (xv).

22. By "cultural difference," I mean differences across social groups in the central tendencies of cultural practices and perspectives within those groups. This is not a claim that all members of a given social group have the same culture. Instead, it is a claim that there is internal homogeneity *relative to* the heterogeneity across groups.

23. Benhabib, "Toward a Deliberative Model of Democratic Legitimacy"; Benhabib, *The Claims of Culture*; Chambers, "Deliberative Democratic Theory."

24. Gutmann and Thompson, *Democracy and Disagreement*.

25. Macedo, "Introduction," *Deliberative Politics*, 10.

26. Ackerman, "Why Dialogue?"

27. Habermas, *Communication and the Evolution of Society*; Cohen, "Deliberation and Democratic Legitimacy."

28. Bohman, *Public Deliberation*.

29. Habermas, *The Postnational Constellation*.

30. Rawls, *Political Liberalism*; Bohman, *Public Deliberation*.

31. Barber, *Strong Democracy*.

32. Rawls, *A Theory of Justice*.

33. Young, *Justice and the Politics of Difference*, 96; Allen, *Talking to Strangers*, chap. 6; Will Kymlicka is one liberal theorist who departs from these arguments. In contrast to most liberals, he supports the recognition and attention to subgroup demands and difference in order to promote the inclusion of subgroups in the life of the broader polity (*Multicultural Citizenship*).

34. King, *Making Americans*.

35. Barry, *Culture and Equality*.

36. Ibid.; see also Kim, "Clinton's Race Initiative" with respect to dialogue.

37. Taylor, "The Politics of Recognition."

38. Barry, *Culture and Equality*, 3, 299; Renshon, "American Character and National Identity."

39. Barry argues that liberals are wrongly accused of focusing on unity while ignoring diversity. He argues that liberals are in fact quite concerned with difference, contrary to multiculturalsts' assertions. He argues that Rawls's prescription to imagine a just society while wearing a "veil of ignorance" that obscures what type of social group memberships we would have was not an attempt to ignore difference but to regard it as important (*Culture and Equality*, 69).

40. Ibid., 77–81.

41. "It is better to be alive than dead. It is better to be free than to be a slave. It is better to be healthy than sick. It is better to be adequately nourished than malnourished. It is better to drink pure water than contaminated water. It is better to have effective sanitation than to live over an open sewer. It is better to have a roof over your head than to sleep in the street. It is better to be well educated than to be illiterate and ignorant. It is better to be able to practise the form of worship prescribed by your religion and to be able to join social and political organizations of your choice than to fear that, if your activities attract the disfavor of the regime, you face arbitrary arrest, torture or 'disappearance' at the hands of bodies organized by or connived at by the state. And so on" (ibid., 285).

42. Ibid., 80.

43. Ibid., 81. However, many argue that dual loyalties such as among immigrants undermines democratic stability (Huntington, *Who are We?*; Renshon, "Dual Nationality + Multiple Loyalties = One America?"). Staton, Jackson, and Canache provide evidence from surveys that dual nationality is negatively related to skills and attitudes that attach people to the American political system ("Dual Nationality among Latinos").

44. Research on intergroup contact emerged in the post-World War II era in conjunction with attempts to overcome anti-Semitism (Pettigrew and Tropp, "Does Intergroup Contact Reduce Prejudice?" 93). Early accounts appeared in 1947 (Watson, *Action for Unity*; Williams, *The Reduction of Intergroup Tensions*; as cited in Forbes, *Ethnic Conflict*, 22), but contact research continues to treat Gordon Allport's *The Nature of Prejudice* as the point of departure.

45. Throughout *The Nature of Prejudice*, Allport carefully avoided explaining why reducing prejudice is desirable. The final chapter makes it clear that he was wary of having his work discounted for being moralistic or driven by his own values. However, in that chapter he implies that his goal is far larger than merely reducing prejudice: the protection of democracy itself.

46. Deutsch and Collins, *Interracial Housing*, 79; Sherif et al., *Intergroup Conflict and Cooperation*; Sherif, *In Common Predicament*.

47. Allport, *The Nature of Prejudice*, 276–78, 489.

48. Ibid., 489; see also 466–73.

49. Ibid., 274–76, 488, 489.

50. Pettigrew and Tropp, "Does Intergroup Contact Reduce Prejudice?," 94; Hogg, "Intergroup Relations," 493; Eller and Abrams, "Come Together"; Forbes, *Ethnic Conflict*, 114–32. Various scholars also emphasize Allport's recognition of the importance of enabling participants to develop friendships (Allport, *The Nature of Prejudice*, 264–68, 489; Cook "Interpersonal and Attitudinal Outcomes in Cooperating Interracial Groups"; Cook, "Experimenting on Social Issues"; Brewer and Brown, "Intergroup Relations," 577–79; Brewer and Gaertner, "Toward Reduction of Prejudice," 452–53; Pettigrew, "Intergroup Contact Theory"; Wittig and Grant-Thompson "The Utility of Allport's Conditions of Intergroup Contact for Predicting Perceptions of Improved Racial Attitudes and Beliefs"), or to

obtain stereotype-disconfirming information (Cook, "Interpersonal and Attitudinal Outcomes"; Cook, "Experimenting on Social Issues"; Marcus-Newhall and Heindl, "Coping
with Interracial Stress in Ethnically Diverse Classrooms"; Wittig and Grant-Thompson,
"Utility"). Others have suggested additional refinements, such as prescribing equal proportions of marginalized and dominant group members within the contact group (Miller
and Davidson-Podgorny, "Theoretical Models of Intergroup Relations and the Use of Cooperative Teams as an Intervention for Desegregated Settings"; Mullen, "Group Composition, Salience, and Cognitive Representations"; Mullen, Brown, and Smith, "Ingroup Bias
as a Function of Salience, Relevance, and Status"); anxiety-free situations (Stephan and
Stephan, "The Role of Ignorance in Intergroup Relations"; Miller and Davidson-Podgorny,
"Theoretical Models"); and social norms in the situation that are supportive of group
equality (Cook, "Interpersonal and Attitudinal Outcomes"; Cook, "Experimenting on Social Issues"). However, Allport's four main criteria continue to receive the most attention,
as scholars attempt to avoid muddying the theory (Pettigrew, "The Contact Hypothesis
Revisited"; Stephan, "The Contact Hypothesis in Intergroup Relations"). See also Amir
("The Role of Intergroup Contact in Change of Prejudice and Ethnic Relations") for an
overview of optimal conditions.

   51. Tajfel and Turner, "An Integrative Theory of Inter-group Conflict"; Lakoff, *Women,
Fire, and Dangerous Things;* Medin and Coley, "Concepts and Categorization"; Walsh,
Talking about Politics.

   52. For example, a study of German-influenced English dialect among people in a
Wisconsin town revealed that contrary to expectations, it was the youngest people in the
community whose speech retained the strongest imprints of German language, not their
elders (Purnell et al., "Structured Heterogeneity and Change in Laryngeal Phonetics").

   53. Abrams and Hogg, "Comments on the Motivational Status of Self-Esteem in Social Identity and Intergroup Discrimination"; Rubin and Hewstone, "Social Identity Theory's Self-Esteem Hypothesis."

   54. Devine, "Stereotypes and Prejudice."

   55. Alexander and Levin, "Theoretical, Empirical, and Practical Approaches to Intergroup Conflict."

   56. Brewer and Miller, "Beyond the Contact Hypothesis"; Miller, "Personalization
and the Promise of Contact Theory."

   57. Gaertner et al., "Reducing Intergroup Bias: Elements of Intergroup Cooperation";
Gaertner et al., "How Does Cooperation Reduce Intergroup Bias?"; Gaertner et al., "The
Common Ingroup Identity Model"; Gaertner et al., "Across Cultural Divides"; Gaertner
et al., "Reducing Intergroup Bias: The Benefits of Recategorization"; Gaertner and Dovi-
dio, *Reducing Intergroup Bias.* This can be either a preexisting or a newly created category
(Gaertner et al., "The Common Ingroup Identity Model").

   58. Gamson and Modigliani define a frame as "a central organizing idea or story
line that provides meaning to an unfolding strip of events, weaving a connection among
them. The frame suggests what the controversy is about, the essence of the issue" ("The
Changing Culture of Affirmative Action," 143).

   59. Kinder and Herzog, "Democratic Discussion." See also Chong, "How People
Think, Reason and Feel About Rights and Liberties"; Chong, "Creating Common Frames
of Reference on Political Issues." The literature on framing in political communication is
voluminous. See Nelson, Clawson, and Oxley, "Media Framing of a Civil Liberties Con-

flict and Its Effect on Tolerance," and Druckman, "Political Preference Formation," for recent prominent works in the field. While the main theme of this work is that political elites play the main role in the public's understanding of current affairs, recent work has revealed the conditionality of these effects (e.g., Druckman and Nelson, "Framing and Deliberation"; Chong and Druckman, "Competitive Framing").

60. Mandelbaum, "Telling Stories"; Briggs, "Culture, Power, and Communication in Community Building."

61. Mandelbaum, *Open Moral Communities,* chap. 6; Mandelbaum, "Telling Stories."

62. Barabas, "How Deliberation Affects Policy Opinions," 699.

63. Mendelberg and Oleske, "Race and Public Deliberation," 187.

64. Snow et al., "Frame Alignment Processes, Micromobilization, and Movement Participation," 477.

65. Macedo et al., *Democracy at Risk,* chap. 3, esp. 67; Nelson et al., "Bridging Social Capital and an Investment Theory of Collective Action," 13; Warren, *Dry Bones Rattling.* Proponents of deliberation at times suggest that citizens cope with heterogeneity in forums by forging a "thin but shared group identity" (Gastil, *By Popular Demand,* 170).

66. Rahn and Rudolph, "National Identities and the Future of Democracy." See also Peter Muhlberger's work on the relationship between city-wide identity and political action ("Democratic Deliberation and Political Identity").

67. For example, Barry, *Culture and Equality;* Gleason, "Sea Change in the Civic Culture in the 1960s"; Renshon, "American Character"; Sears et al., "Cultural Diversity and Multicultural Politics," 71.

68. Sears et al., "Cultural Diversity," 38–39.

69. Ibid., 39.

70. Ibid. These authors equate the melting pot and salad bowl model, but Deborah Schildkraut distinguishes melting pot models that acknowledge the country's pluralistic nature but nevertheless expect assimilation from multicultural models that acknowledge pluralism and seek to ensure continual recognition of it ("The More Things Change"; *Press One for English*). As will be seen in chapter 6, national organizations that sponsor race dialogues distinguish the melting pot from the salad bowl metaphor. The important point is that Citrin and colleagues identify a form of multiculturalism that treats social groups as so distinct that they are "isolated from each other," not tossed into the same "pot" or "bowl."

71. Sears et al., "Cultural Diversity"; Citrin et al., "Multiculturalism in American Public Opinion." Sears et al. also use two phone surveys representative of adults in Los Angeles County in 1994 and 1995 ("Cultural Diversity"). I restrict my attention to the national sample. The L.A. 1994 survey had 921 respondents and through oversampling contained a sample that was 37 percent white, 30 percent black, 25 percent Hispanic, and 7 percent Asian. The 1995 survey had 595 respondents, and was 44 percent white, 12 percent black, 30 percent Hispanic, and 8 percent Asian (45).

72. Sears et al., "Cultural Diversity," 51.

73. Citrin et al., "Multiculturalism," 260. Results by race are not provided for this response.

74. Ninety-one percent of whites preferred identifying themselves as "just an American," while 50 percent of blacks and 80 percent of Hispanics did so. "With respect to social and political issues, do you think of yourself mainly as a member of your ethnic, racial, or

nationality group, or do you think of yourself mainly as just an American?" (Followed by:) "Do you think of yourself as 'just an American' on all issues, most issues, some issues, or just a few issues?" These figures for whites and blacks are from Citrin et al., "Multiculturalism," 258, and for Hispanics, from Sears et al., "Cultural Diversity," 53–54. In Sears et al., "Cultural Diversity," the figures for whites and blacks are reported as 96 percent and 66 percent. In the 1994 L.A. survey, 55 percent of blacks, 56 percent of Hispanics, and 59 percent of Asians said that they thought of themselves as having a dual identity ("just an American, but also as a member of a group") (54). (The combined L.A. surveys include sufficient numbers of Asian Americans to merit inference.) In a study of attitudes toward immigration and multiculturalism among parents of school children in two Detroit-area communities, Pontiac and Hamtramck, Wallace Lambert and Donald Taylor found that among Polish, Albanian, Arab, Mexican, Puerto Rican, black, and white Americans, white Americans were the least supportive of multiculturalism, where support for multiculturalism was measured with self-placements on a scale between these two alternatives: "Cultural and racial minority groups should give up their traditional ways of life and take on the American way of life" and "Cultural and racial minority groups should maintain their ways of life as much as possible when they come to America." See their figure 6.1 for summary results (*Coping with Cultural and Racial Diversity in Urban America*).

75. That is, among whites, 39 percent chose "melting pot" and 30 percent chose maintaining distinct cultures. Among blacks, 37 percent favored melting pot while 41 percent favored ethnic distinctiveness. Among Hispanics, 47 percent preferred melting pot while 31 percent favored distinctiveness. Sears et al., "Cultural Diversity," 55–57; see also Citrin et al., "Multiculturalism," 258–59. This same question was used in the L.A. surveys. The combined sample of Asians indicated that 53 percent preferred the melting pot vision while 29 percent preferred ethnic distinctiveness (Sears et al., "Cultural Diversity," 57).

76. Citrin et al., "Multiculturalism," 263–66.

77. Ibid., 264. Thirty-one percent of those under thirty said that groups should blend into the larger society; 46 percent of those over sixty took that stand.

78. "The More Things Change"; Press One.

79. Smith, *Civic Ideals*.

80. One of the most famous distinctions made with respect to deliberative democracy is Jane Mansbridge's comparison of unitary and adversary democracy (*Beyond Adversary Democracy*). Although this is closely related to the unity/difference distinction I am making here, the two are not the same. The Mansbridge distinction pertains to forms of democracy, while the unity/difference distinction pertains to the nature of deliberation.

81. My gratitude to Eric MacGilvray for clarifying this point.

82. Much of this debate has centered on Habermas's work. For example, Dryzek writes that Habermas's focus on consensus "has long troubled many of those who are otherwise sympathetic to [his] project" (*Deliberative Democracy and Beyond*, 48), and cites the following as examples: Benhabib "Communicative Ethics and Contemporary Controversies in Practical Philosophy"; Bohman, *Public Deliberation*; Dryzek, *Deliberative Democracy*, 16–17; Gould, *Rethinking Democracy*, 18, 126–27; and Mackie, "Models of Democratic Deliberation." See also Benhabib, "Toward a Deliberative Model of Democratic Legitimacy"; Gould, "Diversity and Democracy"; Mansbridge, "Everyday Talk in the Deliberative System," 226; and Dryzek, *Deliberative Democracy*, chap. 3. See Mansbridge, "Conflict and Self-Interest in Deliberation," for an argument that conflict is a central component of the work of Habermas and other deliberative theorists.

83. Gardner, "Shut Up and Vote"; see also Gastil, *By Popular Demand*, 12.

84. Sanders, "Against Deliberation," 362–69.

85. Ibid.; Young, "Activist Challenges to Deliberative Democracy."

86. Williams, "The Uneasy Alliance of Group Representation and Deliberative Democracy."

87. For an overview of related critiques, see Bickford, *The Dissonance of Democracy*, chap. 4.

88. See Dutwin, "The Character of Deliberation," for an analysis of inequality in participation in deliberations.

89. Bohman, *Public Deliberation*; Gutmann and Thompson, *Democracy and Disagreement*.

90. Gutmann and Thompson, *Democracy and Disagreement*, 55.

91. Young, "Activist Challenges," 687; See also Williams, "The Uneasy Alliance."

92. Mouffe, "Democracy, Power and the 'Political,'" 251–52.

93. Cohen, "Deliberation and Democratic Legitimacy."

94. Mansbridge, "Everyday Talk."

95. Young, *Justice and the Politics of Difference*, chap. 4.

96. Some suggest that Barber does not support a politics of unity. See Allen, *Talking to Strangers*; Karpowitz and Mansbridge, "Disagreement and Consensus, 252n; Bickford, *The Dissonance of Democracy*, 12–14. Barber, *Strong Democracy*, 16.

97. See also Connolly, *Identity/Difference*, 87–92; and Schildkraut, *Press One*, chap. 6.

98. Young, *Justice*, 99. Arguments against a focus on unity do not just come from the left. See William Schambra, "Local Groups are the Key to America's Civic Renewal."

99. See also Gould, "Diversity and Democracy"; Phillips, "Dealing with Difference."

100. See for example, Young, *Justice*, 44. In later work, Young departs from a definition of social groups that relies on identity ("Gender as Seriality"; *Inclusion and Democracy*").

101. Allen, *Talking to Strangers*.

102. Ibid., xxii.

103. Ibid., 88–89.

104. Young, *Justice*, 171–72.

105. Ibid., 166.

106. Ibid., 166–67.

107. Ibid., 167.

108. Young explicitly prefers a deliberative model of democracy over an aggregative or liberal individualist model of democracy, but argues for refinements in order for deliberative democracy to promote justice and inclusion (*Inclusion and Democracy*, especially chap. 1). See also Barge, "Enlarging the Meaning of Group Deliberation."

109. Young, "Activist Challenges," 687.

110. Ibid.

111. Gould, "Diversity and Democracy"; Phillips, "Dealing with Difference"; Young, *Justice*; Young, "Communication and the Other"; Young, *Inclusion*; Sanders, "Against Deliberation"; Mouffe, "Democracy, Power and the 'Political'"; Connolly, *Identity/Difference*; Allen, *Talking to Strangers*; Fraser, "Rethinking the Public Sphere." Like difference democrats, John Dryzek also calls for an opening up of the deliberative system, but he poses his argument as an alternative to that of "difference democrats," claiming that while the latter call for contestation across identities, he calls for contestation across discourses (*Deliberative Democracy*, 74–75). However, Dryzek grants that discourses and

identities are intertwined (75), and therefore his arguments are closely related to those of difference democrats.

112. See especially Connolly, *Identity/Difference*; Allen, *Talking to Strangers*; Mouffe, "Democracy, Power and the 'Political'"; Phillips, "Dealing with Difference"; also Welsh, "Deliberative Democracy and the Rhetorical Production of Political Culture."

113. Connolly, *Identity/Difference*; see xxv–xxvi for his distinction between "agonistic respect" and "agonistic democracy." With regard to calls for finding ways to continually contest social group categories, see Phillips, "Dealing with Difference." See Pitkin and Shumer, "On Participation," for a vision in which conflict is not an obstacle but an integral component of democratic politics that requires "not unanimity but discourse" (47). See also Honig, *Political Theory and the Displacement of Politics*.

114. Sanders, "Against Deliberation."

115. Young, "Communication and the Other"; Young, Inclusion.

116. Young, *Inclusion*, 58.

117. Ibid., 75.

118. Mansbridge, *Beyond Adversary Democracy*.

119. Dryzek, "On the Prospects for Democratic Deliberation."

120. Mendelberg and Oleske, "Race and Public Deliberation."

121. Sanders, "Against Deliberation," 371.

122. Karpowitz and Mansbridge , "Disagreement and Consensus," 238.

123. Button and Mattson, "Deliberative Democracy in Practice."

124. Ibid., 620.

125. Mansbridge, *Beyond Adversary Democracy*, chap. 6; Coote and Lenaghan, *Citizens' Juries*, 83–84, 91–92.

126. Mendelberg, "The Deliberative Citizen."

127. Karpowitz and Mansbridge, "Disagreement and Consensus," 246.

128. Ibid., 238. Mansbridge elaborates this need for democracy to include both communication among like-minded citizens as well as challenges to consensus within interest enclaves in *Beyond Adversary Democracy and Why We Lost the ERA*. See also Grogan and Gusmano, "Deliberative Democracy in Theory and Practice," for a call for attention to difference during resident–public official public talk.

129. Gaertner et al., "The Common Ingroup Identity Model," 20.

130. Gaertner et al., "Reducing Intergroup Bias," 398; Dovidio, Kawakami, and Gaertner, "Reducing Contemporary Prejudice." See also Brewer and Schneider, "Social Identity and Social Dilemmas."

131. Hewstone and Brown, "Contact is Not Enough."

132. Hornsey and Hogg, "Assimilation and Diversity."

133. Ibid., 144; Hewstone and Brown, "Contact is Not Enough," 30; Brown and Lopez, "Political Contacts," 283–84; Gurin et al., "Context, Identity, and Intergroup Relations," 137–38, 166–67.

134. Gurin et al., "Context, Identity, and Intergroup Relations."

135. Nagda, Kim, and Truelove, "Learning about Difference, Learning with Others, Learning to Transgress."

136. Brewer, "The Social Self."

137. Brewer and Gaertner, "Toward Reduction of Prejudice," 460.

138. Ibid., 462–66; Pettigrew, "Intergroup Contact Theory."

139. Brown and Lopez, "Political Contacts."

140. Gurin et al., "Context."

141. Gaertner et al., "Across Cultural Divides."

142. Young, *Inclusion*, chap. 4; Phillips, "Dealing with Difference."

Chapter Three

1. "Voting after speaking is to governance what keeping the score is to sports. It changes everything" (Bryan, *Real Democracy*, 139–40).

2. Gastil, *By Popular Demand*, 22. See also Button and Mattson, "Deliberative Democracy in Practice," 610. Others have included individual (cognitive) processes as forms of deliberation (Mutz, "Mechanisms of Momentum"; Lindeman, "Opinion Quality and Policy Preferences in Deliberative Research"), but the present project focuses on group processes.

3. Burkhalter, Gastil, and Kelshaw, "A Conceptual Definition and Theoretical Model of Public Deliberation in Small Face-to-Face Groups," 408.

4. Ibid.

5. McCoy and Scully, "Deliberative Dialogue to Expand Civic Engagement."

6. Los Angeles Region NCCJ, "Neighbor to Neighbor Dialogue Series and Skills Training for Facilitating Interracial Dialogue," 1005.

7. Flavin-McDonald and McCoy, *Facing the Challenge of Racism and Race Relations*, 47.

8. Ibid., 7.

9. Leighninger, "The Recent Evolution of Democracy"; Leighninger, *The Next Form of Democracy*.

10. Sirianni and Friedland, *Civic Innovation in America*; See Boyte, *Commonwealth*; Barber, *Strong Democracy*.

11. Ryfe, "The Practice of Deliberative Democracy"; Button and Mattson, "Deliberative Democracy"; Gastil and Levine, *Deliberative Democracy Handbook*; Lindeman "Opinion Quality"; Price and Neijens, "Deliberative Polls"; Gastil, *By Popular Demand*, chap. 6.

12. Sirianni and Friedland, *Civic Innovation*, 256–58; Matthews, *Politics for People*, 108–9, chap. 10; Yankelovich, *Coming to Public Judgment*, 248–49; Melville, Willingham, and Dedrick, "National Issues Forums: A Network of Communities Promoting Public Deliberation"; Gastil and Dillard, "The Aims, Methods, and Effects of Deliberative Civic Education Through the National Issues Forums"; Gastil and Dillard, "Increasing Political Sophistication Through Public Deliberation"; Ryfe, "Narrative and Deliberation in Small Group Forums"; Gastil, *By Popular Demand*, 115–19.

13. Sirianni and Friedland, *Civic Innovation*, 257.

14. Lukensmeyer, Goldman, and Brigham, "A Town Meeting for the 21st Century." Also, see Polletta, *It Was Like a Fever*, chap. 4, for an analysis of the online dialogue that followed this deliberation.

15. On instances of the former in the United States, Irvin and Stansbury, "Citizen Participation in Decision Making"; Gastil and Kelshaw, "A Conceptual Definition"; Cheng and Fiero, "Collaborative Learning and the Public's Stewardship of Its Forests"; Sokoloff, Steinberg, and Pyser, "Deliberative City Planning on the Philadelphia Waterfront"; Karpowitz and Mansbridge, "Disagreement and Consensus"; Potapchuk, Carlson, and Kennedy, "Growing Governance Deliberately"; Cooper and Kathi, "Neighborhood Councils

and City Agencies." On the latter, see Bonner et al., "Bringing the Public and the Government Together through Online Dialogues." On town meetings in particular, see Mansbridge, *Beyond Adversary Democracy*, chaps. 4–11; Zimmerman, *The New England Town Meeting*; Bryan, *Real Democracy*. For further elaborations of the general trend, see Day, "Citizen Participation in the Planning Process"; Box, *Citizen Governance*; Booher, "Collaborative Governance Practices and Democracy"; Pratchett, "New Fashions in Public Participation"; Bingham, O'Leary, and Nabatchi, "Legal Frameworks for the New Governance"; Leighninger, "The Recent Evolution of Democracy"; Fung, "Varieties of Participation"; Williamson and Fung, "Public Deliberation."

16. See Friedland, Sotirovic, and Daily, "Public Journalism and Social Capital"; Charles, Sokoloff, and Satullo, "Electoral Deliberation and Public Journalism."

17. For the NCDD see, http://www.thataway.org/main/about/about.html. For the DDC, see http://deliberative-democracy.net. Also, Heierbacher et al., "Deliberative Democracy Networks."

18. For an example of using dialogue and deliberation together, see Deveaux, "A Deliberative Approach to Conflicts of Culture," 781. Also, Bohman defines public deliberation as a particular type of dialogue (*Public Deliberation*, 57).

19. Anderson, Baxter, and Cissna, "Texts and Contexts of Dialogue"; Burkhalter, Gastil, and Kelshaw, "A Conceptual Definition"; Cissna and Anderson, *Moments of Meeting*; Pearce and Littlejohn, *Moral Conflict*; Baxter and Montgomery, *Relating*.

20. Pearce and Littlejohn, *Moral Conflict*; Burkhalter, Gastil, and Kelshaw, "A Conceptual Definition."

21. Burkhalter, Gastil, and Kelshaw, "A Conceptual Definition."

22. Diaz and Stennet, "Transforming Relationships through Sustained Dialogue," 11; referring to Freire, *Pedagogy of the Oppressed*; Saunders, *A Public Peace Process*.

23. Schoem, "College Students Need Thoughtful, In-Depth Study of Race Relations"; Schoem, "Teaching about Ethnic Identity and Intergroup Relations"; Schoem and Hurtado, *Intergroup Dialogue*; Gurin et al., "Context, Identity, and Intergroup Relations"; Thompson, Brett, and Behling, "Educating for Social Justice."

24. Gurin et al., "The Educational Value of Diversity."

25. Diaz and Stennet, "Transforming Relationships through Sustained Dialogue"; Treviño, "Voices of Discovery"; Thompson, Brett, and Behling, "Educating for Social Justice"; Nagda et al., "Intergroup Dialogue, Education, and Action"; Miller and Donner, "More than Just Talk."

26. Stephan and Vogt, *Education Programs for Improving Intergroup Relations*; Schoem, "Intergroup Relations, Conflict, and Community."

27. High schools and elementary schools also increasingly use dialogue: Pincock, "Insights from an Intergroup Dialogue"; Fernandez, "Building 'Bridges' of Understanding through Dialogue"; Tiven, "Student Voices"; McKenna and Sauceda, "Students Talk about Race."

28. See Sapiro, "Seeking Knowledge and Information as Political Action"; Oliver, *Study Circles*; Oliver, "Study Circles."

29. Personal communication, Martha McCoy, Matt Leighninger. See also Fanselow, *What Democracy Feels Like*; Houlé and Roberts, *Toward Competent Communities*, esp. 41.

30. Personal communication, Martha McCoy; McCoy and Scully, "Deliberative Dialogue to Expand Civic Engagement," 128.

31. Corcoran and Greisdorf, *Connecting Communities;* Robert Corcoran, personal interview. The SCRC assisted in the development of this program (Martha McCoy, personal communication).

32. Chip Harrod, Executive Director of the National Conference for Community and Justice in Cincinnati, Ohio, personal interview.

33. For example, the National League of Cities produced a pamphlet called "Ensuring Race Equality: Resources for Local Officials," a 1999 Futures Report called "Undoing Racism: Undoing Justice in America's Cities and Towns," a book called *Governing Diverse Communities* (Reichler and Dredge), and a pamphlet called "Talking is the First Step: Governing in a Racially and Ethnically Diverse Community."

34. *One America in the Twenty-First Century;* Oskamp and Jones, "Promising Practices in Reducing Prejudice"; Kim, "Clinton's Race Initiative"; Goering, "An Assessment of President Clinton's Initiative on Race."

35. Staub, "Genocide and Mass Killing."

36. Nelson, Kaboolian, and Carver, "Bridging Social Capital and An Investment Theory of Collective Action."

37. Sirianni and Friedland refer to the work these organizations do as "common work" (*Civic Innovation*, 237).

38. I use in-depth interviews with eight representatives of national organizations either conducting or promoting civic dialogue with respect to race relations. These include telephone interviews conducted in the spring and summer of 2002 with Martha McCoy, Executive Director of the Study Circles Resource Center; Molly Holme Barrett, Project Coordinator and Assistant Editor of the SCRC; Robert Corcoran, National Director of Hope in the Cities; and William Barnes, Director, Center for Research and Program Development of the National League of Cities. In addition, program evaluators for the Study Circles programs, Rona Roberts and Steve Kay, were interviewed in person in June 2002. Interviews ranged in length from forty to seventy-five minutes. Also, several in-person and telephone conversations were conducted with Gwen Wright, Project Coordinator, Racial Justice and Race Relations, National League of Cities, and Deborah George, Manager of Local Government Services at the National League of Cities, as well as numerous additional consultations with McCoy.

39. Mansbridge, "Everyday Talk in the Deliberative System," 221–27.

40. Mendelberg and Oleske, "Race and Public Deliberation."

41. Cohen, "Deliberation and Democratic Legitimacy."

42. The criteria identified by Mendelberg and Oleske map to Mansbridge's labels in the following way. "Meetings are public" and "citizens reflect and decide collectively rather than individually" map to publicity; "Citizens have an equal opportunity to participate" maps to equality of access; "decisions turn on arguments, not on coercive power" maps to free from power; "citizens are fully informed" maps to reasoned; "all alternatives are considered" maps to reciprocity; "deliberation is an ongoing process supported by other institutions" maps loosely to accountability; "arguments are based on general principles and appeal to the common good, not exclusively to self-interest" maps to consensus or common ground ("Race and Public Deliberation," 170).

43. Flavin-McDonald and McCoy, *Facing the Challenge of Racism and Race Relations*, 38.

44. See also Diaz and Stennet, "Transforming Relationships," 32.

45. Leighninger, *The Next Form;* Bill Barnes, personal interview.

46. Marder, "Gender Dynamics and Jury Deliberations"; Sanders, "Against Deliberation"; Kathlene, "Power and Influence in State Legislative Policymaking"; Mattei, "Gender and Power in American Legislative Discourse."

47. Guzzetti and Williams, "Changing the Pattern of Gendered Discussion."

48. Bryan, *Real Democracy*, chap. 9.

49. Bolce, De Maio, and Muzzio, "Dial-In Democracy"; Davis and Owen, *New Media and American Politics*, 146.

50. Huckfeldt and Sprague, *Citizens, Politics, and Social Communication*, chap. 10; Hansen, "Talking about Politics."

51. I make this claim based on interviews with practitioners of particular programs throughout the country, as well as evaluation questionnaires completed by participants in Madison, Wisconsin, and Aurora, Illinois, and the behavior of members of the six groups I observed. Of the 131 Madison participants who completed pretest questionnaires, 74 percent were female. Fifty-seven percent of the forty-five Aurora participants with valid data were women. Of the sixty-four people I observed in actual dialogue groups (excluding the facilitators, of whom six of seven were female), thirty-eight were women (59 percent). See the methods appendix for details on the questionnaires.

52. Fung, *Empowered Participation*, 125–27; see also Bryan, *Real Democracy*, chap. 8.

53. Fishkin, *The Voice of the People*; Ackerman and Fishkin, *Deliberation Day*.

54. Crosby, "Citizens' Juries"; Coote and Lenaghan, *Citizens' Juries*; Barnes, *Building a Deliberative Democracy*; Stewart, Kendall, and Coote, *Citizens' Juries*; Smith and Wales, "Citizens' Juries and Deliberative Democracy." ChoiceDialogues, a project of Daniel Yankelovich and Steven Rosell, are one-day dialogues that use randomly selected participants (Fishkin and Rosell with Shepherd and Amsler, "ChoiceDialogues and Deliberative Polls").

55. Flavin-McDonald and McCoy, *The Busy Citizen's Discussion Guide*, 10–11.

56. Bohman, *Public Deliberation*. See also Fung and Wright, "Deepening Democracy," 19.

57. Hubbard, "Face-to-Face at Arm's Length."

58. Typically, facilitators give people a page of ground rules and then invite them to modify them. However, in five of the six groups I observed, people always agreed on the rules provided. (The sixth generated their rules from scratch.) For example, a study circle program in Kenosha, Wisconsin, uses the following rules, summarized with the acronym "ROPES":

R=Respect/Risk

- Treat each other with respect, even if you disagree. *No putdowns.*
- Only one person speaks at a time. Listen carefully to each other, without interruptions.

O=Openess/Ouch

- Speak honestly. The most respectful thing we can do tighter [together] is to be real. Be willing to say what you really think about each topic. If you hold back, we cannot learn from you.
- If someone or something offends you, it is your responsibility as a member of this Diversity Circle to say, "Ouch." Let the speaker finish, and then tell the group how you were hurt or angered and why.

P=Participation/Pass
- Speak briefly, so everyone has a chance to participate.
- Stay on the topic at hand.

E=Education/Escuchar (Spanish: to listen)
- The facilitators are not experts. They are here to help facilitate the process.
- Everyone has come to the table to learn, grow and share.

S=Sensitivity/Safety
- Use "I" statements. Speak only for yourself, rather than as a representative for any group. Remember the others are only speaking for themselves.
- Confidentiality is important. Speak about what is happening, not who said it.

59. Corcoran and Greisdorf, *Connecting Communities,* 112; FOCUS St. Louis, *Bridges Across Racial Polarization,* 12.

60. Mansbridge points out that Gutmann and Thompson include many other criteria under this dimension, including "the values of mutual respect, the goals of consistency in speech and consistency between speech and action, the need to acknowledge the strongly held feelings and beliefs of others, and the values of openmindedness and 'economy of moral disagreement' (seeking rationalities that minimize the rejection of an opposing position)" and notes that their definition includes Lynn Sanders's call for testimony ("Everyday Talk," 222).

61. Flavin-McDonald and McCoy, *Busy Citizen's Discussion Guide,* 35.

62. Corcoran and Greisdorf, *Connecting Communities,* 112.

63. Ibid., 113.

64. Los Angeles Region NCCJ, "Neighbor to Neighbor Dialogue Series and Skills Training for Facilitating Interracial Dialogue."

65. FOCUS, *Bridges Across Racial Polarization,* 7–8.

66. Sapiro, "Considering Political Civility Historically"; Herzog, *Poisoning the Minds of the Lower Orders.*

67. Young, "Activist Challenges to Deliberative Democracy," 687.

68. Mansbridge, "Everyday Talk," 223.

69. Schudson, "Why Conversation is Not the Soul of Democracy," 308.

70. For example, Cohen, "Deliberation and Democratic Legitimacy."

71. Bessette, *The Mild Voice of Reason.*

72. Sniderman, Brody, and Tetlock, *Reasoning and Choice,* chap. 6; Marcus, Neuman, and MacKuen, *Affective Intelligence and Political Judgment;* Marcus, *The Sentimental Citizen;* Brader, *Campaigning for Hearts and Minds.*

73. Mansbridge, "Everyday Talk," 22–26.

74. Flavin-McDonald and McCoy, *Busy Citizen's Discussion Guide,* 5.

75. Corcoran and Greisdorf, *Connecting Communities,* 74.

76. Ibid., 11; see also Staub, "Genocide."

77. Mansbridge, "Everyday Talk," 224.

78. Young, "Activist Challenges."

79. Flavin-McDonald and McCoy, *Busy Citizen's Discussion Guide.*

80. Flavin-McDonald and McCoy, *Facing the Challenge,* 44.

81. Corcoran and Greisdorf, *Connecting Communities,* 112.

82. Ibid., 111.

83. Mansbridge ("Everyday Talk") interprets this criterion as responsibility to others, but Chambers states that the treatment of accountability in recent deliberative theory is "primarily understood in terms of 'giving an account' of something, that is, publicly articulating, explaining, and most importantly justifying public policy" ("Deliberative Democratic Theory," 308). I use Mansbridge's treatment because Chambers's definition overlaps with the criterion of reciprocity.

84. "We will speak in the first person. We will not speculate on what 'they' think or feel" (Corcoran and Greisdorf, *Connecting Communities*, 112).

85. Walsh, *Talking about Politics*.

86. Sirianni and Friedland, *Civic Innovation*, 245.

87. Flavin-McDonald and McCoy, *Facing the Challenge*, 45.

88. Ibid., 45.

89. http://www.usconsensuscouncil.org/.

90. Merelman et al., "Unity and Diversity in American Political Culture," 781–82.

Chapter Four

1. Allport, *The Nature of Prejudice*.

2. Pettigrew and Tropp, "Does Intergroup Contact Reduce Prejudice?"

3. Putnam, *Bowling Alone*; Varshney, *Ethnic Conflict and Civic Life*.

4. Warren, *Dry Bones Rattling*.

5. Among political scientists, see Schumpeter, *Capitalism, Socialism and Democracy*; Fiorina, "Extreme Voices." Among local officials, see Harwood, *The Public's Role in the Policy Process*; Bramson, "The Deliberative Public Manager"; see Berry, Portney, and Thomson, *The Rebirth of Urban Democracy*, chap. 8, esp. 206–7 for a statement of these arguments, but see results on 208–10 showing that many officials thought participatory democracy resolved conflict although it delayed policy processes; see Schumaker, *Critical Pluralism, Democratic Performance, and Community Power*, 53, 64–65 for evidence that public officials are less supportive of public involvement than is the public at large.

6. For example, Bachrach and Baratz, *Power and Poverty*, 71–73.

7. Edelman, *Political Language*; Greenstone and Peterson, *Race and Authority in Urban Politics*; Irvin and Stansbury, "Citizen Participation in Decision Making."

8. Lasswell, *Democracy through Public Opinion*; Reed, "Yackety-Yak About Race."

9. Habermas, *The Structural Transformation of the Public Sphere*.

10. Kinder and Herzog, "Democratic Discussion."

11. Peterson, *City Limits*.

12. Orr and West, "Citizens' Views on Urban Revitalization."

13. Florida, *The Rise of the Creative Class*; Judd and Fainstein, *The Tourist City*.

14. Clark, "The Presidency and the New Political Culture"; Bennett, "The UnCivic Culture"; Inglehart, *Culture Shift*.

15. Clark, "Race and Class Versus the New Political Culture," 23.

16. Ibid.; Clark, "Structural Realignments in American City Politics."

17. Bennett, "The UnCivic Culture."

18. Clark, "Race and Class," 23; Clark, "Structural Realignments"; Inglehart, *The Silent Revolution*; Inglehart, *Culture Shift in Advanced Industrial Society*; Inglehart, *Modernization and Postmodernization*.

19. Clark, "Structural Realignments."

20. Bennett, "The UnCivic Culture," 755.

21. Berry, *The New Liberalism*.

22. Peterson, *City Limits*, 158–62. Martha McCoy and Patrick Scully, the executive director and deputy director of the Study Circles Resource Center, write: "When people call us to ask about study circles, most are not calling to say that they want to improve public life or enhance deliberative democracy. They are calling because they want to engage people in their community around solving or addressing a particular issue" ("Deliberative Dialogue to Expand Civic Engagement," 130).

23. Clark, "Structural Realignments."

24. Karnig and Welch, *Black Representation and Urban Policy*.

25. Ibid.

26. See Schneider and Teske, "Toward a Theory of the Political Entrepreneur," 743.

27. Polletta, *Freedom is an Endless Meeting*, 206.

28. Warren, *Dry Bones Rattling*; Polletta, *Freedom*, chap. 7; see also Boyte, *Commonwealth*.

29. Browning, Marshall, and Tabb, *Protest is Not Enough*; Stone, *Regime Politics*; Stone, "Powerful Actors and Compelling Actions"; Stone, "It's More than the Economy After All."

30. Additional support for the expectation that inequality is related to the emergence of dialogue programs comes from evidence that inequality spurs collective action on the neighborhood level (Crenson, *Neighborhood Politics*), and that city economic diversity is related to higher interest and participation in local politics (Oliver, *Democracy in Suburbia*, 89, 92).

31. Relationships between the presence of programs and income gaps were analyzed for the gap between non-Hispanic whites and all Census-designated racial groups. Only the white-Hispanic and white-black gaps exhibited statistically significant relationships that remained in multivariate specifications.

32. On Dayton's priority boards, see Berry, Portney, and Thomson, *The Rebirth*, esp. 12–13, 57–58, 67, 69.

33. Karnig and Welch, *Black Representation and Urban Policy*; Welch and Bledsoe, *Urban Reform and its Consequences*; Welch, "The Impact of At-Large Elections on the Representation of Blacks and Hispanics"; Hirlinger, "Citizen-Initiated Contacting of Local Government Officials." I also anticipated that cities with previous experience with mandated citizen participation in the policy process were likely to have less hierarchical local politics (Karnig and Welch, *Black Representation and Urban Policy*). Specifically, I expected that cities that have active community action agencies (remnants of the federal Community Action programs instituted in the 1964 Economic Opportunity Act), or that participated in the federal Model Cities program created in the 1966 Demonstration Cities and Metropolitan Development Act, might have greater citizen-government linkages. Although residents of the affected neighborhoods were often not actively involved in decision-making (Greenstone and Peterson, *Race and Authority in Urban Politics*; Gittell, *Limits to Citizen Participation*; Yankelovich, *Evaluation of the Cincinnati Community Action Program*; see also Thomas, *Between Citizen and City*), several studies suggest that these federal policies paved the way for a larger public role in policy making in the long run (Allard, "Intergovernmental Relationships and the American City"; Sirianni and

Friedland, *Civic Innovation in America*; Marston, "Citizen Action Programs and Participatory Politics in Tucson"; Eisinger, "The Community Action Program and the Development of Black Political Leadership"). Despite this expectation, residents in almost all of these cities had access to a CAP, and very few cities had received Model Cities funding (*HUD Statistical Yearbook from 1974*). Therefore, I exclude these predictors from the analyses. In addition, I hypothesized that cities that provide citizen seats on boards and commissions would be more likely to have civic dialogue programs. However, 90 percent of cities in the sample provided such opportunities. Due to this lack of variation, this variable is excluded as well.

34. Welch, "The Impact of At-Large Elections"; Engstrom and McDonald, "The Election of Blacks to City Councils"; Davidson and Korbel, "At Large Elections and Minority Group Representation"; Karnig and Welch, *Black Representation*; McManus, "City Council Election Procedures and Minority Representation."

35. Black and Black, *Politics and Society in the South*.

36. Walker, "The Diffusion of Innovations Among the American States"; Mintrom, "Policy Entrepreneurs and the Diffusion of Innovation"; Balla, "Interstate Professional Associations and the Diffusion of Policy Innovations."

37. Skocpol et al., "Women's Associations and the Enactment of Mothers' Pensions in the United States."

38. This distinction runs across a range of partnerships. I use a dichotomy for the purposes of these analyses because government-sponsorship is distinct from government-endorsement in its symbolic importance and in its connection to policy decisions. Both facets suggest differences in the factors associated with sponsorship as opposed to mere endorsement. For example, in the racial justice model, we would expect particularly large stores of racial resources to be associated with government sponsorship as opposed to mere government endorsement.

39. Ottensman, "The New Central Cities"; Hill, Brennan, and Wolman, "What is a Central City in the United States?"

40. The hypotheses tested here are derived from theories developed in relation to larger cities. Their applicability to medium-sized cities is an important empirical question that has received far too little attention. This chapter is a step toward such a test.

41. The states include California, Colorado, Florida, Illinois, Iowa, Kentucky, Mississippi, New Jersey, New York, North Dakota, Oklahoma, Oregon, Rhode Island, Texas, Utah, Vermont, Virginia, and Wisconsin. Please see the methods appendix for a list of cities.

42. Diagnostics indicated that one city, Fort Collins, Colorado, exerted undue influence on the results. Fort Collins is therefore omitted from the multivariate analyses.

43. To maximize the number of cases, these three cases are retained. When these cases are omitted, individual coefficients do not differ in their direction or significance, and tests for the significance of sets of coefficients stay the same. Four had multiple programs. The two cases which had both a government-sponsored and a government-endorsed program were coded as the former.

44. A second research assistant conducted reliability checks on the presence of programs, the presence of civil rights organizations, media targeted to marginalized racial groups, and government forms by independently gathering the information and checking the findings against the initial results. All discrepancies were settled with additional research. We paid close attention to cases in which no program or civil rights organiza-

tion could be identified. These were researched until at least three independent sources confirmed the absence of a program or civil rights organization.

45. The 2000 Census collected racial and ethnic data according to the following categories: Black or African American, American Indian and Alaska Native, Asian, Native Hawaiian and other Pacific Islander, some other race, two or more races, Hispanic or Latino, and White. The Census gathers information on Hispanic origin and race separately, first asking whether or not a person is Spanish, Hispanic, or Latino, and then asking for racial background. In this chapter, references to Hispanics or Latinos refer to people who answered affirmatively to the first question. A designation of "non-Hispanic white" refers to people who reported a white racial background but not a Spanish/Hispanic/Latino background. Results with respect to Native Hawaiian and other Pacific islanders are not reported here, because no city in the analysis had more than 106 people classifying themselves in this category in the 2000 census.

46. Interactions are between the dichotomous indicator of status as a high-income city and the independent variable. All variables except those indicating presence of civil rights organizations, nonwhite media, location in the South, and location in a state with statewide promotion of programs were rescaled such that the mean=0 before computing the interaction. Thus, the "main effect" coefficient for "High Income City" represents the effect of that independent variable when the values of other interaction variables are zero.

47. Interactions were retained only if they added explanatory power to the model. A test for improvement of fit showed that inclusion of the entire set of deleted interactions would produce no significant improvement in model performance (Chi^2 = 2.06, 6 d.f., p = .914). See table 4.3 for the full model results.

48. The cities are clustered by state, potentially violating the assumption of independent observations. To the extent that this violation is due to the diffusion of information through a statewide organization, my model includes an adequate control variable. Nevertheless, to minimize any inefficiency due to resulting heteroskedasticity, all multivariate analyses use Huber/White (robust) standard errors. The small number of cases prevents computing weighted least squares with the cluster command in Stata.

49. Separate analyses indicate that the negative sign of this coefficient was not driven by the presence of a particular type of civil rights organization.

50. Checks for multi-collinearity and alternative specifications support the robustness of the results in tables 4.4 and 4.5.

51. Chi^2 = 24.43, 7 d.f., p = .001.

52. Probabilities estimated using CLARIFY (King, Tomz, and Wittenberg, "Making the Most of Statistical Analyses").

53. Pearson's r = .236, two-tailed p = .005, N = 141. Matt Leighninger, an associate of the SCRC, observes that human rights commissions in the Midwest have been particularly active in organizing dialogue programs (personal communication).

54. Schumaker, *Critical Pluralism*, esp. 52–53.

55. Ibid., 53.

Chapter Five

1. For example, see Johnson, Johnson, and Maruyama, "Goal Interdependence and Interpersonal Attraction in Heterogeneous Classrooms."

2. As David Ryfe notes, "an insight . . . is slowly becoming apparent in the broader

literature on the practice of deliberative democracy, namely that deliberation is hard work: it is not easily undertaken, and once undertaken, it is not easily pursued" ("Narrative and Deliberation in Small Group Forums," 73). See also Patterson, "Structuration and Deliberation."

3. Hibbing and Theiss-Morse, *Stealth Democracy*.

4. Eliasoph, *Avoiding Politics*; Mansbridge, *Beyond Adversary Democracy*, chap 6; Hibbing and Theiss-Morse, *Stealth Democracy*.

5. Mutz and Martin, "Facilitating Communication Across Lines of Difference"; Beck, "Voters' Intermediation Environments in the 1988 Presidential Contest"; see also Mutz, "Cross-Cutting Social Networks"; Ulbig and Funk, "Conflict Avoidance and Political Participation." People also appear to interact with people whom they believe have similar political leanings (Huckfeldt and Sprague, *Citizens, Politics, and Social Communication*, 135–36), and the pool of potential discussion partners is influenced by lifestyle choices that are themselves associated with political preferences (Mutz, *Hearing the Other Side*, 44–48).

6. Balfour, "'A Most Disagreeable Mirror,'" 366n; see also Crenshaw, "Color-blind Dreams and Racial Nightmares: Reconfiguring Racism in the Post-Civil Rights Era."

7. Merelman, "The Mundane Experience of Political Culture," 529.

8. Polletta, *Freedom is an Endless Meeting*, chap. 8; Abu-Nimer, *Dialogue, Conflict Resolution, and Change*, especially chap. 1.

9. Merelman et al. note that advocating dialogue on race is subject to attacks from both the left and the right ("Unity and Diversity in American Political Culture," 782).

10. Edelman, *The Symbolic Uses of Politics*, chap. 1

11. Soss, *Unwanted Claims*, 26.

12. Mills, "Situated Actions and Vocabularies of Motive."

13. Mansbridge, *Beyond Adversary Democracy*.

14. In total, forty-two people said that civic dialogues were valuable for helping people become aware of difference (including the fourteen people who said it also helped identify shared categories, values, or common ground). Five people talked about identifying shared categories, values, or common ground, and did not also mention difference. Sixteen people could not be clearly categorized as emphasizing common ground and/or difference, due to short interview length or ambiguity of responses.

15. The one exception is Madison, Wisconsin, in which a Task Force on Race Relations recommended to the city council and mayor a variety of strategies the city could pursue to improve race relations, including a study circles on race program. I discuss this further, below.

16. Kingdon, *Agendas, Alternatives, and Public Policies*, 84–89. Kingdon bases this model on the work of Cohen, March, and Olsen ("A Garbage Can Model of Organizational Choice"). For an argument that city politics does *not* fit this model, see Berry, Portney, and Thomson, *The Rebirth of Urban Democracy*, 114–18. Intergroup dialogues are an exception in the local politics patterns Berry et al. examined because national organizations *have* invested resources to develop solution prototypes.

17. In 2004, he was promoted to direct the statewide Department of Human Rights.

18. Mutz, *Hearing the Other Side*.

19. See also SCRC senior associate Matt Leighninger's observation that practitioners see difference-focused dialogues as ongoing work (*The Next Form*, chap. 3, p. 4).

20. Allen, *Talking to Strangers*, 174.

21. After Bauman was defeated in the primary during her first reelection attempt, the new mayor, a white man, promoted the gradual transition of the city-run program into the hands of an independent nonprofit organization. Reflecting the desire for a program with a greater orientation toward action, the request for proposals was awarded to a local Latina with experience with diversity training who titled the new study circles program: Respectful Dialogues with a Purpose.

22. Pitkin, "Justice: On Relating Private and Public."

23. Bickford, *The Dissonance of Democracy*, chap. 5.

24. Hardy-Fanta, *Latina Politics, Latino Politics*.

25. Cedar Falls is the wealthier and much less diverse city of the Waterloo–Cedar Falls metro area, In 2000, its population was 94.6 percent non-Hispanic white.

26. Sandy Robinson, personal interview; Study Circles Resource Center, "Success Stories: Uniting Springfield's House Divided," http://www.studycircles.org/pages/success/sucspring.html. See also Leighninger, *The Next Form*, chap. 3.

27. Compare to the community action programs of the 1960s. The stipulation for "maximum feasible participation" was not treated as a major part of the federal legislation that created CAPs, but activists who had originated the idea took it literally and pushed for community participation (Moynihan, *Maximum Feasible Misunderstanding*).

28. Bultena and Reasby, "Negro-White Relations in the Waterloo Metropolitan Area." The Teachers College became the University of Northern Iowa.

29. The report noted that one student wrote in his field notes: "Almost all nightly ads are headed 'Attention Colored Buyer.' . . . The ads for homes in the white sections do not say 'No Negroes Allowed.' However, they leave little room for doubt."

30. "In one case when a Negro ordered an egg and toast the waiter brought him a raw egg broken on a piece of bread together with the egg shell" (18).

31. Paton, "The Negro in America Today."

32. Within the class of 1999 across Waterloo's high schools, 40 percent of the African-American females and 70 percent of the African-American males had dropped out by January of their graduating year (*Waterloo/Cedar Falls Courier*, "Another Day Off from Realizing King's Dream.")

33. Racial slurs and swastikas have been painted on city property, private garages, scratched into a car parked outside a multiracial church service, and mailed to interracial couples living in predominantly white neighborhoods (Reinitz "Racial Slurs Painted on Private, City Property"; Reinitz, "Racist Message Left Outside Church").

34. An advisory committee of the U.S. Commission on Civil Rights held a public hearing in 1999 in the city and was told that developers avoid the East side of town (no longer referred to as the North End), and employers such as John Deere do little to hire and retain minority employees (U.S. Commission on Civil Rights, Iowa Advisory Committee, "Race Relations in Waterloo"; Kinney, "Racism Alive in Waterloo, Rights Panel Told"). Employment in general is an issue, as the Rath plant closed in the mid 1980s, and the days of secure, blue collar employment are over.

35. For a similar instance of a public talk program stemming from frustration with other forms of politics, see Karpowitz and Mansbridge, "Disagreement and Consensus," 238.

36. Fernandez, "Keeping It Together."

37. For example, a study circles program in Lima, Ohio, has reportedly involved over

5,000 people, or 12.5 percent of the 2000 Census population. Leighninger, "How Have Study Circles Made an Impact?"

38. Mansbridge, *Beyond Adversary Democracy.*

39. See also Abu-Nimer, *Dialogue, Conflict Resolution, and Change,* 167.

40. Nelson, Kaboolian, and Carver, "Bridging Social Capital and An Investment Theory of Collective Action," 2.

41. Ibid.

42. See also Eliasoph's reconceptualization of rationalist models of political behavior from the question, "Should I participate?" to "What kind of citizen should I be?" (*Avoiding Politics,* 251).

43. Monroe, *The Heart of Altruism;* Monroe with Epperson, "'But What Else Could I Do?'"

44. Soss, *Unwanted Claims,* chap. 3.

45. Miller, "Framing and Political Participation," 2, building on Gamson, *Power and Discontent,* 96; See also Miller, "What Motivates Political Participation?"; Miller and Krosnick, "Threat as a Motivator of Political Activism."

46. Miller, "Framing." "When deciding whether to spend your free time on volunteer or political activities, how important is it that the volunteer or political activity helps you express your personal values, convictions, or beliefs?" ("What Motivates Political Participation?," 42).

Chapter Six

1. Citrin et al., "Is American Nationalism Changing?"; Sears et al., "Cultural Diversity and Multicultural Politics"; Citrin et al., "Multiculturalism in American Public Opinion"; Citrin, Wong, and Duff, "The Meaning of American National Identity"; Schildkraut "The More Things Change."

2. Schildkraut, "The More Things Change."

3. Schildkraut, *Press One for English.*

4. Lane, *Political Ideology;* Hochschild, *What's Fair;* Feldman and Zaller, "The Political Culture of Ambivalence"; Chong, "How People Think, Reason, and Feel about Rights and Liberties." By ambivalence, I mean the state of "simultaneously hold[ing] several contradictory beliefs about the same issue" (Hochschild, "Disjunction and Ambivalence in Citizens' Political Outlooks," 190).

5. Schildkraut, *Press One for English;* Alvarez and Brehm demonstrate that instability in racial attitudes is due more to uncertainty than ambivalence ("Are Americans Ambivalent about Racial Policies?"). However the ambivalence I expect here is not about racial attitudes per se, but about the push and pull of unity and diversity.

6. Merelman, Streich, and Martin, "Unity and Diversity in American Political Culture," 798–801.

7. Merelman, "The Mundane Experience of Political Culture."

8. In the central Wisconsin city, the fifth session took place two weeks after the fourth session and was a joint meeting of all of the discussion groups that had been meeting in the city that spring.

9. The city in central Wisconsin fell just below a population of 50,000 in 2000.

10. Flavin-McDonald and McCoy, *The Busy Citizen's Discussion Guide.*

11. Please see the appendix for a list of participants in each of the groups.

12. Edwards and Edwards, *Aurora*.

13. "Tips for study circle leaders. . . . *Stay neutral!* The *most important* thing to remember is that, as facilitator, you should not share your personal views or try to advance your agenda on the issue. You are there to serve the discussion, not to join it" (Flavin-McDonald and McCoy, *Facing the Challenge of Racism and Race Relations*, 44, emphasis in original).

14. This couple chose to participate in both groups, and reported that they were not asked to do so by the coordinators of the program. However, their participation in both groups, and the fact that in the Wednesday group they were the only people of color besides the facilitator, speaks to the difficulty that relatively homogenous communities have in recruiting sufficient numbers of people of color to participate in interracial dialogues. In the analyses, I was careful to ask myself whether common patterns I observed across the two central Wisconsin groups were due to this overlap in membership.

15. According to the surveys of participants in the Madison and Aurora programs (see appendix), 20 percent of Madison and 56 percent of Aurora participants heard about the program through word of mouth, 22 percent of Madison and 23 percent of Aurora participants heard through other organizations, and 49 percent of Madison and 14 percent of Aurora participants heard about it through local mass media.

16. Jacobs, Delli Carpini, and Cook report, based on a national sample, that most people who participate in face-to-face civic deliberation are recruited through public means rather than through personal acquaintances ("How Do Americans Deliberate?" 21). This differs for New England town meetings (Bryan, *Real Democracy*).

17. For example, an article about the City of Madison Study Circles on Race in one of that city's daily newspapers included a side bar that read: "To take part in the 10-week, free series of Study Circle discussions on race, call Mona Winston at 251–8550, Ext. 26" (Schneider, "Study Circles Seek More Participation").

18. In a study of NEH civic dialogues focused on national identity and pluralism, Merelman observes little talk about action ("The Mundane Experience of Political Culture"). It appears that I observed more talk about action in the dialogues I observed, which may be attributed to the topic of the dialogues (participants did not commonly talk about race or institutional racism in the NEH dialogues), the one-shot nature of many of the dialogues he and his colleagues observed, or to the structure of the curriculum. In addition, many participants viewed the talk as action in and of itself (Merelman, "Mundane Experience," 531). In general, it seems that individuals are more likely to self-select into these forums if they see it as action in itself or as a step toward action, as people are often frustrated when deliberation does not allow people to "mov[e] from a 'deliberative' to an 'implementational' mindset" (Ryfe, "Narrative and Deliberation in Small Group Forums," 84). See also Jacobs, Delli Carpini, and Cook, "How Do Americans Deliberate?" 26–27.

19. The fact that some participants spoke very little in these groups (besides myself) is a challenge to claims made by Theiss-Morse and Hibbing that silence in focus groups is a sign that people disdain participatory democracy ("Citizenship and Civic Engagement," 243). The silent people in the group I observed were volunteers who could have easily chosen to not return the following week. Silence in group conversations is not necessarily a sign of disgust for the process, but of a different style of participation.

20. Thomas, Woodruff, and Thomas, *Building a House for Diversity.*

21. Citrin et al., "Multiculturalism." Likewise, in Deborah Schildkraut's analysis of opinions on national identity and language policy through focus groups and survey data, at no time in the focus groups did people express support for ethnoculturalism or separation (*Press One for English,* 198).

22. I use statements made during the dialogues as indicators of ideology rather than survey measures of ideology because my interest was not in whether people labeled themselves liberal or conservative (or a variant of either) in private, but in the way they behaved in the group and the ideological atmosphere of the group.

23. The one exception in my observations was the group in Madison, a notoriously liberal city. Most of the participants in this group conveyed what could be considered relatively liberal views on race relations, though some were shocked at the conservatism of others' statements. Questionnaires that the participants completed suggested that the average ideology of participants, on a scale including "Extremely conservative, conservative, slightly conservative, moderate/middle of the road, slightly liberal, liberal, or extremely liberal," was between "slightly liberal" and "liberal." See the methods appendix for details.

24. Merelman, Streich, and Martin, "Unity and Diversity," 788–90.

25. Ibid., 794.

26. Leighninger, *The Next Form of Democracy,* chap. 3.

27. Jacobs, Delli Carpini, and Cook, "How Do Americans Deliberate?" 14–16.

28. Of 102 respondents in Madison, 8 percent expressed this belief. Of thirty-eight respondents in Aurora, only one (2.6 percent) did so. Surveys were also given to one round of high school dialogue participants. Of the twelve respondents, none of them said they thought the dialogues achieved unity or common ground.

29. Forty-six percent of the Madison respondents and 36.8 percent of the Aurora respondents felt that this is what had gone on in their dialogues. See methods appendix for details.

30. Karpowitz and Mansbridge, "Disagreement and Consensus," 246.

31. Norton, *95 Theses on Politics, Culture, and Method.*

32. Evaluation questionnaires also displayed many such remarks.

33. In central Wisconsin, past participants continued to discuss the topic of appropriate labels by email.

34. This is an example of what Nelson et al. call the unproductive practice of "gotcha." "The purpose of the interrupter was not to engage in a discussion on respectful names, but to show that the speaker was thoughtless and not to be trusted and that the interrupter was the guardian of true understanding" ("Bridging Social Capital and An Investment Theory of Collective Action," 20).

35. Young, *Justice and the Politics of Difference,* 99.

36. See de Figueiredo and Elkins, "Are Patriots Bigots?"

37. Young, *Justice,* 171–72.

38. The discussions show that the power to label oneself did not always sit comfortably with the participants, and that was most obviously the case in discussions around the use of the term "nigger." Whites, and often people of color, expressed a great deal of disapproval of the use of this term by blacks.

39. Zaller, *The Nature and Origins of Mass Opinion.*

40. My gratitude to Cara Wong for noticing this dynamic.

41. Schildkraut defines a "completed thought" as "(1) the dialogue of one speaker at one time or (2) the minimum amount of comments necessary to communicate the speaker's main point. Definition 1 was used when a speaker said little, and definition 2 was used when a speaker said a lot at once" (*Press One for English*, 95). Because speakers did not tend to speak for long periods of time, the vast majority of the comments consisted of one completed thought. Some turns did include multiple thoughts. Many of the comments were too short to code (e.g., "that goes back to what Adam said.") Therefore, I include only those comments that were longer than 140 characters of type or comments less than 140 characters to which a code could be assigned. This yielded a total of 141 completed thoughts across the five groups. An intercoder reliability check produced 93 percent agreement.

42. Schildkraut, *Press One for English*, 97.

43. Schildkraut found that only 4 percent of all thoughts related to policy used an incorporationist conception of American identity, which includes both multicultural and melting pot incorporationism (135). The large difference from the results here is likely due to the fact that the main topic of Schildkraut's focus groups was language policy, but the main topic of the dialogue groups I observed was race relations, making the topic of multiculturalism more prominent.

44. In the translation from private to public, "we discover connections to others and learn to care about those connections. . . . In the process we learn that we are different than we had thought, that our interests are different than we had supposed. *We discover the way our membership helps to define us*, and the pleasure of becoming active in relation to it together with others" (Pitkin, "Justice," 348, emphasis added).

45. Allen, *Talking to Strangers.* See also Harris-Lacewell, *Barbershops, Bibles, and BET*, 75.

46. Robert Lane's work alerted scholars to the prevalence of ambivalence in American public opinion (*Political Ideology*). Some scholars took his findings as confirmation of Phillip Converse's arguments that Americans lack coherent political belief systems (Kinder, "Diversity and Complexity in American Public Opinion"; Converse, "The Nature of Belief Systems in Mass Publics.")

47. Hochschild, "Disjunction and Ambivalence in Citizens' Political Outlooks."

48. Ibid., 189.

49. Ibid., 204–6. This openness is akin to an important personality trait that psychologists refer to as "openness to experience" (McCrae, "Social Consequences of Experiential Openness." My gratitude to an anonymous reviewer for pointing out the relevance of this literature.) Such willingness to alter one's own perceptions on the basis of new information or experience is akin to the kind of positive ambivalence Hochschild discusses and that we saw operating in the discussion groups. It has particular consequences for race relations, as recent research has shown that whites high in "openness to experience" tend to form more favorable impressions of blacks (Flynn, "Having an Open Mind.")

50. Mutz, "Mechanisms of Momentum"; Lindeman, "Opinion Quality and Policy Preferences in Deliberative Research."

51. Compare to Theiss-Morse and Hibbing, "Citizenship and Civic Engagement," 244.

Chapter Seven

1. McCoy and Scully, "Deliberative Dialogue to Expand Civic Engagement," 117.

2. See Smith, *Stories of Peoplehood*.

3. Ryfe, "Narrative and Deliberation in Small Group Forums"; Merelman et al., "Unity and Diversity in American Political Culture," 795.

4. Polletta states that in practice a story typically has a beginning, middle, and end, a setting, characters, a point of view, and a plot. However, stories can be as brief as "'The king died and then the queen died of grief'" (*It Was Like a Fever*, 8–9).

5. Ryfe, "Narrative and Deliberation."

6. Bruner, *Acts of Meaning*; White, *Metahistory*; White, "The Value of Narrativity in the Representation of Reality"; Ricoeur, "Narrative Time"; Ricoeur, *Time and Narrative*; Taylor, *Sources of the Self*; Perin, *Belonging in America*; Mandelbaum, "Telling Stories"; Mandelbaum, "Historians and Planners"; Mandelbaum, *Open Moral Communities*, chap. 6; Andrews et al., *Lines of Narrative*; MacGilvray, *Reconstructing Public Reason*, chap. 3; Monroe, *The Hand of Compassion*, Appendix A, esp. 273–75.

7. Barthes, *Image, Music, Text*, 79, cited in Cromer and Wagner-Pacifici, "Introduction to the Special Issue on Narratives of Violence," 163.

8. Jacobs, *Race, Media and the Crisis of Civil Society*.

9. Bohman, *Public Deliberation*.

10. Young, *Inclusion and Democracy*.

11. Ibid., 73–74.

12. Ibid., 75–76.

13. Ibid., 76–77.

14. Ibid., 77.

15. See also Sanders's call for testimony ("Against Deliberation").

16. Mandelbaum, *Open Moral Communities*, chap. 6.

17. See Ryfe, "The Practice of Deliberative Democracy," 367.

18. Ryfe, "Narrative and Deliberation," 77; see also Bruner, *Acts of Meaning*.

19. Ryfe, "Narrative and Deliberation," 78–79.

20. Ibid., 79–80.

21. Ibid., 75–76.

22. Ibid., 87.

23. Barnes, "The Same Old Process?" 251

24. Walsh, *Talking about Politics*.

25. Bar-On and Kassem, "Storytelling as a Way to Work Through Intractable Conflicts."

26. A parallel process takes place on the level of mass-mediated public discussion. Even when initial news of an event has multiple narratives, entropy soon sets in and a single narrative tends to dominate (Jacobs, "The Problem with Tragic Narratives"; see also Jacobs, *Race, Media and the Crisis of Civil Society*).

27. Polletta, *It Was Like a Fever*, chapter 4.

28. Ibid., 94–95.

29. Monroe, *The Hand of Compassion*, 275–77.

30. Bar-On and Kassem, "Storytelling," 301.

31. Ibid., 297.

32. Barnes, "The Same Old Process?" 252–53.

33. Fung, *Empowered Participation*, 124.

34. This pattern appears in many aspects of the deliberative system. Ryfe, "Narrative and Deliberation"; Walsh, *Talking about Politics;* Merelman et al., "Unity and Diversity," 795.

35. Although the Aurora evening group did not follow the curriculum, the facilitator asked the participants to talk about themselves at the beginning of the first session.

36. Flavin-McDonald and McCoy, *The Busy Citizen's Discussion Guide*, 35.

37. Ryfe, "Narrative and Deliberation." See also Jacobs, Delli Carpini, and Cook, "How Do Americans Deliberate?" for more on the importance of facilitator style.

38. Coote and Lenaghan, Citizens' Juries, 89–90.

39. Barnes, *"The Same Old Process?"* 256.

40. Walsh, *Talking about Politics.*

41. "Think back to what you learned in school about the history of race relations in this country. What made an impression on you? What do you think kids today should learn about the history of race relations?" (Flavin-McDonald and McCoy, *The Busy Citizen's Discussion Guide*, 10).

42. Bruce had said: "Isn't reverse discrimination more along the lines of being a member of the power structure, the dominant race?"

43. Mansbridge, *Beyond Adversary Democracy.*

44. Bobo, "Racial Attitudes and Relations at the Close of the Twentieth Century," 280–85; Hochschild, *Facing Up to the American Dream*; Kuklinski and Hurley, "On Hearing and Interpreting Political Messages"; Kuklinski and Hurley, "It's a Matter of Interpretation"; Sapiro and Soss, "Spectacular Politics, Dramatic Interpretations," 302–5; Blauner, *Black Lives, White Lives;* Blauner, *Still the Big News,* chap. 13; Walsh, Talking about Politics, chap. 7.

45. Nisbett and Ross, *Human Inference*, 62.

46. My gratitude to Richard Allen for raising these points.

47. Walsh, *Talking about Politics.* See also, McCoy and Scully, "Deliberative Dialogue," 121.

48. Rojas et al., "Media Dialogue: Perceiving and Addressing Community Problems."

49. Compare to claims that storytelling interferes with the process of linking personal lives to broader historical and structural explanations (Merelman et al., "Unity and Diversity," 795).

50. MacGilvray, *Reconstructing Public Reason*, especially chap. 3.

51. Ryfe, "Narrative and Deliberation," 83–84.

52. Polletta, *It Was Like a Fever.*

Chapter Eight

1. Dryzek, *Deliberative Democracy and Beyond*, 67.

2. The guide that these groups used was last updated in 1997. Some of the scenarios provided in the guide that participants could choose to discuss referred to immigration or language policy, but these were optional. At the time of this writing, the SCRC was in the final stages of editing a new discussion guide that differed from the 1997 version in its focus on ethnicity as well as race, its attempt to expand the discussion beyond the

black/white divide, an additional session and other strategies to ensure that people grad-uated from the dialogues with plans for action, a greater focus on inequality, and also an option for affinity sessions, in which people of similar racial backgrounds could engage in separate dialogues before and after the six sessions of the full group.

3. Walsh, *Talking about Politics*; Harris-Lacewell and Mills, "Truth and Soul."

4. This group also discussed reparations during their third meeting, which I could not attend. Group members who attended indicated that the conversation took the same pattern.

5. Whites as well as African Americans in the group struggled with this. One re-marked that she feared that the concern with Hispanics meant that "we're sort of doing a poll vault over black Americans."

6. People did not often use these dialogues to directly confront issues of legitimacy among people of color, possibly due to the relative scarcity of racial minorities other than black Americans in these groups. Various communities around the country have imple-mented interracial dialogues among people of color precisely to provide such discussions.

7. Schildkraut, *Press One for English*, chap. 6.

8. Steve's comments appear in chapter 6.

9. Mendelberg and Oleske, "Race and Public Deliberation"; Sanders, "Against Delib-eration"; Briggs, "Culture, Power, and Communication in Community Building."

10. Patterson, "Structuration and Deliberation"; see also Merelman, "The Mundane Experience of Political Culture," 519.

11. Dahl, *Who Governs?*

12. Bachrach and Baratz, *Power and Poverty*; Bachrach and Baratz, "The Two Faces of Power."

13. Gaventa, *Power and Powerlessness*.

14. Patterson "Structuration and Deliberation"; see also Flyvberg, *Rationality and Power*.

15. These analyses also show that men spoke more than women in these dialogues, ex-cept in the southern Wisconsin group, consistent with previous research on other forms of public talk (Bryan, *Real Democracy*, chap. 9). Thus even though women volunteer for these programs more than men, they actually participate less within them. This dynamic was not due to facilitators asking men to participate more, to compensate. Unless a fa-cilitator asked each of the participants to take a turn consecutively, people contributed when they felt the desire to do so.

These tables display several additional characteristics of note. Facilitators were the most frequent contributors. Lower attendance tended to increase the inequality in turn taking; relatively quiet participants did not speak more when fewer people were present. Finally, there were some people who did talk more than the others, but in none of the groups did one person completely dominate.

16. To conduct this analysis, I coded all transcripts for instances of a participant ask-ing an individual or the group as a whole for justification for claims that had been made within the group. This did not include questions seeking clarification, nor mere chal-lenges to someone else's statements, but clear requests for further evidence or reasons. Some examples include: "Why is past history relevant to whether or not they should be charged?" "Why do you define racism that way?" This coding also does not include justi-fications that people volunteered and therefore underestimates the incidence of justifica-

tion. I use this narrow definition to minimize coding error and because my purpose is to determine the relative incidence of justification across people, not total amounts.

17. Previous work shows the importance of facilitation for the nature of public talk (Ryfe, "Narrative and Deliberation"; Fung, *Empowered Participation*, 179–87).

18. Also, in the Aurora evening group, the most contentious of these groups, fewer demands were made for justifications during the fourth session, in which we sat around one small table rather than a large table as was the case in other sessions.

19. Bickford, *The Dissonance of Democracy*, 156–57; Forester, *Planning in the Face of Power*, 111–12.

20. Mendelberg and Oleske, "Race and Public Deliberation," 186.

21. Ibid., 187.

22. Ibid.

23. Ibid., 185.

24. For further evidence that the mere appearance of listening is not enough to produce meaningful public talk, see Fung, *Empowered Participation*, 179–87.

25. Bickford, *The Dissonance of Democracy*, 156.

Chapter Nine

1. Skocpol, *Diminished Democracy*, chap. 2.

2. Salamon, "The New Governance and the Tools of Public Action," 2.

3. Ibid.; see also Barnes, "The Same Old Process?"

4. Salamon "The New Governance."

5. Barnes, "The Same Old Process?"; Reichler and Dredge, *Governing Diverse Communities*.

6. Briggs, "Culture, Power, and Communication in Community Building."

7. Verba, Schlozman, and Brady, *Voice and Equality*, 349; Abramson, "Political Efficacy and Political Trust Among Black Schoolchildren," 1246–47; Austin and Dodge, "Despair, Distrust, and Dissatisfaction among Blacks and Women, 1973–1987." The finding by Verba, Schlozman, and Brady in *Voice and Equality* is based on the 1990 Citizen Participation Study, which oversampled for blacks and Latinos. The political efficacy of a national sample was measured through a four-item index that includes measures of perceptions of government responsiveness at the national and local levels, and then perceptions of ability to influence government decisions at the national and local levels. Combining the efficacy measures into an additive index (alpha = .79) allows a comparison of mean scores across racial groups. Reanalysis of this data shows that the differences in mean efficacy are statistically significant across racial groups. On a scale from 4 to 16, the average among whites is 9.4, among African Americans 8.8, and among Latinos, 8.4. The difference between whites and both racial minority groups is statistically significant at $p < .001$.

8. Bingham, O'Leary, and Nabatchi, "Legal Frameworks for the New Governance."

9. Smith and Ingram, "Policy Tools and Democracy."

10. Box, *Citizen Governance;* Murphy, "Politics, Political Science, and Urban Governance"; Schuckman, "Political Participation in American Cities"; Macedo et al., *Democracy at Risk*, chap. 3, for an overview.

11. Bramson, "The Deliberative Public Manager"; Harwood, *The Public's Role in the*

Policy Process; see also Schumaker, *Critical Pluralism, Democratic Performance, and Community Power,* 53.

12. Greenstone and Peterson, *Race and Authority in Urban Politics;* Yankelovich, *Evaluation of the Cincinnati Community Action Program.*

13. Moynihan, *Maximum Feasible Misunderstanding.*

14. Berman, "Dealing with Cynical Citizens," 107. Thanks to Christopher Karpowitz for alerting me to this survey. For an overview of literature on public hearings, see Williamson and Fung, "Public Deliberation," 8–9.

15. Williamson and Fung, "Public Deliberation."

16. Fung, *Empowered Participation.*

17. Gastil and Kelshaw, "Public Meetings."

18. For more on the notice-and-comment model, traditionally used in public planning, see Bingham et al., "Legal Frameworks for the New Governance"; Irvin and Stansbury, "Citizen Participation in Decision Making," 57; Beierle, "Using Social Goals to Evaluate Public Participation in Environmental Decisions." See Coote and Lenaghan, *Citizens' Juries,* 2, for more on the citizen-as-consumer model outside the United States.

19. See Fung, *Empowered Participation,* 128–31.

20. Gastil, *By Popular Demand,* 98–101.

21. Gastil and Kelshaw, "Public Meetings"; Fung, *Empowered Participation;* Bramson, "The Deliberative Public Manager"; Button and Mattson, "Deliberative Democracy in Practice"; Grogan and Gusmano, "Deliberative Democracy in Theory and Practice."

22. Button and Mattson, "Deliberative Democracy in Practice," 620.

23. Bryan, *Real Democracy,* 173.

24. Irvin and Stansbury, "Citizen Participation."

25. Bramson, "The Deliberative Public Manager."

26. Karpowitz and Mansbridge, "Disagreement and Consensus," 243.

27. Gastil and Kelshaw place such communication in high regard for its potential to result in policy change ("Public Meetings"). See also Barber's call for "horizontal" as opposed to "vertical" communication between members of the public and public officials (*A Place for Us,* 85).

28. Ren et al., "Linking Confidence in the Police with the Performance of the Police."; Zhao, Lovrich, and Thurman, "The Status of Community Policing in American Cities."

29. Fenno, *Home Style.*

30. Verba and Nie, *Participation in America,* chaps 17–19; Dewey, *The Public and its Problems.*

31. In all of the cases that I observed, public officials identified themselves as officials during initial introductions.

32. This was not the first black man to ever live in the city, but may have been the first black man to reside there in recent decades. Escaped slaves had settled in this town and started a small African-American community, but these residents fled when the Ku Klux Klan reemerged in the 1920s.

33. See Schumaker, *Critical Pluralism.*

34. Schraufnagel, "Testing the Implications of Incivility in the United States Congress, 1977–2000"; Uslaner, *The Decline of Comity in Congress.*

35. Mutz shows that people are most likely to gain an awareness of rationales for crosscutting views when encountering them in a context of civility (*Hearing the Other Side,* 76).

36. Fung, *Empowered Participation*, 186–87. If changes in the format produce changes in the content of the communication, one might ask what we can reasonably learn from observing just a small number of groups. The cases do not necessarily represent what happens in all intergroup dialogues. However, the in-depth examination of these cases, which vary by group composition and facilitator quality among other factors, allows us to observe patterns of behavior that characterize civic dialogues on race across a range of group characteristics.

37. My gratitude to an anonymous reviewer for making this point.

38. Please see methods appendix for more detail.

39. Pitkin and Shumer eloquently note the importance of this kind of exchange: "[W]hile various kinds of knowledge can be profoundly useful in political decisions, knowledge alone is never enough. The political question is what we are to *do*; knowledge can only tell us how things are, how they work, while a political resolution always depends on what we, as a community, want and think right. And those questions have no technical answer; they require collective deliberation and decision. The experts must become a part of, not an alternative to, the democratic political process" ("On Participation," 52).

40. Fung, *Empowered Participation*, 129.

41. Lipsky, *Street-Level Bureaucracy*, 57.

42. Ibid., 60–65.

43. Ibid., 60.

Chapter Ten

1. Schudson, "Why Conversation is Not the Soul of Democracy."

2. Bryan, *Real Democracy*; Mansbridge, *Beyond Adversary Democracy*.

3. Verba, Schlozman, and Brady, *Voice and Equality*.

4. See also Bryan, *Real Democracy*, 68–69, 114–21; Fung, *Empowered Participation*, chap. 4.

5. See a similar argument in Taylor and Moghaddam, in their study of roots of ethnic revolutions of the 1970s (*Theories of Intergroup Relations*, 189).

6. Pitkin, "Justice," 343.

7. Fung, *Empowered Participation*, chap 6.

8. In conversations about American Identity, 14.74 percent of the 2,090 completed thought statements used an incorporationist perspective (*Press One for English*, 98) and just 60.71 percent of these (or 9 percent of the total) used a specifically multicultural perspective (p. 116). (Incorporationism contains both multiculturalism as well as melting-pot assimilationism.) Just 1.9 percent of thought statements about language policy used multiculturalism (p. 154).

9. Wolfe, *One Nation, After All*, 154–63.

10. Key, *Public Opinion and American Democracy*.

11. Lichterman, *Elusive Togetherness*.

12. My gratitude to Amaal Tokars for alerting me to this point.

13. Karpowitz, "The Deliberative Potential and Realities of Public Meetings"; however, see Cook, Delli Carpini, and Jacobs, "Who Deliberates?" for contrary evidence.

14. See also Leighninger, *The Next Form of Democracy*, chap. 3.

15. Ibid.

16. This was true for many of the programs I encountered. See also Merriss and Abercrombie, "Investing in a Community of Stakeholders"; and Gastil and Kelshaw, "Public Meetings."

17. Dean Lovelace, Dayton City Commissioner, and Audrey Norman-Turner, Dayton Dialogues coordinator, personal interview.

18. Leighninger, *The Next Form*, chap. 3; Sandy Robinson, Director Springfield Department of Community Relations, personal interview; Fanselow, "Springfield, Illinois."

19. Robinson, personal interview.

20. Leighninger, *The Next Form*, chap. 3.

21. Fanselow, *What Democracy Looks Like: Vermont*, 3.

22. Fanselow, *What Democracy Looks Like: Kansas City, Kansas*, 5.

23. Leighninger, *The Next Form*, chap. 3.

24. Personal communication, Martha McCoy. See also McCoy, "Art for Democracy's Sake"; Leighninger, "How Have Study Circles Made an Impact?"

25. Rojas et al., "Media Dialogue."

26. An alternative hypothesis is that these dialogues lead to heightened conflict. Berry, Portney, and Thomson studied neighborhood associations with a link to local government, not dialogues on race relations, but their results are instructive for the types of effects we might expect (*The Rebirth of Urban Democracy*). They found that participants did not perceive that the associations led to greater conflict (201–2) but rather, participating seemed to bring about a "strong[er] sense of community" (established through a panel study) (240–41).

27. Merriss and Abercrombie, "Investing in a Community of Stakeholders," 8–9; Walsh, Memo to City of Madison Common Council, December 23, 2002; Walsh, *Talking about Politics*, 193–94; Goldstein and Sturm, "Assessing the Impact-Report 1"; Goldstein and Sturm, "Assessing the Impact-Report 2"; Keniston, Hubbard, and Honnold, "The Dayton Multiracial Dialogues."

28. Gurin et al., "Context, Identity, and Intergroup Relations."

29. Nagda and Zuñiga, "Fostering Meaningful Racial Engagement through Intergroup Dialogues."

30. Nagda, Kim, and Truelove, "Learning about Difference, Learning with Others, Learning to Transgress."

31. See for example Cappella, Price, and Nir, "Argument Repetoire as a Reliable and Valid Measure of Opinion Quality"; Price, Cappella, and Nir, "Does Disagreement Contribute to More Deliberative Opinion?"

32. Allport, *The Nature of Prejudice*, chap. 29.

33. Hayward, "The Difference States Make."

34. Chambers, "Deliberative Democratic Theory," 311, citing Fraser, "Rethinking the Public Sphere"; and Habermas, *The Inclusion of the Other*.

35. Chambers, "Deliberative Democratic Theory," 311.

36. State-sponsored forums that enable members of the public to challenge the status quo do exist. Public universities are one example.

37. Young, "Activist Challenges to Deliberative Democracy," 673.

38. This is reminiscent of the IAF (Warren, *Dry Bones Rattling*).

39. See Gould on the varieties of forms that representation of differences in the public sphere can take ("Diversity and Democracy").

40. Norton, "Review: *Race Relations and the New York City Commission on Human Rights*," 349.

41. http://www.usdoj.gov/crs/pubs/gehrc.htm

42. Berry et al., *The Rebirth of Urban Democracy*, chap. 4.

43. Abramson, "Political Efficacy and Political Trust Among Black Schoolchildren"; Hirsch, *Political Socialization in an American Subculture*; Burns, Schlozman, and Verba, *The Private Roots of Public Action*, chap. 13.

44. An important precedent for these questions comes from the Berry et al. study, *The Rebirth of Urban Democracy*. The focus of their study was on the effects of participation in, and the existence of, neighborhood governance structures in which residents engaged in face-to-face policy decision-making that involved direct contact with public officials. Participation in the structures was not causally related to perceptions of government responsiveness or unresponsiveness at the individual level, but the existence of high-participation neighborhood structures was related to perceptions of government responsiveness (243–47) and trust in government (248–53) among the mass public. In addition, participation led to external political efficacy, particularly in high participation cities (268–70), but not internal efficacy, or perceptions of one's own ability to affect the policy process (265–70). Finally, participation in face-to-face community politics was related to a gain in knowledge about which public officials to contact and awareness of the neighborhood governance structures (270–76). Many of these effects were particularly pronounced for people of low socioeconomic status. See also Coleman, "The Lonely Citizen," 202, for evidence that a greater psychological connection to officials may make citizens more likely to contact them in the future.

45. For example, Gastil, *By Popular Demand*, 179–80.

46. Claibourn and Martin, "Trusting and Joining?"

47. Citizen input is likely to increase perceptions of fairness and legitimacy (Tyler, "The Psychology of Public Dissatisfaction with Government"). However, if the participants are not representative of the broader public, the resulting policy may be perceived as illegitimate (Fiorina, "Extreme Voices"; Smith and McDonough, "Beyond Public Participation"; Williamson and Fung, "Public Deliberation"; Fung, *Empowered Participation*).

48. If the communication conveys lower authority for members of the public than public officials, we might expect negative, not positive effects on political efficacy (Soss, *Unwanted Claims*; Soss, "Lessons of Welfare").

49. Fung, *Empowered Participation*.

50. Berry, Portney, and Thompson, *Rebirth*, chap. 4; Mettler, "Bringing the State Back In to Civic Engagement."

51. See Norton, *95 Theses on Politics, Culture, and Method*, for the utility of conceptualizing phenomena as matters of balancing rather than reconciliation, as well as our resistance to doing so; see also Merelman et al., "Unity and Diversity."

52. Mendelberg and Oleske, "Race and Public Deliberation."

53. The productiveness of contestation calls into question assertions that facilitators ought to be neutral in order for public talk to be effective (such as in Fung, *Empowered Participation*, 210). The evidence presented here suggests that what is needed is not neutrality but fairness woven with a good dose of provocativeness.

54. Schudson, "Why Conversation is Not the Soul of Democracy," 308.

55. Young, *Justice and the Politics of Difference*, 687.

56. Sapiro, "Considering Political Civility Historically."

57. Karpowitz and Mansbridge, "Disagreement and Consensus," 238.

58. Mansbridge, *Beyond Adversary Democracy.*

59. Karpowitz and Mansbridge, "Disagreement and Consensus," 247.

60. Allen, *Talking to Strangers.*

61. MacGilvray, *Reconstructing Public Reason,* 33.

62. Pateman asserted decades ago that participatory democracy is more practical than a model of governance in which citizens play little role, given their comparative potential for sustainability (*Participation and Democratic Theory,* esp. 43–44).

Methods Appendix

1. Two participants stopped attending the sessions, an African-American woman and an African-American man.

2. Bobo, "Race and Beliefs about Affirmative Action," 158.

3. For example, in the southern Wisconsin group, we read over a list of examples of experiences that are manifestations of white privilege, such as "I can go shopping alone most of the time, pretty well assured that I will not be followed or harassed." This was reprinted from Peggy McIntosh, "White Privilege: Unpacking the Invisible Knapsack," (which is available on a multitude of websites, including http://www.antiracistalliance.com/Unpacking.html), and is excerpted from McIntosh, "White Privilege and Male Privilege."

4. Manna, "How do I Know What I Say I Know?"

5. Soss, "Talking Our Way to Meaningful Explanation."

6. Briggs, "Culture, Power, and Communication in Community Building," 5.

7. Soss, "Talking Our Way."

8. Feldman, *Strategies for Interpreting Qualitative Data.*

BIBLIOGRAPHY

Abrams, Dominic, and Michael A. Hogg. "Comments on the Motivational Status of Self-Esteem in Social Identity and Intergroup Discrimination." *European Journal of Social Psychology* 18 (1988): 317–34.

Abramson, Paul R. "Political Efficacy and Political Trust among Black Schoolchildren: Two Explanations." *Journal of Politics* 34 (1972): 1243–64.

Abu-Nimer, Mohammed. *Dialogue, Conflict Resolution, and Change: Arab-Jewish Encounters in Israel.* Albany: State University of New York Press, 1999.

Ackerman, Bruce. "Why Dialogue?" *Journal of Philosophy* 86 (1989): 5–22.

Ackerman, Bruce, and James S. Fishkin. *Deliberation Day.* New Haven, Conn.: Yale University Press, 2004.

Alexander, Michele G., and Shana Levin. "Theoretical, Empirical, and Practical Approaches to Intergroup Conflict." *Journal of Social Issues* 54 (1998): 629–39.

Allard, Scott W. "Intergovernmental Relationships and the American City: The Impact of Federal Policies on Local Policy-Making Processes." Ph.D. diss., University of Michigan, 1999.

Allen, Danielle S. *Talking to Strangers: Anxieties of Citizenship since* Brown v. Board of Education. Chicago: University of Chicago Press, 2004.

Allport, Gordon W. *The Nature of Prejudice.* Cambridge, Mass.: Addison-Wesley, 1954.

Alvarez, R. Michael, and John Brehm. "Are Americans Ambivalent about Racial Policies?" *American Journal of Political Science* 41 (1997): 345–74.

Amir, Yehuda. "The Role of Intergroup Contact in Change of Prejudice and Ethnic Relations." In *Towards the Elimination of Racism,* edited by Phyllis A. Katz, 245–308. New York: Pergamon, 1976.

Anderson, Rob, Leslie A. Baxter, and Kenneth N. Cissna. "Texts and Contexts of Dialogue." In *Dialogue: Theorizing Difference in Communication Studies,* edited by Rob Anderson, Leslie A. Baxter, and Kenneth N. Cissna, 1–17. Thousand Oaks, Calif.: Sage, 2004.

Andrews, Molly, Shelley Day Sclater, Corinne Squire, and Amal Treacher. *Lines of Narrative: Psychosocial Perspectives.* London: Routledge, 2000.

"Another Day Off From Realizing King's Dream." *Waterloo/Cedar Falls Courier,* A4, January 18, 1999.

Arendt, Hannah. *The Human Condition*. 2d ed. Chicago: University of Chicago Press, 1998. First published 1958.

Aristotle. *Politics*. Translated by Ernest Barker. Oxford: Oxford University Press, 1998.

Austin, Roy L., and Hiroko Hayama Dodge. "Despair, Distrust, and Dissatisfaction among Blacks and Women, 1973–1987." *Sociological Quarterly* 33 (1992): 579–598.

Bachrach, Peter, and Morton S. Baratz. *Power and Poverty: Theory and Practice*. New York: Oxford University Press, 1970.

———. "The Two Faces of Power." *American Political Science Review* 56 (1962): 947–52.

Balfour, Lawrie. "'A Most Disagreeable Mirror': Race Consciousness as Double Consciousness." *Political Theory* 26 (1998): 346–69.

Balla, Steven J. "Interstate Professional Associations and the Diffusion of Policy Innovations." *American Politics Research* 29 (2001): 221–45.

Bar-On, Dan, and Fatma Kassem. "Storytelling as a Way to Work Through Intractable Conflicts: The German-Jewish Experience and Its Relevance to the Palestinian-Israeli Context." *Journal of Social Issues* 60 (2004): 289–306.

Barabas, Jason. "How Deliberation Affects Policy Opinions." *American Political Science Review* 98 (2004): 687–701.

Barber, Benjamin R. *Strong Democracy: Participatory Politics for a New Age*. Berkeley and Los Angeles: University of California Press, 1984.

———. *A Place for Us: How to Make Society Civil and Democracy Strong*. New York: Hill and Wang, 1998.

Barge, J. Kevin "Enlarging the Meaning of Group Deliberation: From Discussion to Dialogue." In *New Directions in Group Communication*, edited by Lawrence R. Frey, 159–78. Thousand Oaks, Calif.: Sage, 2002.

Barnes, Marian. *Building a Deliberative Democracy: An Evaluation of Two Citizens' Juries*. London: IPPR, 1999.

———. "The Same Old Process? Older People, Participation and Deliberation." *Ageing and Society* 25 (2005): 245–59.

Barry, Brian. *Culture and Equality*. Cambridge, Mass.: Harvard University Press, 2001.

Barthes, Roland. *Image, Music, Text*. Translated by Stephen Heath. New York: Hill and Wang, 1977.

Baxter, Leslie A., and Barbara M. Montgomery. *Relating: Dialogues and Dialectics*. New York: Guilford Press, 1996.

Beck, Paul Allen. "Voters' Intermediation Environments in the 1988 Presidential Contest." *Public Opinion Quarterly* 55 (1991): 371–94.

Beierle, Thomas C. "Using Social Goals to Evaluate Public Participation in Environmental Decisions." *Policy Studies Review* 16 (1999): 75–103.

Benhabib, Seyla. "Communicative Ethics and Contemporary Controversies in Practical Philosophy." In *The Communicative Ethics Controversy*, edited by Seyla Benhabib and Fred Dallmayr, 330–70. Cambridge, Mass: MIT Press, 1990.

———. "Toward a Deliberative Model of Democratic Legitimacy." In *Democracy and Difference: Contesting the Boundaries of the Political*, edited by Seyla Benhabib, 67–94. Princeton, N.J.: Princeton University Press, 1996.

———. *The Claims of Culture: Equality and Diversity in the Global Era*. Princeton, N.J.: Princeton University Press, 2002.

Bennett, W. Lance. "The UnCivic Culture: Communication, Identity, and the Rise of Lifestyle Politics." *PS: Political Science and Politics* 31(1998): 741–61.

Berman, Evan M. "Dealing with Cynical Citizens." *Public Administration Review* 57 (1997): 105–12.

Berinsky, Adam J. *Silent Voices: Public Opinion and Political Participation in America.* Princeton: Princeton University Press, 2004.

Berry, Jeffrey M. *The New Liberalism: The Rising Power of Citizen Groups.* Washington, D.C.: Brookings Institution Press, 1999.

Berry, Jeffrey M., Kent E. Portney, and Ken Thompson. *The Rebirth of Urban Democracy.* Washington, D.C.: Brookings Insitution Press, 1993.

Bessette, Joseph M. *The Mild Voice of Reason: Deliberative Democracy and American National Government.* Chicago: University of Chicago Press, 1994.

Bickford, Susan. *The Dissonance of Democracy: Listening, Conflict, and Citizenship.* Ithaca, N.Y.: Cornell University Press, 1996.

Bingham, Lisa Blomgren, Rosemary O'Leary, and Tina Nabatchi. "Legal Frameworks for the New Governance: Processes for Citizen Participation in the Work of Government." *National Civic Review* 94 (2004): 54–61.

Black, Earl, and Merle Black. *Politics and Society in the South.* Cambridge, Mass.; Harvard University Press, 1987.

Blauner, Bob. *Black Lives, White Lives: Three Decades of Race Relations in America.* Berkeley and Los Angeles: University of California Press, 1989.

———. *Still the Big News: Racial Oppression in America.* (Revised and expanded edition of *Racial Oppression in America,* 1972.) Philadelphia: Temple University Press, 2001.

Bobo, Lawrence D. "Racial Attitudes and Relations at the Close of the Twentieth Century." In *America Becoming: Racial Trends and Their Consequences,* vol. 1, edited by Neil J. Smelser, William Julius Wilson, and Faith Mitchell, 264–95. Washington, D.C.: National Academy Press, 2001.

———. "Race and Beliefs about Affirmative Action: Assessing the Effects of Interests, Group Threat, Ideology, and Racism." In *Racialized Politics: The Debate About Racism in America,* edited by David O. Sears, Jim Sidanius, and Lawrence Bobo, 137–64. Chicago: University of Chicago Press, 2000.

Bohman, James. *Public Deliberation: Pluralism, Complexity and Democracy.* Cambridge, Mass.: MIT Press, 1996.

Bolce, Louis, Gerald De Maio, and Douglas Mazzio. "Dial-In Democracy: Talk Radio and the 1994 Election." *Political Science Quarterly* 111 (1996): 457–81.

Bonner, Patricia, Bob Carlitz, Rosemary Gunn, Laurie Maak, and Charles Ratliff. "Bringing the Public and the Government Together through Online Dialogues." In *Deliberative Democracy Handbook,* edited by John Gastil and Peter Levine, 141–53. San Francisco: Jossey-Bass, 2005.

Booher, David E. "Collaborative Governance Practices and Democracy." *National Civic Review* 93 (2004): 32–46.

Box, Richard C. *Citizen Governance: Leading American Communities into the 21st Century.* Thousand Oaks, Calif.: Sage, 1998.

Boyte, Harry C. *Commonwealth: A Return to Citizen Politics.* New York: Free Press, 1989.

Brader, Ted. *Campaigning for Hearts and Minds: How Emotional Appeals in Political Ads Work.* Chicago: University of Chicago Press, 2006.

Bramson, Ruth Ann. "The Deliberative Public Manager: Engaging Citizens in Productive Public Conversations." Unpublished manuscript, Sawyer School of Management, Suffolk University.

Brehm, John, and Wendy M. Rahn. "Individual-Level Evidence for the Causes and Consequences of Social Capital." *American Journal of Political Science* 41 (1997): 999–1023.

Brewer, Marilynn B. "The Social Self: On Being the Same and Different at the Same Time." *Personality and Social Psychology Bulletin* 17 (1991): 475–82.

Brewer, Marilynn B., and Rupert J. Brown. "Intergroup Relations." In *The Handbook of Social Psychology*, 4th ed., edited by Daniel T. Gilbert and Susan T. Fiske, 554–94. Boston: McGraw-Hill, 1998.

Brewer, Marilynn B., and Samuel L. Gaertner. "Toward Reduction of Prejudice: Intergroup Contact and Social Categorization." In *Blackwell Handbook of Social Psychology: Intergroup Processes*, edited by Rupert J. Brown and Samuel L. Gaertner, 451–72. Malden, Mass.: Blackwell, 2001.

Brewer, Marilynn B., and Norman Miller. "Beyond the Contact Hypothesis: Theoretical Perspectives on Desegregation." In *Groups in Contact: The Psychology of Desegregation*, edited by Normal Miller and Marilynn B. Brewer, 281–302. Orlando: Academic Press, 1984.

Brewer, Marilynn B., and Sherry K. Schneider. "Social Identity and Social Dilemmas: A Double-Edged Sword." In *Social Identity Theory: Constructive and Critical Advances*, edited by Dominic Abrams and Michael A. Hogg, 169–84. New York: Springer-Verlag, 1990.

Briggs, Xavier de Souza. "Culture, Power, and Communication in Community Building." *Journal of Planning Education and Research* 18 (1998): 1–13.

Brown, Lisa M., and Gretchen E. Lopez. "Political Contacts: Analyzing the Role of Similarity in Theories of Prejudice." *Political Psychology* 22 (2001): 279–88.

Browning, Rufus, Dale Rogers Marshall, and David Tabb. *Protest is Not Enough.* Berkeley and Los Angeles: University of California Press, 1984.

Bruner, Jerome. *Acts of Meaning.* Cambridge, Mass.: Harvard University Press, 1990.

Bryan, Frank M. *Real Democracy: The New England Town Meeting and How it Works.* Chicago: University of Chicago Press, 2004.

Bultena, Louis, and Harold Reasby. "Negro-White Relations in the Waterloo Metropolitan Area: A Class Study Project, Spring Quarter 1955." Typescript, Iowa State Teachers College, 1955.

Burayidi, Michael A., ed. *Urban Planning in a Multicultural Society.* New York: Praeger, 2000.

Burkhalter, Stephanie, John Gastil, and Todd Kelshaw. "A Conceptual Definition and Theoretical Model of Public Deliberation in Small Face-to-Face Groups." *Communication Theory* 12 (2002): 398–422.

Burns, Nancy, Kay Lehman Schlozman, and Sidney Verba. *The Private Roots of Public Action.* Cambridge, Mass.: Harvard University Press, 2001.

Button, Mark, and Kevin Mattson. "Deliberative Democracy in Practice: Challenges and Prospects for Civic Deliberation." *Polity* 31 (1999): 609–37.

Capella, Joseph N., Vincent Price, and Lilach Nir. "Argument Repertoire as a Reliable and Valid Measure of Opinion Quality: Electronic Dialogue During Campaign 2000." *Political Communication* 19 (2002): 73–93.

Chambers, Simone. "Deliberative Democratic Theory." *Annual Review of Political Science* 6 (2003): 307–26.

Charles, Michelle, Harris Sokoloff, and Chris Satullo. "Electoral Deliberation and Public Journalism." In *Deliberative Democracy Handbook,* edited by John Gastil and Peter Levine, 59–67. San Francisco: Jossey-Bass, 2005.

Cheng, Antony S., and Janet D. Fiero. "Collaborative Learning and the Public's Stewardship of Its Forests." In *Deliberative Democracy Handbook,* edited by John Gastil and Peter Levine, 167–73. San Francisco: Jossey-Bass, 2005.

Chong, Dennis. "How People Think, Reason and Feel About Rights and Liberties." *American Journal of Political Science* 37 (1993): 867–99.

———. "Creating Common Frames of Reference on Political Issues." In *Political Persuasion and Attitude Change,* edited by Diana C. Mutz, Paul M. Sniderman, and Richard A. Brody, 195–224. Ann Arbor: University of Michigan Press, 1996.

Chong, Dennis, and James N. Druckman. "Competitive Framing." Unpublished manuscript, Northwestern University.

Cissna, Kenneth N., and Rob Anderson. *Moments of Meeting: Buber, Rogers, and the Potential for Public Dialogue.* Albany: State University of New York Press, 2002.

Citrin, Jack, Ernst B. Haas, Christopher Muste, and Beth Reingold. "Is American Nationalism Changing? Implications for Foreign Policy." *International Studies Quarterly* 38 (1994): 1–31.

Citrin, Jack, David O. Sears, Christopher Muste, and Cara Wong. "Multiculturalism in American Public Opinion." *British Journal of Political Science* 31 (2001): 247–75.

Citrin, Jack, Cara Wong, and Brian Duff. "The Meaning of American National Identity: Patterns of Ethnic Conflict and Consensus." In *Social Identity, Intergroup Conflict, and Conflict Resolution,* edited by Richard D. Ashmore, Lee Jussim, and David Wilder, 71–100. New York: Oxford University Press, 2001.

Claibourn, Michelle P., and Paul S. Martin. "Trusting and Joining? An Empirical Test of the Reciprocal Nature of Social Capital." *Political Behavior* 22 (2000): 267–91.

Clark, Terry Nichols. "Race and Class Versus the New Political Culture." In *Urban Innovation: Creative Strategies for Turbulent Times,* edited by Terry Nichols Clark, 21–78. Thousand Oaks, Calif.: Sage, 1994.

———. "The Presidency and the New Political Culture." *The American Behavioral Scientist* 46 (2002): 535–52.

———. "Structural Realignments in American City Politics." *Urban Affairs Review* 31 (1996): 367–403.

Cohen, Joshua. "Deliberation and Democratic Legitimacy." In *The Good Polity: Normative Analysis of the State,* edited by Alan Hamlin and Philip Pettit, 17–34. Oxford: Basil Blackwell, 1989.

Cohen, Michael D., James G. March, and Johan P. Olsen. "A Garbage Can Model of Organizational Choice." *Administrative Science Quarterly* 17 (1972): 1–25.

Coleman, James S. *Foundations of Social Theory.* Cambridge, Mass.: Harvard University Press, Belknap Press, 1990.

Coleman, Stephen. "The Lonely Citizen: Indirect Representation in an Age of Networks." *Political Communication* 22 (2005): 197–214.

Connolly, William E. *Identity/Difference: Democratic Negotiations of Political Paradox.* Expanded Edition. Minneapolis: University of Minnesota Press, 2002.

Converse, Phillip E. "The Nature of Belief Systems in Mass Publics." In *Ideology and Discontent*, edited by D. E. Apter. New York: The Free Press, 1964.

Cook, Stuart W. "Interpersonal and Attitudinal Outcomes in Cooperating Interracial Groups." *Journal of Research and Development in Education* 12 (1978): 97–113.

———. "Experimenting on Social Issues: The Case of School Desegregation." *American Psychologist* 40 (1985): 452–60.

Cook, Fay Lomax, Michael X. Delli Carpini, and Lawrence R. Jacobs. "Who Deliberates? Discursive Capital in America." Paper presented to the American Political Science Association annual meeting, Philadelphia, August 27–31, 2003.

Cooper, Terry L., and Pradeep Chandra Kathi. "Neighborhood Councils and City Agencies: A Model of Collaborative Coproduction." *National Civic Review* 93 (2004): 43–53.

Coote, Anna, and Jo Lenaghan. *Citizens' Juries: Theory into Practice*. London: Institute for Public Policy Research, 1997.

Corcoran, Robert L., and Karen Elliott Greisdorf. *Connecting Communities*. Washington, D.C.: Initiatives for Change, 2001.

Crenshaw, Kimberlé Williams. "Color-blind Dreams and Racial Nightmares: Reconfiguring Racism in the Post-Civil Rights Era." In *Birth of a Nation 'hood: Gaze, Script, and Spectacle in the O.J. Simpson Case*, edited by Toni Morrison and Claudia Brodsky Lacour, 97–168. New York: Pantheon, 1997.

Crenson, Matthew. *Neighborhood Politics*. Cambridge, Mass.: Harvard University Press, 1993.

Cromer, Gerald, and Robin Wagner-Pacifici. "Introduction to the Special Issue on Narratives of Violence." *Qualitative Sociology* 24 (2001): 163–68.

Crosby, Ned. "Citizens' Juries: One Solution for Difficult Environmental Questions." In *Fairness and Competence in Citizen Participation*, edited by Otwinn Renn, Thomas Webler, and Peter Wiedemann, 157–74. Dordrecht, Netherlands: Kluwer, 1995.

Dahl, Robert. *Who Governs?* New Haven: Yale University Press, 1961.

Dalton, Harlon L. *Racial Healing: Confronting the Fear between Blacks and Whites*. New York: Bantam Doubleday Dell, 1995.

Daniel, G. Reginald. *More than Black? Multiracial Identity and the New Racial Order*. Philadelphia: Temple University Press, 2000.

Davidson, Chandler, and George Korbel. "At Large Elections and Minority Group Representation: A Re-examination of Historical and Contemporary Evidence." *Journal of Politics* 43 (1981): 982–1005.

Davis, Richard, and Diana Owen. *New Media and American Politics*. New York: Oxford University Press, 1998.

Day, Diane. "Citizen Participation in the Planning Process: An Essentially Contested Concept?" *Journal of Planning Literature* 11 (1997): 421–34.

De Dreu, Carsten K.W., Fieke Harinkch, and Annelies E. M. Van Vianen. "Conflict and Performance in Groups and Organizations." *International Review of Industrial and Organizational Psychology* 14 (1999): 369–414.

Delli Carpini, Michael X., Fay Lomax Cook, and Lawrence R. Jacobs. "Public Deliberation, Discursive Participation, and Citizen Engagement: A Review of the Empirical Literature." *Annual Review of Political Science* 7 (2004): 315–44.

Delli Carpini, Michael X., Lawrence R. Jacobs, and Fay Lomax Cook. "Does Political Deliberation Matter? The Impact of Discursive Participation on Civic and Political

Behavior?" Paper presented to the American Political Science Association annual meeting, Chicago, September 2–6, 2004.

Deutsch, Morton, and Mary Evans Collins. *Interracial Housing: A Psychological Evaluation of a Social Experiment.* Minneapolis: University of Minnesota Press, 1951.

Deveaux, Monique. "A Deliberative Approach to Conflicts of Culture." *Political Theory* 31 (2003): 780–807.

Devine, Patricia G. "Stereotypes and Prejudice: Their Automatic and Controlled Components." *Journal of Personality and Social Psychology* 56 (1989): 5–18.

Dewey, John. *The Public and its Problems.* Athens, Ohio: Swallow Press, 1954. First published 1927.

———. *Individualism, Old and New.* New York: Capricorn Books, 1962. First published 1930.

Diaz, Ande, and Roberta Stennet. "Transforming Relationships through Sustained Dialogue: An Experience in Conflict Resolution at Princeton University." Unpublished manuscript, 2005.

Dovidio, John F., Kerry Kawakami, and Samuel L. Gaertner. "Reducing Contemporary Prejudice: Combating Explicit and Implicit Bias at the Individual and Intergroup Level." In *Reducing Prejudice and Discrimination: Social Psychological Perspectives,* edited by Stuart Oskamp, 137–63. Mahwah, N.J.: Erlbaum, 2000.

Druckman, James N. "Political Preference Formation: Competition, Deliberation, and the (Ir)relevance of Framing Effects." *American Political Science Review* 98 (2004): 671–87.

Druckman, James N., and Kjersten R. Nelson. "Framing and Deliberation: How Citizens' Conversations Limit Elite Influence." *American Journal of Political Science* 47 (2003): 726–45.

Dryzek, John. *Deliberative Democracy and Beyond: Liberals, Critics, Contestations.* New York: Oxford University Press, 2000.

Dryzek, John, and Valerie Braithwaite. "On the Prospects for Democratic Deliberation: Values Analysis Applied to Australian Politics." *Political Psychology* 21 (2000): 241–66.

Du Bois, Paul Martin, and Jonathan J. Hutson. *Bridging the Racial Divide: A Report on Interracial Dialogue in America.* Brattleboro, Vt.: Center for Living Democracy, 1997.

Dutwin, David. "The Character of Deliberation: Equality, Argument, and the Formation of Public Opinion." *International Journal of Public Opinion Research* 15 (2003): 239–64.

Edelman, Murray J. *Political Language: Words that Succeed and Policies that Fail.* New York: Academic Press, 1977.

———. *The Symbolic Uses of Politics.* Urbana: University of Illinois Press, 1964.

Edwards, Jim, and Wynette Edwards. *Aurora: A Diverse People Build Their City.* Charleston, S.C.: Arcadia, 1998.

Eisinger, Peter. "The Community Action Program and the Development of Black Political Leadership." In *Urban Policy Making,* edited by Dale R. Marshall, 127–44. Beverly Hills, Calif.: Sage, 1979.

Eliasoph, Nina. *Avoiding Politics: How Americans Produce Apathy in Everyday Life.* Cambridge: Cambridge University Press, 1998.

Eller, Anja, and Dominic Abrams. "Come Together: Longitudinal Comparisons of Pettigrew's Reformulated Intergroup Contact Model and the Common Ingroup Identity Model in Anglo-French and Mexican-American Contexts." *European Journal of Social Psychology* 34 (2004): 229–56.

Engstrom, Richard L., and Michael D. McDonald. "The Election of Blacks to City Councils." *American Political Science Review* 75 (1981): 344–55.

Ensuring Race Equality: Resources for Local Officials. Washington, D.C.: National League of Cities, 1999.

Espino, Rodolfo III. "Minority Interests, Majority Rules: Representation of Latinos in the U.S. Congress." Ph.D. diss., University of Wisconsin-Madison, 2004.

Fanselow, Julie. *What Democracy Feels Like*. Pomfret, Conn.: Study Circles Resource Center, 2002.

———. *What Democracy Looks Like: Kansas City, Kansas, Where Neighborhood Voices Lead to Better Solutions*. Pomfret, Conn.: Study Circles Resource Center, 2005.

———. *What Democracy Looks Like: Springfield, Illinois, Where Conversations about Race Create Ripples of Community*. Pomfret, Conn.: Study Circles Resource Center, 2005.

———. *What Democracy Looks Like: Vermont, Where Deep-Rooted Democratic Traditions Open the Way for Study Circles*. Pomfret, Conn.: Study Circles Resource Center, 2005.

Feldman, Martha S. *Strategies for Interpreting Qualitative Data*. Thousand Oaks, Calif.: Sage, 1995.

Feldman, Stanley, and John Zaller. "The Political Culture of Ambivalence: Ideological Responses to the Welfare State." *American Journal of Political Science* 36 (1992): 268–307.

Fenno, Richard F. Jr. *Home Style: House Members in Their Districts*. Boston: Little Brown, 1978.

Fernandez, Frank. "Keeping It Together." *Waterloo/Cedar Falls Courier*, February 17, 2000.

Fernandez, Tina. "Building 'Bridges' of Understanding through Dialogue." In *Intergroup Dialogue: Deliberative Democracy in School, College, Community and Workplace*, edited by David Schoem and Sylvia Hurtado, 45–58. Ann Arbor: University of Michigan Press, 2001.

de Figueiredo, Rui J. P. Jr. and Zachary Elkins. "Are Patriots Bigots? An Inquiry into the Vices of In-Group Pride." *American Journal of Political Science* 47 (2003): 171–88.

Fiorina, Morris P. "Extreme Voices: A Dark Side of Civic Engagement." In *Civic Engagement and American Democracy*, edited by Theda Skocpol and Morris Fiorina, 395–426. Washington, D.C.: Brookings Institution and Sage, 1999.

Finifter, Ada F. "The Friendship Group as a Protective Environment for Political Deviants." *American Political Science Review* 68 (1974): 607–25.

Fishkin, James S. *Democracy and Deliberation: New Directions for Democratic Reform*. New Haven, Conn.: Yale University Press, 1991.

———. *The Voice of the People*. New Haven, Conn.: Yale University Press, 1995.

Fishkin, James S., and Steve A. Rosell with Denise Shepherd and Terry Amsler. "Choice-Dialogues and Deliberative Polls: Two Approaches to Deliberative Democracy." *National Civic Review* 93 (2004): 55–63.

Flavin-McDonald, Catherine, and Martha L. McCoy. *The Busy Citizen's Discussion Guide: Facing the Challenge of Racism and Race Relations*. 3d ed. Pomfret, Conn.: Study Circles Resource Center, 1997.

———. *Facing the Challenge of Racism and Race Relations: Democratic Dialogue and Action for Stronger Communities*. 3d ed. Pomfret, Conn.: Study Circles Resource Center, 1997.

Florida, Richard. *The Rise of the Creative Class: And How It's Transforming Work, Leisure, Community, and Everyday Life*. New York: Basic Books, 2002.

Flynn, Francis J. "Having an Open Mind: The Impact of Openness to Experience on Interracial Attitudes and Impression Formation." *Journal of Personality and Social Psychology* 88 (2005): 816–26.

Flyvberg, Bent. *Rationality and Power*. Translated by Steven Sampson. Chicago: University of Chicago Press, 1998.

FOCUS St. Louis. *Bridges Across Racial Polarization: A Handbook to Get You Started*. St. Louis, Mo., 2002.

Forbes, H. D. *Ethnic Conflict: Commerce, Culture, and the Contact Hypothesis*. New Haven, Conn.: Yale University Press, 1997.

Forester, John. *Planning in the Face of Power*. Berkeley and Los Angeles: University of California Press, 1989.

Fraser, Nancy. "Rethinking the Public Sphere: A Contribution to the Critique of Actually Existing Democracy." In *Habermas and the Public Sphere*, edited by Craig Calhoun, 109–42. Cambridge, Mass.: MIT Press, 1992.

Freire, Paulo. *Pedagogy of the Oppressed*. New York: Seabury, 1970.

Friedland, Lewis, Mira Sotirovic, and Katie Daily. "Public Journalism and Social Capital: The Case of Madison, Wisconsin." In *Assessing Public Journalism*, edited by Edward Lambeth, Phillip Meyer, and Esther Thorson, 191–220. Columbia: University of Missouri Press, 1998.

Fung, Archon. *Empowered Participation: Reinventing Urban Democracy*. Princeton, N.J.: Princeton University Press, 2004.

———. "Varieties of Participation in Democratic Governance." Unpublished manuscript, Kennedy School of Government, Harvard University, 2005.

Fung, Archon, and Erik Olin Wright. "Deepening Democracy: Innovations in Empowered Participatory Governance." *Politics and Society* 29 (2001): 5–41.

Gaertner Samuel L., and John F. Dovidio. *Reducing Intergroup Bias: The Common Ingroup Identity Model*. Ann Arbor, Mich.: Taylor and Francis, 2000.

Gaertner Samuel L., Phyllis A. Anastasio, Betty A. Backman, and Mary C. Rust. "The Common Ingroup Identity Model: Recategorization and the Reduction of Intergroup Bias." *European Review of Social Psychology* 4 (1993): 1–26.

Gaertner, Samuel L., Jeffrey A. Mann, John F. Dovidio, Audrey J. Murrell, and Marina Pomare. "How Does Cooperation Reduce Intergroup Bias?" *Journal of Personality and Social Psychology* 59 (1990): 692–704.

Gaertner, Samuel L., Jeffrey Mann, Audrey Murrell and John F. Dovidio. "Reducing Intergroup Bias: The Benefits of Recategorization." *Journal of Personality and Social Psychology* 57 (1989): 239–249.

Gaertner Samuel L., Jason A. Nier, Christine M. Ward, and Brenda S. Banker. "Across Cultural Divides: The Value of a Superordinate Identity." In *Cultural Divides: Understanding and Overcoming Group Conflict*, edited by Deborah A. Prentice and Dale T. Miller, 173–212. New York: Russell Sage Foundation, 1999.

Gaertner Samuel L., Mary C. Rust, Jason A. Nier, Brenda S. Banker, Christine M. Ward, Gary R. Mottola, and Missy Houlette. "Reducing Intergroup Bias: Elements of Intergroup Cooperation." *Journal of Personality and Social Psychology* 76 (1999): 388–402.

Gale Directory of Publications and Broadcast Media. Detroit: Gale Research, 2003.

Gamson, William A. *Power and Discontent*. Homewood, Ill.: Dorsey Press, 1968.

————. *Talking Politics.* Cambridge: Cambridge University Press, 1992.

Gamson, William A., and Andre Modigliani. "The Changing Culture of Affirmative Action." In *Research in Political Sociology,* edited by Richard Braungart, 137–77. Greenwich Conn.: JAI Press, 1987.

Gardner, James A. "Shut Up and Vote: A Critique of Deliberative Democracy and the Life of Talk." *Tennessee Law Review* 63 (1996): 421–52.

Gastil, John. *By Popular Demand.* Berkeley and Los Angeles: University of California Press, 2000.

————. *Democracy in Small Groups: Participation, Decision Making and Communication.* Philadelphia: New Society Publishers, 1993.

Gastil, John, E. Pierre Deess, and Phil Weiser. "Civic Awakening in the Jury Room: A Test of the Connection Between Jury Deliberation and Political Participation." *Journal of Politics* 64 (2002): 585–95.

Gastil, John, and James P. Dillard. "The Aims, Methods, and Effects of Deliberative Civic Education through the National Issues Forums." *Communication Education* 48 (1999): 179–82.

————. "Increasing Political Sophistication through Public Deliberation." *Political Communication* 16 (1999): 3–23.

Gastil, John, and Todd Kelshaw. "Public Meetings: A Sampler of Deliberative Forums that Bring Officeholders and Citizens Together." Unpublished manuscript. Kettering Foundation, 2000.

Gastil, John, and Peter Levine. *Deliberative Democracy Handbook.* San Francisco: Jossey-Bass, 2005.

Gaventa, John. *Power and Powerlessness: Quiescence and Rebellion in an Appalachian Valley.* Urbana: University of Illinois Press, 1980.

Gerstle, Gary, and John Mollenkopf. "The Political Incorporation of Immigrants, Then and Now." In *E Pluribus Unum? Contemporary and Historical Perspectives on Immigrant Political Incorporation,* edited by Gary Gerstle and John Molleknopf, 1–30. New York: Russell Sage Foundation, 2001.

Gittell, Marilyn. *Limits to Citizen Participation: The Decline of Community Organizations.* Beverly Hills, Calif.: Sage, 1980.

Gleason, Philip. "Sea Change in the Civic Culture in the 1960s." In *E Pluribus Unum? Contemporary and Historical Perspectives on Immigrant Political Incorporation,* edited by Gary Gerstle and John Molleknopf, 109–42. New York: Russell Sage Foundation, 2001.

Goering, John. "An Assessment of President Clinton's Initiative on Race." *Ethnic and Racial Studies* 24 (2001): 472–84.

Goldstein, Marc B., and Shimon Sturm. "Assessing the Impact-Report 1: MetroHartford Community Conversations on Race." Unpublished manuscript, The Center for Social Research, Central Connecticut State University, New Britain, Connecticut. January 21, 1999.

————. "Assessing the Impact-Report 2: MetroHartford Community Conversations on Race." Unpublished manuscript, The Center for Social Research, Central Connecticut State University, New Britain, Connecticut. May 10, 1999.

Gould, Carol C. *Rethinking Democracy.* Cambridge: Cambridge University Press, 1988.

———. "Diversity and Democracy: Representing Differences." In *Democracy and Difference: Contesting the Boundaries of the Political*, edited by Seyla Benhabib, 151–86. Princeton, N.J.: Princeton University Press, 1996.

Greenstone, J. David, and Paul E. Peterson. *Race and Authority in Urban Politics: Community Participation and the War on Poverty*. New York: Russell Sage Foundation, 1973.

Grey, Mark A., and Anne C. Woodrick. "'Latinos Have Revitalized Our Community': Mexican Migration and Anglo Responses in Marshalltown, Iowa." In *New Destinations: Mexican Immigration in the United States*, edited by Víctor Zúñiga and Rubén Hernández-León, 133–54. New York: Russell Sage Foundation.

Grogan, Colleen M., and Michael K. Gusmano. "Deliberative Democracy in Theory and Practice: Connecticut's Medicaid Managed Care Council." *State Politics and Policy Quarterly* 5 (2005): 126–47.

Gudykunst, William B., and Robin B. Shapiro. "Communication in Everyday Interpersonal and Intergroup Encounters." *International Journal of Intercultural Relations* 20 (1996): 19–45.

Gurin, Patricia, with Eric L. Dey, Gerald Gurin, and Sylvia Hurtado. "The Educational Value of Diversity." In *Defending Diversity: Affirmative Action at the University of Michigan*, edited by Patricia Gurin, Jeffrey S. Lehman, and Earl Lewis with Eric L. Dey, Gerald Gurin, and Sylvia Hurtado, 97–188. Ann Arbor: University of Michigan Press, 2004.

Gurin, Patricia, Timothy Peng, Gretchen Lopez, and Biren A. Nagda. "Context, Identity, and Intergroup Relations." In *Cultural Divides: Understanding and Overcoming Group Conflict*, edited by Deborah A. Prentice and Dale T. Miller, 133–70. New York: Russell Sage Foundation, 1999.

Gutmann, Amy, and Dennis Thompson. *Democracy and Disagreement*. Cambridge, Mass.: Harvard University Press, Belknap Press, 1996.

Guzzetti, Barbara J., and Wayne O. Williams. "Changing the Pattern of Gendered Discussion: Lessons from Science Classrooms." *Journal of Adolescent and Adult Literacy* 40 (1996): 38–47.

Habermas, Jürgen. *Between Facts and Norms: Contributions to a Discourse Theory of Law and Democracy*. Translated by William Rehg. Cambridge, Mass: MIT Press, 1996.

———. *Communication and the Evolution of Society*. Toronto: Beacon Press, 1979.

———. *The Inclusion of the Other: Studies in Political Theory*. Cambridge, Mass.: MIT Press, 1998.

———. *Philosophical Discourse of Modernity: Twelve Lectures*. Translated by Frederick G. Lawrence. Cambridge, Mass.: MIT Press, 1987.

———. *The Postnational Constellation: Political Essays*. Edited and translated by Max Pensky. Cambridge, Mass.: MIT Press, 2001.

———. *The Structural Transformation of the Public Sphere: An Inquiry into a Category of Bourgeois Society*. Cambridge, Mass.: MIT Press, 1962.

———. *Theory of Communicative Action*, vol. 1: *Reason and the Rationalization of Society*. Translated by Jeremy J. Shapiro. Boston: Beacon Press, 1984.

———. *Theory of Communicative Action*, vol. 2: *Lifeworld and System: A Critique of Functionalist Reason*. Translated by Thomas McCarthy. Boston: Beacon Press, 1987.

Hallinan, Maureen T., and Richard A. Williams. "Interracial Friendship Choices in Secondary Schools." *American Sociological Review* 54 (1989): 67–78.

Hansen, Susan B. "Talking about Politics: Gender and Contextual Effects on Political Proselytizing." *Journal of Politics* 59 (1997): 73–103.

Hardy-Fanta, Carol. *Latina Politics, Latino Politics: Gender, Culture and Political Participation in Boston.* Philadelphia: Temple University Press, 1993.

Harris-Lacewell, Melissa Victoria. *Barbershops, Bibles, and BET: Everyday Talk and Black Political Thought.* Princeton, N.J.: Princeton University Press, 2004.

Harris-Lacewell, Melissa Victoria, and Quincy T. Mills. "Truth and Soul: Black Talk in the Barbershop." In *Barbershops, Bibles, and BET: Everyday Talk and Black Political Thought,* by Melissa Victoria Harris-Lacewell, 162–203. Princeton, N.J.: Princeton University Press, 2004.

Hart, Roderick P., and Sharon E. Jarvis. "We the People: The Contours of Lay Political Discourse." In *A Poll with a Human Face: The National Issues Convention Experiment in Political Communication,* edited by Maxwell McCombs and Amy Reynolds, 59–84. Mahwah, N.J.: Lawrence Erlbaum, 1999.

Harwood, Richard. *The Public's Role in the Policy Process: A View from State and Local Policymakers.* Dayton, Ohio: Kettering Foundation, 1989.

Hayward, Clarissa Rile. "The Difference States Make: Democracy, Identity, and the American City." *American Political Science Review* 4 (2003): 501–514.

Heierbacher, Sandy, Tonya Gonzalez, Bruce Feustel, and David E. Booher. "Deliberative Democracy Networks: A Resource Guide." *National Civic Review* 93 (2004): 64–67.

Herzog, Don. *Poisoning the Minds of the Lower Orders.* Princeton, N.J.: Princeton University Press, 1998.

Hewstone, Miles, and Rupert Brown. "Contact is Not Enough: An Intergroup Perspective on the 'Contact Hypothesis.'" In *Contact and Conflict in Intergroup Encounters,* edited by Miles Hewstone and Rupert Brown, 1–44. New York: Basil Blackwell, 1986.

Hibbing, John R. and Elizabeth Theiss-Morse. *Stealth Democracy: Americans' Beliefs about How Government Should Work.* Cambridge: Cambridge University Press, 2002.

Hill, Edward W., John F. Brennan, and Harold L. Wolman. "What is a Central City in the United States? Applying a Statistical Technique for Developing Taxonomies." *Urban Studies* 35 (1998): 1935–69.

Hirlinger, Michael W. "Citizen-Initiated Contacting of Local Government Officials: A Multivariate Explanation." *Journal of Politics* 54 (1992): 553–64.

Hirsch, Herbert. *Political Socialization in an American Subculture.* New York: Free Press, 1971.

Hochschild, Jennifer L. "Disjunction and Ambivalence in Citizens' Political Outlooks." In *Reconsidering the Democratic Public,* edited by George Marcus and Russell Hansen, 187–210. University Park: Penn State University Press, 1993.

———. *Facing Up to the American Dream: Race, Class, and the Soul of the Nation.* Princeton, N.J.: Princeton University Press, 1995.

———. *What's Fair? American Beliefs about Distributive Justice.* Cambridge, Mass.: Harvard University Press, 1981.

Hogg, Michael A. "Intergroup Relations." In *Handbook of Social Psychology,* edited by John Delamater, 479–501. New York: Kluwer Academic/Plenum Publishers, 2003.

Honig, Bonnie. *Political Theory and the Displacement of Politics (Contestations).* Ithaca, N.Y.: Cornell University Press, 1993.

Hornsey, Matthew J., and Michael A. Hogg. "Assimilation and Diversity: An Integrative Model of Subgroup Relations." *Personality and Social Psychology Review* 4 (2000): 143–56.

Houlé, Kristin, and Rona Roberts. *Toward Competent Communities: Best Practices for Producing Community-Wide Study Circles.* Lexington, Ky.: Roberts and Kay, Inc., 2000. http://www.studycircles.org/pages/doc.html#Anchor-Als-36201.

Housing and Urban Development, Department of. *The HUD Statistical Yearbook.* Washington, D.C.: U.S. Government Printing Office, 1974.

Hubbard, Amy S. "Face-to-Face at Arm's Length: Conflict Norms and Extra-Group Relations in Grassroots Dialogue Groups." *Human Organization* 56 (1997): 265–74.

Huckfeldt, Robert, Paul E. Johnson, and John Sprague. *Political Disagreement: The Survival of Diverse Opinions within Communication Networks.* Cambridge: Cambridge University Press, 2004.

Huckfeldt, Robert, and John Sprague. *Citizens, Politics, and Social Communication: Information and Influence in an Election Campaign.* Cambridge: Cambridge University Press, 1995.

Huntington, Samuel P. *Who Are We? The Challenges to America's National Identity.* New York: Simon and Schuster, 2004.

Inglehart, Ronald. *Culture Shift in Advanced Industrial Society.* Princeton, N.J.: Princeton University Press, 1990.

———. *Modernization and Postmodernization.* Princeton, N.J.: Princeton University Press, 1997.

———. *The Silent Revolution.* Princeton, N.J.: Princeton University Press, 1977.

Innes, Judith E. "Planning Theory's Emerging Paradigm: Communicative Action and Interactive Practice." *Journal of Planning Education and Research* 14 (1995): 183–89.

Irvin, Reneé A., and John Stansbury. "Citizen Participation in Decision Making: Is It Worth the Effort?" *Public Administration Review* 64 (2004): 55–65.

Iyengar, Shanto, Robert C. Luskin, and James S. Fishkin. "Facilitating Informed Public Opinion: Evidence from Face-to-Face and On-Line Deliberative Polls." Paper presented to the annual meeting of the American Political Science Association, Philadelphia, 2003.

Jacobs, Lawrence R., Michael Delli Carpini, and Fay Lomax Cook. "How Do Americans Deliberate?" Paper presented at the annual meetings of the Midwestern Political Science Association, Chicago, April 15–19, 2005.

Jacobs, Ronald N. "The Problem with Tragic Narratives: Lessons from the Los Angeles Uprising." *Qualitative Sociology* 24 (2001): 221–43.

———. *Race, Media, and the Crisis of Civil Society: From Watts to Rodney King.* Cambridge: Cambridge University Press, 2000.

Johnson, David W., Roger Johnson, and Geoffrey Maruyama. "Goal Interdependence and Interpersonal Attraction in Heterogeneous Classrooms: A Metanalysis." In *Groups in Contact: The Psychology of Desegregation,* edited by Norman Miller and Marilynn B. Brewer, 187–212. Orlando: Academic Press. 1984.

Jones-Correa, Michael. "Immigrants, Blacks, and Cities." In *Black and Multiracial Politics in America,* edited by Yvette M. Alex-Assensoh and Lawrence J. Hanks, 133–64. New York: New York University Press, 2000.

Judd, Dennis, and Susan S. Fainstein, eds. *The Tourist City*. New Haven, Conn.: Yale University Press, 1999.

Karnig, Albert K., and Susan Welch. *Black Representation and Urban Policy*. Chicago: University of Chicago Press, 1980.

Karpowitz, Christopher F. "The Deliberative Potential and Realities of Public Meetings: Inequality and Patterns of Public Participation." Paper presented to the annual meetings of the Midwest Political Science Association, Chicago, April 2005.

———. "Public Hearings and the Dynamics of Deliberative Democracy: A Case Study." Paper prepared for presentation to the annual meetings of the Midwest Political Science Association, Chicago, April 2003.

Karpowitz, Christopher F., and Jane Mansbridge. "Disagreement and Consensus: The Importance of Dynamic Updating in Public Deliberation." In *Deliberative Democracy Handbook*, edited by John Gastil and Peter Levine, 237–53. San Francisco: Jossey-Bass, 2005.

Kathlene, Lyn. "Power and Influence in State Legislative Policymaking: The Interaction of Gender and Position in Committee Hearing Debates." *American Political Science Review* 88 (1994): 560–76.

Keniston, Leonda Williams, Amy Seymour Hubbard, and Julie Honnold. "The Dayton Multiracial Dialogues: Expanding the Circle of Contact through Dialogue." Evaluation Report for the City of Dayton Human Relations Council. Richmond, Va.: Social Sources, Inc., 2002.

Key, V. O., Jr. *Public Opinion and American Democracy*. New York: Alfred Knopf, 1961.

Kim, Claire Jean. "Clinton's Race Initiative: Recasting the American Dilemma." *Polity* 33 (2000): 175–97.

Kinder, Donald R. "Diversity and Complexity in American Public Opinion." In *Political Science: The State of the Discipline*, edited by Ada Finifter, 391–401. Washington: American Political Science Association, 1983.

Kinder, Donald R., and Don Herzog. "Democratic Discussion." In *Reconsidering the Democratic Public*, edited by George E. Marcus and Russell L. Hanson 347–77. University Park: Pennsylvania State University Press, 1993.

King, Desmond. *Making Americans: Immigration, Race, and the Origins of Diverse Democracy*. Cambridge, Mass.: Harvard University Press, 2000.

King, Gary, Michael Tomz, and Jason Wittenberg. "Making the Most of Statistical Analyses: Improving Interpretation and Presentation." *American Journal of Political Science* 44 (2000): 341–55.

Kingdon, John W. *Agenda, Alternatives, and Public Policies*. 2d ed. New York: Longman, 2003.

Kinney, Pat. "Racism Alive in Waterloo, Rights Panel Told." *Waterloo/Cedar Falls Courier*, A1, December 21, 1999.

Kuklinski, James H., and Norman L. Hurley. "It's a Matter of Interpretation." In *Political Persuasion and Attitude Change*, edited by Diana C. Mutz, Paul M. Sniderman, and Richard A. Brody, 125–44. Ann Arbor: University of Michigan Press, 1996.

———. "On Hearing and Interpreting Political Messages: A Cautionary Tale of Citizen Cue-Taking." *Journal of Politics* 56 (1994): 729–51.

Kymlicka, Will. *Multicultural Citizenship: A Liberal Theory of Minority Rights*. New York: Oxford University Press, 1995.

Lakoff, George. *Women, Fire, and Dangerous Things: What Categories Reveal About the Mind.* Chicago: University of Chicago Press, 1987.

Lambert, Wallace E., and Donald M. Taylor. *Coping with Cultural and Racial Diversity in Urban America.* New York: Praeger, 1990.

Lane, Robert E. *Political Ideology.* New York: Free Press, 1962.

———. *Political Life: Why and How People Get Involved in Politics.* New York: Free Press, 1959.

Lasswell, Harold. *Democracy through Public Opinion.* New York: George Banta, 1941.

Lee, Taeku. "Social Construction, Self-Identification, and the Measurement of 'Race.'" Paper presented to the annual meeting of the American Political Science Association, Chicago, Sept 2–5, 2004.

Leighninger, Matt. "How Have Study Circles Made an Impact? Organizers Report on their Successes." *FOCUS,* Fall 2000.

———. "The Recent Evolution of Democracy." *National Civic Review* 94 (2005): 17–28.

———. *The Next Form of Democracy: How Local Civic Experiments are Shaping the Future of Politics.* Nashville, Tenn.: Vanderbilt University Press, 2006.

Leighninger, Matt, and Martha McCoy. "Mobilizing Citizens: Study Circles Offer a New Approach to Citizenship." *National Civic Review* 87 (1998): 187.

Lichterman, Paul. *Elusive Togetherness: Church Groups Trying to Bridge America's Divisions.* Princeton, N.J.: Princeton University Press, 2005.

Lin, Ann Chih. "Bridging Positivist and Interpretivist Approaches to Qualitative Methods." *Policy Studies Journal* 26 (1998): 162–80.

Lindeman, Mark. "Opinion Quality and Policy Preferences in Deliberative Research." In *Research in Micropolitics: Political Decision-Making and Participation,* vol. 6, edited by Michael X. Delli Carpini, Leonie Huddy, and Robert Y. Shapiro, 195–221. Amsterdam: JAI, 2002.

Lipsky, Michael. *Street-Level Bureaucracy: Dilemmas of the Individual in Public Services.* New York: Russell Sage Foundation, 1980.

Los Angeles Region NCCJ. *Neighbor to Neighbor Dialogue Series and Skills Training for Facilitating Interracial Dialogue.* Los Angeles, Calif., 1995.

Lukensmeyer, Carolyn, Joe Goldman, and Steve Brigham. "A Town Meeting for the Twenty-First Century." In *Deliberative Democracy Handbook,* edited by John Gastil and Peter Levine, 154–63. San Francisco: Jossey-Bass, 2005.

Luskin, Robert, James Fishkin, and Roger Jowell. "Considered Opinions: Deliberative Polling in Britain." *British Journal of Political Science* 32 (2002): 455–87.

Macedo, Stephen. "Introduction." In *Deliberative Politics: Essays on "Democracy and Disagreement,"* edited by Stephen Macedo, 3–14. Oxford: Oxford University Press, 1990.

Macedo, Stephen, Yvette M. Alez-Assensoh, Jeffrey M. Berry, Michael Brintnall, David E. Campbell, Luis Ricardo Fraga, Archon Fung, William A. Galston, Christopher F. Karpowitz, Margaret Levi, Meira Levinson, Keena Lipsitz, Richard G. Niemi, Robert D. Putnam, Wendy M. Rahn, Rob Reich, Robert R. Rodgers, Todd Swanstrom, and Katherine Cramer Walsh. *Democracy at Risk: Renewing a Political Science of Citizenship. A Report of the American Political Science Association's Standing Committee on Civic Education and Engagement.* Washington, D.C.: Brookings Institution Press, 2005.

MacGilvray, Eric A. *Reconstructing Public Reason.* Cambridge, Mass.: Harvard University Press, 2004.

Mackie, Gerry. "Models of Democratic Deliberation." Paper presented to the annual meeting of the American Political Science Association, Chicago, 1995.

Mandelbaum, Seymour J. "Historians and Planners: The Construction of Pasts and Futures." *Journal of the American Planning Association* 51 (1985): 185–88.

———. *Open Moral Communities.* Cambridge, Mass: MIT Press, 2000.

———. "Telling Stories." *Journal of Planning Education and Research* 10 (1991): 209–14.

Manna, Paul F. "How Do I Know What I Say I Know? Thinking about *Slim's Table* and Qualitative Methods." *Endarch: Journal of Black Political Research*, Spring 2000: 19–29.

Mansbridge, Jane J. *Beyond Adversary Democracy.* Reprint with new preface. Chicago: University of Chicago Press, 1983.

———. "Conflict and Self-Interest in Deliberation." Paper presented to the Princeton Conference on Deliberative Democracy, Princeton University, March 9–11, 2006.

———. "Everyday Talk in the Deliberative System." In *Deliberative Politics: Essays on "Democracy and Disagreement,"* edited by Stephen Macedo, 211–239. Oxford: Oxford University Press, 1999.

———. *Why We Lost the ERA.* Chicago: University of Chicago Press, 1986.

Marcus, George E. *The Sentimental Citizen: Emotion in Democratic Politics.* University Park: Pennsylvania State University Press, 2002.

Marcus, George E., W. Russell Neuman, and Michael MacKuen. *Affective Intelligence and Political Judgment.* Chicago: University of Chicago Press, 2000.

Marcus-Newhall, Amy, and Timothy R. Heindl. "Coping with Interracial Stress in Ethnically Diverse Classrooms: How Important are Allport's Contact Conditions?" *Journal of Social Issues* 54 (1998): 813–30.

Marder, Nancy S. "Gender Dynamics and Jury Deliberations." *Yale Law Journal* 96 (1987): 593–612.

Marston, Sallie A. "Citizen Action Programs and Participatory Politics in Tucson." In *Public Policy for Democracy*, edited by Helen Ingram and Steven Rathgeb Smith, 119–35. Washington, D.C.: Brookings Institution Press, 1993.

Mattei, Laura R. Winsky. "Gender and Power in American Legislative Discourse." *Journal of Politics* 60 (1998): 440–61.

Matthews, David. *Politics for People: Finding a Responsible Public Voice.* Urbana: University of Illinois Press, 1994.

McCoy, Martha. "Art for Democracy's Sake." *Public Art Review* 9 (1997): 4–9.

McCoy, Martha, and Patrick L. Scully. "Deliberative Dialogue to Expand Civic Engagement: What Kind of Talk Does Democracy Need?" *National Civic Review* 91 (2002): 117–35.

McCrae, Robert R. "Social Consequences of Experiential Openness." *Psychological Bulletin* (120): 323–37.

McIntosh, Peggy. "White Privilege and Male Privilege: A Personal Account of Coming to See Correspondences through Work in Women's Studies." Wellesley Centers for Women Working Paper 189, Wellesley College, 1988.

McKenna, Joseph H., and James Manseau Sauceda. "Students Talk about Race." In *Intergroup Dialogue: Deliberative Democracy in School, College, Community and*

Workplace, edited by David Schoem and Sylvia Hurtado, 74–84. Ann Arbor: University of Michigan Press. 2001.

McLeod, Jack M., Dietram A. Scheufele, Particia Moy, Edward M. Horowitz, R. Lance Holbert, Weiwu Zhang, Stephen Zubric, and Jessica Zubric. "Understanding Deliberation: The Effects of Discussion Networks on Participation in a Public Forum." *Communication Research* 26 (1999): 743–74.

McManus, Susan. "City Council Election Procedures and Minority Representation." *Social Science Quarterly* 59 (1978): 153–61.

Medin, Douglas L., and John D. Coley. "Concepts and Categorization." In *Perception and Cognition at Century's End,* edited by Julian Hochberg, 403–39. San Diego: Academic Press, 1998.

Melville, Keith, Taylor L. Willingham, and John R. Dedrick. "National Issues Forums: A Network of Communities Promoting Public Deliberation." In *Deliberative Democracy Handbook,* edited by John Gastil and Peter Levine, 37–58. San Francisco: Jossey-Bass, 2005.

Mendelberg, Tali. "The Deliberative Citizen: Theory and Evidence." In *Political Decision Making, Deliberation and Participation,* edited by Michael Delli Carpini, Leonie Huddie, and Robert Y. Shapiro, 151–93. Oxford: Elsevier Press, 2002.

Mendelberg, Tali, and Christopher Karpowitz. "How People Deliberate about Justice." Unpublished manuscript, 2005.

Mendelberg, Tali, and John Oleske. "Race and Public Deliberation." *Political Communication* 17 (2000): 169–91.

Merelman, Richard M. "The Mundane Experience of Political Culture." *Political Communication* 15 (1998): 515–35.

Merelman, Richard M., Greg Streich, and Paul Martin. "Unity and Diversity in American Political Culture: An Exploratory Study of the National Conversation on American Pluralism and Identity." *Political Psychology* 19 (1998): 781–807.

Merriss, Peggy, and Jon Abercrombie. "Investing in a Community of Stakeholders." Paper presented to the ICMA University Best Practices 2000 conference, Savannah, Georgia, March 30–April 1, 2000.

Mettler, Suzanne B. "Bringing the State Back In to Civic Engagement: Policy Feedback Effects of the G.I. Bill for World War II Veterans." *American Political Science Review* 96 (2002): 351–65.

Mill, John Stuart. *On Liberty.* 1859. Edited by Currin V. Shields. New York: Liberal Arts Press, 1956.

Miller, Joanne M. "Framing and Political Participation." Paper presented to the Conference on Framing, Texas A&M University, March 5, 2005.

———. "What Motivates Political Participation?" Paper presented at the 100th Annual Meeting of the American Political Science Association, Chicago, Sept. 2–5, 2004.

Miller, Joanne M., and Jon A. Krosnick. "Threat as a Motivator of Political Activism: A Field Experiment." *Political Psychology* 25 (2004): 507–24.

Miller, Joshua, and Susan Donner. "More than Just Talk: The Use of Racial Dialogues to Combat Racism." *Social Work with Groups* 23 (2000): 31–53.

Miller, Norman. "Personalization and the Promise of Contact Theory." *Journal of Social Issues* 58 (2002): 387–410.

Miller, Norman, and Gaye Davidson-Podgorny. "Theoretical Models of Intergroup Relations and the Use of Cooperative Teams as an Intervention for Desegregated Settings." In *Review of Personality and Social Psychology: Group Processes and Intergroup Relations*, vol. 9, edited by Clyde Hendrick, 41– 67. Beverly Hills, Calif.: Sage, 1987.

Mills, C. Wright. "Situated Actions and Vocabularies of Motive." *American Sociological Review* 5 (1940): 904–13.

Mintrom, Michael. "Policy Entrepreneurs and the Diffusion of Innovation." *American Journal of Political Science* 41 (1997): 738–70.

Monroe, Kristen Renwick, with Connie Epperson. "'But What Else Could I Do?' Choice, Identity, and a Cognitive-Perceptual Theory of Ethical Political Behavior." *Political Psychology* 15 (1994): 201–26.

———. *The Hand of Compassion: Portraits of Moral Choice During the Holocaust.* Princeton, N.J.: Princeton University Press, 2004.

———. *The Heart of Altruism: Perceptions of a Common Humanity.* Princeton, N.J.: Princeton University Press, 1996.

Mouffe, Chantal. "Democracy, Power and the 'Political.'" In *Democracy and Difference: Contesting the Boundaries of the Political,* edited by Seyla Benhabib, 245–56. Princeton, N.J.: Princeton University Press, 1996.

Moynihan, Daniel P. *Maximum Feasible Misunderstanding: Community Action in the War on Poverty.* Toronto: Free Press, 1969.

Muhlberger, Peter. "Democratic Deliberation and Political Identity: Enhancing Citizenship." Paper presented to the annual meeting of the International Society of Political Psychology, Toronto, July 2005.

Mullen, Brian. "Group Composition, Salience, and Cognitive Representations: The Phenomenology of Being in a Group." *Journal of Experimental Social Psychology* 27 (1991): 297–323.

Mullen, Brian, Rupert Brown, and Colleen Smith. "Ingroup Bias as a Function of Salience, Relevance, and Status: An Integration." *European Journal of Social Psychology* 22 (1992): 103–22.

Murphy, Russell D. "Politics, Political Science, and Urban Governance: A Literature and a Legacy." *Annual Review of Political Science* 5 (2002): 63–85.

Mutz, Diana C. "Cross-Cutting Social Networks: Testing Democratic Theory in Practice." *American Political Science Review* 96 (2002): 111–26.

———. *Hearing the Other Side: Deliberative versus Participatory Democracy.* Cambridge: Cambridge University Press.

———. "Mechanisms of Momentum: Does Thinking Make it So?" *Journal of Politics* 59 (1997): 104–25.

Mutz, Diana C., and Paul S. Martin. "Facilitating Communication Across Lines of Difference: The Role of Mass Media." *American Political Science Review* 95 (2001): 97–114.

Mutz, Diana C., and Jeffery J. Mondak. "The Workplace as a Context for Cross-Cutting Political Discourse." *Journal of Politics* 28 (2000): 140–55.

Nagda, Biren (Ratnesh) A., Scott Harding, Dominique Moïse-Swanson, Mary Lou Balassone, Margaret Spearmon, and Stan de Mello. "Intergroup Dialogue, Education, and Action: Innovations at the University of Washington School of Social Work." In *Intergroup Dialogue: Deliberative Democracy in School, College, Community and*

Workplace, edited by David Schoem and Sylvia Hurtado, 115–34. Ann Arbor: University of Michigan Press, 2001.

Nagda, Biren (Ratnesh) A., Chan-woo Kim, and Yaffa Truelove. "Learning about Difference, Learning with Others, Learning to Transgress." *Journal of Social Issues* 60 (2004): 195–214.

Nagda, Biren (Ratnesh) A., and X. Zuñiga. "Fostering Meaningful Racial Engagement through Intergroup Dialogues." *Group Processes and Intergroup Relations* 6 (2003): 111–28.

Nelson, Barbara J., Linda Kaboolian, and Kathryn A. Carver. "Bridging Social Capital and an Investment Theory of Collective Action: Evidence from the Concord Project." Paper prepared for presentation to the annual meetings of the American Political Science Association, Chicago, Sept 3–6, 2004. Available at http://concord.sppsr .ucla.edu.

Nelson, Thomas E., Rosalee A. Clawson, and Zoe M. Oxley. "Media Framing of a Civil Liberties Conflict and Its Effect on Tolerance." *American Political Science Review* 91(1997): 567–84.

Nisbett, Richard E., and L. Ross. *Human Inference: Strategies and Shortcomings of Social Judgment.* Englewood Cliffs, N.J.: Prentice Hall, 1980.

Nisbett, Richard E., and Timothy DeCamp Wilson. "Telling More than We Can Know: Verbal Reports on Mental Processes." *Psychological Review* 84 (1977): 231–59.

Norton, Anne. *95 Theses on Politics, Culture, and Method.* New Haven, Conn.: Yale University Press, 2004.

Norton, Eleanor Holmes. "Review: *Race Relations and the New York City Commission on Human Rights.*" *Political Science Quarterly* 90 (1975): 348–50.

Oliver, Leonard P. *Study Circles: Coming Together for Personal Growth and Social Change.* Cabin John, Md.: Seven Locks Press, 1987.

———. "Study Circles: New Life for an Old Idea" *Adult Learning* 2 (1990): 20–22.

Oliver, J. Eric. *Democracy in Suburbia.* Princeton, N.J.: Princeton University Press, 2001.

One America in the Twenty-First Century: The President's Initiative on Race-One America Dialogue Guide. Washington, D.C.: The White House, 1998.

Orr, Marion, and Darrell M. West. "Citizens' Views on Urban Revitalization: The Case of Providence, Rhode Island." *Urban Affairs Review* 37 (2002): 397–419.

Oskamp, Stuart, and James M. Jones. "Promising Practices in Reducing Prejudice: A Report from the President's Initiative on Race." In *Reducing Prejudice and Discrimination,* edited by Stuart Oskamp, 319–34. Mahwah, N.J.: Lawrence Erlbaum Associates, 2000.

Ottensmann, John R. "The New Central Cities: Implications of the New Definition of the Metropolitan Area." *Urban Affairs Review* 31 (1996): 681–91.

Pateman, Carole. *Participation and Democratic Theory.* Cambridge: Cambridge University Press, 1970.

Paton, Alan. "The Negro in America Today." *Collier's,* October 15, 1954, 52–66.

Patterson, Molly A. "Structuration and Deliberation: A Theory of Power for Deliberative Democracy." Paper presented to the annual meetings of the Midwest Political Science Association, Chicago, April 7–10, 2005.

Pearce, W. Barnett, and Stephen W. Littlejohn. *Moral Conflict: When Social Worlds Collide.* Thousand Oaks, Calif.: Sage, 1997.

Perin, Constance. *Belonging in America: Reading Between the Lines.* Madison: University of Wisconsin Press, 1988.

Peterson, Paul. *City Limits.* Chicago: University of Chicago Press, 1981.

Pettigrew, Thomas F. "The Contact Hypothesis Revisited." In *Contact and Conflict in Intergroup Encounters,* edited by Miles Hewstone and Rupert Brown, 169–95. New York: Basil Blackwell, 1986.

———. "Intergroup Contact Theory." *Annual Review of Psychology* 49 (1998): 65–85.

Pettigrew, Thomas F., and Linda R. Tropp. "Does Intergroup Contact Reduce Prejudice? Recent Meta-Analytic Findings." In *Reducing Prejudice and Discrimination,* edited by Stuart Oskamp, 93–114. Mahwah, N.J.: Lawrence Erlbaum Associates, 2000.

Phillips, Anne. "Dealing with Difference: A Politics of Ideas, or a Politics of Presence?" In *Democracy and Difference: Contesting the Boundaries of the Political,* edited by Seyla Benhabib, 139–52. Princeton: Princeton University Press, 1996.

Pincock, Heather. "Insights from an Intergroup Dialogue: Structure, Separation, and Identity." Paper presented at the annual meeting of the International Society of Political Psychology, Toronto, July 6, 2005.

Pinderhughes, Dianne M. "Urban Racial and Ethnic Politics." In *Cities, Politics, and Policy: A Comparative Analysis,* edited by John P. Pelissero, 97–125. Washington, D.C.: CQ Press, 2003.

Pitkin, Hanna Fenichel. "Justice: On Relating Public and Private." *Political Theory* 9 (1981): 327–52.

Pitkin, Hanna Fenichel, and Sara M. Shumer. "On Participation." *Democracy* 2 (1982): 43–54.

Polletta, Francesca. *Freedom is an Endless Meeting: Democracy in American Social Movements.* Chicago: University of Chicago Press, 2002.

———. *It Was Like a Fever: Storytelling in Protest and Politics.* Chicago: University of Chicago Press, 2006.

Potapchuk, William R., Cindy Carlson, and Joan Kennedy. "Growing Governance Deliberately: Lessons and Inspiration from Hampton, Virginia." In *Deliberative Democracy Handbook,* edited by John Gastil and Peter Levine, 254–70. San Francisco: Jossey-Bass, 2005.

Pratchett, Lawrence. "New Fashions in Public Participation: Toward Greater Democracy?" *Parliamentary Affairs* 52 (1999): 616–33.

Price, Vincent, Joseph N. Cappella, and Lilach Nir. "Does Disagreement Contribute to More Deliberative Opinion?" *Political Communication* 19 (2002): 95–112.

Price, Vincent, and Peter Neijens. "Deliberative Polls: Toward Improved Measures of 'Informed' Public Opinion?" *International Journal of Public Opinion Research* 10 (1998): 145–76.

Purnell, Thomas, Dilara Tepeli, Joseph Salmons, and Jennifer Mercer. "Structured Heterogeneity and Change in Laryngeal Phonetics: Upper Midwestern Final Pbstruents." Manuscript, University of Wisconsin-Madison, 2005.

Putnam, Robert D. *Bowling Alone: The Collapse and Revival of American Community.* New York: Simon and Schuster, 2000.

Quillian, Lincoln, and Mary E. Campbell. "Beyond Black and White: The Present and Future of Multiracial Friendship Segregation." *American Sociological Review* 68 (2003): 540–66.

Rahn, Wendy M., and Thomas J. Rudolph. "National Identities and the Future of Democracy." In *Mediated Politics: Communication in the Future of Democracy*, edited by W. Lance Bennett and Robert M. Entman, 453–67. Cambridge: Cambridge University Press, 2001.

Ramakrishnan, S. Karthick. *Democracy in Immigrant America: Changing Demographics and Political Participation*. Stanford, Calif.: Stanford University Press, 2005.

Rawls, John. *Political Liberalism*. New York: Columbia University Press, 1996.

———. *A Theory of Justice*. Rev. ed. Cambridge, Mass.: Harvard University Press, 1999. First published in 1971.

Reed, Adolph, Jr. "Yackety-Yak About Race." *The Progressive*, December 1997, 18–19.

Reichler, Patricia, and Polly B. Dredge. *Governing Diverse Communities: A Focus on Race and Ethnic Relations*. Washington, D.C.: National League of Cities, 1997.

Reinitz, Jeff. "Racial Slurs Painted on Private, City Property." *Waterloo/Cedar Falls Courier*, B3, February 17, 2000.

———. "Racist Message Left Outside Church." *Waterloo Cedar Falls Courier*, October 31, 2000.

Ren, Ling, Liqun Cao, Nicholas Lovrich, and Michael Gaffney. "Linking Confidence in the Police with the Performance of the Police: Community Policing Can Make a Difference." *Journal of Criminal Justice* 33 (2005): 55–66.

Renshon, Stanley A. "American Character and National Identity: The Dilemmas of Cultural Diversity." In *Political Psychology: Cultural and Cross Cultural Diversity*, edited by Stanley A. Renshon and John Duckitt, 285–310. London: Macmillan, 2000.

———. "Dual Nationality + Multiple Loyalties = One America?" In *One America? Political Leadership, National Identity, and the Dilemmas of Diversity*, edited by Stanley Renshon, 232–82. Washington, D.C.: Georgetown University Press, 2000.

Ricoeur, Paul. "Narrative Time." *Critical Inquiry* 7 (1980): 169–190.

———. *Time and Narrative*. 3 vols. Translated by Kathleen McLaughlin and David Pellauer. Chicago: University of Chicago Press, 1984, 1985, 1988.

Rojas, Hernando, Dhavan V. Shah, Jaeho Cho, Michael Schmierbach, Heejo Keum, and Homero Gil-De-Zuñiga. "Media Dialogue: Perceiving and Addressing Community Problems." *Mass Communications and Society* 8 (2005): 93–110.

Rosenberg, Shawn. "Can the People Deliberate? Types of Discourse and the Democracy of Deliberation." Paper prepared for presentation to the annual meetings of the International Society of Political Psychology, Toronto, July, 2005.

Rubin, Mark, and Miles Hewstone. "Social Identity Theory's Self-Esteem Hypothesis: A Review and Some Suggestions for Clarification." *Personality and Social Psychology Review* 2 (1998): 40–62.

Ryfe, David M. "Narrative and Deliberation in Small Group Forums." *Journal of Applied Communication Research* 34 (2006): 72–93.

———. "The Practice of Deliberative Democracy: A Study of 16 Deliberative Organizations." *Political Communication* 19 (2002): 359–78.

Salamon, Lester M. "The New Governance and the Tools of Public Action: An Introduction." In *The Tools of Government: A Guide to the New Governance*, edited by Lester M. Salamon with Odus V. Elliott, 1–47. Oxford: Oxford University Press, 2002.

Sanders, Lynn M. "Against Deliberation." *Political Theory* 25 (1997): 347–76.

Sapiro, Virginia. "Considering Political Civility Historically: A Case Study of the United States." Paper prepared for presentation to the annual meeting of the International Society of Political Psychology, Amsterdam, The Netherlands, 1999.

———. "Seeking Knowledge and Information as Political Action: A U.S. Historical Case Study." Paper prepared for presentation at the meeting of the European Consortium for Political Research, Turin, March, 2002.

Sapiro, Virginia, and Joe Soss. "Spectacular Politics, Dramatic Interpretations: Multiple Meanings in the Thomas/Hill Hearings." *Political Communication* 16 (1999): 285–314.

Saunders, Harold. *A Public Peace Process: Sustained Dialogue to Transform Racial and Ethnic Conflicts.* New York: Palgrave Books of St. Martins Press, 1999.

Schambra, William C. "Local Groups Are the Key to America's Civic Renewal." *Brookings Review* 15 (1997): 16–19.

Schildkraut, Deborah. "The More Things Change . . . : American Identity and Mass and Elite Responses to 9/11." *Political Psychology* 23 (2002): 511–35.

———. *Press One for English: Language Policy, Public Opinion, and American Identity.* Princeton, N.J.: Princeton University Press, 2005.

Schneider, Mark, and Paul Teske. "Toward a Theory of the Political Entrepreneur: Evidence from Local Government." *American Political Science Review* 86 (1992): 737–47.

Schneider, Pat. "Study Circles Seek More Participation." *The Capital Times,* B1, February 3–4, 2001.

Schoem, David. "College Students Need Thoughtful, In-Depth Study of Race Relations." *Chronicle of Higher Education,* April 3, 1991, A48.

———. "Intergroup Relations, Conflict, and Community." In *Democratic Education in an Age of Difference: Redefining Citizenship in Higher Education,* edited by Richard Guarasci, Grant Cornwell, and associates, 137–58. San Francisco: Jossey-Bass, 1997.

———. "Teaching about Ethnic Identity and Intergroup Relations." In *Multicultural Teaching in the University,* edited by David Schoem, Linda Frankel, Ximena Zúñiga, and Edith A. Lewis, 15–16. Westport, Conn: Praeger, 1995.

Schoem, David, and Sylvia Hurtado, eds. *Intergroup Dialogue: Deliberative Democracy in School, College, Community and Workplace.* Ann Arbor: University of Michigan Press, 2001.

Schraufnagel, Scot. "Testing the Implications of Incivility in the United States Congress, 1977–2000: The Case of Judicial Confirmation Delay." *Journal of Legislative Studies* 11 (2005): 216–34.

Schuckman, Harvey. "Political Participation in American Cities: Deconstructing the Role of Local Political Institutions." Ph.D. diss., University of Michigan, 2000.

Schudson, Michael. "Why Conversation Is Not the Soul of Democracy." *Critical Studies in Mass Communication* 14 (1997): 297–309.

Schumaker, Paul. *Critical Pluralism, Democratic Performance, and Community Power.* Lawrence: University Press of Kansas, 1991.

Schumpeter, Joseph. *Capitalism, Socialism and Democracy.* 3d ed. New York: Harper and Row, 1950.

Sears, David O., Jack Citrin, Sharmaine V. Cheleden, and Colette van Laar. "Cultural Diversity and Multicultural Politics: Is Ethnic Balkanization Psychologically Inevitable?" In *Cultural Divides: Understanding and Overcoming Group Conflict,* edited by

Deborah A. Prentice and Dale T. Miller, 35–79. New York: Russell Sage Foundation, 1999.

Shapiro, Ian. "Enough of Deliberation: Politics Is About Interests and Power." In *Deliberative Politics: Essays on "Democracy and Disagreement,"* edited by Stephen Macedo, 28–38. New York: Oxford University Press, 1999.

Sherif, Muzafer. *In Common Predicament: Social Psychology of Intergroup Conflict and Cooperation.* Boston: Houghton Mifflin, 1966.

Sherif, Muzafer, and O. J. Harvey, B. Jack White, William R. Hood, and Carolyn W. Sherif. *Intergroup Conflict and Cooperation: The Robber's Cave Experiment.* Norman: University of Oklahoma Press, 1961.

Sirianni, Carmen, and Lewis Friedland. *Civic Innovation in America: Community Empowerment, Public Policy, and the Movement for Civic Renewal.* Berkeley and Los Angeles: University of California Press, 2001.

Skerry, Peter. *Counting on the Census?: Race, Group Identity, and the Evasion of Politics.* Washington, D.C.: Brookings Institution Press, 2000.

Skocpol, Theda. 2003. *Diminished Democracy: From Membership to Management in American Civic Life.* Norman: University of Oklahoma Press.

Skocpol, Theda, Marjorie Abend-Wein, Christopher Howard, and Susan Goodrich Lehman. "Women's Associations and the Enactment of Mothers' Pensions in the United States." *American Political Science Review* 87 (1993): 686–701.

Smith, Rogers. *Civic Ideals: Conflicting Visions of Citizenship in U.S. History.* New Haven, Conn.: Yale University Press, 1997.

———. *Stories of Peoplehood: The Politics and Morals of Political Membership.* Cambridge: Cambridge University Press, 2003.

Smith, Steven Rathgeb, and Helen Ingram. "Policy Tools and Democracy." In *The Tools of Government: A Guide to the New Governance,* edited by Lester M. Salamon with Odus V. Elliott, 565–84. Oxford: Oxford University Press, 2002.

Smith, Graham, and Corinne Wales. "Citizens' Juries and Deliberative Democracy." *Political Studies* 48 (2000): 51–65.

Smith, Patrick D., and Maureen H. McDonough. "Beyond Public Participation: Fairness in Natural Resource Decision Making." *Society and Natural Resources* 14 (2001): 239–49.

Sniderman, Paul M., Richard A. Brody, and Philip E. Tetlock. *Reasoning and Choice: Explorations in Political Psychology.* New York: Cambridge University Press, 1991.

Snow, David A., E. Burke Rochford Jr, Steven K. Worden, and Robert D. Benford. "Frame Alignment Processes, Micromobilization, and Movement Participation." *American Sociological Review* 51 (1986): 464–81.

Sokoloff, Harris, Harris M. Steinberg, and Steven N. Pyser. "Deliberative City Planning on the Philadelphia Waterfront." In *Deliberative Democracy Handbook,* edited by John Gastil and Peter Levine, 185–96. San Francisco: Jossey-Bass, 2005.

Soss, Joe. "Lessons of Welfare: Policy Design, Political Learning, and Political Action." *American Political Science Review* 93 (1999) 363–80.

———. "Talking Our Way to Meaningful Explanation: A Practical Approach to In-Depth Interviews for Interpretive Research." In *Interpretation and Method,* edited by Dvora Yanow and Peregrine Schwartz-Shea. New York: M. E. Sharpe, 2004.

———. *Unwanted Claims: The Politics of Participation in the U.S. Welfare System.* Ann Arbor: University of Michigan Press, 2000.

Sotirovic, Mira, and Jack M. McLeod. "Values, Communication Behavior, and Political Participation." *Political Communication* 18 (2001): 273–300.

Staton, Jeffrey K., Robert A. Jackson, and Damarys Canache. "Dual Nationality among Latinos: What are the Implications for Political-Connectedness?" Unpublished manuscript, Florida State University.

Staub, Ervin. "Genocide and Mass Killing: Origins, Prevention, Healing and Reconciliation." *Political Psychology* 21 (2000): 367–82.

Stephan, Walter G. "The Contact Hypothesis in Intergroup Relations." *Review of Personality and Social Psychology* 9 (1987): 13–40.

Stephan, Walter G., and Cookie White Stephan. "The Role of Ignorance in Intergroup Relations." In *Groups in Contact: The Psychology of Desegregation,* edited by Norman Miller and Marilynn B. Brewer, 229–55. Orlando: Academic Press, 1984.

Stephan, Walter G., and W. Paul Vogt, eds. *Education Programs for Improving Intergroup Relations.* New York: Teachers College Press, Columbia University, 2004.

Stewart, John, Elizabeth Kendall, and Anna Coote, eds. *Citizens' Juries.* London: Institute for Public Policy Research, 1994.

Stolle, Dietland. "Bowling Together, Bowling Alone: The Development of Generalized Trust in Voluntary Associations." *Political Psychology* 19 (1998): 497–525.

———. "'Getting to Trust': An Analysis of the Importance of Institutions, Families, Personal Experiences and Group Membership." In *Social Capital and Participation in Everyday Life,* edited by P. Dekker and Eric M. Uslaner, 118–33. London: Routledge, 2001.

Stolle, Dietland, and Thomas R. Rochon. "Are All Associations Alike? Member Diversity, Associational Type, and the Creation of Social Capital." *American Behavioral Scientist* 42 (1998): 47–65.

Stone, Clarence N. "It's More Than the Economy After All: Continuing the Debate About Urban Regimes." *Journal of Urban Affairs* 26 (2004): 1–19.

———. *Regime Politics: Governing Atlanta, 1946–1988.* Lawrence: University Press of Kansas, 1989.

———. "Powerful Actors and Compelling Actions." *Educational Policy* 15 (2001): 153–67.

Sturgis, Patrick, Caroline Roberts, and Nick Allum. "A Different Take on the Deliberative Poll: Information, Deliberation, and Attitude Constraint." *Public Opinion Quarterly* 69 (2005): 30–65.

Tajfel, Henri, and John Turner. "An Integrative Theory of Inter-group Conflict." In *The Social Psychology of Inter-group Relations,* edited by William G. Austin and Stephen Worchel, 33–47. Belmont, Calif.: Wadsworth, 1979.

Tatum, Beverly Daniel. *Why Are All the Black Kids Sitting Together in the Cafeteria?: And Other Conversations about Race.* 5th ed. New York: Basic Books, 2003.

Taylor, Charles. "The Politics of Recognition." In *Multiculturalism: Examining the Politics of Recognition,* edited by Amy Gutmann, 25–74. Princeton, N.J.: Princeton University Press, 1994.

———. *Sources of the Self: The Making of the Modern Identity.* Cambridge, Mass.: Harvard University Press, 1989.

Taylor, Donald M., and Fathali M. Moghaddam. *Theories of Intergroup Relations: International Social Psychological Perspectives.* 2d ed. Westport, Conn.: Praeger, 1994.

Theiss-Morse, Elizabeth, and John R. Hibbing. "Citizenship and Civic Engagement." *Annual Review of Political Science* 8 (2005): 227–49.

Thomas, R. Roosevelt, Marjorie I. Woodruff, and R. Roosevelt Thomas Jr. *Building a House for Diversity: A Fable about a Giraffe and an Elephant Offers New Strategies for Today's Workforce.* New York: American Management Association, 1999.

Thomas, John Clayton. *Between Citizen and City: Neighborhood Organizations and Urban Politics in Cincinnati.* Lawrence: University Press of Kansas, 1973.

Thompson, Monita C., Teresa Graham Brett, and Charles Behling. "Educating for Social Justice: The Program on Intergroup Relations, Conflict, and Community at the University of Michigan." In *Intergroup Dialogue: Deliberative Democracy in School, College, Community and Workplace,* edited by David Schoem and Sylvia Hurtado, 99–114. Ann Arbor: University of Michigan Press, 2001.

Tiven, Lorraine. "Student Voices: The ADL's A WORLD OF DIFFERENCE Institute Peer Training Program." In *Intergroup Dialogue: Deliberative Democracy in School, College, Community and Workplace,* edited by David Schoem and Sylvia Hurtado, 59–73. Ann Arbor: University of Michigan Press, 2001.

Treviño, Jesús. "Voices of Discovery: Intergroup Dialogues at Arizona State University." In *Intergroup Dialogue: Deliberative Democracy in School, College, Community and Workplace,* edited by David Schoem and Sylvia Hurtado, 87–98. Ann Arbor: University of Michigan Press, 2001.

Tyler, Tom R. "The Psychology of Public Dissatisfaction with Government." In *What Is It About Government that Americans Dislike?,* edited by John R. Hibbing and Elizabeth Theiss-Morse, 227–42. Cambridge: Cambridge University Press, 2001.

Ulbig, Stacy G., and Carolyn L. Funk. "Conflict Avoidance and Political Participation." *Political Behavior* 21 (1999): 265–82.

U.S. Commission on Civil Rights. Iowa Advisory Committee. "Race Relations in Waterloo." June 2002. Accessed at http://www.usccr.gov/pubs/pubsndx.htm.

Uslaner, Eric M. *The Decline of Comity in Congress.* Ann Arbor: University of Michigan Press, 1993.

Varshney, Ashutosh. *Ethnic Conflict and Civic Life: Hindus and Muslims in India.* New Haven, Conn.: Yale University Press, 2002.

Verba, Sidney, and Norman H. Nie. *Participation in America: Political Democracy and Social Equality.* New York: Harper and Row, 1972.

Verba, Sidney, Kay Lehman Schlozman, and Henry Brady. *Voice and Equality: Civic Voluntarism in American Politics.* Cambridge, Mass.: Harvard University Press, 1995.

Verba, Sidney, Kay Lehman Schlozman, Henry Brady, and Norman H. Nie. American Citizen Participation Study, 1990. (Computer file.) ICPSR Version. Chicago, Illinois: University of Chicago, National Opinion Research Center (NORC) [producer], 1995. Ann Arbor, MI: Inter-university Consortium for Political and Social Research [distributor], 1995.

Walker, Jack L. "The Diffusion of Innovations Among the American States." *American Political Science Review* 63 (1969): 880–99.

Walsh, Katherine Cramer. *Talking about Politics: Informal Groups and Social Identity in American Life.* Chicago: University of Chicago Press, 2004.

Warren, Mark R. *Dry Bones Rattling: Community Building to Revitalize American Democracy*. Princeton, N.J.: Princeton University Press, 2001.

Watson, Goodwin B. *Action for Unity*. New York: Harper, 1947.

Welch, Susan. "The Impact of At-Large Elections on the Representation of Blacks and Hispanics." *Journal of Politics* 52 (1990): 1050–76.

Welch, Susan, and Timothy Bledsoe. *Urban Reform and its Consequences: A Study in Representation*. Chicago: University of Chicago Press, 1988.

Welch, Susan, Lee Sigelman, Timothy Bledsoe, and Michael Combs. *Race and Place: Race Relations in An American City*. Cambridge: Cambridge University Press, 2001.

Welsh, Scott. "Deliberative Democracy and the Rhetorical Production of Political Culture." *Rhetoric and Public Affairs* 5 (2002): 679–708.

White, Hayden. *Metahistory: The Historical Imagination in Nineteenth Century Europe*. Baltimore: Johns Hopkins University Press, 1973.

———. "The Value of Narrativity in the Representation of Reality." *Critical Inquiry* 7 (1980): 5–23.

Williams, Melissa S. "The Uneasy Alliance of Group Representation and Deliberative Democracy." In *Citizenship in Diverse Societies*, edited by Will Kymlicka and Wayne Norman, 124–52. Oxford: Oxford University Press, 2000.

Williams, Robin M. *The Reduction of Intergroup Tensions*. Social Science Research Council Bulletin, no. 57. New York: Social Science Research Council, 1947.

Williamson, Abby, and Archon Fung. "Public Deliberation: Where Are We and Where Can We Go?" *National Civic Review* 93 (2004): 3–15.

Wittig, Michele Andrisin, and Sheila Grant-Thompson. "The Utility of Allport's Conditions of Intergroup Contact for Predicting Perceptions of Improved Racial Attitudes and Beliefs." *Journal of Social Issues* 54 (1998): 795–812.

Wolfe, Alan. *One Nation, After All: What Middle-Class Americans Really Think about God, Country, Family, Racism, Welfare, Immigration, Homosexuality, Work, the Right, the Left, and Each Other*. New York: Viking, 1998.

Yankelovich, Daniel. *Coming to Public Judgment: Making Democracy Work in a Complex World*. Syracuse, N.Y.: Syracuse University Press, 1991.

———. *Evaluation of the Cincinnati Community Action Program*. Cincinnati: Daniel Yankelovich, Inc., 1967.

Yin, Robert K. *Case Study Research: Design and Methods*. 2d ed. Thousand Oaks, Calif.: Sage, 1994.

Young, Iris Marion. "Activist Challenges to Deliberative Democracy." *Political Theory* 29 (2001): 670–90.

———. "Communication and the Other: Beyond Deliberative Democracy." In *Democracy and Difference: Contesting the Boundaries of the Political*, edited by Seyla Benhabib, 120–36. Princeton, N.J.: Princeton University Press, 1996.

———. "Gender as Seriality: Thinking about Women as a Social Collective." *Signs* 19 (1994): 713–38.

———. *Inclusion and Democracy*. Oxford: Oxford University Press, 2000.

———. *Justice and the Politics of Difference*. Princeton, N.J.: Princeton University Press, 1990.

Zaller, John R. *The Nature and Origins of Mass Opinion*. Cambridge: Cambridge University Press, 1992.

Zhao, Jihong, Nicholas P. Lovrich, and Quint Thurman. "The Status of Community Policing in American Cities: Facilitators and Impediments Revisited." *Policing: An International Journal of Police Strategies and Management* 22 (1999): 74–92.

Zimmerman, Joseph F. *The New England Town Meeting: Democracy in Action.* Westport, Conn.: Praeger, 1999.

Zuberi, Tukufu. *Thicker than Blood: How Racial Statistics Lie.* Minneapolis: University of Minnesota Press, 2001.

INDEX

Note: The letter *t* following a page number denotes a table.